FriesenPress

One Printers Way
Altona, MB R0G 0B0
Canada

www.friesenpress.com

ISBN
978-1-03-915307-3 (Hardcover)
978-1-03-915306-6 (Paperback)
978-1-03-915308-0 (eBook)

1. BIOGRAPHY & AUTOBIOGRAPHY, ENTERTAINMENT & PERFORMING ARTS

Distributed to the trade by The Ingram Book Company

ALL IN WITH LOVE

my journey to the hero within

JAMES GARDINER

TABLE OF CONTENTS

ACKNOWLEDGEMENT

Writing one's life story is impossible without the support, inspiration, and encouragement of so many. None of this would have been possible without the currency of relationships, of which I have had many over the years and became a better person from them.

To my mom and dad, little Jimmy's secret guardians on the night, thank you for always allowing me to hoist my sail and seek the lands of adventure. And always welcoming me back when I learned whatever it was that the universe was trying to teach me: the good, the bad, and the ugly. To my Scottish sage, Malcolm, and my grandmother Myrtis, you were everything a boy would want growing up as grandparents. Your life lessons while fishing, sipping ice cold lemonade in your backyard, or devouring a plate of buttermilk pancakes gave me the ability to dream.

Close friendships are great, lifelong friends are a blessing. To my co-pilot, Dave, from the Cydot Drive crew, you have been my wingman for forty seven years and counting. So much of my life journey has been shared with you. Without you and our conversations of lost innocence this book would not be. Likewise for my adopted brothers Steve, Ed, and Big Jon, together we have created the unbreakable bond that spans the pull of time. Our late night sing-a-longs and rock and roll road trips to take over the dance clubs of Rhode Island are legendary. As are you three. Thank you for always being there while I was off chasing dreams.

To the brotherhood and sisterhood of the oar, without you and the sport of rowing I simply would not be the man I am today. My life has been defined by everything I learned as part of the University of Rhode Island Crew team. To Coach Jack and Coach Steve, I owe you everything. To the boys in blue from that magical ride, I am everything.

Carolyn, Kevin, Ken, Brian, Tom, Brendan, Gregg, and Jim…there are no words of gratitude big enough. To the full circle rekindling of that magical sport in the Pacific Northwest and the men in red: one word - glorious. And lastly to all the rowers of Vancouver Rowing Club and Deep Cove Rowing Club, thank you for the gift of "swing" once more.

To music, my secret weapon and trusty sidekick that never failed me on my journey, I have to acknowledge my sonic six shooters: Queensrÿche and Dream Theater. Geoff Tate, Chris Degarmo, Michael Wilton, Eddie Jackson, and Scott Rockenfield - you gave me music that lit my fire, inspired the artist within me, and captivated my imagination. Geoff, your voice and storytelling has been my muse for thirty three years and counting. To the boys from Dream Theater: James LaBrie, John Petrucci, John Myung, Jordan Rudess, Mike Portnoy, and Mike Mangini your music has scored my adult life more than any other. I have grown emotionally and spiritually because of your lyrics, melodies, and stream of consciousness. Quite simply, your music provided me with an emotional tapestry to go inward and grow.

I would be remiss if I didn't acknowledge a seemingly insignificant right hand turn into a small watering hole in New York City back in 1995, where its owner, Mike, took a chance and offered a naive young man a bartending gig. The Ye Old Triple Inn and its colorful cast of characters became a nucleus to my growth as a man learning the ropes of the concrete jungle. Without them and their support, my artistic endeavors would never have seen the light of the stage and screen.

They say a clown car is far more enjoyable with other clowns. To Tina and Nicole, my two sisters of middle age, I love you dearly. Tina, quite simply this book "is" because of your guidance and coaching. Your unwavering belief in me and my abilities kept me going each and every day towards the dream. And for you, my little Nicole, what would I be without your love for the arts and our deep connection championing me to get back to the artist I was meant to be.

Working with FriesenPress to get this book to fruition has been a fantastic experience. I would like to thank the president, my publishing specialists, the editor, and the designers who have all had a hand in bringing this dream to life. Their dedication to my vision along with their unique creative genius has helped me produce a work of art that I am deeply proud of.

Lastly, to my little angels, who will always remain little to me. The gift of childhood lives in these pages and in the lessons you taught this aging old man. I love you more than you will ever know. Perhaps one day you will see that this book is my attempt to understand life and find peace in it. I hope that one day you feel the love I have in my heart for you and understand adult life a little better from my journey.

Love Always,

James, Jim, and Jimmy

CHORUS: *INTO THE FREY*

Consider if you will this story, a lifetime of roles to self-discovery on the stage of life. To be or not to be, for that truly is the question of any arena. This symphony has been penned by the sword of ego, and now the weary composer stands at the threshold. His soul has been weighed; it has been measured, and it is found wanting.

Finally, at nearly fifty, the Primus of the Coliseum has called him to its grand stage. The warrior stands gathering himself at the only sense of home he has ever known: the water's edge. The glow of early autumn twilight highlights his pending battle and allows for reflection.

His chronicle begins as any other: a seedling of innocence and the dawning of curiosity. Sweet youth is a kindling laid at the belly of a cast-iron forge, the spark of wonder gives life to the fires of conquest and adventure. The sun now rises on his story in the first of many arenas that will accompany this tale. The actors await their cues, and the orchestra is ready to ignite the sonic undercurrents. Behold the man and his journey to the boy.

The chilling winds of October intensify as the trumpets summon him to his mark. The door of the hallowed ground opens. If it pleases, enter the arena with us and bear witness to the play. For inside the greatest battle of one's life will be found among the frey... love, the heroic quest of the day.

RHODE ISLAND ARENA

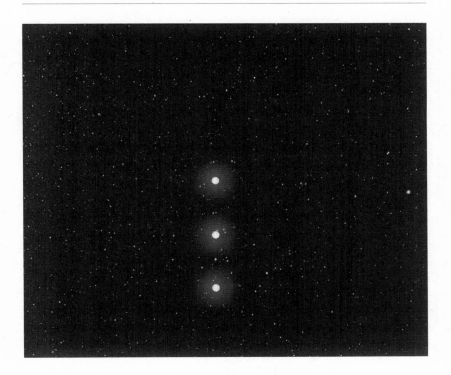

The Captain's Chair

New England in the fall of 1976 was simply October rust. It was a true kaleidoscope of sights and colors accompanied by the fresh smell of fallen leaves, the northeast winds blowing in off the Atlantic, and the smiling faces of jack-o-lanterns bellowing the early darkness. For little boys and girls, it was just one day closer to lots of candy and the

Christmas countdown. To a blond-haired, seven-year-old elf from Cydot Drive, it was *the* time... just about five p.m., when the Gardiner household stood still and life began, three feet away from a floor-model Zenith television set.

"Dad... is it time?" the elf excitedly asked.

Little Jimmy knew it was close because his dad's finger was buried knuckle deep in his double Manhattan, stirring, the ice cubes clinking the glass as if announcing it. As usual, he would grab his son by the shoulders and slide his tiny frame back two feet so Mom didn't have to remind him "he would go blind."

"Yep, Jimmy, it's time," his dad said while slurping the excess whisky off his finger. With a flip of the switch, the screen shimmered to life with static before the picture radiated in full focus and color. The channel knob then slowly clicked from one channel to another.

"Dad! Dad! That's it. Stop. That's the channel," Jimmy ordered.

There he was. His mustard shirt, his pointy-eared friend by his side. The man, the myth, the legend: James Tiberius Kirk. Once a Trekkie, always a Trekkie. Little Jimmy *Gardiner*, aka the Cydot Drive elf, desperately wanted to be James *Kirk*, Captain Kirk, the seer of worlds, the savior of civilizations, the man who swooned more ladies than Bond and got more behind than a toilet seat.

"Arena!" I cried out, beating my dad to the punch and pumping my fist. No one could ever beat me in naming the episodes. For those of you non-Trekkian heathens, "Arena" was the episode with the Gorn, that silly rubber lizard that hunted the mighty Kirk at the slowest speed you've ever seen. Yup, that one. But to the eyes of a seven-year-old, it was, well... "fascinating."

Ah yes, the world of *Star Trek* opened Jimmy's eyes. The mustard shirt, the phasers, the USS *Enterprise*. The crew of that silver/gray spaceship gave him the permission to dream and began his fascination with being a hero. Ironically, thirty years later, he would have a run in with the man who wore the mustard tunic, but for now, the hero who overcame all odds, illness, and limitation was everything Little Jimmy wanted to be, especially as a kid who spent days in the hospital, trying to breathe. He was born with severe asthma.

Jimmy was always an imaginative kid. It was a tool, a carefully crafted weapon to help him deal with the stress and anxiety of feeling like he was going to die. He created worlds, creatures, and conversations like those he saw on his parent's TV. It would ease his affliction, and above all else, provide companionship when he was stuck in a breathing tent. Jimmy never wanted to be alone, but for much of his young life, he had no choice. With his ability to dream and his trusty sidekicks by his side, he could take on anything, even a Gorn if he had to. The boy from Cydot was rarely seen without his tattered red squirrel, Rusty, clutched in one hand and his seven-inch mustard-tunic action hero in the other. The piece de resistance, his favorite adventure book featuring a pirate mouse set on plunder. With these three characters for company, handbook by his side, and a yellow brick road to follow, Jimmy was armed with the most powerful weapon against any foe: love and the ability to dream.

Yet somehow, *Star Trek* reruns were never quite as fascinating through the plastic walls of an oxygen tent. Jimmy's scene always played out like this:

Cue 1974–1987 . . .

"Breathe," his mom softly whispered while attempting to mirror her son's inhalations and exhalations.

"I cannn't, Mom . . . I'm . . . I'm trying," he struggled to respond.

His mother, a schoolteacher, store clerk, and "hearer of all things that go bump in the night," would shoot up out of bed like a flash, and shimmering, briskly float into his room in her ancient nightgown to prop him up. She would begin the "breath dance" as Jimmy liked to call it, softly trying to help him relax. Swaying gently, the two would move in unison back and forth.

"You must . . . be a good dancer?" Jimmy sputtered before sinking his head back onto her chest.

His mom just smiled before softly taking her index finger and placing it under his chin. "Lift your head up, sweetie," she whispered.

She would gauge the severity of the attack by that small space at the base of his throat. The harder it was for him to breathe, the deeper that space would indent with each struggling inhale. A slight indent would equate to Jimmy sucking air through a snorkel—no real issues. The deeper it went, the smaller and smaller that snorkel would get until it was the size of a cocktail stirrer with the tiniest space for air. That was an asthma attack. Plus, of course, there was the sound. That unmistakable wheeze of constricting pipes yearning to expand. Mom gave Jimmy the nod that he was hoping to avoid.

"Do you have... to... Mom?" Jimmy sputtered.

The defeated words were getting harder to get out. In true super-hero fashion, she was gone, vanishing to the medicine cabinet and back again like Samantha on *Bewitched*. Jimmy knew what was coming, so he pulled up his loosely fitting *Star Trek* pajama sleeve. He always watched with curiosity, each time she ripped open the alcohol swab and applied it to the back of his arm.

Inch by inch, Jimmy would watch the needle move closer. Looking away was not an option because every injection was a step towards the captain's chair, or so he told himself at the time. Sometimes he winced, sometimes he screamed, and other times he would take it like a hero. It was always a crapshoot with the back of his tiny arm looking like a pincushion from overuse. Jimmy always wondered if it would be the gentle prick of Mother Teresa or the searing death blow of the slow-moving Gorn.

The needle went in, causing him to wince slightly. When it came out, Jimmy waited before giving his verdict. "No blood. No pain. Good one, Mom."

"Five minutes," she said softly.

Even now, I remember the wait that would ensue. She passed the time by rubbing my blond locks, the best bowl cut east of the mighty Mississippi. She was my mom. My defender from the dark space beneath my bed and the angelic nightlight of my sleep. She was my savior. Within seconds, I would start to feel the adrenaline flowing, my heartbeat increasing, and my wheezing diminishing slightly. She would observe, listen, and then decide. Within five minutes, if the wheeze in my lungs hadn't stopped, to the hospital I would go.

This particular scene ended with the patented Carolyn Gardiner look as it did many nights, and Jimmy knew it well. His left hand reached for his red bushy-tailed soulmate to comfort him. The soft fuzz on his worn, knitted cheek seemed to say, *"Everything will be okay."* Jimmy gave him a soft kiss, not because he asked for it but because the boy needed one.

They were friends for life, Rusty and him. Some days, Jimmy would cry, and others, they would have a sense of adventure about the whole thing. He reached out his other hand to the nightstand. On it was the original 1973 Mego Captain Kirk action figure. The boy from Cydot needed him tonight too.

✧ ✧ ✧

South County Hospital was the Land of Oz, and the yellow brick road would usually take his dad's '74 off-green Pontiac Scamp about twenty-five minutes to get from the front door of home to the sliding doors of admission. That night, like most, his mother sat in the back seat, watching over him.

"Do you think I'll stay?" he asked, innocently. "I'm not sure I want to this time, Mom."

She whispered back, "I don't know," in the calmest tone she could.

She didn't know because it was in the emergency room where the man behind the curtain would tell him how long he would stay. Jimmy looked down at Rusty and Kirk, each clutched firmly in his tiny hands. At least he had the Scarecrow and the Tin Man with him. Jimmy was on a quest for courage.

The faraway land of Emergency Room was full of people and energy, or that is how the older version of Jimmy remembers it all these years later. Doctors, nurses, patients. And a cold sterile smell permeated the air. But above all, there was his dad. The comfort from his shoulder and his laughter made Little Jimmy feel okay. His dad knew what to do to keep the mood light upon entry, always choosing a lighter approach to life. His six-foot-three frame always seemed to ease the fear that would come. With his mom, Jimmy was safe; with his dad, he was protected.

Dad carried Jimmy that evening, as he always did, his head on his shoulder, his arms around his neck with his two besties, Rusty and Kirk, tucked in for the ride. Mom carried Jimmy's overnight bag as it was always packed and ready to go. As soon as they entered, Dad would turn his head, and Jimmy would slightly raise his. A bushy eyebrow signal would connect the two and warn his mother of impending tomfoolery.

Out came what would become a Gardiner household phrase through the years:

"Leigh, don't you dare," Mama Gardiner proclaimed.

Down Jimmy's dad would quickly duck with the shortest of drops. "Whoa!" his dad said, followed by a slight smack from Carolyn. Jimmy would whisper, "Again," because there was always time for one more. His dad would frantically duck down again. "Whoa! Did you see that one!?" he said then, staring bewildered towards the ceiling.

Jimmy squeezed his dad a little tighter with the biggest of smiles, one that even Mom had to give in to. For you see, they were ducking from the staff. They were on the yellow brick road after all, and to Little Jimmy, some of those nurses definitely flew through the hallway on brooms.

The true palace of Oz was upstairs in the pediatric wing. It was a magical place that held the power to cure Jimmy, or at least, provide him all the ice cream a young boy would ever want. It was a fairytale world of flying wheelchairs and mythical creatures, but he had to be granted access.

It usually took about fifteen minutes for the wizard to appear. The Cowardly Lion always made an appearance and sat with Jimmy as they waited. Together, they hoped the man behind the curtain would make him better this time. Just a few more struggling deep breaths, and then the curtain whooshed open and in walked the wondrous wizard. His cape was a pristine white coat with popsicle sticks in one side pocket and cheap click pens in the other. But it was his magic wand that held his true power, slung ever so careful around his neck. On one end, magic earphones, and on the other, the dreaded circle of ice.

"Hey, little guy," the doctor said.

He knew Jimmy. They all did. There were five doctors that rotated and worked upstairs in the pediatric wing. This wizard, Dr. Ryan, was one of his favorites for sure. But as he approached, Little Jimmy was only focused on one thing: that dangling piece of ice-cold metal that was about to send shivers through his tiny body. Ask any seven-year-old, and he or she will tell you. The impending cold doom of that damn stethoscope landing on a bony chest is the worst!

Jimmy nearly shot off the table when it found his skin. Deep breaths, or at least as deep as he could manage, was the protocol. From there, it was simple: another stronger dose of adrenaline to add to the war wounds on the back of his arm, and then wait. If the wheezing subsided completely, then he could head home, ever mindful of the flying brooms on the way out. If it didn't work, then upstairs he went, access granted.

But for now, Jimmy puts his jammy top back on and nestles in on Mom one more time.

Tonight, he doesn't want to stay. He wants to go home. The ice cream isn't tempting, and even his sidekicks can't convince him everything is going to be okay. The wetness of the impending tent seems cold and scary. But that night, like many before and so many after, Jimmy, Rusty, Kirk, and the lion within would continue their quest for courage upstairs, alone.

A tiny finger moves down the plastic, making a temporary dry streak. Jimmy sits propped up in bed, covered in layers of hospital blankets to keep him warm. Rusty lays on top of his chest, the red-knitted head the only thing visible. *Squirrels get cold too.*

Little Jimmy's left hand is immobilized on a small board, the IV needle secured with layers and layers of white tape. Anywhere that hand wanted to go, the board went with it, which presented a problem when he wanted to go on an adventure, especially on one of his favorites, down to the self-serve snack shack. The IV stand and his young age made that impossible. He was held hostage, and he hated it.

Most of the visits were the same, each with their own aspects that made it memorable at the time. Some stays would be four or five days, some more than a week. Freedom would usually come around day three or four when the IV was removed and access to the wheelchairs were granted.

Jimmy loved being able to wheel around the halls, dodging nurses and making them laugh. Because of his frequent flyer miles, he truly felt like the captain of the third floor. At a young age, this is where he first learned how to leverage some Kirk charisma.

There was a secret society of beautiful beings that would make an appearance during his stay, and to Jimmy, they were the closest thing to the "green chick" from *Star Trek* he had ever seen. When it was time, he would sit up in his bed, making himself presentable, and occasionally hiding Rusty beneath the blankets to diminish the possibility of feeling embarrassed. They would approach with a veil of angelic light surrounding them. Their uniforms reminded him of Christmas; their red lipstick made him think of his fashionista grandmother who always looked like a million bucks. It was quite the phenomenon, affecting not just Little Jimmy but all the boys of the Pedi-unit. It was real, and it was powerful.

Jimmy officially had a candy striper "crush." These beautiful beings with their sparkly eyes and soft, whispering voices made him feel like the captain as he held court. All their smiles and eyes were fixated on him and the book he was holding in his hand. Even at his age, it felt normal to have an audience in front of him. The seeds of attention were being cultivated, and his secret weapon was a book: *Scuttle the Stowaway Mouse.* This picture book, written by Jean and Nancy Soule, was a random item in the lobby that became a staple for his home away from home, so much so that his mom eventually bought a brand new one to protect the hospital copy from further wear and tear. (It's sitting here beside the author as this is written, forty-five years later.)

Not too shocking, it's an adventure book, one about a mouse who escapes a dreaded mob of wharf rats by finding refuge as a stowaway on a pirate ship destined for plunder and chaos. When Jimmy was on the ward, they would all congregate to hear the tales of Scuttle told word for word by the Cydot elf. It was the beginning of something brewing inside him. He loved the attention and how their emotions were caught on his every word and action.

"Shiver me timbers!" the little elf mouse said.

Jimmy had them hook, line, and sinker. There was something magical about the affection he was getting. It stimulated him, like a better shot in the arm than his usual dose. He gave them what they wanted, which was to feel, and in return, he got something too: self-worth. For twenty minutes, he would continue in all his glory, unleashing botched accents and multiple swings of an imaginary sword. The stripers lived and breathed through Jimmy and Scuttle saving the day. Together, the two survived broadside attacks, billows of cannon smoke, and pirate ships colliding in chaos. Scuttle finally found some clothes and fancy new boots to cover his hairy mouse toes. He stood proud and tall, for Captain Scuttle was now richer than them all. And with that Jimmy became Captain Jimmy. He had indeed found his chair.

As the applause faded, and Jimmy grew strong again, it was time for the once Cowardly Lion to accept his medal of courage and head home. The protocol was always a first-class escort out of the building, being pushed in a wheelchair by one of his favorite nurses. Sure, he was leaving the magical land of make believe, but he was excited. He was heading to the wonderful galaxy that was far far away, and yet closest to his heart, back to the joys of his neighborhood.

The Possibility Playground

Kirk had the crew of the *Enterprise*, and the galaxy was his playground. For my younger self, I had the Cydot Drive crew under my command as we explored the vast landscapes surrounding it. One of the greatest gifts of any childhood is to grow up in an amazing neighborhood with a bunch of awesome kids living in it. I had it and still have it etched in my mind. Each and every day, we would play. The classroom of life has never been more enjoyable, and all I need to do is close my eyes and listen to the youthful shouts of pure joy from long ago.

Cydot Drive was a true mecca of snot-nosed dreamers, tearing up and down the road on banana-seat bikes, playing football in the street, basketball games on old rickety backboards, hide and go seek, and spying on the neighbors, which never went over well when we got caught. There were snow forts and snowball fights in the wintertime and springtime bike-riding excursions to the faraway land of "the next street over." Mystical early summer morning walks by the river would melt into carpool excursions to the town beach for greasy fries and a sunburn. Lastly, the fall was pure magic in its colors, sights, and sounds. It was the time for football rivalries, school lunch kit shopping, pumpkin carving, costume creation, and the greatest thing of all: the Christmas season. It was truly the time of make believe.

Years later, it does seem like a faraway land, just a dream of images and emotions that pass like a gentle offshore breeze. Stories vaguely tangible and yet wrought with innocence and wonder accompany almost every single memory. The Cydot crew assembled daily, a roll call for the day's adventure. Little Jimmy would be the first to emerge to scout the weather, temperature, and assess the day. His first mate, Dave, would eagerly pop his head out his second-story window with a wave and soon emerge with a Wilson football in his hand, its surface worn and tattered from daily use. It was their ritual—their time before the other kids joined in.

There were two different Jimmys that returned home from the hospital in those younger years: one puffed out on steroid pills and barely recognizable; and the normal, scrawny boy that had endless energy at his disposal to become the hero of the day. To either Jimmy though, when the pig-skin leather was in his hand, there was only one hero: Roger Staubach, the quarterback for the Dallas Cowboys.

Quarterbacks were captains and led their teams to last-minute victories, just like "Roger the Dodger" and his famous Hail Mary. Just a year earlier, in the 1975 playoff game against the Minnesota Vikings, his team had been losing with only seconds left on the clock. In heroic fashion, he'd let a fifty-yard bomb fly to Drew Pearson for the come-from-behind win. In a post-game interview, he'd said that he threw the ball and said a Hail Mary. And so, the term was born and has been used ever since when it came time for a desperation toss, of which there would be many on Cydot Drive.

Jimmy would call the plays, and Dave would run the patterns. The street was the playing field with the two telephone poles in front of their houses marking each end zone. The grass on either side marked out of bounds. Dave would run his receiving routes and dance along the sidelines with the agility of Baryshnikov as Jimmy would lay the ball perfectly into his outstretched hands. Little Jimmy knew it was likely as close as he would ever get to playing quarterback as he just didn't have the physicality or stamina.

After a few rounds of last-minute heroics and amazing tightrope catches, Cydot began to come to life. Dave's younger sister, Christine, would join in. Little "Weenie" as she was called had the knack of always pissing Dave off, which I suppose is often the case for that brother/sister dynamic. Next to follow would be Jennifer from the house next to Dave on the other side. Her younger brother, Jason, would join more in the coming years as he began to get a bit older. The McDades resided at the top of the street with Mickey joining in on the day's adventure. Last but not least was Peter, who lived on the other side of Jimmy. He was always the last one to show up and the first to have to answer the dinner cry of "Peter!" (usually right in the middle of some amazing Cydot Crew initiative).

"Goose," as Peter was called by everyone, entered the street huddle last. There they were each morning, coming together like a team bent on another adventure. They were committed to making the most of each day, understanding that it held whatever they wanted and that the magic of possibility was right around the corner. This day, like many, the quarterback elf gave the signal, and everyone went in the direction of their bikes. With a slight hill smack dab in the middle of the street, it allowed for good speed in either direction. Nothing says freedom more than the wind through your hair as you sail towards the unknown, no matter your age.

As a playground, Rhode Island is a postcard of perfection. Nicknamed the "Ocean State," it sits flush with the Atlantic in the colonial hotbed called "New England." It is charming in its simplicity, combining the modern with the majestic old world. Stone walls endlessly stretch across fields and through dense woods, marking ancient land barriers of ownership. Historic cemeteries are as common as the seagulls who jockey for position on the town docks throughout the state, and of course, the mighty Atlantic in all its magnitude and force. Its gentle breath can be that comfort of a close friend, while its seasonal northeast gales have brought many a sailor to the cold loneliness of the deep. Lighthouses are strategically poised along the coast to honor safe passage amidst the rocky minefields scattered about. Bridges span Narragansett Bay and connect a handful of islands leading to elusive treasure buried by William Kid, the famed pirate. The state is perfect, and the ocean gives it life. Perfect indeed.

As are the harbor communities from which it feeds. Nothing says Rhode Island like the small-town villages nestled at the water's edge, inviting tourists and locals to step back to colonial times. One village in particular, in the middle of the state, sits exactly one mile from Cydot Drive, straight as the bike rides.

Wickford Village was first settled back in 1637. It comprises two main streets: Brown and Main. Brown was the throughway, either side laden with art shops and little mom and pop stores selling knick-knacks and touristy keepsakes. Two main stores have been there since the dawning of the 1900s: Earnshaw Drugs and Ryan's Market. Like any small town, it can be a rumor mill, however, Earnshaw Drugs was the hub of rumor control, and at the helm was the fact-giver: Carolyn Gardiner. When Jimmy was ten, she decided to leave teaching and work there in the center of town. She did so for thirty-nine full-time years until retiring just shy of her eightieth birthday.

Directly across the street was Ryan's Market, your one-stop grocer for the small town. Owned by a family of butchers, it had sought-after meats drawing people from two counties away to buy the choice cuts. Ryan's also holds the distinction of being Jimmy's first-ever place of employment, as a bag boy extraordinaire for its patrons.

But it was Main Street that was synonymous with the essence of Wickford, postcard worthy in every aspect. Both sides of the street were lined with old colonial houses proudly displaying date plaques like badges of honor. Though most of these were now homes, they were governed by strict painting and display guidelines, historic in every sense. "Ye olde Narragansett Bank" would be etched in a hand-carved wooden sign with a date plaque reading 1750. Other houses had belonged to famous poets, congressmen, and so forth. American flags would hang at just the right angle as if announcing the throughway, guiding guests on a trip back in time to a truly unique destination, the town dock. It was here where boisterous characters reminded little Jimmy of Scuttle the mouse and the band of dangerous wharf rats he encountered.

Like Knights of the Round Table, Jimmy and Dave would ride, always on the sidewalk, and usually while getting yelled at by some snobby lifers (or Wickfordites as they were known). These lifetime inhabitants never liked anyone or anything mucking with their sanctuary, but they were quick on their feet and had to be. They would jump out of the way in terror as the bikes approached, fishing rods extending through the handlebars as though the riders were young warriors, jousting for a princess. The boys didn't care at all. And why should they? Fishing was on their minds, that sense of excitement as the red and white bobber goes under for the first time trumping all. As they made the last few pedals before entering the dock area, they looked at each other and each took a deep breath. On they traveled, into the land of Scuttle's wharf rats.

The town dock was a mix of three types of men: quahoggers (or clammers to anyone outside of New England), lobstermen, and the fishermen. You would think that three distinct brethren of the sea would be bound by some brotherhood and/or code. In their defense, they probably were. However, that didn't stop them from getting into fist fights, yelling, swearing, and throwing pots and buoys around like grenades. The quahoggers were like the Neanderthals of the wharf; to Dave and Jimmy, they were gargantuan beings and usually hairy as hell. Their weapons were long poles with a clawed basket on one end. These bull rakes provide muscles where there shouldn't be any. The lobster-men were shorter in stature but still tenacious and not willing to back down from the larger and louder quahoggers. Lastly, the fisherman were more refined, if there was such a thing in that setting. Being of a more slender build, they would usually side with whomever they thought was right in any given situation. It was a recipe for chaos, but Jimmy was determined to get through these creatures and their world-record "F" bombs. Because on the other side was the Promised Land, the uncom-fortable wooden planks of the dock on which they would sit down and cast their lines. And when they did, the loud curses and chaos would always subside.

Some days, the bobber would dance with its rapid movement, and others, it would lay as still as an August low tide. Regardless, there was always one universal constant: conversation. Those innocent exchanges have been carried away by time, adrift on the breeze of what was. But back then, it was uncorrupted by age and full of wonder.

For Jimmy and Dave, there was always one more tradition to cap off their town-dock escapes: the corner store. This was the mecca of all things sweet and yummy. A wonderland of tasty treats that could be purchased for next to nothing with a handful of change kept neatly in a baggie safely secured at the bottom of a backpack.

They leaned their bikes and jousting lances up against an old white-stone wall, and in they'd go, the clang of a bell on the door announcing their arrival. Like a pack of wolves, they circled their targets, salivating, eyeing, and intimidating the unsuspecting prey. They lunged in unison without hesitation, knowing precisely the prize. Dave homed in on his plunder lured by its perfect golden hue. Inside of it was a trove of white creamy filling—yes, the one and only Twinkie. Jimmy would always go for the Honey Bun, a sweet cinnamon experience worth every penny, many of which soon filled the countertop, much to the chagrin of the store clerk.

They exited the store and walked a few hundred feet to the Hussey Bridge, which marked the entrance in and out of Wickford. There they began the ceremonious unwrapping of their treasures while staring out at the harbor through the green metal railings of the bridge. As they grew older, they would jump off that bridge into the water below, earning another badge of courage on their Boy Scout sash of life. But for now, they were content savoring their plunder and saving some strength for the venture back home. The return trip had a major hill to pedal up with their small legs, but the reward, at 92 Prospect Ave, was oh so sweet.

Both Jimmy and Dave were out of breath as they hopped off their bikes in the driveway, leading to an off-yellow Cape Cod style house. The house was typical of New England, with the colonial yellow-painted siding, the dark-green wooden shutters on every window, the lamp post leading the flagstone walkway to the front door, and the black ceramic eagle hung high above the garage door. It was a special house for many reasons. The owner had built it from the ground up, piece by piece, a few hours every day after his shift at the naval base. It also happened to be the house that Jimmy's mom had grown up in, only half a mile from his own house.

They ditched their bikes and fishing rods and opened the screen door to the family room. "Grampy! Grammy!" Jimmy announced as they entered. The boys peeked into the kitchen and spotted the owners through the window, sitting out back, enjoying the peace and serenity of the backyard.

Another screen door was flung open, this one leading to the backyard oasis of beautiful green grass with large oak trees and a simple home-made clothesline with its occupants swaying gently in the air. There was a large bird fountain in the middle of a gorgeous flower bed, and behind it, the hammock to end all hammocks. Sitting quietly in their lawn chairs were Malcolm and Myrtis Matheson, enjoying some freshly poured lemonade and showcasing the biggest smiles as Jimmy and Dave disrupted their peace. Jimmy went for the hugs; Dave for the hammock.

Malcolm, ever the Scotsman and always the prankster, was a tall man with white curly hair, his face tanned from a retirement life shared between a boat and a large garden. All of Jimmy's friends enjoyed his humor, and it wasn't until sometime later that he realized it was enhanced by a brown liquid called scotch! Myrtis was the opposite, in that while her husband sported the latest in worn and tattered ten-year-old fashion, she was a regal queen dressed for a night out. Always. She was also lightning quick to give Malcolm the stink eye of disapproval when he misbehaved.

Grandparents are special to all kids lucky to have them and have a relationship with them. Mine were special for sure. Living so close allowed for a lot of quality visits, sleepovers, favorite meals, and fishing trips on the boat, all adding to the adventure of growing up. I wish I could recount all of those memories, but many have joined the conversations with Dave on the edge of the dock, adrift on the wind.

But this particular day stood strong against the cold march of time. It marked the very first time the two friends had made it up the large hill on their bikes without stopping. A swift breeze of perfection rose up as they sat cross-legged on the soft green earth while the hanging garments on the clothesline rejoiced in a liberating dance. The ice-cold lemonade was exactly what the doctor had ordered, and with Malcolm switching to a darker version, the jokes flew and laughter ensued. But secretly, there was something else in the air that magical late afternoon. Jimmy had conquered that hill, and the tiniest spark of something took hold of him—a spark that was about to ignite something... more.

Cydot Cinema and a Field of Dreams

Some children know immediately what they want to be when they grow up. Dreams fuel ambition and possibilities are not limited by reality. Looking back, I sure spent a lot of time alone. While my dad worked, and later, my mother, I always seemed to find myself alone with my thoughts. But even now, I choose to think that my younger self wanted it this way, so that Little Jimmy could spend time with his most important friend: his dreams.

As with most boys, my dreams were of space. All of that was due to *Star Trek,* but I was also taken by the real-life idea of a man climbing into a tiny capsule while sitting atop a huge rocket, which seemed the greatest test of courage. Just like *Scuttle the Stowaway Mouse* and all the episodes of *Star Trek* that he knew by name, Little Jimmy had an infinity to be "all in" on the things he loved. He knew the names of all the Mercury 7, Gemini, and Apollo astronauts that had dared the greatest adventure of mankind.

Jimmy would climb into the cockpit of an F-4 Corsair and take his place alongside Pappy Boyington and the Black Sheep Squadron to face off against the Japanese Zeroes. This World War Two fighter plane reminded him of the seagulls that would strafe Dave and him at the dock, their wings in a bent gull shape as they descended for the attack. His grandfather Malcolm held a true connection to these fighter planes. He had wanted to be a pilot in the war but a detected heart murmur put an end to that. So, he'd opted to work as a flight mechanic on the F-4's at the naval base when Jimmy's mom was just a toddler. Gramps would tell them both of the guttural power of the engine on start-up, and the pilot's ability to maneuver the craft with the precision of a race car. Jimmy's imagination did the rest.

To Little Jimmy, a hero was someone who overcame great odds, and the idea filled his tiny heart with a wee bit of extra juice. Two things became clear to him in his childhood. First, that the hero didn't have to be real because the story they were in was real to them... and to Little Jimmy. The ability to put himself in Captain Kirk's story, or others', and feel what they were feeling was real. Actors held the passage to his imagination and began to paint the tapestry of emotions that would layer his personality over time.

The common denominator that binds us as adults is that we were all children once. As children, we were all geniuses, Beethovens, with the ability to compose our very own "Ode to Joy" on a daily basis. We could make up stories of faraway lands and save the day against insurmountable odds. We had the ability to paint a canvas where each step in the woods was leading us towards a distant "X" that marked the spot. Childhood for Jimmy meant being in the moment, being alive in the story he was creating. Truly, that is the goal of any actor, and the way a story could be told through the magic of movies spoke to him and to the hero he wanted to be.

Watching *Star Wars* for the first time was like walking through the wardrobe to Narnia. Indiana Jones was Jimmy on another adventure, one where he too hated snakes. *Rocky* was his struggle with being a nobody with asthma. *Jaws* just plain scared the crap out of him on the couch one night. (Disclaimer, when that one-eyed head popped into view from the hull of Ben Gardner's boat, he nearly shat himself.) There was the courage of *The Right Stuff,* which made astronaut Jimmy think there should have been a Mercury 8 program instead, just one more to include him. But it was one summer night in 1982, when his thirteen-year-old world had ended. He wanted desperately for E.T. to stay with Elliot. So much so that he cried and cried and cried as if a part of him was missing. There would be more pivotal films as he grew older, but for now, it was all about the films of Steven Spielberg. Little Jimmy was content with reenacting scenes of movies that inspired him and living the emotions that accompanied them—providing he didn't need an intermission to go and see the wizard.

The second childhood pull was athletics, and the thought of being an athlete. He would sit around and watch athletes compete with wide-eyed wonder, wanting to "feel" what they did and stand before the roar of the crowd. To him, there was nothing greater than representing one's country during the once-every-four-year spectacle called the Olympics.

As soon as he could swing a bat or dribble a basketball, he did. Like most young boys and girls, he found himself learning through recreational sport programs and team gatherings. But he was quick to realize that reciting lines from a book in a hospital bed was safe. Stepping up to home plate scared the bejesus out of him.

"Time out!!" the coach bellowed from the dugout.

The umpire signaled time, and the petrified little ball player made his way over to his coach—well, actually, to his dad. Thankfully, his father had joined him in his first ever season of Little League. Back then, during the fantasy of play, names didn't mean as much as they do now.

Jimmy's dad was the coach, and he was the center fielder of the Indians. Just like the scripted movies, Little Jimmy found himself at the plate with the tying run just sixty feet away.

There was just one issue with this potential Hollywood ending: Poor Jimmy was absolutely terrified at the plate. Only two things had happened the entire season: He either got a walk or was called out on strikes. He was scared to swing the bat, and that was his curse.

Jimmy made his way to the sidelines to meet with his coach, who took to a knee so that they were at eye level. His dad adjusted his green "I" baseball cap and looked into his eyes. There was no athlete before him, just his scared son.

"This moment is not about winning the game, son. It's about you winning the moment. Being scared is part of life."

One of his first life lessons was unfolding before his terror-filled eyes. He was about to unsheathe his sword for the very first time. Jimmy looked at the bat, and it felt different. He looked back at his father, his eyes reddening with the internal conflict of fear and courage.

"Swing... and you won't be scared anymore," his dad said as he swiped the brim on Jimmy's helmet.

His words resonated, but it was the look they exchanged that was life changing. Within his dad's eyes, Jimmy finally saw that, no matter what, he was loved. Scared or not, win or lose, strikeout or not, it didn't matter. His dad's words, and the one's unspoken, fueled his walk to the plate.

He dug in and squeezed the rubber grip of the handle with all he had. Jimmy took a moment, looking at the sword in his hands, the shiny aluminum perfectly matching the weapon of a brave knight. He took his position, staring forty-six feet away at the movement coming off the raised mound. The white ball began its motion toward the plate, causing Jimmy to grip even tighter than he thought possible. As it came closer to the strike zone at what seemed warp speed, he did the unthinkable; he forcefully closed his eyes and swung that mighty sword of his as hard as he possibly could. "Thwap!" into the catcher's mitt the ball landed. Jimmy's eyes only opened as he struggled to prevent himself from an embarrassing fall.

He looked over at his dad, who just nodded in affirmation. Jimmy took a deep breath and stepped in again, this time feeling a bit more in control. His tiny hands tightened, the rubber almost squeezing out between his fingers. He tracked the ball being released, and this time, his eyes matched the speed off the mound. The ball was coming high, but he knew he was meant to do one thing: "Swing and you won't be scared anymore." His eyes remained open as he stepped into the pitch and swung with his tiny frame. "Thwap!"

"Strike two!" called the umpire. No near fall this time; Jimmy stood still and immediately repositioned himself. Jimmy stood in the batter's box, catching one last nod from the coach, and dug in. This was it.

He cocked his elbow up and swirled the head of the bat causing it to feel like a coiled snake ready to spring. Jimmy perfectly tracked the ball coming off of the mound. Everything was slowing down for him. He could already hear the crack of the bat and see the ball carry out of the park and land in the underbrush of left field. It was the most powerful swing he'd ever had.

"Thwap!"

"Strike three! You're out!" called the umpire. His powerful swing had caught nothing but air.

As the triumphant team cheered, Jimmy began to smile. He could feel something beginning to pulsate within him, something wondrous. He felt the warm tingle of courage. As he left home plate, his head was up, his eyes fixed on only one thing: the eyes of his dad, his coach, and in that moment, his hero. Curse lifted!

That moment of "try" spurred him on to more Little League seasons, where in his last one, he led the team in batting. Jimmy began to build confidence, but the seedling hero in him associated greatness with one thing: the long ball. He didn't have the size or strength for the heroic homerun shot, which to him was a sign of greatness. His only glimpse came in his final year with a monstrous shot that was sailing onward, over the fence marking the heroic from the ordinary. It abruptly ended when the center fielder contorted his body over the chain fence and robbed him of his crowning moment. With that catch, there would never be a heroic homerun for the boy (or the man, for that matter).

Jimmy could sense that he was lagging physically. The other boys seemed to have some magical growth formula, which became more apparent as he entered middle school. He was determined to give baseball one more try in the hallowed ground of school sports, where players had to make the team. It was a different level of competition. *But that's what real athletes do,* he thought. *They compete for the right to play.*

Unfortunately for Jimmy, he missed the week of tryouts while visiting South County Hospital on another asthma getaway courtesy of the gods, or fate, or whatever the hell was pulling the strings at that time. He asked his mother to phone the coach to see if he would be willing to give him a tryout once he was back at school. It was granted.

Jimmy showed up after school, glove in hand. But he wasn't the boy who had led his team with his batting average. He was more like Jimmy in his green uniform, looking for a father on the sidelines for support. But this time, there was none. Just big kids who intimidated him with their physiques and abilities. Jimmy was afraid. He barely made it through practice that day and never returned to baseball again. That dream, that role, had ended.

Jimmy never returned to basketball either. His fond memories of playing H-O-R-S-E with his dad, whom he could never beat, was overshadowed by the fact that he never really won much of anything back then, even a coin toss. Yes, a coin toss. It was the last day of basketball tryouts for the middle school team, and Coach Smith called Jimmy and a boy named Pat over. As the coach stood there with his arms laying atop what appeared to be a pregnant belly, he flipped a coin. The toss went to Pat. Walking into his grandparent's house afterwards, the four sets of anticipating eyes that greeted him over dinner were too much. He went straight into the kitchen and cried.

Even now that I've been a coach most of my life, it still baffles me in its absurdness. A fucking coin toss? Really? I do take comfort in remembering the guy struggling to bend over and pick that coin up off the ground. Well, that night, I wasn't forced to eat seafood, which I loathed (and still do). My family knew I was devastated. There would be no more competitive sports in middle school for me, which as I look back now, was just fine. The memory of wiping away the tears over a large stack of buttermilk pancakes, complete with melted butter and tons of confectionary sugar, was worth it. It was a feast for my soul and one that my grandfather always made with love.

A Stairway to Cold Steel

As a grown man now preparing to enter the last stage of his life, I don't know if I am any clearer on the true definition of this mysterious thing called "love." It's arguably the most powerful force surrounding us. It can launch a thousand ships, topple the mightiest empires, and make little boys and girls giddy with love notes and slow dances. I think love first came to me through the boob tube as opposed to the boob itself. Perhaps it was episode twenty-eight: "City on the Edge of Forever" where Kirk had to sacrifice his love and the life of Joan Collins' character. Or maybe it was the full effect of Sean Connery's charm with Pussy Galore. The stakes always seemed higher when it was associated with a woman, and way more heroic. The hero would save the day and always get the girl. I've come to learn that's not always the case, not now and not back then.

Everyone remembers their first kiss. To Jimmy, Jessica was his leading lady in elementary school. She also lived on the next street over, which made excursions across the stone wall even more adventurous. Girls at that age seem way bolder than boys, or at least they did to Little Jimmy. He marveled at her courage when she ask their fourth-grade teacher to move their desks so they could sit next to each other—which they did. Of course, it was all just the naïve and innocent warm fuzzies that accompany boys and girls at that age. Until one day.

After school, Jimmy had skillfully maneuvered the stone wall leading to the Promised Land. It was a rendezvous at Jessica's house, complete with a neighborhood friend and her cousin (all girls). Before Jimmy knew what hit him, he was upstairs in her bedroom on the floor with three girls and an empty Coke bottle. The girls wanted to play Spin the Bottle, a game in which players would, duh, spin the bottle on the floor and kiss whomever the mouth of the bottle pointed to when it came to a stop.

Feeling trapped and definitely not channeling his inner Kirk, he watched as Jessica spun the bottle, afraid of what would happen next. The glass bottle stopped its rotation and pointed directly at Little Jimmy. Time stopped. But his heartbeat didn't. In fact, if he didn't know better, he would have thought he'd just been given a double dose of adrenaline in the back of the arm. He gulped, trying to keep his heart from coming up through his mouth, and then it happened. Just like in the movies. That slow-motion approach, the wordless language, the anticipation, and for Jimmy, complete 100 percent terror! His eyes grew as wide as saucers as their lips met. Complete and utter silence engulfed the room. Jimmy could feel a trance-like state overtake him. Pure serenity... until the bliss was broken by Jessica's bark of "Next!" as she abruptly ended the kiss.

Just like that, the moment was gone. He had no time to process, as her cousin moved in to take a crack at the game. Away the bottle went, round and round until it stopped once again on the asthmatic boy wonder. Rampant panic shot through his head, as did thoughts of Kirk and Bond. *Nope,* he thought as he dodged the incoming cousin who was salivating for a lip assault. Exit stage left, pronto. Out of the house, Jimmy ran. No stonewall shortcut this time; he took the long way home.

Needless to say, the J&J thing was never really the same after that. Grade five came and went. So did a few more trips to the hospital and run-ins with the candy stripers (sans the spinning bottle). It wasn't till the following year, entering grade six and middle school, that he began to get somewhat more courageous, thanks in no small part to two amazing school creations: lockers and school dances.

The thought of having your own locker was a new lease on social life back then. It was a great way to send anonymous notes to unsuspecting cuties by taking a bathroom break and sliding a carefully folded-up paper through the tiny slot of a certain locker. It was his only course of action because he just didn't seem to show up on the girls' radar, which Jimmy attributed to one thing: not making the sports teams. The girls that roamed the halls only wanted the athletes. This was further confirmed under the shimmering lights of a disco ball.

The introduction of the school dance was like stepping into a whole new world full of sights, lights, sounds, and energy. Sixth grade marked another huge moment in Jimmy's life: meeting Steve for the first time in homeroom. The two immediately bonded, and this Greek/Italian wingman would become his friend forever. Along with Ed, a friend from a few streets over, the three became inseparable wherever they went, including the middle school dances. They would sit in what would become known as "Single Alley," folding steel chairs that lined both sides of the cafeteria (aka, dance floor). That's where boys and girls would sit and wait for someone, anyone, to ask them to dance. Sure, during the faster-paced songs, Single Alley thinned out, but during the slow dances, and there were a lot, it would host the souls of boys like Jimmy, who waited for invitations like doe-eyed orphans.

Many times, the wait would be in vain. No takers. Of course, all the jocks had their dance cards full (or at least that's the way Jimmy saw it). Nonetheless, there was always a pivotal moment during the night when Jimmy, Steve, and Ed would have to make a fateful decision. As the lights dimmed, and the acoustic guitar began, the time would be at hand. It was the final song, and it was always Led Zeppelin's "Stairway to Heaven," which was epic at more than eight minutes long. Eight minutes is an eternity to either A) sit alone on a cold steel chair or B) be in the embrace of someone you don't really want to dance with. But you had to choose and accept your fate. Jimmy's fate was isolation on the chair that night, as well as most others. He watched Steve and Ed dance under the stars of the room. They were content, and he was not.

The drive home was unusually quiet as Jimmy didn't say a word to his father. When they got home, he made a beeline for his room. "Do not pass go; do not collect $100." Inside his room, in the sanctuary of *Star Trek* action figures, assembled painted models, and a Roger Staubach poster, he began to cry. *No one likes me,* he kept thinking to himself. *How can I be a hero if no one likes me?* His dad entered then, and Jimmy was just too defeated to turn away. "No one wants to dance with me," he said through tears. Sometimes a hug is all you need, and sometimes it is not.

Jimmy's neck strained as he gazed toward the night sky. Before him, the cosmos sprawled out like a buffet of possibilities. Up there, Captain Kirk was saving the galaxy somewhere. There were ancient gods and untold stories of conquest. But this night was about the magic on earth. About a young boy following his dad's long arm as it extended upwards, pointing and connecting the dots of a constellation. Up there, among his childhood heroes, Jimmy imagined his own constellation taking shape alongside them. The memory of the cold steel chair slowly faded as the night sky and his dad's voice made him feel loved.

I often wonder why my parents didn't force feed me the secrets to life; sometimes things would have been a hell of a lot easier. But then again, I wouldn't have searched so hard for the answers. Under that starry night, I remember thinking that those answers weren't going to come from my parents or even the safety of the Cydot playground. Glimpses of both the questions and answers I would need were going to be found on the big screen. Movies opened up a doorway for me to investigate life and begin to piece together the hero of my own story. My first step on that path was high school. Love can hurt. It can lift, and it also has the power to heal. Especially when it comes in the form of an embrace, or a trip to the soft serve for a yummy cone, or even a game of H-O-R-S-E when the outcome is never in doubt. It can be the gentle touch of wind as a bike speeds into the unknown, or the view of a starry sky, full of possibility.

The Paper Hero

Ah yes, the wonderful time of life called high school still sparkles as it did all those years ago. It was an undiscovered country that was synonymous with one word: "freedom." The hall pass to explore life on a different level was granted when I walked onto the campus as a ninth grader at North Kingstown High School. Unlike most high schools, this one was laid out like a traditional college campus; a handful of buildings were spread across tree-covered walkways and sports fields. Parking lots were littered with second-hand cars further stamping independence for many teenagers. The young adventurer in me needed a map to navigate this foreign land . . . or just a couple of close friends to explore it with.

Jimmy had tucked Rusty and Captain Kirk away on a shelf of forgotten wonder with other items that used to ride along with his imagination. Now he had Steve and Ed by his side to brave this new world. Jimmy's neighbor, Dave, was still in middle school, so natural evolution began to happen with new friends and new circles forming and old ones fading away. High school was a culmination of every type of kid that Jimmy would see on the television and in the movies. There were the heavy metal dudes with their leather jackets, the nerdy introverts, the degenerates, and the preppies (the grouping Jimmy would most likely fall under).

I don't think I necessarily considered myself a preppy per se. Looking back, I think I was more like Judd Nelson's character in *The Breakfast Club*. Well, on the inside maybe, but the upright collar on my short-sleeved polo shirt and clean-cut innocent look spoke otherwise. But there was one other group of kids at the school I always kept an eye on. They all had these jackets, which gave them a certain sense of identity as they walked among the other kids. Just like the pilots of my dreaming youth, they had clout. The jacket's dark-brown exterior was perfectly balanced with customized white-stitched lettering, each with the owner's name proudly displayed for all to see. And on the back, their discipline. I had just walked into the land of varsity sports.

It might have been the energy of the moment, fueled by his new sur-roundings, or perhaps the thought of earning a spiffy jacket, but there was one other sport that he thought he should give a whirl. Fueled by the comeback hero on his wall and countless tosses with Dave, Jimmy joined the freshman football team.

"What!? Come off it!!" His mom's booming voice probably inter-rupted every dinner on Cydot Drive.

"Carol, relax," his dad chimed in, always calm and collected.

"We get our equipment tomorrow and hit the main field after—" Jimmy was quickly cut off by his mom again.

"I don't think this is a good idea. What if—" Now his mother was the one interrupted.

"This will be good for him," offered his dad with a proud and smiling demeanor. "Besides, the doctor put him on some new pills. He'll be fine."

His father's big mitt of a hand thudded down on his little shoulder. "Man in the making," he proclaimed.

The white painted lines and hash marks he had only seen through the television were now beneath Jimmy's cleats. The man in the making surveyed the scene. Two large bleacher sections flanked the field, and he was quick to imagine the cheers coming out to reach him.

"What position?" barked Joey, the young coach who looked like he had just graduated a few months earlier.

Jimmy pulled down on his oversized helmet, cleared his throat, and tried to muster a lower octave. "Quarterback."

Joey pointed towards some of the offensive men and then turned away, leaving Jimmy to jog over to the group and pick up a football, which immediately fell out of his hand. He hadn't take into consideration that the ball he was able to rifle to Dave on Cydot was a bit smaller than this official scholastic ball.

It was evident from the millisecond throwing began who the starting quarterback was. Ronnie had swagger and ability that would never sit on the cold steel chair of any high school dance; that's for sure. He was going to lead the team from the huddle, a team composed of players that had earned their chops in Pop Warner. To his credit, Jimmy was probably the only one there who had never played organized football before. He was the outsider without even trying. When the coach told the boys to line up for hitting practice, Jimmy almost pulled an Elvis and left the building.

The lines were set. Each player had to blast off their mark and collide on impact. Now Jimmy had honed the skill of avoiding contact at all costs out of sheer survival. But here, he was standing willingly for the onslaught. The last thing that went through Jimmy's head (other than the player across from him) was this: *I thought quarterbacks didn't do this stuff.* Down they went into a stance. Jimmy eyed the boy in front of him. Cue some epic Spanish music and a large red cape. The steaming and foaming bull wanted blood, and as the whistle blew, the rabid creature steamrolled right over Jimmy. It wasn't a block. It was a massacre. Back up off the ground, the little elf stood, and then back into formation he went with a tug on his own helmet. The whistle blew for a second time with pretty much the same result. Jimmy was beginning to wobble but still made it back to the line for the third and final blow of the whistle. The coach signaled the onslaught, and Jimmy launched forward, meeting the player a little lower this time. For a split second, he felt the player's movement slow and a shift. The quarterback wannabe dug in, creating some leverage that seemed to help him, before his tiny legs began to buckle, and he was abruptly upended and pancaked with a thud. He groaned and winced in pain. But then something remarkable happened, or at least something he hadn't experienced with this type of licensed bullying before. The assailant outstretched his hand to help him up. "My name is Williston," he said. "Hang in there."

Just like that, Jimmy felt welcomed into the fraternity of footballers. Williston and many others became friends outside of the gridiron arena. Finally, he felt the privilege of being part of something bigger. It was a brotherhood to some degree and meeting every afternoon for practice became the highlight of each day.

Jimmy learned the snap count and would always run plays as the backup QB, which he was content doing, as he would see his dad standing over by the fence watching some of the practices while he strolled up under center and called the play. To Jimmy, each afternoon on the practice field was an adventure.

Speaking of which, the three-ring circus that is the locker room was a whole new experience for him. On game day, it became a thing of movie legend. The leaders of the team held court, and the antics were eye popping to say the least. Players would have different rituals, some of them bordering on primitive and obnoxious, while some would sit quietly in reflection on what was about to take place. It was the first time in his young life that the seedling warrior within was going to battle, and he loved the atmosphere.

A taped finger presses the "play" button on a large silver boombox. The thumping begins with the drums announcing the riffing guitar. "Bang Your Head" by Quiet Riot would send its metal shrapnel through the young men. This infectious drug stimulated every part of the boys in that locker room. Heads would bob, mouths would scream, and blood would flow this day. It was glorious.

The team, however, was not. They weren't winning any of their games, but as the season progressed, that didn't stop their attitude or work ethic. Jimmy was content on the sidelines, for it was there that he had a front-row seat to the game and the mythical creatures with pom poms. It wasn't the cold steel chair of middle school, but it wasn't the spotlight either. That movie storyline came near the end of the season.

As happens in many sports, athletes get injured. Ronnie, the quarterback, banged up his ribs, and as a result, had to sit out the last away game of the season, which left one person (the only other quarterback on the team) to step in. Jimmy was going into the huddle for the first time ever in a real game.

When I took the field on that fall afternoon, I felt like a young boy living a dream. Not in the grand sense but in a simple close-the-loop moment. I recalled countless times, sitting in my room with my Dallas Cowboy gear on, just gripping the football. I would fantasize that I was the paper hero on the wall. Now it was my turn to call the plays, not Mr. Staubach.

Jimmy surveyed the scene before him and took an extra breath. "Twenty-eight slant left," he commanded. The team broke the huddle with a clap, and there it was: the walk-up under center and then the stare right down the pipe at nasty-looking linebackers who definitely smelled fresh meat.

For a split second, he panicked, but then steadied himself. His hands were poised under the center and the signal began. "Set! Odd Set! Red – Set Go!" The snap was secured, and Jimmy pivoted perfectly away from center to meet the running back in stride. Handoff successful. Let the games begin.

Hand off after hand off was orchestrated by the rookie quarterback. Before the end of the second quarter of a scoreless game, a pass play finally came in. The snap count began, and thoughts of Roger Staubach dropping deep in the pocket to unload across the center of the field filled Jimmy's mind. Now, Roger was also known as Roger the Dodger because he was able to evade linemen out for blood. At the snap, Jimmy and Roger dropped back into the pocket, their eyes scanning. In an instant, they could feel the protection breaking down, and it was time to run for their lives and hold on to the damn ball. Jimmy the Dodger tucked the pig skin tightly into his body, then zigged and zagged, making two linemen miss his scrawny frame. As he approached the line of scrimmage, a linebacker had him dead to rights. But just before that monster sent him back to the hospital, his buddy Williston came across the line and levelled him, sending the linebacker about four yards out of the way. The life-saving gesture opened up the lane, and Jimmy was able to scramble back to the line of scrimmage and was able to get another five yards before he was tackled. A few of his teammates helped him up and slapped his helmet with enthusiastic bravado. *What a rush,* he thought. That first near-death experience on the field seemed to heighten his intensity.

It stayed with him through half time and into the third quarter. He started to take command of the young men, reminding them of their assignments and keeping them focused on the task at hand. Most importantly, they were all in with him. The game remained scoreless, and Jimmy and the men were driving again. They were only fifteen yards away from the end zone, and Coach Joey decided to call another pass play. This time, it was a designed roll out, where Jimmy would drop back to the left and have two targets to choose from. A left roll out is a bit tougher for a right-hand quarterback to throw on the run, and Jimmy knew it. But he also knew the coach had called it for a reason.

Under center, Jimmy scanned the field. "Set! Odd Set! Red – Set Go!" He took the snap and began to orchestrate the roll out. The nimble elf had to run back a bit further so he could see over the lineman and running backs blocking for him. The two optional targets were cutting across the field, matching Jimmy's roll out, one near the goal line, the other in the end zone. He was running out of real estate, and he knew he needed to get rid of the ball. Jimmy couldn't see the receiver in the end zone clearly but reared back and decided to heave it as best as he could. In the air it flew, its tight spiral cutting through the sky. It was sailing towards the open receiver as Jimmy and the team watched in anticipation. The ball began its downward descent towards the target, but it abruptly landed in the end zone, a few feet short of glory.

I do find myself reminiscing on that seemingly insignificant moment in the playbook of life. Just a few more feet, and it would have sealed the heroic day. Roger, Jimmy, and I would have had a glorious moment in the annals of history. Instead, I got an earful from Coach Joey as I had missed a wide-open receiver. Did I mention he was wide open? Coach did, like five friggin times.

Jimmy slapped his own helmet hard and went back to the huddle determined to get the boys into the end zone. A few more running plays, and they were sitting on the two-yard line. Same play as how they'd opened the game: "Twenty-eight slant left." A handoff. The ball was snapped, the handoff was delivered, and Mike busted through the line for the touchdown. Jimmy and the team went wild over what would be the only score of the game. The freshman football team won their first and only game of the season that year... led by a boney, fragile dreamer spurred on by a paper hero.

I never played football again after that season. Even the Cydot Drive sideline passes to Twinkle Toes Dave and his dazzling footwork stopped being thrown. The ball found its resting place somewhere in a garage of forgotten dreams along with items that no longer served a purpose. Football vanished. But that season gave birth to an identity in the making.

Cheeseburger in Paradise

Two cans of ice-cold Pabst's Blue Ribbon beer gently come to rest in a bed of pine needles before gently being covered over with some greenery. Yes, new identity indeed. That little football excursion into the land of the hero further awakened the freedom I was now beginning to experience in high school. Nothing says Independence Day like a bunch of friends smuggling and stashing beer for the evening fireworks. It was July fourth in America after all.

With the special day came another tradition: the Matheson backyard cookout. Everywhere one looked there were hot dogs, hamburgers, chips, and endless Sunkist orange soda cans peeking out from an overstuffed cooler. There was backyard badminton, horseshoes, croquet, and "jarts" (that insanely dangerous game where one chucks projectiles that could pierce a tank high into the air towards the opponent's side of the lawn). Fun and somewhat scary, especially when the adults started to indulge in the libations that were flowing.

Throughout his youth, Jimmy was always surrounded by adults, but it would just be him at these backyard soirees, culminating with a walk down to the town beach for music and fireworks. However, being an only child, Jimmy had one other kid he could count on to make an appearance: his grandfather Malcolm, who would always have that boyish twinkle in his eyes and the endless smile that would be a lighthouse for good times. As Jimmy got a bit older, Steve and Ed would start coming by to enjoy the festivities and provide their best friend with a suitable reprieve among a sea of blabbering adults. They loved Malcolm's stories and antics too, which would occur as the blended scotch was opened. Specifically, his technique for cooking cheeseburgers, which has now garnered a place among the hallowed halls of memory within those three young men.

In his defense, my grandfather hated cheese (come to think of it, my mom does too, which is just down-right ludicrous). In any event, the apron-clad Malcolm was fired up on some Cutty Sark liquid gold as the three of us boys stood eagerly by the grill, paper plates in hand.

"One slice or two, Steve?" Malcolm sputtered.

"Two," said Jimmy's best friend, who had an identical bowl cut to mine. Ed too for that matter.

"Not sure why you boys want to corrupt a perfectly good burger with this—" He quickly scanned for Myrtis and her disapproving eyes. Seeing that the coast was clear, he whispered, "Shit."

The boys laughed hard. But then, as he took another sip from his plastic cup and their plates thrust forward, eagerly anticipating their meals, he did the unthinkable.

Jimmy, Steve, and Ed witnessed the horror of Malcolm flipping three perfectly melted cheeseburgers over on the grill. The cheese immediately oozed through the charred grates and disintegrated all over the briquets. The boys stood in shock, waiting for Malcolm to realize what he'd just done.

"You three going to the beach tonight?" he asked as if nothing had happened.

After a long moment, Ed broke the silence. "I'll... have a hot dog."

This sent all us boys into an uncontrollable fit of laughter, which finally helped Malcolm to clue in to his faux pas. He looked down at the gooey sacrilege and back to the boys.

"Whoops," he said simply.

It didn't take long for us to get new and delicious cheeseburgers made perfectly the second time around. To be fair, my grandfather was a great cook, and I miss those special evening sit-down dinners where he held court. He always seemed to bring his boyishness wherever he went, and I loved him for it. We were in paradise, and as we enjoyed our burgers under the shade of a large oak tree, we began to plan our shenanigans.

The secret beer stash grew with each strategic visit throughout the day, in preparation for our big adventure that evening. Not that it was some epic quest, but to young teens, it was time alone without adults, enjoying soothing friendship and the first warmth of liquid courage. As darkness hit, the boys loaded up as many pockets as they could with their precious cargo and left the house for their walk to the beach. With a ritualistic peel back of beer tabs and a clanging of cans together, down the hatch they went. Freedom was ingested.

The walk that evening felt different. Of course, Jimmy was getting a buzz for the first time, but it was more than that. They were the masters of their fate, captains of their own souls with the freedom to explore. After the second can was emptied, Jimmy started to feel fearless for the first time. Liquid courage was real, and the new yellow brick road led him and his friends to the town beach.

The pomp and circumstance of Independence Day was in full effect. Music from the horn, wind, and string sections swirled together off the bandstand and created a blanket of celebration over the grass field. Rows and rows of lawn chairs were sprawled out like soldiers saluting the night sky while the band's composition was punctuated with colorful explosions from above. Three thunderous booms echoed over the beach, signaling the boys' arrival, the beers spurring on a heightened state of existence punctuated with sonic accuracy in the night sky.

It was my first of many "symphonic moments" as I have come to understand them over the years. A movie moment, if you will, where all senses converge to elicit a greater emotional depth of life. I have come to live for these moments and also realize that, for most, our willingness to explore and seek wonder disappears at the other end of a risk. But that night, all Jimmy had to do was look over to his right, between the rows and rows of chairs and spectators. at one man in particular who sat in wonder, aging and old but never so young at heart. The boy was still alive in Malcolm.

The Sweetheart with Pom Poms

The brown fitted jacket acted like a magnet, attracting smiles and glances from the young girls who lined the walkway between the "A" building and the cafeteria. Jimmy walked ahead of his wingmen, for he was the chosen one—the athlete, the young man, the hero—and everyone took notice.

"Plop" was the sound as an errant seagull (or possibly pigeon) connected its payload smack dab on Jimmy's right shoulder. His off-pink polo shirt, collar up mind you, took the brunt of it, bringing him back to reality. He stood alone, watching some of the boys from the football team with their spiffy jackets entertaining the swooning girls that followed them like little puppies. Jimmy felt like he was still stuck in middle school.

They say that getting shat on by a bird is good luck. Perhaps, although Jimmy would never grow into a gambling man. But things did really start to change during his junior year as Steve, Ed, and he made friends with some of the cheerleading squad. Like the mythical candy stripers from the Land of Oz, these creatures and their magical pom poms hypnotized many under the night lights of football games or in the basketball gymnasium. To Jimmy and his wingmen, they were known as friends and good ones, some of whom still cheer him on to this day.

Cheerleaders had clout in that, if you were friends with some of them, you were friends with all of them. That provided the non-jock Jimmy with a little extra swagger during those final two years of high school. More importantly, the group gatherings around campus grew between classes or at recess with his wingmen and the pom-pom girls. They developed into quite a group that would spill out to after-school outings and even weekend parties. Jimmy had finally established a solid group of friends as he approached his senior year.

Senior year held status, at least in his eyes. It came with an air of elitism that coincided with knowing you're the top dog on campus. But the magic of senior year is also where that worry-free oasis of high school begins to give way to talks about university and life beyond. It's like a veil of safety that begins to dissipate, and a clock starts to tick away.

Those ticks were growing loud for Jimmy as he entered that final year. He was without a girlfriend and without the coveted brown varsity jacket. But it was the magical year of high school, the one where anything is possible, like taking an unsuspecting stroll into Ralph Henry's grade-twelve physics class to sit at a random desk only to lay eyes upon a sight to behold. There she was on the first day of class: Jimmy's future queen (or at least high-school sweetheart).

Her dark curly hair accentuated her fair complexion and perfectly framed her freckled cheeks. Her smile could light the Bunsen burner on the room's workbench, and in fact, probably did. The connection was immediate, the infatuation instant, and those warm fuzzies that can burn brighter than a thousand suns were unleashed. Her name was Allison, and of course, she was a cheerleader.

When you feel something like that as a teenager, it can move mountains. Jimmy began to spread his romantic wings and soon found himself writing epic love notes that called to her as if from the big screen. There were surprise flowers and evening visits at Almacs, the grocery store where she worked. Endless phone calls lasted into the late hours of the night. And much like the rest of Jimmy's life, there was a musical score that always overlaid the emotional thread of their scenes.

For Jimmy and Allie, it was Lionel Richie. Period. Trips to the library together, make-out sessions, and slow dances were as common as the between-class rendezvous on campus. Love had taken hold, and it smacked them both upside the head. This is where Jimmy learned the deeper sense of love and connection at a young age. Allie was his teacher, sharing sexuality and sensuality with him as they moved through their senior year, innocence fueling exploration and growth.

The light of a candle's flame, flickering against skin, allows an artist to capture shadows and subtle nuances on canvas. Jimmy sat across the table from the universe's creation and marveled at its beauty. Her eyes glimmered, and her soul hypnotized the onlooker. Valentine's Day began with an evening meal for two at the romantic colonial stone and candle paradise that was the Pump House restaurant.

Jimmy broke the trance and fumbled with the wine list as the waitress approached. He tried his best to be all "Bond-like" with his attempt to order some alcohol.

"We would like a bottle of the... Frex-e-net," Mr. Bond said while bastardizing the pronunciation of the cheapest bottle on the menu.

"The Freixenet it is," the waitress repeated while rolling the proper French pronunciation off her tongue. She gave a smirk and then vanished, leaving the two love birds alone again.

To this day, I still can't imagine what went through her mind to let a seventeen-year-old who looked not a day older than fourteen order champagne. Simpler times, I suppose. In any event, she returned, and soon, Allie and I raised a glass of bubbly, toasting to the future, or so I assume. God, I wish I could remember for sure what we toasted to. Whatever it was in that moment was alive and all that mattered, I suspect. I have come to find out that such is the true gift of life: the moments that make up the moments.

The dangling light-blue piece of plastic dances as the key finds its way into the lock of Room 24 at the Bob Bean Motel. The door opens, and the young couple move into second part of their night to remember. Jimmy carries with him the black bottle of Freixenet from the restaurant and moves through the dimly lit no-frill room to a strategically placed radio cued for romance. Allison approaches him as his finger finds the play button. Mr. Richie begins his serenade while Allie reaches for the card addressed to her. Its contents are ripe with affection and the four-letter word that would come to be Jimmy's quest in life.

Allie's eyes move up from the card to greet Jimmy's. There are no words to describe the feelings exchanged through the silent stare. Their bodies move closer, their lips connect, and the dance of love begins. Cue Lionel Ritchie's "Wandering Stranger", which was (and is) my all-time favorite Lionel Ritchie song.

It's a song that would become interwoven with the sonic tapestry of my endless search in life. That night was everything we'd both ever wanted and was a postcard to the amazing experiences that high school can truly deliver. Life was perfect, and I think I'm going to stay here with that postcard a bit longer...

A Silver Spoon of Courage

As the cold New England winter gave way to the spring's warmth of possibilities, time was soon to come to an end for Jimmy and the graduating class of 1987. While it was a mad dash for university applications and next steps for most of the seniors, it was rather simple for Jimmy. Both his parents had graduated from the University of Rhode Island, so he had a guaranteed admission spot should he choose to go there, which he would, following on the path of anthropology, specifically archaeology. The idea of combing through sand and dirt with a toothbrush and comb wasn't the allure so much as the thought of visiting faraway lands of ancient people and their remnants (bullwhip and fedora optional). But first there was one more high school item to be checked off his list: that damn Varsity letter and jacket.

The year before, Jimmy had managed to make the tennis team, having put all those youthful tennis lessons with the recreation department to use. It just so happened that the teacher way back when was the current head coach of the high school team. Frank Caine was a different kind of coach. Not the fire and brimstone of other athletic leaders but more refined and chill with a touch of class. To the boys on the team, he was hip (partly due to his convertible Corvette in which he would drive around, and on occasion, chauffeur the boys to local matches).

Tennis as a whole was better on his asthma than most sports. He had progressed through high school aided by those magic pills, but the adrenaline shots were always the backup and still used when needed by Jimmy himself. He no longer had to rely on his mother to swoop in and save the day.

As spring blossomed with tennis, romantic beach walks with Allison, and dreams of post-graduation tales yet unwritten, it also provided allergens, which wreaked havoc on the airways and sinuses of asthmatics. Through most of his youth, if you didn't know better, you would have thought he was a dog. His nose was always wet, always running, and worst of all, seemed to be triggered by kissing as well. Poor Allie.

The night started the same as most others, with a long phone call with Allie and then straight to bed. There was a tennis match against rival East Greenwich the next afternoon. At about midnight the spring nasal drip set a series of events in motion that would alter his life forever. The drip often caused Jimmy to begin coughing in his sleep. He propped himself up in bed, nearly choking from the series of snot-laden coughs, and as usual, his mother immediately chimed in from her bedroom.

"Are you okay, Jimmy?" Her voice floated through their small rancher.

Now much older than the child that used to cuddle his mother and sway with her during the attacks, Jimmy just rolled his eyes as usual. "I'm fine!" he snarked back. Realizing that he needed to go pee, he popped up out of bed and headed for the bathroom.

His eyes squinted in the light in the bathroom, but he was able to find the edge of the sink and brace himself. As his eyes adjusted, he began to take hold of the man in the mirror. He could see the telltale sign at the base of his throat, sucking in hard. He glanced left at the hall cabinet that housed the pincushion relief and then looked back at himself one last time. He gripped the counter for additional leverage before trying to take a powerful breath in. Next, there was nothing but blackness.

The old Zenith television set of Jimmy's childhood would turn on with a small dot at the center of the screen. From that dot, the screen would start to come to life, expanding in a circle as if an eye were opening, exposing a new world. Jimmy's eyes similarly opened, and his pupils slowly tuned into the channel before him. Two paramedics were kneeling next to him, strangers in the Gardiner household. Jimmy's initial response was rather colorful:

"What the fuck are you doing in my house?" the teenager candidly asked from his sprawled-out position on the floor.

He lifted his head to see a police officer talking to his mom and dad in the hallway. He slowly sat up then, gauging the situation, and then embarrassment shot over him. That snot-nosed dog within him had just pissed all over the bathroom on his way to the floor, doing his best to mark his territory.

He had completely stopped breathing from the attack, something that had never happened before. The paramedics advised that he had to be taken into the emergency room for monitoring and a doctor's once-over. The only thing going through his mind at this point was the fact that he had a tennis match that afternoon and that this needed to be a quick trip.

Jimmy was heading down the yellow brick road once again, but the fantasy world that he so desperately needed to help the scared child was gone. The sliding doors whizzed open as they carted him into the emergency room. He kept an eye out for witches on low-flying brooms, but sadly, they were gone. As were the beautiful candy stripers eagerly awaiting his rendition of *Scuttle the Stowaway Mouse*. It was all gone. Even the wizard behind the curtain seemed cold and sterile. Those times had vanished, and the young man would need to earn his lion's courage the following afternoon on the tennis court, not upstairs in an oxygen tent.

The Gardiner three returned home from the emergency room around three a.m., weary from the night's adventure. Jimmy laid in bed, reviewing the story from his folks while staring at the ceiling. The thud of him hitting the tiled landing had caused both parents to shoot up out of bed. When they dashed into the bathroom, they saw their son sprawled out before them, turning bluer by the second. His dad, being a Vietnam vet and Boy Scout leader, knew he had stopped breathing. When he'd tried to administer CPR, he couldn't get his son's jaw to release, Jimmy having clenched it shut in a spasm.

"Get me a spoon!" his dad had barked to Mom who ran down the hall.

His dad began to use the spoon to pry open his son's mouth, and in doing so, had chipped the bottom of Jimmy's two front teeth. But it worked, and he was able to pump some air back into Jimmy's lungs as they waited for help to arrive.

Jimmy was beginning to finally drift off as he slowly ran his fingers over the two jagged front teeth, wondering what Allison would think of them, but even his love for her was overshadowed by the pending conquest coming after school. A battle was looming.

It was a glorious spring afternoon as the boys met behind the girl's gym at the fences that surrounded the tennis courts. They would be travelling today, and since it was the next town over, it would be a car-pooled trip, which meant one thing: Someone would ride shotgun in a black, sixties corvette. That lucky someone was Jimmy.

As the cars pulled out one by one on their procession to the match, Jimmy felt the warmth of the red leather against the back of his thighs. The sun was beaming down on their heads, and the wind was combing his blond locks, taking him back to the freedom of Cydot. Only one thing was missing, one key component to every magical scene as it unfolds.

Coach Cain pushed a cassette into a newly added audio player and cranked the knob. He looked at Jimmy with his mirrored sunglasses and gave a smile. What transpired next would imprint on Jimmy: One song played that, no matter where he was or who he was with, would always take him back to this moment. The two sped down the highway of life, belting out nine minutes' worth of massive air guitars and an unforgettable chorus. Freedom was found with "Free Bird" by Lynyrd Skynyrd.

The white sneaker laces were synched up a bit tighter as Jimmy put the finishing touches with a double knot. He then picked up his oversized Prince racquet and took to the court. During the school matches, there would be multiple games being played right next to each other at the same time with spectators, which included team members, cheering for whomever from outside the surrounding fence.

As a tennis player, Jimmy was average to say the least. He had managed to secure the last of five singles spots on the team and now would be up against the number-five player from the competition. As the match began, the two young combatants traded shot for shot. Jimmy didn't know his opponent, nor did he care that day. On the other side of the net was a monster, an alter ego that had been tormenting him for eighteen years: asthma. It was relentless in its pursuit, and the East Greenwich player was much the same. The two wouldn't give an inch, stubborn in their quest for victory. The first set went to his alter ego, the second to Jimmy. The third back to the rival. As the fourth commenced, the other athletes from both teams became engrossed spectators.

Jimmy was playing out of his skin as if possessed by some competitive spirit that was inhabiting his soul. He was diving at the net to stop blistering passing shots, fully committing his body to the hard surface of the court. He was making the most miraculous plays he had ever made and had the war wounds to prove it. Blood poured from his knee down onto his white sock and sneaker. The fourth set went to Jimmy on another Boris Becker style aerial assault that landed about as hard as it looked to the cheering fans.

After he scraped himself off of the pale-green landing pad, Jimmy walked back to the fence to fetch a towel. He was starting to feel the wear and tear. That was obvious. Both legs had bloody reminders now. Behind the fence, the entire team was now standing and rooting for him. He stood for the first time on the main stage, and it seemed familiar.

He wiped off his face with the towel and thought about wiping the blood from his legs, but he liked the sight of it. It meant he was in it, and it got him fired up. Back out he went for the fifth and deciding set, where much of the same ensued with a back-and-forth spectacle trading points and games. At the midpoint of the last set, Jimmy's body began to shut down, dehydration and cramps began to take hold. The pain mounted, but to Jimmy, it just made it more dramatic. He wanted all of that symphonic bliss on this day. Another dive to save a point to the roar of the small crowd. His blatant disregard for his body continued to the point where he could barely move. But these are the battles that are remembered, and ones where both combatants deserve to win.

As if scripted for greatness, it went into a fifth-set tiebreaker. Win by two. At this point, Jimmy's tank was empty, and when the match concluded on a ball that was beyond his diving attempt, he accepted the death blow, his body crashing to the court one final time. Face down, he stayed there for a moment before he could pry himself off the court and meet his opponent at the net with a respectful hug. But it was the walk towards his team, with their cheering love, that he would remember most.

There would be no Corvette ride home that evening. Just a back seat in the team captain's car, where Jimmy sat broken, not mentally (as the loss didn't bother him) but physically. He was in pain. Sure, his knees were sore, and his body felt tight, but it was a level of discomfort he had never felt before, with his body full of lactic acid, causing nausea and headaches. He would come to know this painful pleasure on a much deeper and intimate level in university. Perhaps his future sports endeavors were born this very day in the arena where he had entered and fought a battle for the Little Jimmy who couldn't. As he sat motionless on the ride home, he reviewed the last twenty-four hours of his life. Into the darkened window, he mustered enough energy to move his lips. His reflection looked back at him, and a slow victory smile took over his face.

A Queen's Touch

To this day, I still have a romantic notion of a warrior searching for his queen because when he finds her, he fights for her, honors her, loves her, and when weary from life (or in this case, a tennis match), he can find refuge in her arms. My younger self needed Allie more than ever after the battle against my archnemesis. I was a broken warrior, and only my queen could offer reprieve.

A finger slowly moved to press the doorbell. Jimmy barely had the strength to stand and wait for her to open it. When she finally answered, her smile cut through the darkness of the night and the pain Jimmy was feeling. There was his queen, with her arms outstretched. It was an invitation to safety, and Jimmy accepted. They spent the next few hours together, mostly with the soothing power of the unspoken word, Jimmy lying on the couch stretching his sore legs, his head cradled in Allie's lap. As he spun the tales of his heroic conquest from earlier, she would gently caress his head, much like his mother would do when he couldn't breathe. For his part, he was touched by an angel. Nothing in the world felt more sacred than a warrior returning home to the embrace of safety and love.

In the many years since that tennis match against my alter ego, I am still drawn to Allie's couch. It was that moment of tenderness where a woman became my champion, listening to my deeds, tending to my scars, and nursing me through my pain with a gentle touch. I don't think I've felt that since—not in the pure form it took that night so long ago. A "wandering stranger" indeed.

Just like Lionel's song eventually Jimmy was called to find himself and would hope someday Allie and he "would make it together." That someday never came. They did make it to the senior prom: a beautiful evening that unfolded at a stunning mansion in Newport, Rhode Island. But even they couldn't escape the setting sun as the magic drew to a close. Jimmy was growing restless as the warrior within evolved. A beacon was now calling him to explore and push the boundaries of what he thought he could do and/or be. Allie did her best to try to keep him by her side, but warriors are called to far-off lands, the lure of adventure running deep in their blood. And so, Jimmy turned away from the birth of love in his life and walked away, leaving Allie and Lionel in his memory.

Even now, high school seems like some faraway land concocted by little Jimmy, but I take comfort in knowing that it was my reality. Many relationships that were built, fostered, and embraced fell apart and eroded. It is the currency of time. The debt that all kids must pay to grow up. The simple walks with Allison and the beer-laden adventures by the railroad tracks would join Rusty, Kirk, and Scuttle on the shelf of memory, as would one more item from that time: a beautiful North Kingstown High School Varsity team jacket.

Jimmy finally got his badge of honor.

A Blue Key to Dream

Many things had changed over the course of the last eighteen years in the life of Jimmy and his folks. One thing that had always remained constant, however, was the air of excitement when his dad pulled up the driveway after work. Sure, the old green Scamp had been replaced by a silver truck, and even the old games of H-O-R-S-E grew dormant. But there was something about Dad coming home that was always a highlight of Jimmy's days, made even better during the eighties with the invention of the VCR player and their tandem love of movies.

It was commonplace for Dad to return home with some plastic VHS rentals pinned under his arm, sometimes juggling the occasional paper bag containing whiskey for his Manhattan. That early summer day, I met him in the kitchen upon arrival.

Dad shuffled in, juggling his keys and three plastic containers. "Hey," he offered.

"How was work?" Jimmy asked, sticking his hand out for the offerings.

"Not much to choose from to be honest. Although, I thought you might like this one." His dad passed the top VHS rental to the outstretched hand of his son.

That simple choice his father had made altered the course of who his son was to become and forever be synonymous with him. He had chosen a nondescript eighties movie starring Rob Lowe, and Jimmy chose a life path.

Just like in days of old, Jimmy sat in front of the Zenith television, although this time at a more acceptable distance, even managing to sit on some furniture. The magic box came to life, and with it, a world where a fellowship was born out of discipline, culture, and an oath to one's self for the good of the boat. The movie was called *Oxford Blues,* and it centered around the sport of rowing.

Rob Lowe played an egomaniac American rower, who was infatuated with some highfalutin British woman played by Amanda Pays, going to school at, you guessed it, Oxford University. There was an immediate and common thread between Jimmy and Rob's character, not the egomaniac part but rather the outsider part, willing to champion a romantic connection across the globe. But it was the introduction to the world of rowing that truly captivated Jimmy. It was steeped in tradition and culture, a code by which one governed themselves and others in unwavering commitment. The training was fierce, and the loyalty was even fiercer. Jimmy felt a deep soulful connection and calling to the sport like nothing he had felt before. Perhaps it was the water, the rhythm, the synchronicity, or the honor. Who knows? Whatever it was, it spoke to him, and he listened. Twice!

He watched the movie two times that evening, back to back. He immediately went through all his printed materials from the University of Rhode Island until he found it, staring at him from the page. The university did, in fact, have a rowing team, though it was a club sport, not a varsity program. The next day, when his mate Ed came over to throw the football, Jimmy shared his thoughts about joining the team, to which the usual dry and droll Ed said something to the effect of "You're out to lunch. Get real."

I don't do well with proposed limitations. Never have and never will. Whether that comes from a close friend or (just a few days later) my pulmonary specialist.

"I would highly advise against it. Rowing is one of the most demanding sports in the world," Dr. Walter Donat said to me from his leathered throne and white coat of stern conduct.

He was a nice enough fellow, but he didn't know me. Neither did Ed for that matter. No one truly knows the heart within each of us or what it is capable of.

As the doctor sat in his optic showdown with Jimmy, just a few feet across from him, it became apparent that all the degrees behind him and thousands of dollars spent on his academic journey wasn't going to sway the calling of a young man.

The doctor moved his hand to retrieve something from his desk drawer and slid it across the wooden desk. An odd-looking device now caught Jimmy's gaze. The off-blue covering housed a small canister.

Smirking, the pulmonary specialist said, "This will provide you immediate relief, and you can take it with you everywhere."

Jimmy smirked too. He picked up that beautiful blue puffer and knew that it was going to unlock his athletic future. He had just punched his ticket to freedom.

Field Redemption

The blue cloudless sky and its September sun provided the perfect backdrop to greet university students in the fall of 1987. The University of Rhode Island is situated in Kingston about ten miles or so inland from the nearest ocean wave. It's nestled on a hillside with the gymnasium complex and sporting fields anchoring the base of the incline. Dormitories and housing units would lead the progression upward to the cafeteria and memorial union, with all the various academic buildings adorning the summit.

In typical New England fashion, many of the buildings were made of stone, giving the allure of colonial history and charm. The university was known for the quadrangle, a large perfectly manicured grassy area complete with cement walkways and benches. Surrounding the square were these remnants of colonial education buildings like a 150-year-old Monopoly board.

The air was one of freedom and exploration, the strum of an acoustic guitar synchronizing with the early fall breeze welcoming in the beginning of freshman year.

Jimmy reached the quad on the second full day of school, a young man on a mission. Once again, he was in the land of team swag and searching for the prized sighting. The rowing team (or crew as it is called in the United States) have the coolest, most original jackets designed specifically for the sport. The brown varsity jackets of high school seemed to pale in comparison. These majestic offerings were dark blue with white strips on the cuffs. A white zipper extended from another white-striped collar down to mid-chest. The white logo on the front were the letters U-R-I in the shape of a boat with a rower sitting on top. The back was bold; big white letters proudly stated, "Rhode Island Crew." To top it all off was the unique butt covering, an extra piece of material that was longer and hung down over the ass to keep it dry.

I don't know if the Red Sea parted for the big "M" or not. Nor do I recall myself standing on a precipice with a rod and staff. I certainly didn't have a long-ass beard; that's for sure. However, my head was on a damned swivel, and when I caught a glimpse of two beautiful blue jackets appearing through the parting of passing students, a light from the heavens shone down on me, and the angels approached. The two women clad in their spiffy blue outerwear came right up to me, waving a piece of paper. Little did I know that it would be the key to everything I would ever want in life, or at least, the courage to search for it. The paper read, "Monday 7:30pm, Room 101."

Thankfully, I can go back to the moment that started it all at will and do so often. Sometimes, I see Jimmy sitting there, always early, and nervously watching the large classroom fill with interested young men and women. Sometimes, I decide to join him, folding down the auditorium seat next to my younger self and watching everything unfold together. I know what the future held that evening for the boy next to me, but Jimmy did not. He sat there wondering, pondering if any of these strangers that filled the seats would become his blood brothers in battle. I know one thing for sure: My younger self wanted to know if rowing was as cool as Rob Lowe and *Oxford Blues* had made it out to be.

The lights dimmed, the projector came to life, and on a large white screen began a "Welcome to Rhode Island Crew" montage video, complete with epic music and imagery. That night, it only took U2's stadium anthem "Where the Streets have no Name" playing for thirty seconds for Jimmy and many others to fall under the spell and hear the call. Rowing would become Jimmy's rock, his lighthouse to weather all the crashing storms in his life. His first test would be the very next day when novice-team run would commence at the field behind the gymnasium at precisely four p.m. Oh, and it would be a three-mile run to boot.

"Pheft! Pheft!" The puffer shot its airy juice into Jimmy's lungs. He wished its sound was a bit more subtle, so it didn't announce to the world his vulnerability. Thirty new potential recruits filled the grassy area behind the gym. Out of those attending, only about twelve were men, the rest women. The novice coach, Mark (who was a former rower himself), stepped up and took command. He laid the groundwork for the three-mile run: the number of loops required, "fitness is first and rowing second" kind of stuff. As clear as day, Jimmy heard him proclaim, "This is not a race."

Jimmy gathered himself and eyed two young men in particular who were edging toward the front of the line, as if getting a clear trajectory for the speed they would unleash. Jim and Gregg were two best friends from the same town in New Hampshire and would become part of Jimmy's brotherhood, which commenced in three, two, one...

"Go!" the coach yelled.

"This is not a race" immediately echoed in Jimmy's mind in response to Jim and Gregg blowing off the line in a sprint. It was followed by a "what the hell" news bulletin, as Jimmy wasn't in Kansas anymore. He had never attempted to run this far; hell, he had never run more than half a mile, and that was with walking intervals. Flashbacks from walking around the field at middle school before losing the coin toss for that final basketball spot replayed like a bad song in his head, over and over.

But the boy from Cydot kept pushing forward despite his lungs crying out. He was able to keep the shortness of breath in check, periodically slowing to a trot while he fumbled for his inhaler, which was along for the ride in his shorts' pocket. After what seemed like an eternity, he turned the last corner and headed down the final stretch, trying his best to pick up the pace.

Those two fields that accompanied two very different school experiences sit with me now like two figures perched atop my shoulders. The horned one is a field of shame, loneliness, and failure with its forked tongue feeding my younger self with limitations and fear. And then there's the haloed one—the one where, as an eighteen-year-old, I witnessed all the boys led by Jim and Gregg standing at the finish line cheering me, a stranger, to the end. There was this sense of strength and unity that is still hard to put into words all these years later. I still get emotional about it as an older man when I tell of the moment that I crossed the line and saw them there. That onscreen brotherhood was now a reality. I had officially entered the world of crew.

Just the Facts, Ma'am

Hear ye! Hear ye! And if I had a bell, I would ring it! It is not a kayak, nor is it a canoe, and for God's sake, rowers do not use paddles!! They are called oarsmen, or oarswomen, not paddle men or women. Even though it is one of the oldest collegiate sports on record, and one steeped in ritualistic traditions and legendary rivals, there are a lot of misconceptions and unknowns about the sport of rowing.

This is rumor control, and here are the facts: The boats are called "shells"—yes, as in clam shells or the gas station chains in North America. These shells are meticulously crafted layers of woodwork, and in the new era, carbon fiber and graphite, that are designed to be as light and strong as possible to support its crew. Shells and their cargo can range from the single scull (one man) to a double, a four-man shell, and the big kahuna, a coxed-eight ticket to glory. Now where it gets a bit tricky is that there are two types of rowing disciplines for all the boats except the eight: sculling and sweeping, with sculling and sweeping oars coinciding with the appropriate boat. The smaller more fragile sculling oars are about eight feet long, while the more robust sweeping oars are massive, twelve feet long and built for power and leverage. At the end of all oars, there is a blade, a finely constructed surface that is designed to slice into the water and catch it to propel the boat forward. Sculling boats consist of having one oar in each hand, keeping the rower centrally stabilized over the boat. Think of your grandmother sitting down and knitting you some cozy slippers, dainty and precise, with both hands holding her tools. As for the other type, think barbarians at the gate with huge lances bent on destruction. This is predominantly found in university rowing and on the Olympic stage. Sweep rowing consists of one twelve-foot oar for each rower in alternating fashion down the boat, so that there are four on one side and four on the other. This, my friends, is the moment that usually defines most collegiate rowers and marks them for life: the arbitrary boathouse lineup where a coach labels you port or starboard, and your life sentence is cast.

It is also true that rowing is the only sport where one gets to sit on their ass and cross the finish line backwards. The placement of each rower within an eight-person shell is strategic as each seat has its role and purpose for the collective. Since rowing is ass-backwards, so is the pecking order. The back of the boat or stern is the front to those in the boat. Bear with me.

The *coxswain* (or coxie, or little creature with big mouth) is the brains of the crew. He or she is the only person to know what the heck is going on, since they have the only view. Rowers don't look; they trust. They put all their energy into letting this ride-along yet important piece of luggage gauge the sixty-foot vessel against other competitors, steer the shell straight, and give designed tactical moves in coherence with a race plan. They are also vicious pitbulls when it comes to keeping discipline in the boat, and a task master on blade timing and power application: two components that are crucial to success. If they could carry a whip like the slave ships of old, they would.

Next up, in seat *eight* is the "stroke" of the boat. This is usually labelled the leader of the boat, the best rower, and the one that can establish the one component necessary for all things in rowing: rhythm. They have a barbaric switch within them, and when the cox calls for that extra summoning of valor and courage, it is the stroke that has to go into the darkness first and lead the way for the others to follow.

The stroke is backed up by the *seven* seat, a skillful channeler of technique and courage to feed off the rhythm the stroke is laying down and set the pace for their side of the boat.

In the middle of the boat sits the engine room, the big guns who just hang and bang on those oar handles and let controlled chaos reign. Seats *six* and *five* are the true hammers within the group and usually the biggest of the athletes, sometimes coined "the Neanderthals" of the group. Their main role is to pull as hard as they possibly can each stroke. Joining them in the middle of the boat are seats *four* and *three* who continue the engine-room concept, though not quite as powerful as the other two savages.

Last, but certainly not least, is the bow pair, seats *two* and one (or '*bow*' seat, as it's called). These two are the skillful, smooth applicators of blade work and timing. The shell narrows quite a bit at the bow, so it is imperative to have finesse with each stroke because the narrower the shell, the more sensitive it is to movement.

The rowers themselves are usually of taller stature since the sport is based around power and length of stroke, which creates more leverage. In other words, the taller the rower, the more effective their reach or "stroke length" in the water. What the movie of Jimmy's youth didn't get into is that there are different weight classes for competition: heavyweights and lightweights. This boded well for Jimmy and his two New Hampshire friends, Jim and Gregg, since they were smaller and built like lightweights. The boat needed to average 155 pounds between all eight men with no one athlete to exceed 160 pounds. The heavies were just that: big, tall dudes with weight and power at their disposal. Yes, size does matter apparently, although in rowing, it truly comes down to one's power-to-weight ratio, which is honed through incredible amounts of training.

Oh yes, the training. Relentless hours rowing, running, weight training, stadium steps, body circuits, and the steel gauntlet by which all is measured in the sport, the rowing ergometer. This piece of present-day torture would put the athletes through a series of soul-shredding reality checks and bring each of them to their breaking point many times throughout their careers. The benchmark was the two-thousand-meter test. This simulated the competition-racing distance, and nothing says, "I'd rather be dead" than a "2k." It is a grueling distance, requiring all the physiological stamina one has with a psychological iron will to go into that deep, dark abyss where the creature awaits, ready to devour them. That beast can be described in the one word above all others that describes rowing and racing: pain.

What makes rowing unique is that it requires the athletes to blast off the line with as much power and speed as possible. This sprint from dead stop to top speed requires vast amounts of power and blade-work agility as the stroke rates (number of strokes per minute) are extremely high. After about 250 meters, the boat settles into a race-pace cadence where the athletes begin to feel the burn, and the dreaded knowing that the worst is yet to come begins to creep in. In rowing, it is always a tactical advantage to have the lead so that you can react to the other boats' moves. Sometimes that speed comes with a price, and there are many who have crashed and burned at the halfway point. In university rowing, the real race begins at the one-thousand-meter mark. Crossing into that third five-hundred-meter stretch is the marker, the dreaded abyss that is unavoidable as the crews push to the line. As if the sheer pain and darkness the athletes feel during this section isn't bad enough, it is only matched with an "all in" call as the crews must pick up the power and rate to sprint in the last five hundred meters and then hit the line, all perfectly executed by their coxie so that not one ounce of energy remains. It is truly soul sucking and twistedly soul fulfilling, knowing that easing off is not an option. Period. It's not an option because of one simple fact: the code.

Rowing is not a sport; it is a discipline. One that stems from the concept that everything is for "the boat." It is a perfect chain bound by nine links, on and off the water. No one is greater than the whole, and the bond formed is one of loyalty to each other *above all things*. Boats live, bleed, and die together. They may not all like each other, but they respect what each is there for. No one backs off, and no one gives in without the guilt and unimaginable anguish of letting down your boat mates. It truly is the ultimate team sport, for in a race, there are no time outs, no huddles, and no off plays. Just an all-out selfless commitment to the brotherhood.

A Coin Toss Among Friends

The young men stood outside the small URI boathouse. In reality, it was like a glorified tin shed, albeit a large one that stood atop a small hill leading down to the hallowed water sanctuary that is Narrow River. It was the moment that all new rowers wait for.

"Port, starboard, port…" Coach Mark just went down the line of men with his finger point of destiny. It wasn't a coin toss, but pretty damn close if you asked Jimmy. The coach soon branded him, "Port," which was exactly the side of the coin he was hoping for. The quarterback from Cydot already had aspirations of leading a boat from the stroke seat.

Once each oarsman accepted their rowing fate, they entered the boathouse and took in the atmosphere of what would become their home away from home. The air is permeated with the unique smell of used equipment stained by the sweat equity of mileage in a wet environment. It is a welcoming smell like the familiar scent of belonging. The large sixty-foot vessels span both sides of the boathouse. They sit idle like giant payloads tucked in their racks, waiting to be deployed.

Jimmy's hand carefully glided along the dark-brown wooden surface. The color strikingly resembles that of his old high school varsity jacket. But the hull radiates stories of past battles waged and stories yet written. The sixty-foot walk led him to the weapons area. He stood, neck craned before the rows and rows of twelve-foot oars, standing tall and defiant. One of these would soon become an extension of him, a powerful instrument to do his bidding and carve his path through the water jungle on his way to glory.

But it was past glory that stopped him in his tracks. He now found himself before a wall with haphazard picture frames of past champions, each with an unknown story on their way to victory and legacy. One picture in particular, the men's lightweight eight from 1985, caught his attention. This gold-medal national-champion boat was full of nondescript athletes that had come to the sport just as he had and had stood where he stood now. The paper heroes from young Jimmy's bedroom walls were now replaced by glass-framed heroic moments in time. He wanted to be on that wall. And he knew that, if he was to get there, he had to get to work.

Nine Hearts: part one

Anticipation was high going into winter training of Jimmy's second year on the team. The lightweight men's eight felt something special about their chemistry based on the racing results from the fall. The URI Crew Club prided itself on its intense winter training: two and a half months of indoor and outdoor hell in the dead of New England winter. The river would freeze, but the passion to out-train the other varsity programs, which were fully funded and rowing in the luxury of indoor tanks or taking training excursions to warmer places, was white hot. This was gorilla-style training at its best, club training doing whatever and using whatever they could to get the physiological advantage, and by default, a psychological one too.

They had to build the mental resolve to go the distance. The squad was already facing a huge uphill battle with their competition. The larger and more robust programs had two or even three boats deep of athletes from which to choose the top eight lightweights to put together the fastest boat. This environment incubated intense competition and the ability to push day in and day out, ensuring the best of the best were chosen. On the contrary, the boys from URI were the only lightweights on the team, eight rowers for eight spots. The only heat of competition would be self-administered and self-governed. However, there would be a conductor for this motley crew, a secret weapon if you will. Someone who knew what this climb was about firsthand.

Their coach, Jack, was a feisty red-haired fireplug who had graduated from the school a few years earlier. What made Jack special was that it was his picture that adorned the boathouse walls, the one that captivated Jimmy. He was the stroke man of that legendary crew, though at first glance, he seemed quite unassuming. But make no mistake, underneath was this tenacious warrior who would hold them accountable to the code and to the brotherhood, even when all hope seemed lost.

Jack knew that one of the keys to success would be the bond. It was just going to be them, day in and day out on the water. He needed to create an environment where they would literally bleed for one another. Each day, they would attack a ghost on the early morning water of Narrow River, pushing against imaginary opponents, and even more challenging, their own doubtful inner voices. They had to be all in, and they were, albeit in their own unique ways.

Working as an extension of Jack, in the cox seat, would be Carolyn. She was an experienced coxie who (for the most part) had no problem controlling the egos and testosterone running amok. She was the brains to everyone else's brawn, to put it bluntly, and would oversee the two fundamental rules during practice and racing: There is absolutely zero talking in the boat; and she would threaten to castrate anyone who looked out of the boat. This is a rowing cardinal sin and breaks the trust between a squad and their coxie.

Setting the rhythm for the boat at the stroke seat was Kevin (Kmart as he was nicknamed) who was a starboard rower, so the rigging of the boat would be different than normal, not that this affected the crew at all. Kmart was a brash surfer dude with longer hair that was always kept in check by a yellow ball cap. Following him was his partner in crime, big Ken, sitting at seven seat. As the tallest guy in the boat, Ken would set the stroke length for the port side and make sure the aggressive Kevin would stay long and strong with each stroke.

The engine room was made up of Brian and Tom. Brian was a beast, plain and simple. He was a physiological specimen of cardiovascular fitness and the fittest guy in the boat by far, as well as the one with the warmest soul. He would be the buffer between the experienced guys and the newbies in the back. Matching Brian was Tom, nicknamed "the Hammer," and he truly was. This guy only knew how to do one thing with "every goddamn stroke": Pull that oar like his life depended on it.

The bow four were made up of the four lightweights from the novice year and the field of destiny. Sitting at four seat was Mr. Ralph Loren and socialite Brendan, who (ironically) bonded with Kevin and Ken more than his sophomore mates. This left the bow three composed of Jimmy, Gregg, and Jim at bow to round out the 1989 Men's Lightweight Varsity Eight. They were an unusually tall crew, ranging from 5'11 to 6'3, which boded well for stroke length and leverage. As the ice gave way to the spring sun, they hit the water, nine hearts on a mission.

I don't think we really knew if we were a good crew, a great crew, or just another crew. We were young, fueled by fire, and I think that innocence coupled with naivety led to this "Well, why not us?" approach when we hit the season. We didn't know any better, and frankly, that's the beauty of it... of being young. The world is a lot less limiting through that lens. Regardless, we needed a unified goal, something to strive for, and as coach, Jack would clearly explain to us that it needed to be a realistic one.

Since Jack had been where these boys wanted to go and knew the path firsthand, he suggested the goal of making the finals. The previous year, both the novice boat and varsity boat had been eliminated in the very first round. It had been four long years since a URI boat had been in the finals, and the rationale was that, once you made it into the finals and were one of six boats vying for three medals, anything could happen. All things considered it was a fairly quick discussion and decision. The goal was to 'make' the finals. The end game to the big dance in Philadelphia, PA was set. The road to get there would be paved with weekly match racing.

Match racing is a tradition of one or sometimes two schools being pitted against each other, *mano a mano*, or in this case, boat versus boat. Each school would pit their boats and their designated weight classes against the other team, side by side for two thousand meters. At stake was not only a victory but something even more precious: your team colors. The tradition had begun nearly a century earlier on the water. At the starting line, the coxies would set the terms of engagement with their rivals. After crossing the finish line, the losers of the race would have to pull their boats alongside the winners and remove their racing jerseys, passing them to the victorious man sitting in their seat. Over time, this tradition evolved to take place on land after the race as the crews returned to their boat trailers.

Nothing is more humiliating than the walk of shame after losing a race. Jimmy and the others got quite adept at the process, making trip after trip to the winning crew's trailer post-race. The first three weeks of racing saw three straight blowouts. Wesleyan University heavyweights trounced URI, which was to be expected, but right out of the gate, a loss is never easy to digest. Next up the Coast Guard Academy, our archrival. Well, Brendan found himself overnight at a young lady's house and missed the bus. A novice sub was placed in, and the walks of shame continued. It was a shirt giveaway so far, leading up to a big race with Georgetown University and Temple University, two powerhouse programs that were consistently in the finals at nationals. The boys in blue finished a distant open water behind both.

The boat just couldn't find its swing. The swing is the holy grail of the sport. It is the Zen state where power, rhythm, and timing are in perfect sync. The result is a magical ease and bliss when everything becomes effortless. The squad had achieved this from time to time in practice but couldn't seem to uncork it under the stress of competition. With the losses, tensions were beginning to mount between the stern four and the bow four.

Discipline began to crack, and chatter in the boat escalated, causing a division between the experienced and young boatmates. The straw that broke the camel's back was when the stern four asked Coach Jack to break the boat up into a Lightweight Four for the nationals. An emergency meeting was called, and the wrath of God ensued.

It was a mid-April afternoon as we surrounded Jack outside the boathouse perched atop its small hill. I remember Jack staring silently out at Narrow River. None of us knew what would transpire as Jack always seemed to keep a level head. We dared not speak and waited with heads hung low, staring at the dirt beneath our sneakers. Jack slowly turned. I can still see his young freckled face and reddish hair glistening with the touch of the sun through the budding trees. He looked at each of us and right through us to what lay inside. This was his superpower: his ability to know our potential, our hearts, and how bad we needed some semblance of honor from all of this. Like the conversations with Jimmy and Dave on the edge of the dock, the magical words of that moment have been set free to recede into an unrecognizable voice, lost with the tick of the clock. However, the message remains.

It will stand beyond the lives of the nine hearts gathered that day. Jack's heart spoke to them, reminding each of the power in doing something for the person across from them. Not for themselves, not because any one person was better than any other but because they loved and respected each other. That is the code that binds oarsmen. That is the undercurrent of finding the swing and the willingness to go into the abyss and meet that beast of pain. It is the fundamental concept of belief and the unconditional love that will champion one to greatness. Through all Jimmy's older years, and countless journeys, he would always come back to this singular moment—that conversation between a handful of boys and a man, not much different from little Jimmy facing fear with his dad.

They stood frozen by the delivery of Jack's crew soliloquy. Slowly, their eyes began to interlock with each other's. Jimmy and Kevin seemed to connect first as if the two sub leaders of the boat instinctively knew that they would play a huge part in keeping that belief and unity going. That day was about surrendering, about submitting with selfless love. And moving forward, the nine would be inseparable, their unbreakable chain held strong by the links of love. There would be extra workouts and weekly trips to Torry Road, a long steep hill that would bring every URI oarsperson to their knees. These punishing runs had the pleasure of ending with an unmistakable chorus of vomit and guttural pain from pure exhaustion. But they ended together, always. The weaker athletes in the boat would never finish without the company of their brethren who would circle back around to make sure they always crossed the finish line together. Even Carolyn would put herself through the trials and tribulations of voluntary discomfort for the boys; and they loved her for it.

Water practices became a ritualistic excursion into the abyss of suffering. The boat would hit every session like it was the last time they would ever pay tribute to the gods of Narrow River. It was a sacrifice of the soul every day. They would be the first ones into the boathouse every morning and the last back onto the dock as the sun began to spread its morning wakeup. The scene would unfold the same, some days more dramatically than others, more given and more sacrificed. This particular morning, Carolyn navigated a perfect dockside landing of the sixty-foot vessel. As she softly spoke the words "One foot, up and out," the boys exited their shell after another valiant conquest of battling their lonely selves. They didn't stand and step, instead crawling out of the boat. Weary warriors lay spewed all over the dock, eight bodies done and dusted. A true postcard of a time of great personal sacrifice and honor.

The season itself progressed with a home win, their first of the season. Followed by another two losses before the upcoming race in Camden, New Jersey. The boys never faltered, even though the season was marred by losses. In fairness and true URI fashion, the boats would always hit their stride later in the season due to the limited water time in comparison to the other schools. It had been a proven track record for winning crews before them, so the boys took comfort in that.

Everyone else around them, however, started to become the doubting voices that rained down on the underperforming gladiators on the arena floor. The boys did their best to maintain a positive energy, but others on the team began chirping in the shadows and reminding them that they hadn't really done well at all. Worse than that, their bravado came across with a hint of arrogance. Their teammates saw them going all in every day but began to chalk it up to a bunch of guys with big hearts and no boat speed. Jimmy's parents were no different.

They came to as many races as possible, and Jimmy's teammates would get to know them as the bearers of Allie's Donuts, delicious fat pills that would be distributed at every race. Each week, Jimmy would tell his folks of the boat's potential and how amazing the training was going, the speed, the power, and the determination. He would pump the boat up only to have to come up with reasons and excuses why they kept losing. Jimmy could even sense that his dad was growing skeptical, not in a negative way but in a supportive one. The boys in blue desperately needed a shot in the arm to get their momentum going.

The tiny needle that would puncture Jimmy's childhood skin on a regular basis was replaced with a sixty-foot one. The boys had been rowing in a Kaschper shell, an older wooden boat named after the recreation department head, Art Tuveson. The Tuveson was a heavy boat and much harder to row because its hull shape made it extremely difficult to balance. Contrary, all the big-funded programs had elite racing shells at their disposal, usually easier to row, lighter, and faster. Inside the boathouse, sitting unused on a rack since the previous year, was the golden yellow ticket. It was the Indy car of racing shells, an Empacher. This German feat of engineering had been bought used and designed exclusively for lightweights. It was much lighter, and its hull shape allowed for a smooth, more solid set during each stroke. It also had an ominous thunder sound that would sing from the tension filled oarlocks at the end of each stroke. That music would begin to echo on the early morning water of the Narrow and beyond.

Camden, New Jersey, was a fairly new racecourse and one that Jimmy would come to know quite well the following summer. At hand was one of the last races before the big dance. It was a meet that included a handful of schools, most notably the Army Military Academy. As one would suspect, these men were known for their discipline and being monstrous oarsmen. When the dust had settled, the URI crew and their German rocket ship had blown the doors off of the big men. It was the first time the boat had really flown the way it did in practice, and for the first time in a race, they had found the effortless beauty of swing. Only better than the row perhaps was the walk of shame those big guys from the military academy had to endure to come and shake hands with the bean poles of URI. Shirts were exchanged, congrats given, and Coach Jack brought the men into a circle. The match season was over; in two weeks would be the New England Championships, and a week after that, the nationals.

The crucial last piece to any athlete peaking at the right time is the sought after and never quite perfected DaVinci Code of training called the "Taper." In a nutshell, this is the culmination of large amounts of training and intensity with a scheduled decrease and backing-off phase, allowing athletes to recover both mentally and physically. If dialed in perfectly, it can be a wonder drug containing extra energy and increased ability. However, if the timing is off, it can have a devastating effect, spelling disaster for high-level performance. Rowing presented a unique challenge to the coach as an individual taper was out of the question. Coach Jack had to choose something that would be universal for all eight rowers and trust that it was just the right recipe for success.

Leading up to the New England Championships, the boys brought everything they had to the intensified training and ended the home-water season as usual, sprawled out like dead fish on the dock. Their work was done, and now it was time for the secret sauce to kick in. The great thing about rowing is that you can lose every seasonal-match race, which they almost did, and still get a shot for glory. This Cinderella squad was heading north to Worcester, Massachusetts.

Lake Quinsigamond, which appeared more like a river, was the home to many races throughout the years and a second home course for teams like URI. In particular, Jimmy would race more on this course than any other over his career, one which culminated with a twenty-three-year return to chase glory later in his life. The regional championship race would be a straight six-boat final with some of the powerhouse teams that demoralized URI earlier in the season vying for the medals and top seeding the following week at nationals.

As a spectator sport, rowing isn't exactly a stadium sell-out. With the races stretching out over one and a quarter mile, the only visible energetic section is the last five hundred meters. But in all fairness, that's the point you want to be at, watching the boats charge to the line, waiting for some crew to drop a sprint from hell and pull off a miraculous victory. At this race, there would be no grandstands at the finish line, just a large mass of cheering people, school chants, and a stroke-by-stroke commentary blaring from the loudspeakers.

As the lightweight eight approached the last five hundred meters of the race, the URI contingent surrounding Jimmy's parents started to hush. It was evident even from the skewed optics that the long yellow boat was not up with the leaders. In fact, at this point, they were a distant fourth or fifth out of six crews. The current situation seemed to confirm some of the thoughts that the other teammates would share out of earshot of the lightweights. Jimmy's mom and dad knew their son would be devastated, especially after the momentum gained over the last two weeks.

Coach Jack stood watching stoically. He took the last few counts on his watch to indicate what stroke rate his crew was rowing at and did a quick calculation in his head. His head dropped as he made his way toward the landing dock. Hitting the line first was Tufts University, followed by the Coast Guard Academy about half to three-quarter's of a length down. Third was UMass, and approaching in fourth place, a length of open water behind them, was the yellow boat with the boys in blue.

Back at the trailer, the boys finished setting the boat in its wooden stretchers. The air was thick with frustration and anger as Jack waved them over to the shade of a nearby tree. Something was different about this loss. There wasn't any moping or finger pointing, just the unmistakable smell of raw anger. Kevin was the first to speak.

"I couldn't get the fucking rate up no matter what I tried," he said while his hands rested on his hips.

"My legs were shot," the powerhouse Brian chimed in.

Jimmy put a finger to his nose, pitching off one side of it and blowing a snot rocket onto the grass. "We had a great start... and then the boat just got heavier and heavier with each stroke," he said while wiping any remnants from his nose.

Coach Jack interrupted the supercharged banter. "According to my rate checks, Carolyn, I had you crossing the five hundred-meter mark at thirty-one strokes per minute. That's three to four beats lower than our race-plan rating," he offered as his investigation commenced.

She chimed in, "Yeah, we hit a thirty-two here and there, but it wasn't coming today."

Jack dropped his head in thought and walked in a slow circle while the coxie continued.

"The boys were solid. It was a set row. Great discipline. We just didn't have the legs on the drive sequence to sustain the rate," she said, concluding her assessment.

Jack scanned the boys and spoke in a gentle, soft tone. "Fuck 'em. It was the taper. You guys aren't there yet, and you shouldn't be. Your bodies are recovering. Trust the process. I'm telling you right now, you guys are fast. I've seen the times in practice. Fresh legs and a thirty-four-stroke rate will work for you."

We all felt let down after that race, but giving up was not an option. Our love was too strong. The only thing we could pin our hope on was Jack's assessment. We knew he was right about the stroke rate. It is the magical formula for success, a mathematical equation to cover the race distance and chew up real estate on the way to the finish line. But it has to fit the style of the crew and be able to maximize their power and length with each stroke.

All good on paper. What needed to happen was for the boys in blue to forget about the past season, forget about today's blowout by Tufts and Coast Guard, who would be at nationals, and just trust in the journey of it all. Jack brought them into a tight huddle and instigated the cheer. A revenge-laden "Fuck 'em!" exploded from the young men, while Jimmy remembered an ancient Klingon proverb from his *Star Trek* youth: "Revenge is a dish best served cold."

Nine Hearts: part two

The Dad Vail Regatta is hosted in Philadelphia, Pennsylvania, on the Schuylkill River that runs through parts of downtown. Philly has quite an old rowing tradition with its own boathouse row and massive historical odes to tradition rivaling that of the mighty Charles River in Boston, Massachusetts. Many schools and Olympians have waged war on this river, and many have found their identity in the process.

For the stern four in the boat and Carolyn, this course was old hat, but for the bow four, it was like Little Jimmy going to the Land of Oz all over again. Thousands of people would line the riverbanks leading to a finish-line grandstand, which held a few hundred screaming fans. It was an epic setting to the end of a conquest. One that would end on the medal dock for the lucky crews, smack dab in front of the grandstands.

The Dad Vail Regatta was the national championship outside of the national championship. To clarify, rowing in its historical tradition was an Ivy League sport, the founding fathers of American education: the Harvards, the Yales, the Brown Universities of the East Coast. They were in a different league and a close-knit group that had their own designated championship. The Dad Vail was for all the other rowing teams that wanted to come to Pennsylvania and wage war on the murky waters of the Schuylkill; the west coast, the south, the Midwest, and even from across the border in Canada of all places. This arena was rich with diverse programs and individual legacies.

Of course, Jimmy's parents made the trip down to support their son and their team. His dad would be sporting his usual blue USA rowing hat while Mom never went anywhere without her Wickford T-shirt proudly representing her home turf. For the boys in blue whose folks didn't make the trip, Jimmy's mom and dad provided some recognizable comfort.

The night before the first race, Coach Jack called a meeting in his hotel room. He was surrounded by the nine hearts situated around the room, some on the bed, some in chairs, and some even on the floor. The air was heavy with the anticipation of the unknown. Jack was going over the logistics for the quarterfinal race coming up the following morning. He instructed Carolyn to use a visualization technique to take the boys through the race plan in crisp detail. The rowers closed their eyes and allowed her voice to take them through the two thousand-meter race, doing their best to breathe vividness into each stroke.

The start sequence would consist of a few short, quick strokes to get the boat moving. There is a lot of dead weight off the start, so a few short bursts did the trick to generate momentum. It would consist of five strokes in the following sequence: ¾ slide, ½ slide, ½ slide, ¾ slide, and full slide. This would immediately be followed by a series of high strokes to deliver maximum power while bringing the boat up to full speed.

The lightweights from Rhode Island would rip off twenty strokes at around forty-eight strokes a minute before Carolyn called the "settle."

"In two strokes, one, two, on this one," Carolyn's soft voice filled the hotel room.

The first stroke of the settle had to be spot on with precision and power. The rating would drop down from high forties to race pace without the speed diminishing. Forty-eight to a thirty-four just like that, and if done properly, this crucial shift would set the tone for the entire rest of the campaign.

The rowers continued their personal visualization from varying points around the room, each lost in their own race but connected spiritually. Carolyn's commands drove them into a continuous rhythm of power and grace. They would now be approaching the bridge that spanned the river, under which the crew would do a slingshot move, marking the 750-meter mark. The goal was to enter the bridge span and take a power ten, a series of strokes with a little more pop to the blades and speed of the boat.

Coming out the other side, they would set themselves up for the thousand-meter mark, the point that separated the great crews from the good ones. At this point, which happened to be right at the URI boat trailer, the boys would take a twenty-stroke push to either separate or stay in contact with crews going into the home stretch. Every rower knows this as the Deadman's Zone, the unforgiving section that seems like an insurmountable stretch to stay composed as the pain begins to really take hold. Especially with the inevitable painful push of the last five hundred.

Carolyn sat up in her hotel chair and called a focus ten as her men crossed into the last five hundred to help get them ready for the final go. With about three hundred meters left, all the crews would be passing by the grandstands. This is where she would call the sprint.

"Up two in two, one, two, on this one." Her voice took a slightly sharper tone in the dimly lit room. The rating would jump a few beats into the high thirties, gaining boat speed. The crew would hold for ten strokes and then repeat for another ten-stroke burst, reaching into the low forties. And finally, expending every ounce of energy they had left, the brave souls would empty their tank at about forty-five strokes a minute, perfectly timed with Carolyn counting the number of strokes to hit the finish line.

"Paddle." She concluded the visualization with the call to ease off pressure and take it easy. Six and a half minutes or so, and the race would be over. In the upcoming quarterfinals, you had to make the top two spots to advance into the semis. A tough order indeed. But it's not the six minutes and change that mean much; it's what *happens* in the six minutes that can create heroes. Jimmy came out of that pre-race coma like he'd just had a spiritual awakening. From the wordless glances around the room, he wasn't alone.

Quarter finals. Race day had arrived, and it was the moment of truth for the boys, both on the water and on land. Like a herd of scrawny cattle, they stood outside the trailers, rows and rows of lightweights waiting for their turn to step on the scale. It was the morning weigh-ins.

Those lucky enough to make weight exited out the other side with their newly acquired stamp of approval, which usually sat somewhere on their right arm. The average boat weight of 155 pounds between all eight didn't come easy for the Rhody crew, and they soon found themselves waiting for Brendan to lose whatever he had wolfed down the night prior. In true GQ style, he made the whole process look like a fashion shoot with his choice Ralph Lauren layering of sweatpants and hoodies before hitting the road for a run. It took two additional visits to the trailer before every ounce of water was rung from his body, and he got stamped certified.

To keep things a bit light after the stressful weigh-in, the boat jester and recent sweat hog Brendan had a surprise. Kevin and he had been farting around with some old children's toys during the season and would bring them to the boathouse as playful mascots. There was one in particular that seemed to keep resurfacing, and it had accompanied the crew to Philly.

The boys stood around their rowing shell, eyes fixated on Brendan as he ceremoniously unveiled what lay hidden underneath a small towel. And there it was, secured to the bow deck. Its olive green and yellow stripes perfectly matched the sixty-foot yellow missile beneath it. Battle Cat was its name, the legendary ride of the great He-Man from *The Masters of the Universe*. Coach Jack rolled his eyes, but those freckled cheeks of his couldn't contain the smile. The boys found joy in the playful simplicity of it, and even he wouldn't dare take that away. In an ode to the powerful Vikings who had never gone anywhere without a figurehead on their ship, the boys in blue now had theirs.

The christening was followed by the ceremonious oar walk to the dock before the boat was carried down. Each rower made the walk in their spiffy blue crew jacket, their weapon in hand. This was more a show of unity and strength as other teams would have the coach do it or even other team members. But not Rhody. This was their psychological play, like a rooster puffing its chest to gain attention. They wanted people to take notice, and in a sea of regatta hustle and bustle, it worked.

The walk back to the boat played out in Jimmy's mind. Time slowed, their cadence drifting into slow motion as he was called back in time. Back to an early hero moment (in movies, of course): The famous scene in *The Right Stuff* when the Mercury Seven astronauts turn the corner dressed in their spacesuits and walk towards the camera in slow motion. The music swells as these heroes take the stage, ready to launch the space program. Now, Jimmy had finally found his Mercury Eight, which he had dreamed of as a child.

The last pep talk from Jack commenced with one instruction only: "Before anyone lays a hand on the boat, each must commit, a life for a life."

They broke with their traditional "F" bomb chant and took their place alongside the boat, standing as ordered, each waiting for the other to commit when they were ready. One by one, the boys committed in their own minds and slapped hands on the boat as an exclamation point to their brief internal conversations. They all looked at Carolyn, salivating.

"Up and over the heads. Ready? Up!" she barked. With military precision, the boys lifted the racing shell high over their heads as if it were light as a feather. "Shoulders, ready. Down!" she barked. The boat descended to its resting place, upon the alternating shoulders of the crew. Destiny was now in motion.

The most nerve-racking moment for many coxswains is backing their sixty-foot-long vessel into the stake boats that sit at the starting line. Sometimes, like in the Olympics, this would be a large floating platform, or in this case, six anchored poles tethered to a small skiff that held one person. That person would sprawl out in the boat with their hands holding on to the stern deck of the racing shell. Once those hands took hold of the shell, the coxie had to keep on their course point by making small adjustments, particularly on a river like this with some current. There would be six lightweight crews attached to six stake boats, awaiting the umpire, who stood underneath a tent on the riverbank to set the alignment. It would be a blind race for URI, meaning that they had no idea about the other five boats in the race, as they all were from different parts of the country. The umpire held a large red flag that would accompany the starting commands. At this regatta, traditional starting commands would be given in French. *"Et vous pres? Partez!"* (Loosely translated, "Are you ready? Go!") Then the flag would drop. Everything was about ready to go. Now the umpire was waiting for one thing.

As the cox makes his or her last-minute adjustments, they have to have a hand in the air to signify to the umpire that they are not ready. Carolyn's hand was high in the air in lane two and was having Jim in the bow seat use a few tiny strokes to adjust the boat's position. The boys took their final deep breaths and sat firmly at attention, awaiting her voice.

Jimmy took one last look around before the tunnel vision would commence, to the inside of the boat where his blue asthma puffer was secured with duct tape, and then it came, the soft voice through the boat's speaker system:

"My hand is down. Sit ready," Carolyn affirmed softly. The blades locked their footing in the water with all the slack removed from the rowers' bodies, just pure connection waiting to lever the shit out of a twelve-foot carbon oar.

"We have alignment!" barked the umpire from the shoreline. *"Et Vous Pres? Partez!"*

The red flag dropped and what had been utter silence gave way to the symphony of chaos: forty-eight bodies springing to life, supercharged by the static voices exploding from the speakers within each shell.

"Three-quarter!! Half!" Carolyn took them through the start sequence. Her body was catapulted back by the magnitude of the start, so much so that you could hear her wince as she had to fight the powerful surge of the boat and stay absolutely still. "Build!" she barked as the boys were laying everything they had into the wooden handles.

The stroke rate skyrocketed and so did the speed of the yellow missile. Jimmy was indeed on his way to outer space. Halfway through the twenty high strokes, URI already had a half-length lead on all the other crews. It was incredible. Nothing had ever felt like this before, and the boys knew it. But there was no time to process it before the next stroke came. Discipline to every single moment requires being absolutely present.

Carolyn set them up as she had done the night before, two more strokes leading into the big drop in rate and the settle to establish race pace. If they hit it as one, it was game over. Well, she called it, and Kevin perfectly landed the decrease in stroke rate to a thirty-four; pure precision and pure power were perfectly executed. The boat was unstoppable. Crossing the five hundred-meter mark, they were clearly in the lead, and by the time the slingshot move under the bridge was dropped on their opponents, they had clear water over all the other five boats. By the thousand-meter mark, the chants of "U-R-I" could be heard from the bank-side trailer. Jimmy's mom and dad had opted for this mid-race view, although his dad would watch it through the lens of a video camera, recording the deeds unfolding. They watched as their son and the others passed the halfway point in command and showing no signs of relenting. The boys were going to the semi-finals.

✧ ✧ ✧

That evening might as well have been an eternity for the nine-hearts club. Sleepless banter kept the mood light, but they knew with the impending sunrise came a chance for glory. The two semi-final races would be held in the morning with the finals taking place later that same day. This was the question though: How to expend just enough energy to make it into the finals without expending it all and then not having enough gas for the actual race for the medals?

The field had been cut down to twelve boats, which would compete in two semi-final races. In rowing, as you progress in the quarterfinals, there is a lane assignment depending on the outcomes. The winners of each quarter-final race get lanes three and four respectively since those are considered the most favorable lanes. It also allows the coxies to better gauge the competition since they are in the middle of the action. From the center lanes, the next places in the quarters slot into lanes two and five, with the last qualifying spots assigned lanes one and lanes six, the outside smoker positions.

The semi-final would see only one other boat that URI had raced that season: the juggernaut Georgetown University. Other than this crew, which was "the" crew, all the other known powerhouses were battling it out in the second semi-final, which had Tufts, Temple, Coast Guard, and U-Mass all vying for the three spots into the final.

Knowing that the seeding was working in their favor, Jack instructed Carolyn to carefully gauge where she was, and if (and only if) she was in a qualifying position, she had the green light to (as he put it) "Keep the horses in the barn." In effect, he wanted them to save some gas in the tank for later. It was also a strategy play, as a race plan is sacred. It is full of moves, countermoves, and specific calls. Once this bag of tricks has been deployed, it becomes knowledge to your competition in another race. Like most things in life, it was a calculated risk.

Up at the start, the sixty-foot rowing shells were scattered in the water way as each coxie began their arduous task of alignment. The yellow missile was in its lane and was now just waiting to get securely fastened to the stake boat.

"Stern pair, back it down," Carolyn muttered softly.

Kevin and Ken would use a backwards motion with their oars to slowly move the boat back towards the outstretched arm of the stake-boat holder. This was the last free ride any of the other men would get before contact with the stake boat was secured.

"Locked on" came the microphone call. "My hand is up. Bow seat, touch it," Carolyn calmly said. Jim, in the bow, would gently touch the water with his blade, bringing the bow of the boat to Carolyn's desired target, the large lane marker down the course.

Each rower has their own ritual in that dead space between aligning and the call to sit ready. Some tinker with nuts and bolts and triple check their tightness, while others sit in absolute silence, having some moment of "last will and testament" with themselves. Jimmy's ritual became something that his older self can still call upon anytime, anywhere. To this day, it is as familiar as brushing his teeth.

Jimmy tucked the wooden handle beneath his armpits, so his arms had an unobstructed path to his quads. His hands would rub and shake those pistons in an effort to keep them relaxed and loose. He then gave two distinct glances. First to the right and then to the left. The recipients would be the enemies sitting in his seat in the other boats. No matter what, Jimmy would out-pull them this day. When those energetic daggers reached their desired targets, he bent forward and gave Brendan a pat on the bold white RI lettering resting proudly across his back. His right hand would then slip behind his back and link up with Gregg, as he out-stretched his. He would then do the same to Jim in the bow. The crackling call of "Sit ready" broke the ritualistic moment and the link between the bow three. The boys took their positions at three-quarter slide.

As the red flag dropped, and the umpire unleashed the beasts from their cages, much went as planned. The boys in blue blew off the line like a gunshot and had an "oh shit" moment when Carolyn told them they were dead even with Georgetown. As they approached the bridge, it was fairly evident that three boats had surged out from the rest. URI and Georgetown were joined by a mysterious dark horse, Western Ontario, for the top three spots. Approaching the thousand-meter mark, these three crews had established a dominant lead over the field. Carolyn craned her neck to glance behind her stern. It became clear that the other three boats in the semi-final had lost contact with the leaders. She knew what this meant. The likelihood of them regaining contact was a lightning strike at best. Now it was time to play cat and mouse.

The three boats were dead even, with each surging ahead for a brief lead as they headed down the back stretch towards the grandstands. The winner would get the prized spot of lane four in the final, second place would get lane number two, with third getting assigned the outside sixth lane. Approaching the last 250 meters, Georgetown was pushing into the lead. Carolyn had a quick decision to make and decided to let them go in an effort to save some juice for the final. She also knew that her boys needed to be surrounded by the other crews to feed their blood lust. Lane six was not a position she wanted to be in for the finals. She adjusted her microphone with her left hand and calmly spoke, setting up the situation to the men.

"Do it," Kevin muttered back from the stroke seat. Carolyn leaned forward just a touch in anticipation of the move.

"Okay, boys, shifting up two beats, steady and together. On this one."

The boys responded by driving down the legs a bit harder on her command. The back pry off the legs created more leverage. And each of the eight oarsmen punctuated the call with snapping the wooden handles into their bodies with a bit of extra aggression. The boat lifted out of the water, and the yellow craft sprang forward, hungry for the line. Carolyn issued the call, and the boys delivered a flawless application. The extra gear helped punch their ticket to the finals in the lane that she wanted. Crossing the line, the mood was silent, part pain, part

"There's more work to do." Kevin reached out his hand for Carolyn's headset. He mustered up his breath and spoke to his boatmates through the microphone, straining to turn backwards so they could see him.

"Fuck 'em. Nobody believed in us. We still have one more race, one more job to do," he said, reminding them. He was right; they did. There was no time to celebrate.

As the boys approached the trailer, carrying the boat, you would have thought they'd lost. They had faces of stone. Their teammates were congratulatory, which they acknowledged with quick smiles or head nods. But shit had just gotten real for them, and they knew it. As did Jack. He approached them and said, "Congratulations. Now anything can happen in the finals."

No one dared to bother the boys as they sat alone, rehydrating and contemplating how that six-minute race had just validated every hard practice and every loss on their way to being where they were now. There was a satisfaction looming in the air, but their pallet had tasted a hint of glory, that sweet nectar that lures gladiators back into the arena, addictive in nature. Glory and the path to one of three medals were only six minutes away.

The finals took place later on that beautiful Sunday afternoon in the beginning of May. The energy from thousands of spectators lining the banks of the river covered the course like a blanket of electricity. Down at the jam-packed grandstands, the spectators, rowers, and parents were all jockeying for the best vantage points to watch the ensuing race. Jimmy's folks were there along with a contingent of URI rowers. Races would come down every fifteen minutes or so with the commentary delivering stroke by stroke updates through the speakers.

Back at the yellow boat, with its growling figurehead poised for battle, the air was calm. Never had the boys seemed so focused. Movement was kept to a minimum, every glance or deep breath powerfully intentional. One last circle brought them together. "Hands in" went the call. But this time, there was no shout, no sonic "F" bomb. Instead, the boys laid down the softest most intense "Fuck 'em!" imaginable. They were done with aggressively proving things to everyone else; this time, it was just for them.

The men took their positions, standing by their seats and going through their internal checklists. Jimmy took one last deep puff from his inhaler and secured it firmly for the ride with a strand of prepared duct tape. "Hands on!" came the call from Carolyn. The boat and the men were on their way. They walked away from the trailer to the cheers and well wishes of fellow boys and girls in blue. Nothing would be the same after today, and they all knew it. No matter the result, the boys instinctively believed that this race would come to define them in some way. Which way that would be was up to the rowing gods as they gathered to watch the spectacle.

Up at the start, the last of the six finalists were locking on to the stake boats. The race was shaping up to be a barn burner for sure, with the best of the best joining in. Lane One was the Coast Guard

Academy, which had beaten the boys twice this season and fairly easily. Lane Two held the boys and their yellow rocket. Lane Three boasted the New England Champs: Tufts University. Lane Four held the juggernaut Georgetown crew. Lane Five was the home-course heroes (and equally powerful) Temple Crew, who along with Georgetown had beaten URI by open water mid-season. Rounding out the field in Lane Six was the crew from Western Ontario in all black. URI was up against four boats that had destroyed them this season and one unknown.

The boys were locked on. Carolyn whispered through her headset as the crew made last-minute adjustments. The always somewhat-reserved Carolyn assured the boys that she would do whatever it took and would say whatever needed to be said to motivate them. They were her boys, and she knew how to reach inside each one of them if and when it was necessary. Taking a page from Jimmy's book, she said, "Link up!" As the call came down the boat, each team member locked hands, from Carolyn down through to the bow seat. "Bring it," she said then, and they broke the chain and took their positions.

A dead silence engulfed the starting area, fifty-four figures completely still. This was it. All the boats were in their proper alignment. The flag went up, and the umpire moved the microphone close to his mouth. "We have alignment. *Et Vous Près? Partez!*"

The blastoff ensued, controlled chaos in motion. The boys in blue began to unleash all of God's fury into their individual weapons. Jimmy was giving everything his 154-pound frame could deliver on each stroke. As the boat surged off the line, the boys began to build the stroke rate as designed. Up they went.

Carolyn barked off the strokes: "Three, Four. Forty-two rate. Six, Seven! Forty-five. That's it! Forty-eight! Nailed it! Ten more! Here we go!" A quick glance at her left. "Four seats up on Coast Guard!" She was in the zone, gauging distances, keeping a course, and counting the strokes.

"Twelve! Three seats up on Tufts! Fifteen! Even with Georgetown. Here we go! Still moving out. Oh yeah! Big fucking settle in two now! One! Two! On this one! And... send it."

Before the movie *The Matrix*, and bullet-time special effects, there was this very moment in time. In a perfectly synchronized movement, the boys went from nearly fifty strokes per minute to what seemed like a morphing, slow-motion, powerful convergence onto one stroke, slowing their recovery and timing to connect with a thunderous sonic boom.

"Yes!! Thirty-four and a half, baby!" Carolyn fired with excitement.

The boys had exploded off their launchpad and used the high strokes to climb further and further into the sky. When they perfectly nailed the settle stroke and established their assaulting rhythm, it was like they'd left the earth's atmosphere. Ten strokes into the settle, and the boys were moving out. Carolyn looked to her left. Coast Guard was already done, eating the yellow missile's wake. She gave a quick double take and strained her neck backwards, sticking up her hand to wave.

"See ya, Coast Guard!" their rabid coxie shouted.

Kevin muttered back under his breath with the exhale of a stroke, 'Yeah!'

Like a savage beast, Carolyn hunkered down and scanned to her right as this was where all the action would come from.

"Next!" the hunting predator barked into her microphone.

The boys were moving effortlessly as the elusive swing was in full effect. The yellow boat was singing at the top of its lungs. The oarlocks popped at the finish of every stroke in a synchronized roar of thunder. Jimmy was super focused, they all were. No roaming eyes, no heads on a swivel, just pure tunnel vision. Each man focused on the stroke at hand and on keeping the boat balanced.

As the crews approached the five hundred-meter mark, Carolyn decided she wanted to put another crew to bed early. She glanced to her right and was making out the distance on lane six, the outside smoker.

"Okay," she said, "time for the Canadian crew to fuck off. Their bow man is hanging on me. Get him off me! Breaking contact with the 'bow four.' Here we go, fellas. Lead us off. Ten strokes bow four, pulling for the stern four in two! One! Two! Hit it!" She drove her team to work.

"Let's go, B!" Jimmy said just loud enough so Brendan could hear. The bow four gave it. They all did. You could hear a more profound exhale as the oar handles came into their bodies. Snarling, Carolyn was calling off the strokes. "Oh yeah! Fading away! That's it, boys!"

A move like this was a brilliant call since the stern four would auto-matically give a tiny bit more and contribute to an increase in speed, and it was working brilliantly. By the end of the tenth stroke, they had broken contact with Western Ontario. Another victim fell to the wayside. At this point, two crews were now out of the medals picture.

The race was shaping up with the remaining four crews. Before the bridge, Georgetown and URI were dead even in the lead. Temple in lane five and Tufts in lane three were not quite half a length back. It was a highly contested battle as they approached the slingshot move under the bridge. Carolyn could see the structure's shadow on the water before the yellow boat as they approached.

"Here we go, boys! Get ready for the slingshot. Together now! Get ready to lay it down!" Her hand adjusted the tiny microphone.

Through the bridge, the coxies had to steer their boat slightly to their right to compensate for the small bend in the river. If done correctly in conjunction with the power move, it could gain a few seats over the competition. "On this one!" she commanded. The boys began to dig in and fire down the legs a bit more. The boat jumped. It entered the dark shadow of the bridge, and as the yellow rocket passed beneath it, the boys in blue felt the surge. Even through the most intense tunnel vision, rowers can feel when they are moving, their peripheral vision acting like a sixth sense. Tufts in lane three was falling off slightly. Carolyn adjusted her rudder perfectly, and as they came out the other side of the bridge, she realigned her course flawlessly. The large lane-two marker down at the grandstand bridge was in her sights.

"Yes!" she barked. "Now swing! Breathe. That's it." Her voice took on a softer tone to keep the men poised. Carolyn surveyed the landscape to her right. The move had worked. Tufts in lane three had fallen back a few seats about three-quarters of a length off URI. Temple in lane five had fallen back slightly, as had Georgetown. The boys from Rhode Island had the lead. They were one seat up on Georgetown University as they approached the thousand-meter mark.

This is where the race begins, and each rower starts to question their sanity, knowing the impending gauntlet of pain that awaits. At this point, most of the tricks were out of the bag for all crews, so Carolyn knew that Georgetown would put on a move crossing the thousand-meter mark. And so did her boys. The only question was whether or not their move could match Georgetown's.

On the shore, the URI team members who'd opted to view the race from the halfway point were going ape shit at what was unfolding. Their lightweight men's eight had the lead over the field. Coach Jack, who'd been able to score a bicycle from another team, was perched with the other coaches. The bikes allowed them to follow the action from start to finish and cover the full course. One of the nearby coaches leaned over to Jack, and surprisingly, said, "URI is in the lead." To which the always cool Jack calmly responded, "I know," as if he'd never had a doubt.

But doubt, or rather anxiety, was starting to creep into the boys' rhythm a tiny bit. They just needed a few more strokes to get their lungs back and reset. If Georgetown and Temple could just wait a little—

Boom! Just like that, Georgetown began its assault. Carolyn saw their boat surge forward, almost reclaiming the lead in just a few strokes.

"We gotta move now! Here we go! Twenty strokes! On this one!" She cracked the whip. The boys did their best to snap out of the recovery mindset and back to that of a hunter/killer. The move itself was designed to create an increase in power, not so much the rating. This is hard enough, especially when the suffer bucket is beginning to fill. They did as commanded, and to their credit, the boat did pick up a bit of speed. However, Georgetown's move was epic; it had both power and a rating shift. Their boat began to move, picking off the boys in blue one at a time. The coxie, who just a few moments earlier had been slightly behind Carolyn, was now sitting across from Brian in six seat and still moving. The URI boys kept their focus, even though they could sense they were getting walked on. This is that helpless feeling in rowing when not even Odin or the rest of Valhalla could prevent a crew from just moving away, stroke by stroke. The Georgetown crew had almost surged ahead a full length on the field. Undimmed, Jimmy and the boys were keeping their shit together, and their move did serve a purpose in the battle of positioning. While getting walked on by Georgetown, they only managed to lose a few seats to Temple, who now were in second place, though just barely. Thankfully, Tufts in fourth place, didn't gain any ground, nor did they lose any. They sat back almost a length off with their bow man even with Carolyn. A dangerous nuisance in the very next lane.

The move at the thousand-meter mark, which all crews had inevitably taken, propelled the boats towards the 750-meter mark. The positions hadn't shifted much, other than it was getting increasingly difficult for Carolyn to gauge how many seats she was down on lane five, Temple. One thing she did know, as they crossed the 750-meter mark, was that they were in the top three. To this point, the boys had been rowing their race, meaning they were in the zone, confident, and in that flow state, moment to moment.

Unfortunately, Carolyn changed that in a millisecond by uttering these exact words: "Seven hundred and fifty meters to go, and we have a medal."

Perhaps it was the distance reminder, or the fact that there was some hardware right there for the taking. Whatever it was, it took the boys out of the flow state and into a tightened-up sense of anxiety. There is nothing worse than when a rower's mindset switches to "just hold on." Every stroke becomes reactive, with thoughts switching from a "playing to win" mindset to one of "playing not to lose."

The boat started to seize up a bit. Worse, there was an air of complacency permeating. They had to hang on at least to the 250-meter mark entering the grandstands, but it seemed an eternity away. Crossing the five hundred mark, Georgetown had maintained its full-length lead. Temple was definitely in second place, but still only two or three seats up on Rhody in third place. But Tufts was beginning to surge. They moved up two seats with their bow man now sitting on Ken in the seventh seat. Still not too alarming. But Carolyn knew they were getting ready to move. She had to keep her crew as calm as possible, which seemed a challenge, especially as the noise from shore began to build.

The roar was growing as the crews approached the grandstands. Four boats were jockeying for three tickets to immortality, fueled by the chanting mob. The thunderous cheers were filling the air with energy and making their way out onto the course, fueling the boats, and apparently, Tufts was cashing in on that fuel. Their boat was picking up speed and moving through URI. The bow man had moved up two more seats and was sitting on Tom in five seat. Carolyn was beginning to get panicky, and the boys could sense it. They were trying, but nothing was working. Someone in the boat let out a frustrated "Come on."

Carolyn responded, "Quiet! Stay focused!"

A few strokes later, she tried again, pleading desperately, "Come on, guys! Stay on it! We're almost there!"

They were at roughly three hundred meters to go and almost at the sprint time (not that it was going to help given the way the boat felt). Carolyn quickly surveyed the scene. Georgetown was one length up, Temple now four seats up, and that pesky Tufts crew had gained even more real estate. Now their bow man was even with Jimmy in three seat and surging forward. They were almost even!

This was the moment. The single point in time for Carolyn to make the most important call in her life. She got furious. She didn't have time to think or to plan. She went with her impulse.

"Fuck this!" she screamed. The loudness of her distorted voice from the speakers was deafening to the men even over the guttural sounds of pain and chaos. More importantly, it seemed to snap them awake, as if they'd been lost in some lucid trance of trying to just survive.

Carolyn was relentless. "Listen to me! I want you to look out of the goddamn boat! Do it!!

She'd just asked them to break a cardinal sin in rowing, especially for an entire boat. "Do it!" she screamed with every ounce of her tiny frame. The boys turned their heads to the left. They saw Tufts was just about even. "That's our fucking medal they want! Our medal! "Fuck that!"

The boys' heads snapped back into the boat like some military regiment. "In two!" she bellowed. "One! Two! On this one!"

Jimmy cried out, "Do it!" Kevin followed suit with some primal noise as the boys dug in.

In two strokes, the boat jumped from thirty-four to thirty-nine strokes per minute. Carolyn looked down at her stroke meter "Forty hold!" Immediately, Tufts fell back one seat. "Here we go now, Kevin, and Ken this is for you: Pull!! The boys just ripped it. "Yes! Yes!! Here we go! Brian and Tom, pass that bowman up! Get him off Brendan!" The boys continued their aggravated assault. "Yes! Forty-one! Yes! Pass that fucker up to Brian!" It was like Carolyn was possessed, and the boys flipping loved it. The fact that they'd just moved three seats back up on Tufts was like an adrenaline shot in the back of the arm for the Rhody Crew.

As she was getting ready to engage with Brendan and Jimmy, she noticed that her boat was actually gaining on both Georgetown and Temple. "Jesus Christ! You guys are moving on Temple." She quickly glanced back at Tufts, their bowman now sitting on Ken. Now Tufts was at the receiving end of being walked on, and there was nothing they could do about it.

Carolyn now went in for the kill. "Here we go! Brendan and Jimmy, put them to bed!" Never before had Jimmy felt so powerful. It was like he had been born for this moment, and every stroke he would take vanquished a trip to the hospital or a wet and damp night alone in an oxygen tent. "See ya!" Up went the call from Carolyn.

In a matter of fifteen strokes, Rhody went through them like a hot knife through butter, and there was still real estate left. Now the grandstands were thumping, and the boys could sense the continual roar of thunder and begin to distinguish the unmistakable U-R-I cheers.

"Gut-check time! I want Temple!" Carolyn growled. "Bow pair gonna lead us off on this shift. On this one. Send it!" Gregg and Jim were backing up Kevin's increase in rate. "Forty-five! Out fucking standing! Yes! One seat down on Temple!" shouted the rabid, foaming coxie.

It was getting increasingly hard to gauge the actual distance on lane five as there was a slight stagger when approaching the line. But Carolyn did know one thing for sure, her boys were moving through Georgetown too. Never had pain been so pleasurable; this was their moment. "Four seats down!" A quick glance to her far right. "Temple almost even!" By the time she looked back, URI had gained another seat on the leaders.

These are the races rowers live for, as does the crowd, which now stood in awe of the spectacle. Jack arrived at the finish line, tossing his bike in excitement. He ran down to the water's edge, caught up in what was playing out. This was it. About a hundred meters to the line, and the race would be over.

"Last ten, boys! Through the roof! I love you!... On this one!"

At this point, another gear would require the utmost commitment in power, speed, and willingness to go into the tunnel of death—that ever closing portal where one's vision begins to close down, the body's starvation of oxygen meaning shutdown is imminent. But this would not play out like it had for Jimmy that fateful night on his bathroom floor. This was their moment, with nine hearts living the Journey stadium anthem, "Don't stop believing." Ever. The boys gave it. The rate jumped up a few more beats. Now the chips were all in. "Forty-eight!" she cried. "Unbelievable Yes! There goes one seat!"

The boys were on fire; the battle cat seemed to be screaming as it chewed its way through the leaders. The yellow warcraft was coming, and they knew it. "Another seat!... Yes! Everything you got!!" Temple was still there, but Carolyn couldn't effectively gauge the distance. "Five more strokes! Everything comes down to this!" The Rhody crew surged again, taking another seat off Georgetown. Only another ten feet or so to pull even.

I wish I had a magic wand to grant the ability to check in with each one of us in that moment to hear what was going through our minds on those last five strokes and how it would come to define each of us over the years. But I can only speak for Jimmy. The weak boy, the timid dreamer, the athlete wannabe. He had dared to grace the stage, and for a brief moment, became the hero of his own story.

The tunnel was closing fast, and Jimmy responded by slamming the wooden handle into his body with even more force. "Four! Three!" With each stroke, he thought, *Swing and you won't be scared anymore!* It was just like his dad had told him, instead of the missed ball landing in the catcher's mitt, it was the handle landing with a thud. Carolyn cried, "Yes!! Two! Everythiiing!!!"

The finish-line horn sounded as the red flag dropped. Then the flag rose one second later with another horn blast. And then finally, a third and final simultaneous salvo signifying third place. In less than two seconds, all three boats punched the line.

"Paddle," she said softly, the command to ease off all pressure and continue rowing spread throughout the boat. But when the stakes were this high, and so much had been given, rowers just collapse in pure agony. Rowers have their own unique way of expressing pain. Some cry out in horror, some are silent, some fall back in the boat, and some barf over the side. As their vision begins to return, and the pain gives way to the present moment, it begins to hit them.

Another five strokes was all they would have needed. Georgetown couldn't have stopped them. No way. But on this day, there wasn't enough racecourse left to complete the ultimate Cinderella story. But the boys had medaled and were thrilled. A third-place finish was settling into their consciousness when Coach Jack came to the water's edge as the yellow boat drifted by. Kevin at stroke had his hand in the air, three proud fingers to his coach. As always, cool Jack just shook his head no and began to smile. He raised his arm back to the boat. Outstretched at the end of his right hand stood two fingers.

The boys in blue had earned a silver medal at the nationals. And then came the moment that would be captured forever and stand the cruel fate of time. Kevin passed his oar handle to Carolyn and stood up on the tiny platform by his seat. He turned to face his crew and threw his hands up in the air, arched his head back, and screamed to the heavens. The captured image would adorn the front page of the city paper and stand as an iconic picture to never stop believing. There was only one thing left for Carolyn and her motley crew to do now: take a trip to the medal dock and greet the cheering mob.

Once life re-entered the bodies of the rowers, the referees instructed the three medaling boats to make their way to the grandstands and the awards dock. The bronze medal would be awarded first. Temple University pulled up to the dock to the cheers from their hometown crowd. Once alongside, the regatta stewards would come to the boat and hang the bronze medals around each of their necks. The Temple faithful were cheering in the stands but unfortunately the boys in that boat weren't too thrilled about the result, some of them even taking off their medals and tossing them into the hull of the boat. The dejected oarsmen then left the dock and rowed their way back to their boathouse. It would be the last time Temple would field a lightweight program. I am not sure if it was their lack of sportsmanship or perhaps its contrast to what happened next that sealed the fate for that program.

It was our turn. Approaching a grandstand full of people all cheering in the name of achievement is something I will never forget. Numerous blue jerseys and familiar faces were nestled among a sea of anonymous cheer. With eagle-eyed precision, I can still home in on two figures as easily as I did that day. I can see my father waving at me from beneath his blue rowing cap only momentarily pausing his recording of the day's events. I can still see my mother's smile as she adjusted her glasses as they slid down her nose. She was wearing her Wickford shirt, as always. I often wonder if this moment was perhaps the proudest moment for my mom and dad.

As Carolyn steered the boat to the side of the awards dock, Brian (the only senior in the boat) jumped out onto the dock, almost falling in in doing so. The stewards were on their way, but no one had told the boys in blue that only the first-place squad was supposed to get out and stand. Before anyone knew what was happening, Jimmy and his team were taking over the dock. There were hugs, high fives, and tears as the nine hearts came together in a massive huddle.

Unlike Temple's response, you would have thought they'd won the Olympic final. Well, to them, they had, and the crowd absolutely loved it. The huddle broke, and the oarsmen took their places, standing by their seats. If the boys were on the dock, you bet Coach Jack was going to join them no matter what, and he did. Jack assisted the stewards in handing out the shiny silver hardware. He began with Carolyn and moved down the boat, hanging the medals around each of their necks. Each crew member had their own personalized moment of recognition with Coach Jack, some getting a hug and others a stoic handshake.

With one more final wave to the adorning crowd, we climbed back into the yellow warcraft. I often wonder if anyone in the crowd saw the fierce battle cat poised atop the bow deck. When we pushed off, we took the longest, slowest row back to the loading area, perhaps wishing the moment would never fade.

In the grand kaleidoscope of time, it was a mere blink of an eye (or more precisely, eighteen blinks), leaving its legacy on the group of young men and one woman, one that would come to serve each of them as the inevitable road of life presented different pathways. It was a special boat and a special time with ordinary folk stepping onto an extraordinary stage.

The Malcolm Suite

I. The Dark Veil

Four years passed in the blink of an eye, and Jimmy found himself nearing the doorway of adulthood. He was standing in his bedroom, which had become more of a museum display to the Little Jimmy of old. His older self was starting to take the shape of a man, his athletic physique now adorned with muscles and his hair slicked back into a lengthy ponytail. His dress slacks and unbuttoned dress shirt announced an impending event that he was getting ready for. But that took a back seat to taking in the menagerie of memory around him. Shelves housed playful toys and models from the sandbox of the past, including the mustard captain and the ever-faithful Rusty. The fading paper hero was still there, proudly displaying the courage of the quarterback. But things had changed, and Jimmy was aware of it. Even his bed looked small, and the visions of his mother swaying during the breath dance seemed like a storybook fable.

The warrior in me was changing, and I could sense the coming departure. My foundation of courage was in place, but I was beginning to come to terms with another layer to the emotional complexity of life: mortality. This veil descends on all of us at different points as we age and begin to grow our own relationship with death.

Through the eyes of a child, "death" seems like just another word from the land of make believe, not rooted in a concrete understanding of any emotional magnitude but rather a simple thought or an exchange. Like the sound of a doorbell that gives way to a father telling Little Jimmy and Dave that "Peter won't be coming to school today" or the innocent walk to the bus stop, unaware that their neighbor's mom had been sick for quite some time and was now gone.

Sometimes it can come suddenly and overtake the smile of a young boy being greeted by a playful puppy who didn't know what a road was or the car that took its life. The brief final struggle and then utter stillness play on a never-ending loop of memory for this older version of that innocent boy.

The impact of the word knows no bounds. Even the most heroic of adventurers are not impervious to its mighty grip. Jimmy had tried to hide his tears as he and his classmates sat stunned while the space shuttle *Challenger* exploded in front of their eyes. Another piece of innocence from the dreaming astronaut was peeled away in that moment, and this veil continued its descent whether from the far reaches of our atmosphere or right down the road.

Life gives us a handful of moments that will never fade or be swept away by the tides of time. Instead, they are seared into the fabric of our soul and stay with us always. Some are joyous, like the rebellious nine hearts taking over the grandstands, and then some make your heart sink no matter how many times you revisit it. I remember pulling into the driveway of my grandfather Malcolm's house and sitting in the car. It was a late spring evening of that glorious Cinderella season, and I wondered why my mother, who had been the angel of the night to an asthmatic boy, wasn't going to be there for her dad to comfort him. Why me? What could I possibly offer? My grandfather was home alone, waiting for the phone to ring regarding the status of his wife, and more importantly, her heart. It took more courage than an afternoon tennis match for me to get out of that car that evening. My footsteps to the front door had never been shakier.

Jimmy entered the dimly lit family room, his entrance divinely announced by the ringing of the phone. As Malcolm slowly picked up the receiver, Jimmy sat down on the edge of the couch, watching for any clues from his grandfather. In reality, only seconds passed before the silence was broken with two words.

"Oh dear," Malcolm uttered. The phone was placed back in its cradle, its user staring deeply at the floor beneath his feet. "She's gone," he said softly. "Oh... Jimmy, she's gone." He rose from his chair and began to aimlessly look around the room, his flowing eyes surveying his new solitary life and trying to process it all in a millisecond. Jimmy didn't know what to do or what to say. He stood up from the couch as Malcolm fell into his arms, sobbing.

Two opposite emotions took the stage for me that night: sadness and anger. I see the young me trying to understand it all, feeling the grief swell. But I also distinctly remember the anger that rose within me. Anger at my mother. In the coming days, and over the years, I would think to myself, *How dare she put me in that position?* Come to think of it, I have never told her of that moment and the pain it left on my heart. Hmm. Well, I forgive you, Mom. You will always be my angel of the night, and that is enough. The younger me slowly forgave himself as well for not being more of a rock for Malcolm that night. I vowed to champion our bond over the coming years, and in return, that bond and my grandfather's voice would spur me on to greater achievements.

II. Echoes of Glory

Jimmy looked in the mirror and slowly began the ritualistic buttoning of his dress shirt, starting at the bottom and working his way up. He paused halfway and leaned forward onto his dresser as if bracing himself and his thoughts. His reflection gave way to two distinct picture frames, proudly adorning the dresser on either side of the mirror: rowing moments captured in time, a victorious medal-dock pose and standing on a podium behind Olympic rings.

With my grandmother's passing, four years earlier, my grandfather and I had grown even closer. Never being much of an athlete, sports wasn't his bag, per se. However, that had all changed during my grandmother's memorial service when a slight commotion broke out in the back of the church as the other eight hearts filed in to support their brother in his loss. Malcolm had given them the once over and then looked at me. With that gesture, I knew that he understood everything there is to know about the sport.

Jimmy now picked up one of the pictures. In it, his slightly younger self stands alongside seven other men, a cox, and their coach, gold medals around their necks. The boatmates however were not the familiar faces of his Rhody blue crew but another organization. The memory took hold and into the past he went.

"Ergs don't float," Malcolm said through the phone receiver.

"They sure don't, Gramps. Wish me luck tomorrow."

Malcolm did, of course, and their conversation done, Jimmy hung up the cordless phone.

He had needed that Scotch-filled pep talk because he was in uncharted territory. This marked the second time he'd been told he wasn't good enough but had done something anyway. The year after his magical silver-medal season with Rhody, the offer was extended to go to a national training camp and compete against others from all over the country. Halfway through the very first practice, the coach had stopped the two rowing eights and moved Jimmy up from the four seat to that of the stroke seat in the top boat. The moment he had dreamt of while standing in the tin shed of a boathouse for the first time, three years earlier, was now his. He assumed the quarterback position once again and now had to defend that seat in the fallout of a devastating ergometer test score.

The phone call to his grandfather had recounted how his stroke seat was in jeopardy after a piss-poor two thousand-meter test score on the rowing machine. The worst in the entire camp. But Malcolm had reminded him that, even though he hadn't been able to fly the mighty F-4 Corsair back in the day, he had known he'd been born for that cockpit, and that if he'd ever gotten the chance, no one and nothing—not even a heart murmur—would have been able to say no to him in the face of his ability to fly the craft better than anyone else.

Malcolm's words reminded Jimmy of his own secret formula: Little Jimmy's ability to make things real through the power of make believe. Simply put, Jimmy believed he was invincible in a rowing seat, surrounded by others. That seat was his, and no one would ever out-row him for it. So, after hanging up the phone with his Scottish sage, he showed up the following morning for seat racing.

There are two undeniable truths in life: Ergs do not float, and bears *do* poop in the woods. The concept of "seat racing" took the *perceived* fitness of the rowing machine and put it to test on the water, where the myriad of variables that make up rowing can affect one's ability to move a boat. Rowing a boat takes skill and rhythm, while any gorilla can pull an erg handle. Seat racing itself entails breaking the squad into smaller boats (fours in this case). They would race at a designated and capped stroke rate over a specified distance. Times would be taken by the coach, and then certain athletes would be swapped in and out to see who moved the boat better.

Jimmy became a sniper with deadly precision, picking off one rower after another, until the dust settled, and there were no more bodies for him to vanquish. When the few days of seat racing had passed, there were zero questions left unanswered. Jimmy had established himself as the top port rower at the camp and would go on to own the stroke seat for all the top boats. The year before, Jimmy had found his identity through the sport, and this summer, had made a name for himself in the national system as the one to watch.

"Are you almost ready?" His dad's voice bellowed from the other room, breaking his son from his memory trance. Jimmy replaced the picture back on the dresser.

"Almost!" he responded while continuing the procession of buttons up to his neck. Once again, the mirror gives way to a memory, his gaze shifting to the other framed-picture bookend. In it, his long blond hair is held back by a makeshift white headband, while his right arm extends skyward, a bouquet of flowers in his hand. Around his neck hangs a large gold medal that accents his white and yellow Olympic attire. The majestic sound of the Olympic anthem began to fill the room then and swell as he surrendered to the memory.

Jimmy and another rower, Brady, walked along the bank of a canal, decked out in their matching Olympic swag. The two Rhode Island boys had travelled across the country in the summer of 1991 to the sunbaked arena of Los Angeles. Brady was a tall blond-haired transfer student who had rowed with Jimmy, Gregg, and Jim during their senior year at university, finishing third at the nationals in the lightweight four. Just eight weeks earlier, back in Rhode Island, the boys had had a fateful decision to make, and for Jimmy, he had sought out some of that wise Scotch council.

Two lawn chairs, two men, and two glasses of Scotch sat in the back-yard sanctuary of Malcolm's home. "They want me to go to Boston for the sweep-rowing camp," Jimmy said.

"That's the next step for the national team?" his grandfather asked. Jimmy's affirming nod lacked inspiration. "But?"

Jimmy fidgeted in his chair. "It's just that, well... the camp environment is cutthroat. I like the idea of doing things outside the system," he confessed, "like Coach Steve."

The Steve he was referring to was Steve Peterson (now a URI legend, Olympian, and world champion). He had been Jimmy's coach and mentor over his last two years of university rowing. Steve was going to row at a small club up in New Hampshire with a handful of elite national-team athletes. The great thing about the U.S. system was that you didn't need to be in the system to make the team. Technically, you can put a boat together, show up at trials, and if you win, you punch your ticket to the world championships.

But it was more than that. It was that lingering feeling of comfort. Jimmy was dealing with the fact that his collegiate rowing was over, and the thought of saying goodbye to four years with his buddies Jim and Gregg was hard. Brady and he still wanted to row, and Steve still wanted to coach them.

"Sculling?" his grandfather asked. "Like an oar in each hand?" He did his best pantomime.

Jimmy laughed as the Scotch was grabbing hold. "Yes. We would have about four weeks to learn how to scull before the race off for the Olympic Festival spot.

"So, what's the dilemma then?" Malcolm fired off.

"Well," Jimmy said, "with the success I had last summer, Boston is what they want me to do."

"'They' being the rowing system." His grandfather nodded and then downed the rest of his Scotch before leaning forward in his chair. "You know, loyalty is the glue that binds you, Jimmy. This... this *sport* is about loyalty. It's about the journey of that loyalty. Like the boys that came to the church. That's what heroes do." With that, he rose from his lawn-chair throne.

"I have to go see a man about a horse." He left to take care of his personal business.

He'd always had a way with words and had gotten to know me better in the four years after Grammy's death than anyone. *That's what heroes do*, I thought as I honored my bond with coach, boatmate, and the Olympic dream (even if it was a pseudo one). The "Olympic Festival" is *not* the Olympics. Period. That said, it does recreate the full symphonic experience down to the slightest of detail. This major event in the United States was held every non-Olympic year, bringing the best athletes from the north, south, east, and west to compete in the largest amateur sporting event in the country.

Brady and I arrived in New Hampshire, and in four short weeks, we learned how to use the miniscule eight-foot sculling oars and promptly punched our ticket west with an all-out thrashing of the other boat vying for the spot. On the canals of Long Beach in Los Angeles, that thrashing continued, with us never losing a race during festival competition and ultimately winning the gold medal by multiple lengths of open water.

When our names were called for the gold-medal podium, my younger self was living out yet another dream. Our heads bowed as the large gold medals found their home. We were each handed a bouquet of flowers, and the Olympic anthem played. Those flowers rose to the sky, and the young heroes in us stood, bound by loyalty and the wisdom of some twelve-year-old Scotch.

III. Primate Pilgrimage

The blue fabric was flung around itself before being cinched tight by Jimmy's pinching fingers. He checked the length in the mirror, staring for a moment at the reflection. Slowly, his fingertips began to dance on the tie as if pressing invisible keys. His eyes closed, and the memory of a saxophone sound began to dance in his mind. Into the past he went again, to the Sunday evenings of yesterday.

✧ ✧ ✧

Malcolm's fingers danced along with the notes emanating from the old record player in his living room. Every ounce of his soul was connected to the upbeat tempo, and as the sax hit a sustained climax, so did the glass of Scotch to the sky.

After the note concluded, Malcolm turned down the volume. "Rest in peace, Charlie Parker." He glanced at his grandson as he moved to his comfy green throne. "There hasn't been another like him." Next to him in the adjacent chair, once reserved for his grandmother, sat Jimmy.

"Damn shame," Malcolm proclaimed, sipping his whiskey. "His whole life ahead of him, and he died alone in a hotel room in New York

City. Gotta make the most out of the time we're given, Jimmy. So... PhD, huh?"

"Well, yeah," Jimmy answered. "I mean, I'm thinking of doing the Jane Goodall thing, maybe work for *National Geographic* or something. Maybe become a professor. I don't know."

"I think you belong on stage. You're a performer. When you were younger—"

"Not the candy stripers again please," interrupted his embarrassed grandson. They both laughed.

"So," Malcolm said, once he'd settled a bit, "tell me: Do they poop a lot?"

"Who? The candy stripers?" Jimmy laughed.

"No, the monkeys. This is only my first Scotch, Jimmy."

Still chuckling with his grinning grandfather, Jimmy nodded. "Yes, the monkeys poop a lot, Grampy."

Jimmy smiled and laughed to himself remembering their exchange, his grandfather's humor a welcome co-pilot on the sixteen-hour drive down to Atlanta, Georgia. His grandfather was no different than most people in that almost everyone is fascinated by primates. These hairy humans captivated Jimmy too. So much so that he had hung up his bullwhip and fedora and shelved his archeology focus for that of primatology. Doing so was made easier by the fact that his university had its very own behavioral-research lab on campus with a harem of patas monkeys.

When I officially graduated, I took up the head-coaching position for the URI Crew team while working closely with my mentor and professor Dr. Jim Loy and his colony of monkeys. It was there, as a glorified poop scooper, that I had decided to apply for post-graduate studies with a world-renowned husband-and-wife team down in Georgia. Sue Savage Rumbaugh led the primate facility, which housed a world-famous bonobo chimpanzee named Kanzi. Sue had created a lexigram and computer-based communication system that allowed Kanzi to speak with the team using a keyboard of sorts. It was both fascinating and groundbreaking. Spurred on by my new sense of "I can do anything" I had attained through rowing, I'd written a letter to the famous duo, complete with some letters of recommendation, and before I knew it, I'd been extended an invite down to Georgia to meet them and see if this was the life for me.

Jimmy arrived at the compound located outside of Atlanta and stepped into the world of *National Geographic*. There were hairy little humans everywhere in the compound and teams of specialists working feverishly on recording all sorts of data. He was immediately welcomed into their world, and he marveled at his surroundings.

When the big unveil came to meet Kanzi, Jimmy could hardly contain his excitement. As the big dark-haired bonobo chimp approached, it was immediately clear that he was capable of all the same emotional interaction as the humans on the outside of the bars. Bonobos are 99.9 percent genetically human, and up close, it truly was another human being looking back into Jimmy's eyes. It was a mischievous one at that, in fact, they all were. At one point while visiting another holding pen, Jimmy marveled at a few of the chimps seemingly laughing at one another. Unknown to him, one of them had sucked some water out of a nearby bucket before casually sauntering up to the bars. The cheeky monkey (well, chimp) spit a stream of water all over Jimmy's borrowed white lab coat and then stood there laughing.

The lab itself was a blurry sea of white. Jimmy was surrounded by people in lab coats carrying clipboards, moving about like fine-tuned robots. But in those machine-like movements, he began to observe that it all seemed monotonous. After a few days of observations and deep philosophical discussions with the famous trailblazers, it was time for Jimmy to begin the long trek back home. There was only one thought on his mind: *I don't know if I can do this the rest of my life.*

My internal voice kept repeating that over and over for sixteen bloody hours. The thought of doing the same thing for the rest of my life suddenly seemed scary. I craved romance, drama, and adventure like in the movies. As I turned up the volume on "Promentory," from *The Last of the Mohicans* movie soundtrack, my artistic soul took over. I felt the swell of emotional symphony within, and my passion seemed to bubble up to the surface. Something my grandfather had said, his words about being a performer, stayed with me while the music fed my soul.

Sixteen hours later, one chapter of my life had closed, and a new one was about to begin.

IV. Runway Stroke

"One minute!" Jimmy shouted while cinching up the last of his Windsor knot and smoothing out his tie. He then reached for his suit jacket and slipped it on over his shirt. He checked himself out and made sure his ponytail was neat and tidy. There he stood, like he had just stepped out of a magazine, which was exactly what he wanted. He'd come a long way from being the wallflower, stuck on his cold, steel folding chair. *"Are you a model?"* whispered a female voice at his reflection.

"She actually said that?" Malcolm's voice responded, inviting Jimmy back into memory one more time.

Malcolm stood over his stove, buttermilk pancakes on the watch.

"Yes, she did as a matter of fact," Jimmy offered with some defensiveness.

"Well then, we better get you signed up for that John... uh..." His voice trailed off as he flipped the pancakes over, unable to come up with the name.

"Casablanca," Jimmy said, finishing it for him.

"They teach you everything you need to know in that school?"

"As far as I know," Jimmy said while passing a plate to his grandfather.

John Casablanca's School of Modeling did in fact teach me the ins and outs of the business. It was there that I took my muscular frame, hardened looks, and whispers, and turned them into fuel towards my growing passion. The allure of photoshoots, far-off locations, and walking runaways consumed me. But it was also a potential doorway to my grand vision. Those sixteen hours alone in the car on my way home from the primate research facility had evolved into a full-on desire to see what I could do in the acting world.

I guess I couldn't shake Little Jimmy's dream, and now it was definitely taking center stage for me. The more I sat in thought, and in council with my Scottish sage, it became clear that acting had all the components to serve me well. It would give me the ability to elicit emotions from people and take them to magical places to escape their day-to-day monotony, allow for me to experience different roles and/or experiences to escape said monotony myself, and in the process, attract more of the attention that I was now beginning to crave. I wanted to be somebody.

"I think you'll do great." Malcolm laughed as he took his seat and watched me dive into the piping-hot stack of pancakes.

We talked some more, when my mouth wasn't full of food, and we laughed. We always seemed to laugh no matter what. But mostly, I remember him just sitting there, sipping on his tea, and staring at my younger self wolfing down his creation. The simple act of eating a pancake gave us both so much joy, and his words gave me life.

When my grandfather had a stroke soon after that last supper, we continued our meetings in the confines of a nursing home, one that would remind me (every time I entered) of one thing: death. It had this unique scent that wasn't enticing but rather served as a warning: We all grow old and die. The conversations, minus the Scotch, still ensued, though they now only went one way.

Grandfather and grandson sat at a small table, with Malcolm's wheel-chair locked into position. The stroke had taken the use of his right side, which was the better option since he was lefthanded. That mischievous Scottish charm was still there behind his cataract eyes and drooping, voiceless mouth. It was his left hand that spoke now by tapping the table if something was funny or exciting.

"So, there's this thing coming up," Jimmy said. "It's a contest—well, actually, it's a pageant." He quickly deduced that his grandfather wasn't quite following. "It's a modelling contest," he added. Malcolm's eyes grew wide as he connected the dots.

"Yeah, the New England Model of the Year pageant will be held in Providence."

Malcolm immediately tapped the table in approval.

"Contestants from all over New England will be there, walking the runway and doing their thing. But the kicker is that the judges will be talent agents from New York City. Acting agents, Grampy."

The whole left side of Malcolm sprang to life with the energy of love. His one expressive eye grew even wider in awe and excitement. A heartwarming smile broke its confines and travelled upward into his left cheekbone. And that left hand of his tapped faster and faster. The boy within the old shell was still very much alive.

✧   ✧   ✧

The boy in the present-day mirror, however, seemed sullen. Jimmy took one last look at his reflection and then buttoned up his suit jacket to signal that he was ready. He took a deep breath inward and then gave the signal.

"I'm ready!"

With that, he exited his childhood sanctuary.

✧   ✧   ✧

Jimmy slowly approached the pristine wooden box, catching a glimpse of the plush fabric within. It wasn't until he arrived that the image he'd been dreading came into full view. There his grandfather lay, resting comfortably in a coffin. The Scottish humor was no more, that boyish twinkle extinguished, and the sage's wisdom silenced forever.

It hit me hard, as it does most people. I remember feeling this emptiness inside me, swirling with sadness, anger, and fear. My safety net was gone, and the last tether I had to any semblance of childhood was severed. I can't remember how long I stood there, just taking in the sight of my Scottish hero, but I do remember what happened next.

My eyes filled with tears. When my dad's hand found my shoulder, it didn't faze me at all. I shrugged it off and turned, not giving any attention to those gathered at the funeral home to pay their respects. A fire was burning within me as I moved to the exit. My walk was purposeful and my intention definitive.

Like Andy Dufresne would famously say a few years later on the big screen, it was time for me to "get busy living or get busy dying."

I walked past the mourners, knowing I would never again hear my grandfather's voice when I needed it most. But I did remember one thing he said as clear as day: *"You belong on the stage, Jimmy. You're a performer."*

You're goddamn right I am, Gramps.

✧   ✧   ✧

Jimmy owned that stage. He strutted down the runway and peeled off his jacket effortlessly with a turn and dramatic pose for good measure, his long Fabio-like hair punctuating the move. The adventurous spirit of Malcolm, and maybe a hint of Scuttle the mouse, possessed him as he strutted and commanded attention at the two-day modelling pageant.

When he was awarded the large trophy and designation of "New England Model of the Year," he knew the Scotsman was by his side. Jimmy immediately signed a contract with a talent manager and would be heading to New York City in a month. A new course was charted, a new and vast jungle laid ready for exploration. Jimmy would be no more. Instead at the con, minus the mustard-colored tunic, would be a young man from Cydot Drive. His name was Jim.

CHORUS: *THE SOUTHERN LANDS*

The sirens and their luring whispers of fame have beckoned our fledgling hero to book passage south to a foreign land. The applause of the homeland arena no longer serves his growing blood lust for achievement. Armed with a watery brotherhood of courage filling his sails, this new land shall be his.

Unknown to our wayward hero is that passage here requires a toll being paid. It is a ferry ride between two worlds, one where lost innocence is the token of entry for on the other side lies a carnival of lights, sounds, and creative heartbeats. Life in all its technicolor glory breathes here amongst its concrete streets and sidewalk caravans. But be warned: It is also a world ripe with the dark underbelly of greed, lust, and murder. The dark force of expectation cracks the strong, the courageous, and even the warriors who come here to claim their legacy. It is a splintering of two worlds, where boys are torn from men.

But alas, we beseech you, throw caution to the wind as does our blue-eyed warrior. For he only knows that somewhere out there lies his destiny. His travelling gaze turns upward to the legacy lights of seekers before him. Over the centuries, ancient myth and tales of glory have been born from the magic of these night candles and their glow. In them is also comfort, their flickering, soothing and hypnotic, call to a boy devastated from life lessons learned at a school dance. And now this new land will indeed pay for it. The stage is set. The young man with the boy by his side ferries to adventure. Unto Manhattan does our scene jet.

NEW YORK CITY ARENA

The Concrete Jungle

The candles of the gods have been replaced by the lights, sounds, and midnight dreams of this concrete world: Manhattan, the Big Apple, the City that Never Sleeps, the Center of the World. The city that was once synonymous with "old blue eyes" Frank Sinatra himself was now home. The currency here wasn't soft-back roads and floating sailboats on picturesque postcards but rather street hustle... dirty, gritty, real life breeding itself in every sensory capacity within everyone who walked the streets. On the other end of each person's stride was "an objective." The bluffs of New England were for dreamers. The streets of Manhattan existed to get shit done.

That energy that people talk about in New York isn't city energy. No. That's too simple. It's the vibration of eight million people with a singular focus to 'make it there, so they can make it anywhere.'

From the intersection of Brown Street and Main Street, in historic Wickford Village, to standing on the corner of 25th street and 2nd avenue, Jim felt like he was on a different planet. Everywhere he looked, there were people, each living their own life, tucked into their own little oasis that they called home. For Jim, "home" was a studio apartment in a pre-war building, with one large room containing a small kitchen area, enough space for a couch futon to double as a bed, a folding table, and a chair. Nothing fancy, nor did it need to be, as it was just a place to hang his hat. The apartment only had two old windows situated above even older floor-mounted pre-war radiators. Overall, it was pleasant enough. The only real eyesore was a large stain on the wooden floorboards by the kitchen. It looked like something had been spilled and then sealed over with a glossy finish. Strange, but again, Jim wasn't in Kansas anymore. Those yellow bricks of his youth had led him right to the heartbeat of the world.

That very first night, in the winter of 1994, was something he would never forget. For the first time in his life, he truly felt the wind at his back. The youthful dreams of adventure were now a reality, and he was living in it. Those old twin radiators were pumping and hissing their dry Savanna heat, which caused him to open both windows to cool off the apartment. That's when it hit him. Immediately, Jim was struck by the heartbeat of the city. Its pulse was hypnotizing and layered with different sonic textures; it was the Big Apple's symphony welcoming its newest member into its cultured brotherhood. Nearby police sirens layered with those in the distance. The thunderous bass from the neighbor's speaker system was paired brilliantly with the staccato of taxi horns. Intermittent dog barks could be heard, as well as homeless banter, periodically infused with shouting matches from a relationship gone awry.

Jim sat straddling the ledge of the window, one leg securely planted on the floor of his apartment, the other dangling free in the winter air high above the street. He craned his neck upward to check for those magical night-sky lights. They were gone, replaced instead with all the lights emanating from below. Two sets of blue eyes sat on the sill that evening, the younger pair ready to create his masterpiece. The older, scoring his imagination. Cue Mr. Sinatra and "New York, New York."

Ah yes, the chairman of the board was right. I did find my small town life melting away and knew it was my time to make a brand new start of it. I felt obliged to honor Mr. Sinatra's moral contract and take my shot in the Big Apple. In actuality, if I could survive and thrive in the arena of rowing, I knew I could, in fact, make it anywhere. However, far be it from me to challenge a legend. The last thing I wanted was to end up six feet deep in the end zone of Giant's stadium next to Mr. Hoffa.

Soon, I stumbled upon a newspaper called *BackStage*, a weekly publication and staple for every actor and wannabe actor in the city. It published union and non-union casting jobs, along with acting tidbits, available classes, and teachers who offered instruction. I settled in on a commercial-acting class since that was a way to land quick cash and learn about the business. It was there that I met my first friend and acting coach, a guy named Brian. He was a big, imposing fellow and a former Vietnam vet turned actor. His blend of intensity and approachability landed him various stage productions as well as a beautiful scene opposite Tim Robbins in *The Shawshank Redemption* as Dekins, a prison guard seeking accounting advice.

Not much happened for me out of the gate as I was really just getting my bearings over those first few months. My manager was doing her thing, and I started to do mine, mostly staying on top of the ads in *Backstage* and seeing what was out there. One day, I saw a casting call for extra work on a big budget film and thought, *Hell yeah! I am in!* At least this would open my eyes firsthand to the glorious world of a film set. I sent my headshot over to the casting office, and boom, next thing I knew, the Christmas junkie in me was heading for the upper west side to work on my first official film.

The project was a remake of the holiday classic *Miracle on 34th Street*. Jim showed up on set wide-eyed and ready for his close-up with Mr. Deville. Instead, what he got was his glorious image of film life pooped on. All day, he stood in the freezing rain, his hand holding onto a rope tethered to a large inflatable balloon. The scene being shot was recreating the famous Macy's Day Parade. Hours and hours would go by, and there was Jim, teeth rattling and doing his best to channel the little Cydot elf within. There *was* one notable win for Jim though, during those hours of balloon wrangling: He had his first celebrity sighting and crush.

Years earlier, Jim had sat in a movie theater with his eyes yearning for the actress Elizabeth Perkins, who played opposite Tom Hanks in the movie *Big*. To Jim, she was a shout-out to the golden-era screen gems like Judy Garland with her classic beauty and charm. The big screen has a way of romanticizing many characters and the actors who play them. Jim fell victim to this spell, especially now that Elizabeth was standing across the street.

As the shoot wrapped, the cold and wet Jim stood motionless while the "Somewhere Over the Rainbow" type beauty began walking directly towards him. She was on her way to her trailer, but the shortest path between two points is a straight line, and that straight line took her right through Jim. While his limbs may have been frozen, his brain surely wasn't. This was the moment—the moment when John Cusack holds the boom box over head in *Say Anything*. The kiss at the end of detention in *The Breakfast Club* or the romantic telescope scene in *Can't Buy Me Love*. The coke bottle from his youth slowed its spin, the surrounding sounds muted, and everything paused except for her. She looked his way and then immediately did a double take as if something had caught her eye about the Rhody man lost in the big city. Her gait deliberately slowed, and she smiled. Her dimples sprang to life on either side of her lips as their corners lifted. It was stunning, if the simple act of a smile could be such a thing. It was obvious to Jim that she was willing to engage in a conversation. This was it. *Carpe diem* and all that rah-rah crap. But the old romantic scenes were immediately replaced by his weak inner voice from middle school. *What do I do? Stars don't talk to extras. She's just being nice.* These thoughts all came at him in rapid-fire succession.

She was coming closer, step after step, and then slowed... waiting for Jim to spring into action. But all he could feel was himself falling down onto that lonely steel chair. His heart leapt into his throat.

"Hi," Elizabeth said, perfectly timed in the slight pause between two walking strides.

Jim responded with a slight nod and his own attempt at "Hi," which fumbled from his mouth.

Elizabeth seemed to wait a split second in between those two steps. Anything audible enough would have made her stop and opened a doorway for Jim.

"*Slam!*"

The sound of a table falling to the ground nearby brought the real world back into consciousness. The actress smiled again and resumed her normal pace. The door closed. Or rather slammed in his face.

Jim watched her walk away, hoping for that iconic movie turn around, but no. A moment in time and possibility vanished. His inability to *carpe diem* burned his soul as he moped all the way home. It was a long frigging walk in the cold with that chain of events eating at him, so much so that he made a vow: If he ever had an opportunity like that again, he would seize the moment. People are people regardless of what they do for a living, and opportunities may never come again.

✧   ✧   ✧

"Struggling actor in need of a big break? Have you thought about hiring a publicist to help you get seen?"

The ad headline caught Jim's attention later that week from one of the pages of *Backstage*. It warranted an investigation, so he made the call. *Why not?* he thought. On the other end of a phone conversation was a man who introduced himself as Leonard Fink, a publicist with a downtown firm.

Jim hopped off the 6-Train and found his designated target easily. Walking into the office, he took in the surrounding environment, which was not what he expected. From the way it looked, it appeared Len's office was in a publicity war zone, with a clear blast radius of papers, folders, phones, and multiple scattered desks. It was exactly the opposite of what he'd hoped for, and the thought of a quick backpedal occurred to him. Then a scurry of feet from a man hidden behind one of the large paper mounds signaled his arrival. Len turned the corner, standing about five-foot-four on a good day and probably weighing 125 pounds soaking wet. As he escorted Jim through the war-zone debris, they paused at another desk, occupied by an older gentleman who was waiting for the desk's owner to return. As casually as if introducing a best friend, Len introduces the man to Jim.

"Jim Gardiner, I'd like to introduce you to one of our clients: Tony Bennet."

The crooner extended his hand for a shake. "Hi, Jim," he said with his signature velvet voice.

"Mr. Benn..." Jim had to clear his throat quickly to remove the quiver from his voice. "Mr. Bennet. Pleasure." They shook hands, and then Jim continued on to Len's corner desk.

Well shit, Jim thought, *if Tony came all the way from San Francisco to this rat's nest of an office, perhaps it can work for me too.* The meeting went a lot better than he'd anticipated after walking into the office, and it ended with a signed agreement for five hundred dollars a month for Len's services in getting him more visibility through special-event invites and personalized introductions to people in the business. He became Jim's doorway to networking.

Things began to happen for Jim, albeit slowly. He started to get out more now that he had an *in*, so to speak. He was also realizing that his naive upbringing was being challenged almost on a daily basis. New York was realism personified, and as he would come to find out, very lonely for a city full of people. Living an apartment lifestyle was an adjustment for sure. The walls were paper thin, and he learned pretty early on that it's hard to keep your personal shit personal. Case in point: His next-door neighbor was a French "sexhibitionist," if there is such a word (and if there's not, then there should be). In the lobby, or even in an elevator, this baguette-toting angel of a nymph would speak with the softest, most unassuming tone you could imagine. That was until her boyfriend (or boyfriends) came over, and then seventh-level carnage would ensue at all hours. In fact, Jim would have a tennis ball strategically placed bedside and at the ready for throwing at the walls during those late-night pagan rituals. That poor wall of his took a beating.

He finally managed his first date in the city after almost six months of flying solo, although it wasn't really a date per se but more of a charity move on her part to get him out of the apartment. She lived at the other end of the hall and had met him outside his door on a midsummer evening.

Jim pulled his door closed to lock it when his attention was drawn to a sticky residue on the door itself. He uttered "Weird" under his breath before turning to greet his date, who was approaching.

"There's sticky shit all over my door," he mentioned to her.

She joined him and gave the door a brief once over before following up with a nonchalant response: "I guess they didn't tell you about the apartment?"

"Tell me about... No. Why?"

"Are you sure you want to know?" she asked, knowing that, of course, he would.

She took him by the shoulders and backed him up against the wall a bit further from the door, so he could see the entire doorway. Slowly, it came into view. The heat from the summer air had brought the residue of that sticky substance to life. It surrounded the door and also went across it in different directions.

"Those sticky lines are the remnants of police tape," she said.

His eyes bulged as he stood frozen in disbelief.

"Come on," she said, whisking him down the hall. "I'll explain it in the taxi."

She did alright, with all the gritty details. Jim's apartment had once been a crime scene. A year earlier, the former occupant, who was heavily into drugs and involved with a shady crowd, had gone missing. No one had seen him or his two cats around the building. About a month later, in the dead of the stifling August heat, a fellow tenant (not the savage French porn-star neighbor) had reported hearing eerie screeches from behind his door. As the legend goes, the man had died of a drug overdose in his apartment, or just outside the kitchen to be more precise. That dark stain on the floor that had perplexed Jim was where he had been for a month, decomposing into the floor. In a grim twist of storytelling fate, the starving cats had started to nibble at him to survive.

Well, "F" me sideways. As you can imagine, that made for a memorable night when I returned home to my crime scene—I mean apartment. I wasn't sure I bought the corpse eating cat part of the story, but that stain was there, and far be it from me to challenge a story with proof like that *and* the sticky door tape. I had no choice but to accept the situation and just take a lighter approach to it. For the next six months, I would just refer to the kitchen stain as "Frank." At the end of those six months, I would bid the ghost of Frank *adieu* and move out of the tiny apartment in which I had started my journey. The old East 25th Street building is still there, fighting the good fight against Father Time.

Schools of Fish

The creative alchemy of the bohemian time frame at the turn of the century seems like it would be a fun place to visit, with writers, artists, poets, dancers, and entertainers all letting their individual love for art give them life. It is a romantic notion for sure, and also one that breeds the allure of creation, the intrinsic force within each of us to honor the artist. Outside of my love for movies and continuous make-believe scenarios of youth, I never dove into the concept of creation at its purest form until Len approached me about an idea.

"I want to write a play with this idea I have," the publicist said to me. "It would be a one-man show for you to star in."

"I... am... in." Those were the exact words uttered by my twenty-five-year-old self.

Even though I was as green as actors come, I knew this was another one of those "meet at the field tomorrow afternoon" moments. Hours upon hours were spent in the smoky war zone of Len's office as we two bohemians went to work, crafting the story. The concept would be based around Len's true-life experience, pursuing self-improvement at the hands of a snake-oil salesman in the deep south. He contributed a lot as a writer and was gracious enough to give me co-writing credit on the piece.

Being my first of many journeys into the world of creative writing, I feel the need to honor the artist within me. I didn't know it existed outside of an emotional pull towards a visual medium like movies or the sonic medicine that is music. But the concept of writing something from a seedling of an idea to seeing it take shape and be performed is one of the greatest gifts within each of us. The ability to birth art.

This artistic newborn needed a director to help bring the words to life on the big stage. The choice was rather easy for Len as he had a close relationship with a known director. Ken Dashow, who ironically lived across the street from me, was a famous radio disc jockey on a high-profile NYC FM station. Like many in the big city, he loved the arts, specifically writing and directing. Ken had written and produced several small plays throughout the years and would be a perfect conductor to helm the initial run of our show, which would begin in the fall. I was about to make my acting debut in New York City as I took to the stage of the Westbeth Theater.

Schools of Fish would debut for three shows and would see Jim solo onstage for eighty minutes, playing three different characters. His folks made the trip down. This time his dad had to forgo the video camera, but rest assured, Mama Carolyn was there in her freshly pressed Wickford T-shirt. Len did his job well, helping to fill the venue to capacity. From backstage, Jim peeked out through the curtains for the first time in his life, and it hit him: All of these people were coming to see *him*. They were coming to watch the play, but it was acted by *him*. The acceptance of the story and its believability would rest on Jim's broad shoulders. He immediately thought of the candy stripers, and the book proudly recited from his hospital bed, and all the backyard pretending. Too bad Rusty wasn't in the change room with him to share the moment. *What a journey,* he thought as the five-minute warning came in from the director.

Though there was no water present, he couldn't help but think he was about ready to blast off the starting line once again. Backstage was eerily quiet and dark—par for the course for a one-man show. It was Jim in his rowing single, backing into the stake boat, and steading his nerves with his famous ritual. Sizing up his competition was replaced with thoughts of the first character, the triggers he would use to hop into his skin and stand before hundreds of peering eyes. The last thing that went through Jim's mind before he made his grand entrance was this: *Well,*

Little Jimmy, you asked for this all those years ago. Here we go. With that, the director dropped his red flag, and he blasted off the line once again.

✧   ✧   ✧

Blackness envelopes the crowd as a thunderous guitar riff and drumbeat overtakes the room from the sound system, accompanied by the lyrics from the rock song "Cult of Personality," which talks about being in the spotlight and exploiting the adoration of the masses.

Jim appeared out of nowhere in the back of the room, charging through the crowd to the rhythm of his entrance theme like a professional wrestler assuming the persona of Tony Robbins, but so much more: one quarter rock god, one quarter slick hustler, one quarter inspired genius, and the remaining quarter completely full of shit.

Lambs to the slaughter, he thought as he high-fived a random audience member.

In theater, there is something called the "fourth wall," which separates the audience from the stage and the actors on it. It's not a real wall. It's invisible, but its main job is to divide the two worlds, and rarely does an actor break the fourth wall. But this play was designed to do so. The audience members were interacted with as lost souls from all over the world, desperately seeking salvation at the hands of the mystery man before them, their gateway paved through a late-night cheesy infomercial that promised redemption from a world that had done them wrong.

With a running leap onto the stage, landing with the added drumbeat for dramatic effect, stood Alfred Holderman, his arms outstretched, embracing his flock, and holding court. He surveyed the masses before him, locking eyes with them and commanding their attention. His hair was slicked back like a weasel's, and his body was adorned with a painted jean jacket complete with his logo and catch phrases.

"Greetings my beloved souls," the charismatic figure said, welcoming his newest arrival of doe-eyed followers. He then began his delivery of charm and intellect, superbly greased with the slickness of evangelical cheese, dripping with the rapid-fire delivery of an auctioneer. Len and Jim had created this section based on Len's firsthand experience at the manipulative hand of one of this type of individuals. Manipulation can come from a multitude of angles, and that was the way Jim approached his delivery of Alfred's complex emotional tapestry.

Revisiting this twenty-five years later, I think I drew on all those times in my youth when I was able to get what I wanted. Being an only child comes with a sense of entitlement that you only begin to understand as you get older. For me, I wanted. Period. Whether I wanted to ride bikes as opposed to playing hide and seek with the Cydot crew or convince my parents that I was going to play football or have a tennis match against my archnemesis, I wanted. When I wanted something, I usually got my way. Much like Alfred did that evening, I charmed. I made people cry, feel bad for me... Hell, I even bullied to get my way. The EGO is a powerful weapon and a devastating one if wielded selfishly. Alfred was a master swordsman.

About halfway into the forty-five-minute act, Alfred started to become disorientated and seemed to be losing his focus. After his big emotional salvos, he would stagger and then catch the eye of his flock. "I do apologize for the heat," he muttered. "The AC is on the fritz. But rest assured, your refreshments are on their way."

Behind him, beneath the large banner that read "The Family of the Hosts," a large glass with red liquid was illuminated by a single spotlight. As he turned for a reprieve, Alfred saw the juice.

"Thank you! Just what the doctor ordered," the re-energized figure proclaimed.

As Alfred picked up the glass, it was as though two souls were reunited. He took a big gulp, took a breath, and then turned to his flock.

"Don't worry. Yours will be here shortly," he said enthusiastically. He took a beat and then shouted, "Yes!!" Now where was I ...?"

The juice had the similar effect to a shot in the back of the arm to the actor underneath. His heartbeat would increase, energy would surge through his veins, and just like that, he began to dive back into twisting the minds of those in front of him once again. Each time he would begin to lose his bearings or feel the need for a pick-me-up, back to the red juice he went.

The climax of the audience's journey with Alfred involved an all-out auction as the weary and disorientated babies gave their candy to the man in the form of money. Alfred was on fire, dancing and prancing all over the stage in a bidding frenzy, his followers on their feet. As the money rolled in, and Alfred stood before the masses, the time was finally at hand: Their juice, their salvation, had arrived.

"Wonderful!" he cried. "Your juice is finally here! Please, pass it around..." He motioned for quiet. "And remember, only *one* cup each."

Alfred raises his cup to the audience, to his flock. "Welcome to the family," he said as the lights faded to black.

Jim entered the off-stage wing, peeling off his sweat-soaked clothes. No time for him to process his first-ever gig or even think about how it went as the clock was ticking. Jim had exactly three minutes to change personas. In front of the curtain, two large televisions on either side of the stage sprung to life, showing the audience images conveying different forms of manipulation, power, and greed throughout the years, all set to a powerful musical score. It would take the audience on a short journey and keep them occupied while Jim was a frantic mess backstage.

It was actually controlled chaos. Jim was shedding the skin of one character and stepping into the life of another. Before his feet, the remnants of ego and misalignment lay strewn about, the pile of Alfred's clothes discarded without a thought. They were now being replaced with dress slacks, dress shoes, and a pressed shirt complete with a tie. Jim violently shook a towel over his hair to remove the slick look and then, after a quick blow dry, he parted his hair on the side with a non-assuming combover. He looked at himself in the mirror and ritualistically put on the final touch: a pair of non-designer glasses. He shifted his stance slightly to lead with his left hand, another character choice to help differentiate from the previous one. In those last few moments, Jim gazed at the reflection in the mirror. CUE: Warren.

The images and music ceased. The lights began to rise. Warren Hutchinson slowly entered the stage and stood before the audience. He appears fragile in nature, soft and timid as he surveys the audience, much like his predecessor.

"People of the court, members of the jury, what has unfolded over the past few weeks is another example of misguided trust and brainwashing at the hands of a man without any moral conduct." His intellectual voice fills the room. "He preyed on the innocent."

Once again, the fourth wall is non-existent as the audience is addressed directly by the district attorney, Warren Hutchinson offers his closing statement, revisiting the details of that fateful night at the hands of Alfred Holderman.

"Dexedrine—for all intent and purposes, speed—was laced in his coveted red juice. He used this as a plot device to strengthen his ability to 'con,' to brainwash, to suck the life out of those unsuspecting people before him."

It is evident from the start that this is Warren's crusade, that perhaps he himself could have been one of those doe-eyed puppets being pulled along a string by Alfred. His demeanor and energy isn't the *Law and Order* type attorney that we have come to know. But rather just another unassuming human, doing their part to win at the game of life.

"And what of Barbara Farrah? That poor woman, wife and mother of two, who arrived at Alfred's doorstep seeking help, only to ingest some of Alfred's drug-laden juice that evening and have an adverse reaction to its secret contents? She will never return home to her family. Gone, at the hands of a master con man." His voice cracked with vulnerability.

I always enjoyed playing Warren as I felt there was a gentleness about him. His movements would be small and never calculated. His timid undercurrent stemmed from my youth, those days riding the steel chair at middle-school dances. When I wasn't claiming my spoiled entitlement, I retreated to the quiet, wimpy version of Jimmy, someone comfortable in the shadows. Warren was like that, all heart and no backbone, but tonight, he was taking his stand.

He would slowly move back and forth downstage, closest to the audience, while making his case. His twenty-minute closing statement would convey the facts, play on the audience's emotional strings, and plead the case for second-degree murder. The retelling of the brainwash journey was deeply affecting this man, and as he stood center stage, he concluded with his final words:

"The choice is yours." His voice cracked as he said this, and as tears began to fall from beneath his glasses, the lights slowly faded.

Jim darted backstage while the televisions sprang to life once again, keeping the audience entertained with more images of manipulation, greed, and turmoil at the hands of public figures and the media. This character change was even shorter, at two minutes in length, during which time Jim did his best to remove the emotional pull of Warren and replace that with an uneducated, blue-collar demeanor. The exchange began with Jim trading in dress slacks for dirty work jeans, and his shirt and tie for a stained off-white, wife-beater tank top. Jim's hands shook the comb over into a "not giving two shits what one looks like" rat's nest. With some final makeup touches on his face to give the appearance of being unshaven, the third and final character was born. With a few seconds to spare, Jim cocked his head to the side and rounded both shoulders forward. His eyes began to burn with fire.

The televisions fell silent, and the blackness lifted. There at the end of a long table sat Frank Green, surrounded by a series of empty chairs at the table. In his hands are scraps of paper that he is tallying. Once the counting has concluded, he throws down the papers in disgust.

"I don't understand you people!" his southern drawl exclaimed in disgust. "We've been sequestered here for two whole days!"

Frank rises, scratching his head and then his nipple, before launching into a fiery, twelve-minute, uneducated and yet powerful exchange to the invisible jury members before him.

"People are not sheep! We have the ability to make our own choices! That's what makes us human fucking beings! Not some dumb sum bitches that want the easy way to happiness! I for one am not a sheep!" Frank proclaimed this at the top of lungs with the power of absolute conviction. And he was just getting warmed up.

"Barbara Farah chose to drink that juice. As did the others. My pigs have more common sense than those bastards!"

Frank Green came naturally to me, and for my part, I enjoyed jumping into his world the most. He was a man much like the young warrior I was. There's something refreshing about being totally committed to your own belief that everything around you is black and white. It's yes or no. Right or wrong. He was a simple man, but I found his unwavering ability to hold true to what he believed powerful. "Damn the consequences," I would always say when I would think of Frank. There were times in my life where I lived out Mr. Green, that warrior backbone with zero compassion. Right or wrong, bodies would fall in his wake, in my wake. Much like the jury members at the whim of Frank and his ability to cut through the bullshit and get to the brass tax.

As his powerful plea comes to a heightened close, he calls for another vote. He scribbles on a piece of paper and then collects all the votes. He slowly goes through each ballot until he has finished the count. His head rises.

"We have a verdict," he says. The backwoods pig farmer stands. "The jury has found Alfred Holderman..." Then the stage went dark.

Sure. I suppose we could have tied it up in a bow for the audience and force fed them. But Len and I knew what we were going after: the ambiguous power of individual choice. We had hoped that the ending would cause an introspective question in each audience member after they themselves had been manipulated for the last eighty minutes. Were they, in fact, part of the school themselves or the lone fish that would swim to the beat of their individual verdict?

In the dark, Jim makes a beeline for the safe-haven of backstage to collect himself. He stands for a moment, taking it all in, and then he hears it, much louder than in the hospital wing, and it is one of the sweetest sounds he has ever heard.

From the back-stage darkness, he appeared once again to take center stage and reap the applause of the few hundred people in attendance, homing in on his proud parents and a few familiar faces. But it was the applause coming from the strangers that was the reward. It filled his soul with purpose, and he wished the moment would never end. The adventure would continue as the show ran for a total of nine months, allowing Jim the opportunity to dive deeper into the three dynamic characters, damn the consequences. The acting fires were lit, and from their flames was birthed a signature weapon. The sword of ego would begin to consume his quest to stardom.

That bloodlust for applause and for creative attention has led many to an inevitable showdown at the crossroads in their acting careers. One where they stand before the devil and bargain for their right to the spotlight. It is definitely not a business for those with thin skin, nor is it a healthy business for those who want shallow fame. Jim and his ego were caught somewhere in the middle.

That middle found him, as it did most times, surrounded by actors in a nondescript casting office. This particular office was run by a well-known casting director, and Jim was auditioning for an underwear campaign. Surrounded by men, he patiently waited until the latest model exited the room and his name was called. In he went.

He was greeted with a drooling wet smile, soft eyes, and an even softer voice from the man behind the desk.

"Those are some tight jeans, Mr. Gardiner," the devil said.

To which Jim responded, "Thanks. It's hard finding jeans that fit right."

"Where did you get those legs?" the man then whispered.

"Rowing," Jim responded.

The man looked down at Jim's headshot and then casually said, "Please, take off your jeans."

It was an underwear campaign after all, so off the jeans went. The casting director's eyes peered up and fixated on their prey as though he were some ravenous beast on the Serengeti. Jim could feel the man's eyes burning through him, or rather, through his crotch. Then the casting director slowly stood, and as if Satan himself was speaking, said the following: "Take your underwear down."

There was a moment of contemplation. That's what this business can do to one's soul, looking for that next ego win. In this case, the always quick on his feet Jim nodded and responded, "If they go *down*, you'll be picking *up* your teeth."

I can still see that weasel cowering behind his desk. I wonder how many victims he'd had over the years, how many young men at his beck and call with their hopes and dreams cradled in his greasy palms. I quickly got dressed and made a beeline for the door, but I distinctly remember turning back and shooting that creep the middle finger for good measure. Needless to say, I never got a call back from that casting office, and as I walked home on the streets of New York City, I was sure it wouldn't be the last of my trips to the crossroads. The actor's life is a double-edged sword for sure.

A Monkey Under the Big Top

Another transformation was happening via Jim's pursuit of his acting life. His yearning for deep and powerful emotional work, bringing characters to life, gave birth to a brooding demeanor. *This is what real actors do,* he thought. They brood. They sit and ponder the existential existence of darkness and the unanswerable "why" in all things. All the "real" actors in his mind had this air of darkness about them. Not evil but rather a formidable state of contemplation, as though they were always searching for something. Well, that was Jim. The searcher. Alone for the first time in his life, what he needed was a compass to help him navigate this foreign land with his newfound ego. It arrived in the form of a couch and a woman, about eight years removed from the comfort of Allie's gentle touch.

Carmen walked into Jim's life late into his first year in the city. They met at a gym, but not just any gym mind you; this was a legendary underworld staple of city iron. Johnny Lats was a dingy, twenty-four-hour mecca of iron, sweat, and mutants. In the early morning, amidst the gym gorillas, there were two normal people training. She was a stunningly beautiful Puerto Rican princess in phenomenal shape, with an artistic spark and intelligence that gave her position among men in the corporate ladder of her business. She was the first "sexy" woman to ever glance his way. Ever. That invite off the chair onto the dance floor found the two of them moving into a midtown apartment together.

Living with someone is a huge step for anyone, although in city life, it was probably more common than in rural America. Walking home to the comfort of a partnership in the sea of loneliness that is the Big Apple can be a cherished gift. She became Jim's rock, and although he didn't have the bloody war wounds of a tennis match, he did have the mental anguish and internal voices of a struggling actor. For nine months, during the *Schools of Fish* run, she was there for him. During that brief interlude with the drooling slime ball, they had laughed, and during some of the struggles she would share about her estranged father, they had cried. The warrior in Jim had finally found his queen. If only life could be that simple.

The brooding actor of New York City was no longer the curious boy of wonder from Cydot Drive. Jim was feeling his first signs of being suffocated. Not by his relationship but by the current lack of momentum in his career, and for that matter, his life. When the applause died, life seemed to stall. The dreaded "M" word appeared again: monotony. It began to surge through him like it had at the thought of working in a monkey lab for the rest of his life. He also needed to find some stable income to help pay the bills while Carmen was busy working.

It's no secret that most actors end up waiting tables or becoming bartenders, mostly because such jobs allow for flexibility during the day for auditions. The ego that had been lit from those stage lights began to whisper to Jim, suggesting that being behind a bar might hold some of that same allure. It wasn't just his ego talking. Jimmy got into the act as well, reminding him of a movie that had opened up his eyes to the possibility of what he saw living out on the big screen. That movie was *Cocktail* with Tom Cruise, and no one made nightlife look cooler from behind the bar than Mr. Top Gun. The aerial dogfights from his Maverick days were quickly replaced with liquor bottles dive bombing in unison to converge on glassware to the delight and cheers of the crowd. Jim saw another opportunity to step on stage and cash in on the spotlight that comes with it.

But the truth was that, outside of sneaking some Seagram 7 from his dad's cabinet and cutting it with water back on Cydot Drive, he'd never mixed a drink. He was quick to stumble upon an ad in his trusty *BackStage* paper for a bartending course, and with its eventual completion, would chart a course over the coming years, slinging drinks for New York's rich and famous. But first things first, monotony and brooding was driving a wedge between him and his queen.

Carmen was a huge fan of the artist Frida Kahlo. She loved the fact that Frida always had one thing she could count on: the company of her pet monkey. Carmen was in love with Jim, a former monkey man who also loved the concept of having a cuddly hairy little human, especially since it seemed he was allergic to every other creature in the animal kingdom.

The two took a ride out to an exotic pet store in Long Island to spice up their relationship and came back with (you guessed it) a monkey. Yup. Let the Ross from *Friends* analogies fly: anthropology degree, NYC, and a monkey. It turns out they weren't alone as there was a whole society of Big Apple primate owners. For now, though, it was Carmen, Jim, and Jimmy Fox, together in midtown.

Jimmy Fox, named after Fox Mulder from the *X-Files,* was a baby squirrel monkey that would fit in the palm of their hands. It was Jim's first adventure into being a dad, feeding it with a tiny bottle and changing homemade diapers as it grew a bit older. The three became quite the center of attention wherever they went, most notably to the downstairs laundry room or out for walks in the concrete jungle. Jimmy Fox would always perch himself on top of Jim's head; that was his spot, and his alone, from which he would view the world from a safe distance.

Nothing says attention-seeking like a monkey crown as you stroll around the streets. That was me for sure. It was my "in" for conversation, for double takes, and to make someone smile. Oh, and here's a newsflash: A guy with a dog ain't got nothing on a man with a monkey. He was my real-life Rusty, and ironically, the same size for much of that first year—not that Rusty would ever fully be replaced (that's just sacrilege).

Unfortunately, the relationship with that amazing woman and cute sidekick wasn't strong enough to withstand the crashing waves of me "wanting more" out of life and my upstart career. After things ended, I saw her and Mr. Fox only a handful of times over the next ten years in New York. One particular time, I was riding the bus and saw her standing on a busy street corner. I wanted to *carpe diem* my ass off that seat, get off that bus, and see how she was doing, but I didn't. That image of her getting smaller through the condensation of a bus window is my last memory of "What if?" I did take comfort knowing that Carmen and Jimmy Fox went on to a better life without me. I know they did. The fantasy of it all eroded under the sweeping tide of reality, and that monkey within me would soon find a home under the circus lights.

The Ye Old Triple Inn was a small rickety looking establishment across the street from the midtown gym Jim now frequented. Quite honestly, he would never have thought about going in if not for walking by it every day. As he pulled open the squeaky wooden door, he was immediately transported into a big-top carnival of lights and sound. Colored Christmas lights greeted the Little Jimmy inside him, and you'd swear one could see snow coming down through the warm glow of lights. Everywhere he looked, there were knick-knacks hanging on the walls and from the ceiling. Conversations were loud, and laughter filled the smoky air. This was pub life in the big city, and Jim smiled at its discovery. A long wooden bar top with countless untold stories and late-night musings was a beautiful sight to behold. It was a throwback to a bygone era where conversation and dreams flowed as easily as the poured alcohol. A large jukebox delivered the soundtrack to its daily story, and a lone dartboard was the gravitational pull for the regulars. There was a stage too, and many of the usual suspects could be found on it during the countless open-mic nights. Their headshots were forever immortalized on the wall surrounded by fellow actors, musicians, and comedians. This was the place to be.

An older man stood behind the bar, diligently cleaning the inside of a pint glass with a white towel as Jim approached.

"What can I do for you?" the gentleman asked. His demeanor was as inviting as the inn's Christmas lights.

"I'm wondering if you need a bartender?"

"Have you bartended before?" The man leaned on the wooden bar and pushed up his glasses.

"Well, to be honest, I just completed a course, but I feel like I know what I'm doing," the confident rower in him offered.

The man nodded for a moment, slung the white towel over his shoulder, and said, "Hi, I'm Mike, and this is my place."

"Jim," the future bartender said as he outstretched his hand for a shake.

"Come by tomorrow evening at six, and we will get you started," Mike replied, taking his hand off his hip and meeting Jim's.

Their eyes, smiles, and hands met, beginning a friendship and a loyalty that would transcend time. As Jim exited through the double doors of the big top, he was greeted by the air of the city streets, which smelled a little sweeter. It was the scent of possibility.

Over the years, I have honed my bloodhound schnoz to pick up that beautiful allure whenever it drifts by. Sometimes the scent is stimulated in a simple conversation, the energy behind the words creating visions of a possible future reality. That sweet smoke from a spark is sometimes all we need to take the next step into the unknown. Possibility, the sweet "what if" of life. Back then, the adventure of bartending was just beginning. Sure, it was new and exciting, but it was a doorway to a new world, new choices, and the excitement of the unknown. I had to learn the ins and outs of the business, and it first started with ungodly hours: 6:00 p.m. to 4:00 a.m. It was the city that never slept after all, but I (for one) had never been a night owl.

Nighttime at the Triple was indeed a circus; that's the best way to put it. Those Christmas lights really came out during the evening, as did the veil of smoke that covered its three rooms like a mist on the Scottish moors. It was still the age of "smoke 'em if you got 'em" indoors, and the regulars didn't disappoint. Each night "the wood" (as the bar is called) had its cast of characters, each with their own special unique gifts. There would be whiskey and pontification being served up by Johnny and his wire-rimmed glasses. He was saddled up next to Pauly the dart meister, noted for the Halls lozenges he would keep close at hand for his nose candy trips to the bathroom. Good old Andrew with his Heineken and Jägermeister would try to stump Jim on the names of *Star Trek* episodes (which he never could). And let's not forget Merrit (or "Merritolius" as Jim would call him). His signature brave-bull cocktail would accompany his rantings on the artistic superiority of Bruce Springsteen and legacy of the New York Mets. The jukebox would be thumping and Crazy Judy would start dancing wherever she was and with whomever she could get her hands on.

If one didn't know better, you would bet the curb outside this bar would be home to multiple clown cars. While each night was fun and exciting, it became evident to Jim that there was tragedy under the surface of the clowns in this circus. This was their safe haven, a big top where they could escape the world with Ringmaster Jim providing the liquid popcorn and peanuts. Each seemed to be seeking shelter from their own tiger that had escaped and was running loose outside its four walls. Inside, they were safe. Each and every night, they would return to the Greatest Show, and Jim would see the downward spiral of his friends. It was a vicious circle. The admission ticket came with a sense of relief. The warm and medicinal libations would silence the tiger and replace it with laughter and pure joy, only to have that laughter and fun silenced as they began to lose a grip on reality and motor function. Their eyes began to drift, and their souls grew quiet. It was haunting seeing the evolution of ghosts at the hands of alcohol.

Jim was on a different path. When he took his place behind the wood, it was like the stage lights came up, and he began to grow a following. His name was quickly replaced with "Buff Boy," and it stuck like a fresh piece of Velcro. His eyes rolled, but he played along with the masses, partly because (deep down) it fed his egoic fire a little more each day. The ladies liked it too. They would enter Buff Boy's circus, make eye contact, share some conversations, and maybe even take part in some red-checkered tablecloth play, or bathroom-stall romp into the wee hours of the morning. Buff Boy Jim had indeed found a new stage, and goddamn it, he was going to make that steel chair pay for all its mental abuse. But as the spotlight faded and the door locked at the end of each shift, the post-show let down would return, and Jim the actor would go home to wherever he was staying, peel off his ashtray- and cologne-smelling clothes, drop them at the foot of his bed, and lay awake, staring at the ceiling. His soul was losing control to the power of his ego. It became a constant bloodlust for more attention, more of the spotlight, culminating in a fateful decision that would create a scar of shame to haunt him. Jim would soon have his own tiger lurking outside the Big Top of the Triple Inn. Now it was his turn to stand with the devil at the crossroads once more.

Friends at the Window

One can only speculate whether or not Blues legend Robert Johnson did, in fact, make a deal with the devil at the crossroads to play guitar the way he did back in the early 1930s. Jim knew one thing for sure: Ralph Macchio of *Karate Kid* fame sure did when he starred opposite the guitar god/devil, Steve Vai in the movie *Crossroads,* loosely based on the mythical legend. There have always been tales of Faustian pacts where one trades their soul with the devil in exchange for talent, fame, women... The list was endless. Now it was Jim's turn.

The wind blew in and circled Jim's feet like a mini tornado, the dirt from the barren road moving upward, circling his body. His eyes squint for protection as they peer out into nothingness. Before them lies a wasteland, an intersection of two roads, two worlds that converge on nothing more than a simple choice. The figure in black appears like the ferryman of ancient Greece waiting to take someone's soul over the River Styx. He is the tollkeeper at the fork in the road, and his hand is outstretched. The price of passage is Jim's soul.

That's how my artistic older self envisions it, looking back all these years. A defining moment where my youth chased applause at any cost. That dream would often overtake real life, and in some cases, bully it into a corner, damn the consequences (Frank Green style). But behind every doorway of opportunity is that sweet air of possibility. Even on a barren dust-filled backroad, bargaining with the man in black.

When my friend and director Ken Dashow wrote a screenplay for a new movie, the offer was extended for me to play the lead. This would be my first fully paid gig to be on the big screen and be the star I dreamt of being as a child. I could feel the excitement pump through my veins, immediately erasing the memories of Carmen and Jimmy Fox slipping away from my unhappiness, and counteracting the "just a bartender" late-night self-talk.

"If" is such an aloof word. But if I could go back in time… "The horror," as Marlon Brando would say. If I had just turned left when the man in black held out his hand, who knows what could have happened? But in my usual genetic DNA fashion, I went all in with every cell of my being.

The starring role that had Jim jumping out of bed in the morning was for television's infamous late-night crowd, and not exactly the Academy Awards crowd either. In the nineties, many of the cable stations like Cinemax would have their late-night offerings of cheesy "R" rated T&A movies. For those of you unfamiliar with "T&A," it stands for Tits and Ass. Yup, commence the eye rolling. "Skinamax" as it was called would showcase these poorly acted and shitty plot devices for the evening sex addicts, loners, and whoever the "F" else of society. At the end of the day, sex sells. But in this case, it was a key to a doorway for Jim, a doorway to another mystical fantasy land that outweighed his sense of reason: a real film set.

Of course, the real Jim (who by this point had been relegated to the shadows of his soul) would whisper questions: Was this a good move or not? Was this aligned with what I had set out to do when stepping through the door to the concrete jungle from Rhode Island? Sometimes I feel like I failed him, the real Jim, like I let him down when he needed me the most. But the "James" that I eventually became was, at that point, barely a fetus on a long road to birth.

I knew I was in for an experience (to say the least) during the initial rehearsal and read through. To be blunt, I was surrounded by people who couldn't act their way out of wet paper bags. Hearing some of the actors read their lines was like nails on a chalkboard pumped through a nightclub stereo system. However, the silver lining was Camille, a beautiful blonde model who seemed different from the others. There was something genuine about her underneath the celebrity aura she seemed to have. She had risen to some fame by being an MTV dancer and being seen under the arm of Marcus Shankenberg, the famous male supermodel, and Nuno Bettencourt, the amazing guitarist from the band Extreme. But this was my show. In that room and in the lead role, I was the supermodel now.

"I'm Jim. I'll be playing Sam Drake," I said to her as she took a seat next to me.

"I'm Camille," she said playfully.

That was all she needed to say. We became inseparable and together would comfort each other as the gratuitous sexual storm and downright cheesy content would batter our psyches. We were there for each other, and somehow, I think we would be again, even all these years removed. Sure, our lives went down separate paths, hers to fame and glory in Los Angeles and mine to self-exile in the Pacific Northwest. Through the years, we tried to shake that albatross, but it was bigger than both of us.

To this day, there is nothing better than the energetic hustle and bustle of a film set. It will always remain a magical place full of the power of creative make believe. For Jim, that first day, stepping foot onto a Brooklyn soundstage was twenty years in the making, from the wide-eyed stage of the pediatric wing to the watery-eyed showing of *E.T., the Extraterrestrial*, to the biggest stage of them all. That boy within the young man was beaming like Christmas morning. Jim had brought all of his sidekicks and memories along for the ride, mentally at least. This was a celebration and one that Rusty, Scuttle, and the mustard Captain all needed to witness. Along with Little Jimmy firmly in tow, they were escorted through the various hand-built sets, side-stepping dolly tracks and light stands as they went.

His youthful sidekicks were also there with him in the make-up room when people were tending to him like royalty. He even caught a glimpse of their smiling faces in the large mirror as he sat on his throne. Like the applause after opening night on stage, Jim felt like he had arrived. Where, exactly, was the question. Especially when a production assistant approached and unraveled what looked like a red sock.

Jim quickly covered Little Jimmy's ears and told his trusty internal wingmen to scram.

"You want me to do what with that exactly?" he asked in shocked bewilderment. Jim stared intently at the red covering and slowly reached out his hand.

God help me. Yes. The red sock. *The* red sock, actually, for it was a lifesaver back then and a must in those types of movies. It was a fitted John Thomas covering, if you will, that served two purposes. Since there was no male genitalia allowed to show on camera, this sock would act like a giant red flag, warning the cinematographer that someone's tool was in the shot. Likewise, it would serve as a barrier when close to a female co-star, in terms of easing her mind.

In his dressing room, Jim fumbled with the sock like a teenager who was all thumbs trying to figure out how a condom works. A perfectly placed elastic band to secure it firmly on the package, and there was lead actor, Jim Gardiner, standing before the mirror in all his glory or agony, depending on which personality you asked. His head started to shake, one bushy eyebrow higher than the other. *There are some things in life that need to be experienced,* he thought. *This isn't one of them.* A knock at the door caught his attention

"Five minutes, Mr. Gardiner," the production assistant bellowed.

Jim secured his bathrobe with a firm tie of its sash, took a deep breath, and plunged into history. *No time for caution,* he thought. *I'm an actor.*

Oh, he was an actor alright. Nothing says an actor like a boom mic six inches from your ass cheek while laying completely naked, keeping your floppy red flag from blowing in the breeze while trying to respect your co-star who is completely naked and exposed in front of thirty crew members. Not exactly what Little Jimmy had in mind, I'm sure. However, among a multitude of firsts in this endeavor was the privilege of sharing his first ever on-screen kiss, and there was no better dance partner to share it with than Camille.

The softness of her lips would make Jim lose his bearings. The boom mic vanished, the crew disappeared, and time slowed once again. They didn't have to "act" their passion or their connection. It was readily available and couldn't be contained. It came naturally, and Jim even thought to himself at one point, *Thank God for the sock.*

"Cut!" cried the director. "Fire in the duct tape!"

Some scrawny production assistant blew in like the wind, snapping Jim from his slow dance, his bony claw holding out a roll of gray duct tape to the actor.

"What the hell is that for?" Jim asked.

The nervous assistant tried to utter a response. "Well, the director—"

Jim didn't want an answer from him and turned to the director. "What the hell is this for?"

His friend Ken, sensing his agitation, stepped in for the director and tried to soften the moment with reason. "You gotta... tape down... your sock, Jim. You're in the damn shot."

"For fuck's sake, Ken." Jim surrendered and grabbed the duct tape.

The ripping of the tape echoed the sentiments of Jim's soul dividing more and more with each day of the shoot that passed. The story itself revolved around a detective, one Sam Drake, who was called to investigate a murder in "Clue" fashion. The backdrop was a stunning mansion where the who-dun-it yarn spun around a throughline of every female character successfully seducing Mr. Drake in an attempt to throw him off the trail.

Years later, I think this was payback for me from running away from that spinning coke bottle and being so goddamn naive about life. Well, here I was, or rather there was Jim waiting for that next spin to stop. It would land on the nurse. Up next, the wife's sister, and then the maid.

Each day, Jim would return to his apartment room, the dirty-ashtray clothes replaced by the growing scent of filth and sleaze.

The snapping point came in the final days of shooting. It was a scene that involved Sam Drake in the kitchen with the maid and a candlestick. (Actually, it was whipped cream, not a candlestick, and a lot of it.) A few things played out in a perfect storm if you will. First and most importantly, Jim hated whipped cream, always scooping it to the side of any dessert offering. Secondly, the woman who played the maid reminded Jim of a female Michael Jackson, with a face that had gone under the knife a few times and come out the other side with a warped sense of reality. Lastly, his internal moral compass (in terms of little Jimmy and the real Jim) were barking words of regret from the window in his mind.

That scene found the Academy Award winning contender covered in a white disgusting mess of dessert topping, sprawled out on the kitchen counter. On top of him was the King of Pop, her boobs being caked with more and more whipped cream, over and over.

"BANG!" A loud internal knock rattled his consciousness. *"Stop it!"* cried a younger voice, a pure voice, from the windows of his soul. *"Walk away! This isn't you!"*

White. Just white. That was all Jim could see. Then there was that sickly smell of sugar and sleaze, his hands covered in it. A boom mic dropped into frame right above the carnage that was happening. Jim's eyes drifted to the microphone and then to the man holding it, to the lights above him as he lay helpless on the counter being held prisoner by a naked maid in wolf's clothing. It was then that he heard it.

The tiny sniffles of a nose running with emotion from the upstairs window of his soul. The world around him stopped, and for a brief second, a soft tap replaced the loud banging on the window.

"This is not what we wanted when we saw E.T.," Little Jimmy softly whispered through his tears.

For a moment, Jim could see with perfect clarity. It was crystal clear. "Stop," he said softly, but his scene partner couldn't hear him through the sound of sloppy self-lathering.

"Stop!" he shouted, and then snapped at her. "Get off me."

"Cut!" the director said. "Jim, what's the matt—"

"What the fuck is going on here?" Jim shouted as he pushed the boom mic out of his space. "Seriously, this isn't a movie! It's fucking joke!"

Jim jumped off the table, fueled by his companion at the windows of his soul. "Ken, this isn't art! This is... this is shit! Three-ring-circus bullshit! I mean... look at this!"

Jim was standing in the kitchen, red sock and all, half covered in whipped cream, his arms outstretched and pointing to the war zone that was the kitchen counter, the stunned actress mounted on top of it like some trophy.

From Schools of Fish *to this*, he thought. Taking one more look at the battlefield of self-destruction, he then walked off set, no bathrobe, no nothing.

I am proud of that brief moment, in which my younger self connected (or better yet, reconnected) to my truth, even if it was at the end of the shoot. Some of my younger decisions that have served to create lasting scars are also interwoven with radiating moments of redemption, like the sun beaming and clouds clearing in the eye of a hurricane. It is a pure moment, a loving moment before the inevitable clouds gather and the storm ensues. Through the years, I would plead my case that this was, in fact, just another movie (albeit a bad and boob-filled one), but it fell on deaf ears and judging eyes. I have paid the price to the ferryman with that decision, and now, I stand with it in acceptance, not against it.

On a side note, I still hate the sight and smell of whipped cream.

The stroke of her hand felt oddly familiar as his eyes closed. Camille gently massaged his head while the mentally exhausted actor did his best to recharge his soul. Memories of the tennis match came flooding back to honor this present moment, to the comfort he was now receiving, lying in her bed. There was no blood or aches and pains for Camille to tend to, just a soul rife with torment and longing. Once again, the simple touch of a woman's gentle hand seemed to erase the pain. Unlike his time with Allison, this one was cut short by the ring of a phone. She twisted herself free of Jim and went to answer it.

With that call, possibility blew in and filled her sails. After what was to be their last embrace, Camille had received a call to go out with some friends for dinner. Lying in her bed, Jim watched this beautiful woman before him talking on the phone.

"I got invited out with some friends. Do you want to come?" she asked him.

"Go, you idiot! Play! Have fun," pleaded that voice from the window, and yet Jim just smiled at her beauty.

"Nah, you go," he said softly. "Have fun. I'm tired."

The truth was that he felt insecure. The sideline of the school dance is also safe, and its chair comfortable with a customized fit. Let's face it; he wasn't a famous supermodel or a famous lead guitarist. Nope. He was just Jim, renting a room somewhere and slinging drinks, trying to make a dream a reality. She was somebody, and Jim wasn't. As he drifted off that evening, he knew things would be different when the sun rose.

While Jim was lost in a sleepy dream in her bed, Camille met Kelsey Grammer at dinner, and the rest was Hollywood history. That doorway opened for her, and she walked through it to a wonderful life. They would keep in touch here and there over the following few years, with Camille calling from Kelsey's estate in Los Angeles to check in on her buddy. She knew just where to find him: on a chair engaged in another dream.

The Starlet and the Clown

The New England coastline will always be the marker by which I gauge beauty in all things. Even as I sit here on the stunning shores of the Pacific Northwest, I am drawn back to its rolling greens, its endless stone walls, and the bold Atlantic sweeping in on jagged bluffs to greet old colonial lighthouses.

Trips back to Rhode Island were fairly frequent in those first few years, like a baby weaning away from its loving mother. The passage originated from beneath Madison Square Garden at the Amtrak train station. A view through a window on a train is a precursor to life, especially the older we get. Snapshot images caught in a split second, and then quickly replaced by the next, greet one's eyes in a blurring tapestry of what was. As I sat there on many a trip home, always on the right side so that my eyes could capture that coastline romance, I would reflect and try to understand the great arena of life.

One particular ride home, Jim sat pondering a next phase looming for many, specifically for one of his best friends. Highschool wingman Ed was getting married. He was the first of them to take the plunge, and the event would mark a series of firsts for Jim. It was the first wedding that he had ever been to and his first wedding-party duties. It also marked the first time in his life that a woman dropped him dead in his tracks. There are connections, and then there are *connections*.

Jim approached the church with his arm around his other best friend, Steve, as the two shared a deep laugh at one of his legendary one-liners. It was a beautiful summer day, and Jim felt the pull of the big city melt away as the laughter and never-ending friendship warmed his heart. Steve, ever the gentleman, opened the door to the church and in they went, Jim first.

I am not sure what it's like to have a divine sighting or to see the Virgin Mary in a grilled-cheese sandwich, but I do know what it is like to stare into the face of God's beauty. The opening of the door and Steve's loud voice signaled their entrance. The gathering of bodies peeled back, perfectly choreographed by universal design to expose her. There she stood, radiating, while the chorus of angels accompanied Jim's thunderous heartbeat.

Tanya was in the bridal party and was the most beautiful woman Jim had ever laid his eyes on. She was indeed the browned-eyed girl to this blue-eyed boy as only Bono would decree, definitely the sweetest thing. Her long brown hair perfectly paired with her Italian features like a robust Sangiovese dancing with the softness of fresh ricotta on one's pallet. The symphony of life had surely orchestrated this synchronized movement, even their smiles were perfectly in tune.

"This is Tanya," the groom said.

Jim didn't even acknowledge his best friend Ed. He just moved closer to Tanya. "Hi," he said, lovestruck.

He felt her eyes going straight through his and down to the very base of his soul. She touched him deeply without speaking, her energy instantly filling his void.

"Hi," she said softly and secured a place in Jim's soul for the rest of his life.

The two would be walking together as part of the wedding party, and they immediately started bonding. Jim couldn't help but think about how all of this was playing out as if orchestrated by a higher power. Tanya was a former Miss Canada winner who was also living in New York City, trying to make it in the business. She had made the trip up because of her friendship with Ed's soon-to-be wife.

For the entire weekend, the two big-city goofballs seemed insepa-rable, two sets of smiles and two sets of enamored eyes lighting their way with playful schoolyard banter. But it was their slow dances that would become the stuff of legend. The way the two moved and the wordless stares between them would make any newlyweds jealous. The weekend was a perfectly scripted coming-of-age eighties romance movie. It just happened to take place six years after that glorious decade.

Back in Manhattan, the two immediately connected again. There would be long walks in Central Park and endless romantic discussions about love, life, and the pursuit of dreams. Their favorite fantasy was driving across the country via the old southern way on the famous Route 66.

"Convertible," Jim said with a smile. "Gotta have a convertible."

"And music to dance to on the side of the road," Tanya added eagerly.

The two moved closer, almost nose to nose, their bodies starting to move to the music of their hearts. "And soft kisses," the lovestruck man whispered.

"Every hour on the hour." Her brown eyes punctuated the words as they left her lips.

We didn't care if we were in a coffee shop, movie theater, or standing in line for a slice of Ray's Pizza. There was no one else around us when we were together. It was a fairytale, a dream where each waking day I got to unwrap a beautiful present. But underneath was a whisper in my head that asked, *Will I be enough?*

I think it was natural to have some skepticism, especially given my Camille experience. I had a belief (and perhaps still do) that, "I don't get girls like this," and if I do, "I don't have anything to offer them." Sure, that was fear talking back then, but then my whisper was confirmed on the steps of a New York City brownstone apartment, and I felt like the dejected outcast banished once more to the steel chair of solitude.

"I'm kind of seeing someone else," Tanya said. "It's more of an on-again-off-again thing." Her voice pierced Jim's armorless body. "Plus, I'm thinking about moving to LA."

His heart was just punctured, and he could feel his spirit bleeding out through the open wound.

He could barely find the strength to respond. "I don't... understand."

"He's a lawyer," she said, beginning an explanation.

The sound of a record being deliberately scratched fills my ears now as much as it did Jim's back then. Nothing else after that opening statement mattered, not her dreams in Los Angeles or anything else. I'd like to believe Jim could have wooed her with the only currency that matters (or should matter): love. But my younger self had yet to fully realize the power and magnitude of that word. Unfortunately, love is not money, and it doesn't pay the bills. Kelsey had it. Obviously this lawyer had it. All Jim had was a heart tied to a dream with zero stability in his wallet.

Adventure and exploration of the world comes at a price. While others are building careers and laying foundations, the dreamers and seekers embrace wanderlust simply to build their emotional depth. I have learned that it is rich beyond measure; however, in a society and culture built upon the expectation of stability, it can be hard to navigate. It would circle back around in my life and my journeys, rearing its ugly, monstrous head numerous times. But for now, it was all about Tanya as her conflicted soul stood in line, waiting to either catch a ride on the stability bus or take the love train.

The bus ticket (or rather a one-way flight to Los Angeles) was punched, and just like that, she was gone, pursuing her dreams, the luggage of true love left behind on a street corner.

We never fully disconnected over the years. She went on to fame as a television host and inspirational speaker. Years would pass and sporadic check-ins would manifest from thin air on both our parts. We always would cheer each other on in spirit. Time definitely softens pain. However, back on the streets of NYC, pain was beginning to become part of my life.

✧ ✧ ✧

"Thud! Thud!" The hollow sound echoed in the late-night air. Jim's foot orchestrated this music as it forcefully found a home in some guy's body. The sidewalk was a war zone. Two male figures were being decimated at the hands (and feet) of the Triple Inn's bartender. Jim turned back to see a few of the regulars in the doorway, watching their gladiator at work.

As he reentered, and the colored lights illuminated him, he was drawn to the crimson sight of fresh blood streaming from his two knuckles.

"You!" he shouted to some New Jersey meathead, likely over for the weekend. "Out! Now!"

As the guy left, exiled to scrape his two buddies off the pavement, Jim took his position behind the wood once more. His lightness had gone away, replaced by a hardened warden left to oversee the inmates of the asylum.

Jim had morphed into a miserable and angry young man, hell bent on self-misery and looking for anyone to take his frustrations out on. Each day, the whirlpool seemed to suck him in deeper and deeper. There would be more stitches, depending on who decided to challenge the warden behind the bar. After a few weeks, the whirlpool finally pulled him down to a breaking point, alone in the darkness beneath the Triple Inn. The basement was only illuminated by two solitary light bulbs casting ghostly shadows. Among the endless cases of beer, liquor bottles, and dusty storage boxes sat Jim, perched atop a keg and crying uncontrollably.

I was probably down there for thirty minutes before Mike, the owner, came to check on me. I wish I could remember what he said to me as I sat there sobbing. Much like that pep talk from Coach Jack back in the glory season of the boys in blue, it escapes me. The young man sitting in the basement was far removed from the gold-medal winner who took the podium, or even the defying rebel in the face of an asthma doctor. I think it was my first broken moment, and it happened in a basement underneath a circus. Mike sent the sad clown home that evening, and as I strolled the magical night streets of Manhattan, I knew I had to find the courage within. Every crusader has to look inside and find that inner resolve to carry on. Back then, and to this day, I would always turn to one thing to help me rise.

Sonic Six Shooters

Music has flowed in my veins for as long as I can remember. Not a day goes by that I don't get caught up in a moment of sonic bliss and step outside of myself. Quite simply, it has become my dog whistle. Songs have a way of capturing moments in time and securing them forever, even if they are temporarily forgotten. Soundtracks have become as essential as food in my adult life with their wordless scores allowing me to capture that film moment and repurpose it to fuel myself. Like the pulsating rhythm of the Atlantic, music would flow with my current moods and pendulum swings of emotions, always constant and always scoring that exact moment in my life.

Much like movies, it has always had the ability to transport me down a six-lane emotional highway, arriving at a destination filled with love, sadness, reflection, aggression, softness, and inspiration. When I first came upon music, it was delivered through the speakers of my dad's transistor radio.

The backyard patio would find Little Jimmy (and Rusty) sitting across from his mom and dad as they sat around the radio, much like they did with its big brother, the floor-model Zenith. Except there was no image, no visual storytelling. Just voices and sounds allowing for the listener to create their own visions.

For Little Jimmy, it was an angelic voice that first pierced his tiny young heart. The voice of Karen Carpenter would drift effortlessly out of the black speaker mesh and begin to dance in the thick summer air. It was music for the soul, and Jimmy would watch his parents close their eyes and be transported somewhere known only to them.

As he began to get older, Jimmy started to latch on to music as much as his trusty sidekicks. In his high school days, his musical collage began to expand with his love of Lionel Richie, Neil Diamond, Journey, and a rock band from Canada (No, not the trio known as Rush but another powerful rock trio) called Triumph. With Gil Moore on drums, Mike

Levine on bass, and the one and only Rik Emmitt on guitar, this was the band for Jimmy. And, come to think of it, Steve and Ed as well. It was good old-fashioned rock, and it was written with uplifting and inspirational lyrics that would intertwine with his day-to-day adventures while he was destined to "Fight the Good Fight,' "Never Surrender,' and "Carry on the Flame" with a certain "Magic Power" leaving most "Spellbound," and as "Time Goes By," Jim never forgot to "Hold On" even when it appeared he was "Headed into Nowhere." This band was his "Battle Cry" all through high school and beyond. It wasn't until later that two other rock bands would take the altar of Jimmy's ongoing personal anthem. During that amazing Cinderella year back in 1989, with the boys in blue, Jimmy would come across a band that literally impacted his life more than any other.

"Who killed Sister Mary?" was the question that rockers all over the world would be asking themselves. This was it, ladies and gentlemen: the definitive rock concept album that took storytelling to a whole other level. Among a musical scene of cheesy lyrics and screaming nonsense came a thought-provoking story. The depth, darkness, and intelligent weaving of the current political landscape in this concept album is heralded as one of the greatest rock albums of the eighties and beyond. Queensrÿche's magnum opus, "Operation: Mindcrime," centered around a secret underground revolutionary faction bent on political assassination. Their crusade was carried out by homeless street addicts with a drug den masquerading as a church to distribute heroin and manipulate weary soldiers seeking salvation. At the center of it all was a love story between Nikki and his needle of redemption: Sister Mary.

If the concept alone didn't stand out enough to lure people in, there was the double axe attack of leading guitars that created a sonic canvas with their searing dueling riffs and harmonic inflections worthy of the gods. But it was the man himself that delivered the soaring vocals and emotional depth of the characters. There are singers, there are even rock gods, but there is only one true God to hold a microphone: Geoff Tate. He was unparalleled in his ability to hit a four-octave range, delivering power and grace while letting the music and his soul speak with stage-commanding emotion and presence. His operatic style and thinking-man's lyrics lifted this band's music way ahead of its time. Geoff would become another hero to Jim through the years, one he dreamt of meeting.

To say I was obsessed would be an understatement. The very next day, I drove to the record store and bought all their cassettes and began to go all in, losing myself in their music. They took a seat at my table of heroes, and their music has never left my side. I did eventually meet my hero, around the same time that I was grieving my own murdered nun. Wait, I'm getting ahead of myself. Sideline that for now.

The second band that would be Jim's other weapon in his rock holster came a bit later, once he was out of university. It was a progressive rock band that, unsurprisingly, was highly influenced by Queensrÿche. The members were all aficionados at their instruments and had attended the prestigious Berkeley School of Music in Boston. Backing the powerful lead singing of James LaBrie was the otherworldly guitar playing of John Petrucci, and the pocket rhythm of the one and only Mike Portnoy. The band's name was Dream Theater, and they created epic songs about the stream of consciousness and the poetic power of spiritual emotion. One word comes to mind when I try to describe them to people: epic. To this day (and some fifteen albums later), I have come to trust their sonic escape more than any other musical offering.

When I arrived through the saloon doors of New York City, I was strapped, with Queensrÿche on my right hip and Dream Theater on my left. Other powerful pieces from bands like Fates Warning, Triumph, Journey, Boston, Rush, and The Cult would combine forces with the more subtle Lionel, Enya, Whitney, and Celine. The tapestry would also weave in an ongoing assortment of movie soundtracks and classical compositions to keep me armed and ready for whatever comes across my path.

During that first period of feeling lost as I drifted away from Carmen, it was Geoff's medicating voice with the song "Someone Else?" that would soothe my soul, speaking as it did about crossroads in life and self-perception. I encourage all of you to look up its lyrics and spend some time pondering their wisdom.

It moves me every time, ever since it first dropped back in '94. Probably more than any other song, it is the true anthem of "me." I also have a reminder on my left leg to remember the journey. I paid tribute to the band, the song, and the album by having the famous New York tattooist Spider Webb forever symbolize the bond between the band's music and my soul.

Similarly, the boys of Dream Theater would permeate my headphones as I searched for answers post Camille and Tanya. There wasn't any magical formula for me to climb out of the anger and sadness when Tanya flew to Los Angeles. I just needed time to allow for a reconnection to the boy who had strived so hard to reach the podium. With my sonic inspiration, I began to rekindle the fire that Daniel Day-Lewis and my other acting heroes had once ignited within me. In honor of my lower leg, it was time to "Take Hold of the Flame" and burn that fucker bright.

Who Killed Sister Rita

Tony Robbins has always said that the key to everything is mindset. Even before him, Napoleon Hill would utter the words "Believe and you can achieve." Jim was unaware of their teachings at this point in his life, but I sit here knowing the immense power that resides within each of us. What Jim did have going for him, thanks to Little Jimmy, was the ability to say, "Well, why not me?" He had that dreamer mindset. Getting something takes a dream in the form of a vision, and the steps to make it a reality.

He finally secured his own apartment again in Hell's Kitchen just a few short blocks from the Triple Inn. There would be no more walks of shame to a rented room in some stranger's place. As lightness began to come back to his personality, he would let his childlike humor and demeanor peek out as he slung drinks and stirred up conversations from behind the wood. It is always about taking the first step and keeping one's eyes open for what may show up.

Like a random audition from a casting director out of the blue.

"Do you play baseball? We are looking for good baseball players," the casting director said from behind the camera.

"Hell yeah! Played all my life. Shortstop, First Base, you name it," Jim said without missing a beat.

* Business note. In any audition, pending life or death, when a casting director asks if you're good at something (and you're not), you lie and then deal with it on set. Just like the "rules to fight club," there are a set rules for actors booking gigs. This was one of them.

Luckily for Jim, he did know how to play baseball. So what if it had been fourteen years since he'd actually thrown a ball? When Jim received the call that he had booked the gig, he was excited. It was extra money, and a spot in a national commercial for the allergy medicine Claritin, but it wasn't till he arrived at a ball field in New Jersey and suited up in a baseball uniform that it hit him.

"Hi, I'm Mike," said the large man through a mouthful of bubble gum.

"Jim. Jim Gardiner," he answered, feeling dwarfed by Mike.

"Let's throw the ball while we're waiting," Mike suggested playfully.

Jim smiled. So did Little Jimmy from within. The man on the other end of the playful catch was the future Baseball Hall of Famer Mike Piazza. He was playing for the New York Mets at the time and a hero to many young kids growing up in the Little League arena. Jim couldn't help remembering the dejected kid that day at middle school, when he'd walked off the field, never to return. *Not too shabby*, he thought to himself as his glove secured another toss from big Mike.

Life is a series of serendipitous moments if one chooses to see them as such. Intentions and energy can be enough to create doorways of opportunity, and then sometimes, people just have to roll up their sleeves and take matters into their own hands. Especially in the creative world. Artists die without expression, and Jim knew he needed to create to live.

What better place to be the nucleus of that creation than the Triple Inn? It served as the backdrop for many friendships that arose during that period of his life, including one with a woman from the west coast. Sarah was a red-haired creative genius who now was living and pursuing the arts in the Big Apple. She was there to try her hand at directing. *Perfect*, Jim thought. He had an idea.

It wasn't long before the two had established an independent theater production company. Threads of Humanity Productions was created to be a vehicle for both of them and their respective talents. Over the next three years, they would go on to produce a number of plays that would be showcased in the midtown area and allow the artist within Jim to live. He had achieved external applause and validation but still was on that elusive quest to find a sacred role. One that would allow him to channel the brilliance of Daniel Day-Lewis and disappear from his own reality to channel some of that darkness he had acquired. For Jim, that opportunity came in the form of a priest.

The flicker of candles brought the only movement to the stillness of the altar, their shadows dancing behind the statues like playful spirits unleashed from their confinement. Hand-crafted stained-glass artwork covered the only visible windows, showering the interior in hues of red, blue, and green. The smell of aged wooden pews would circulate in the air, along with the dust of those who had visited it over the past century. The old church on 42nd Street was rich in its history and its story, much like the colonial buildings of Jim's youth. For there he sat, alone in its vastness with only the candles and his thoughts for company. This was his immersion into the energy and mythos of a religious framework. He was punching his ticket on a one-way transformation journey, DDL style.

Jim went all in on his prep for this role. The tortured soul of Father Rivard had the meat actors crave. Actually, it had the meat, a side of potatoes with two servings of veg, and a beautiful wine with which to wash it all down. *The Runner Stumbles* was a play written by Milan Stitt, and after a successful Broadway run, it had gone on to be a major Hollywood film. In a beautiful twist of fate, Jim found himself in a turn-of-the-century murder mystery just like *Operation: Mindcrime.* He'd spent endless hours listening to Geoff Tate spin the tale of Nikki and Sister Mary, and now found himself playing out an eerie similar concept album, one where dialogue replaced music. Where the actor and character became one, and reality warped.

Her eyes spoke the innocence of a pure heart as she approached Jim in that opening scene. Her habit perfectly fitted around her soft cheek-bones, her lips trumpets to the angelic voice within. It was the energy, the eyes that would break down any wall of strength that Jim ever had. He was powerless against that yearning for connection, damn the consequences. It fueled his walk, and as he approached the downstage mark, Father Rivard could feel something fiery igniting in his pious heart. Sister Rita had cast her spell.

When two older nuns contract tuberculosis, Sister Rita is forced to stay with Father Rivard at his rectory. The internal struggle raged within the priest as Rita would chip away his armor of faith one laugh, one cherished gaze, at a time. The slightest touch of an errant hand would send shivers through Rivard's soul. The goosebumps would spring to life and work their way up Jim's arm like a feverish virus taking over his faculties. The softness of skin, the combustible energetic transference, would charge his soul and feed the author to this day.

Father Rivard felt this and was drawn to Rita regardless of his surrounding dogma. She would transform him from a life of service to a life of love . . . of joy. His grip on reality began to loosen, and the insanity of love started its own disease of consumption. "Why do I always walk away from love when it begins to scare me?" Jim's internal voice would ring like a five-alarm bell. Was it self-preservation, self-worth, monotony, the fear of being tied down when his sail wants to fill with the billowing wind of adventure? Inevitably they would be gone by his own doing or theirs.

When Sister Rita was found murdered outside the church, all peering eyes focused on the prime suspect. The priest's ever diminishing grip on reality began to question whether it had been his hands that had wielded the shovel to the back of her skull. He sat in his cell, the darkness of the stage illuminating the regret and betrayal sweet Rita had suffered from his actions. But he was also filled with an uncontrollable rage now that she was gone. Like that which filled the actor underneath the priest's skin, still angry that the opening of his heart had been rewarded with a one-way plane ticket west. He felt betrayed. Left stranded by that four-letter word: love.

The trial concluded and determined that Father Gardiner was innocent of the murder that was now pinned on a loving, religious housekeeper trying to protect her priest from the "evil" that was Sister Rita. The weary man rose and staggered his way to center stage. Each night, he would be visited by the ghost of the departed. Sister Rita would make her way from behind a curtain and walk to a point just out of reach of Jim's hand, smack dab in front of the audience. Jim and the priest tried desperately for one last touch, but it wasn't meant to be. As the ghost of Rita and the others from Jim's past faded back into the darkness, the broken man's soul cracked open, unleashing a torrent of bubbling snot and tears.

As the lights dimmed, I crumpled to the floor. It took everything I had to pick myself up and make it backstage behind the safety of the curtain. I continued to sob as the other actors went out for the curtain call, each to a thunderous applause. But I couldn't move until the director finally approached, and with her gentle touch, reminded me that my job was not finished.

I made my way back to the stage, each footstep a struggle between reality and fiction, between abandonment and abandonment, between failure and failure. I couldn't shake the anguish of Rivard as I accepted the loud standing ovation that unfolded. My watering eyes scanned members of the audience and noticed that many were weeping themselves, white tissues signaling a surrender to something that transcended the four walls of the theater. Unlike *Schools of Fish,* I wouldn't crack a smile. I just couldn't. I was locked in a prison of anguish that would take time to escape. The applause continued as did the tears of two men, both searching for love only to somehow fail it.

I look back on that week-long run at some obscure off-Broadway theater house, and the time I shape-shifted into an alternate reality. I think actors are like rowers. We both search for that elusive "swing" where magic happens. The boys in blue found it when it counted, and I think Jim found it on the stage in the role of Father Rivard. The organic freedom that came from connecting on some deep subconscious level provided a performance that has become my most cherished acting moment. I like to think that I did find my Daniel Day-Lewis moment, even if it has drifted into obscurity.

The Dance of Eternity I.

It took me some time to shake out the cobwebs of Father Rivard and fully step back into the skin suit that was Jim—not that actors ever truly shed a role, especially one that consumes them. Instead, I like to think that each personality leaves a tiny imprint from which we add more color to our lives and walk around as richer human beings. That's my two cents anyway. In that time of reflection and reclaiming "me," I also started to realize something very powerful. Only a hint of it, like the waft of a summer barbecue from two streets over. Tasty and alluring.

Jim started to look at these serendipitous moments not as chance encounters or "one offs" but rather as if they were orchestrated by some universal design. One day in particular, he went for a walk and found himself navigating a sea of people on 5th Avenue, his trusty headphones and the aspirational music of Dream Theater's "Lines in the Sand" serenading him. Something happened on this walk, he could sense a change in the perception of what was around him as the lyrics filled his soul, James LaBrie singing to him about introspection, faith, and creating our own realities.

I still don't know why it happened in that very moment, but a seed was planted in me that I am still cultivating today. Perhaps it was my loneliness among a sea of strangers. Or the random couple lost in a romantic dance on the corner of 5th and 34th street. I realized that I never had to truly be alone... that I had my own dance partner in life.

The universe, God, the source, whatever energetic label you want to put on it surrounds us and is with us. In that random or perhaps designed moment, Jim could sense it with him on that street corner. It was the start of a long pilgrimage for one elusive and then intangible word: truth. His truth. For now, that would consist of nothing more than trusting that, if he focused on his passion, his newly acquired dance partner would open up some doorways for him.

Then it happened, seemingly out of the blue. The boy from Cydot Drive found himself on a Times Square billboard alongside Mr. Supermodel Marcus from the Camille days. Celebrities, sexy cologne, and fashion signs littered the skyline on 42nd and Broadway. Jim stood on that corner and gazed up at the masterpiece. The gorgeous ad was for a clothing company and featured three guys sitting in Central Park. Jim looked great—well, parts of him anyway. The back of his broad shoulders, two beautifully shaped ears, and a gorgeous head of hair was captured forever. The other two clowns in the spot were in full view and basking in the limelight. Jim stood there on that corner among strangers and began to laugh out loud at his "big" unveil. Too bad it didn't lead to any ear modeling over the years. They looked good up there, if I do say so myself. And for the record, it was still a billboard in Times Square.

Thankfully that dance continued, albeit in an unorthodox way, as Jim navigated the corridors of the studio for the daytime soap opera *All My Children*. It was his first of many visits to the show as a bit player over the next handful of years. A universal run in with Kelly Ripa, which sent her script flying, reddened those prize ears of his with embarrassment. But thankfully, her soothing voice and calming eyes quickly doused any fear over the mishap. He received a first-class star escort to his own dressing room that day and never forgot his experience on the show with Kelly and the icon Susan Lucci, with whom he shared lines in a courtroom scene. It dawned on him that conversation is what binds us all, celebrity or not.

"Kids today, they need positivity more than ever. Whether in music, sports, actors... they need us," said Ice-T from his side of the table.

The legendary gangsta rapper turned actor sat and continued on with an educated ease and flow of positivity. I remember sitting there so inspired by this man whose life to get to where he sat now hadn't exactly been all rainbows and Cydot Drive unicorns. This was the man behind the famous "Cop Killer" anthem, and here he was playing a cop sitting with me, discussing views on life in between takes on the set of *Law and Order: Special Victims Unit*. Sure, when the cameras were rolling, we were "different," but sitting idle, we all held the same status on our resume: human beings who need human beings.

My dance partner afforded me a taste of "set culture," and I loved it. It was another brotherhood if you will, one bigger and more visual than what a theater could provide. With this realization came the need for my creative life to expand. Among the colored lights and endless spins from the bar jukebox, a movie project was born. Bob (nicknamed "Chumley") was a guy that everyone loved. He was big in stature and gentle of heart while having the most infectious laugh that could make anyone smile. Bob became the producer while I began to write the screenplay for the film, which I would direct and star in.

Over the years, I have learned that going all in requires a toll to be paid, much like the bargain at the crossroads. Something needs to be sacrificed or offered to the gods in return, creative ones or not. Unaware of this tax, I worked feverishly, and within two weeks, banged out a script that both Bob and I were happy with. *A Pleasant Shade of Gray* would be a full-length feature film with a story that mirrored some of my recent relationship struggles and trying to make sense of life. Much like my younger self, the lead character, Chase, would be on a quest of self-understanding, loss, and hope as the story unfolded.

This was the dawning of the independent film and digital age, which allowed filmmakers the ability to create their artistic expressions with a digital medium for a lot less money.

Bob was able to put together the funding for the $20,000 budget, and Jim went to work securing the cast and crew for the three-week shoot.

Filming commenced throughout Manhattan, including the Triple Inn (and its regulars), upstate New York, and even New Jersey. Inspired by Kevin Costner and Mel Gibson's double duty behind and in front of the camera, Jim dove into his art unaware of the true complexity of the task that he'd so eagerly thrown himself into. Setting up shots and storyboarding a visual medium was a process that he was learning more about with each and every day that passed as the shoot commenced. In a throwback to the time Jimmy took the huddle at QB that day on the football field, he was surrounded by the crew, explaining to his camera-man how the shot would unfold and what he needed the camera to capture. The lighting team would be on his left, with Jim laying out the scene and movement for them so they could properly illuminate the moment. Behind them, the sound guy would carefully listen so he could plan his way to capture the best sound from all the various angles available. After the crew huddle broke, it was onto the actors, making sure they knew the dynamics of the scene and what he was looking for from each of them. Lastly, he would take a moment to himself and try his best to switch from his intellectual creative mind to that of Chase, the life-searching lead character. Then into the scene he went.

"Quiet on set!" the assistant director called, taking over.

Everyone hit their choreographed positions and quiet ensued.

"Camera," said the assistant director softly.

"Camera," the cameraman answered, indicating his readiness back to the A.D.

"And... action." The dance of filmmaking ensued.

So it went, day in and day out during the shoot. With each passing day, I juggled all my duties, some better than others. There were days of inspiring creative freedom and days of near complete exhaustion and surrender. I worked myself to the bone in that time frame, at one point barely able to function while being sick. Going all in sure does come with a price. But life is one big sweeping flow of perseverance. Just like rowing. I felt comfortable leading the troops into battle no matter what, and hopefully, inspiring those around me.

When it came time for the film project to finally have its debut moment, about a hundred people filed into a theater to be swept away by Jim's creative vision. He sat at the back of the theater as the lights went down and the shimmering eyes of everyone around him became fixated on the large screen. The music began and the opening scene faded in as did the thought of Little Jimmy and all those younger dreams. (This aging and older man wishes he could pull up a seat next to both of them and relive that moment.)

I don't know if I was too hard on myself or if I wanted the audience to desperately fall in love with the story, or what. I knew the movie wasn't all that and a bag of chips; however, I also knew how much blood sweat and tears had gone into this story of a man seeking answers. I do remember one thing to this day, actually two things. First, I smile when I think of sitting there in the darkness like Little Jimmy and watching something I had created in all its visual imagery, dialogue, story, and soundtrack springing to life and filling the room.

And second, I remember some guy coming up to me afterwards, putting his hand on my shoulder, and saying, "You'll do better on your next one."

I can barely recognize his face, though if memory serves, he was a filmmaking friend to the assistant director. But the feeling of it stays with me twenty-some years later. My mind still translates his statement as "That wasn't very good." Who was I to argue? I'd just followed my creative spark, which would not be everyone's cup of tea I suppose. I do take comfort in knowing that, the next time, I did do better. A number of years later, I turned the *Schools of Fish* play into an independent film, which premiered on both coasts. Still, of all the well wishes and handshakes I received that night, it was the quick passing exchange with a stranger that seemed to stop the music.

The Dance of Eternity II.

Effortless. Their white and gray bodies glide along the rush of wind currents, greeting his face with a welcoming kiss. Beavertail Lighthouse sits over Jim's shoulder, the last marker before the endless Atlantic and the faraway lands that lay somewhere over the horizon. It is his throne, upon which he has always sat when returning to Rhode Island with only the seagulls for an audience and his thoughts for company. Young or old, it will forever remain his sanctuary.

Jim's eyes stray from the sea birds' air dance and back out to the ocean and the waves that have been building in momentum out beyond sight. Slowly, from a birth in obscurity, they rise and finally spring to life with a furious explosion onto the rocky bluffs. The spray up into the heavens is their celebration. Their story.

As those water fireworks diminish into the air and retreat to the rocks and ocean, Jim couldn't help but think of his own life and what to do with it. He felt like he was somewhere out there in the blue, building momentum but never arriving for his own crescendo.

I took a break at thirty years old and pressed the pause button on the movie of my life as I thought it was to play out. After the film screening, I desperately needed the welcoming wind of the Atlantic to rejuvenate my soul. Creativity fuels the heart but not the bank account. I sat for hours on the rocks of Beavertail in nearby Jamestown, trying to come to grips with what was next. While I was off playing actor, Steve and my friends were already well into the lane of life and building financial nest eggs and families. All I had to show for my efforts to this point was a bunch of rowing medals, some neat experiences, and some cool stories to share as we sat around drinking and reminiscing.

Returning home to Rhode Island this time felt like I had missed out. My parents had moved into Malcolm's pancake sanctuary, and my childhood home was now home to another family without even a proper goodbye. I have often wondered about this word "home" and its meaning. Only now am I beginning to understand that, for me, "home" is where I hang my soul, not my hat. Back then, I suspect my mom felt the pull of the word and the history of that yellow hand-built Cape Cod house my grandfather had built. For her, it was comfort and a chance to stay closer to the memory of her own parents.

Jim felt it too but in a nostalgic sort of way. There was a comfort that permeated the air, the streets, the ocean. It all felt nice and "known," as if life here would be simple. *What more could one ask for?* he would think to himself. With that, the internal chatter would begin. Jim would conjure up stories to himself that life would be more manageable in Rhode Island as opposed to Manhattan or anywhere else. For one month, he toyed with those stories while trying to come to some conclusion.

It was in the middle of Malcolm's backyard, basking in the glorious September sun, that some clarity broke. He sat propped up against the once-sturdy clothesline pole, which now had grown weary and old, like much of its surroundings. The pristine yellow paint had begun to fade in a losing battle with the sun. A toppled-over bird bath lay strewn across a once-flourishing flower garden, now nothing more than an ancient ruin fallen under the weight of time. Jim wondered if he would become stale and old like his surroundings should he stay. As he sat there alone, he closed his eyes and tried to sense if Malcolm was with him. He longed to hear his voice, and for his humor to guide him on what to do next.

"What do I do?" Jim softly whispered, hoping the ghost of Malcolm would appear and deliberate, Scotch in hand. Silence. For twenty minutes, Jim sat engulfed in the solitude of blue sky, rays of sunlight, and memories. His mind drifted back to that street corner in New York

City when Dream Theater had been in his headphones, and he was willing to let the universe take the lead. Surrender slowly overtook him, and he let his body slide off the pole to the comfort of the grass. The silence filled his soul, and he waited, peacefully, for the dance partner to grab his hand. At the end of that twenty-minute slice of silent heaven, his cell phone sprang to life. It was time to tango.

The late fall air is cold and heavy. Plumes of hot exhaled breaths shoot like flares into the artificially lit night as shadowy figures move in unison. Their movements are calculated and tactical, barely visible in the tall grass. Gunshots ring out, piercing the night and echoing into the distance. Chaos ensues. The men, soldiers in green camouflage, begin with counter fire, taking up positions to guard their escape. The men deploy a leapfrog-style covering system, two waves of men working together to allow for both cover and escape. As the first wave lays down a suppressing cover fire, the second wave retreats.

More gunshots from the darkness. This time, a bullet connects with a soldier, immediately dropping him, his leg useless to retreat. Jim does what any navy seal would do. Immediately, he moves into action, rolling his wounded comrade up over his shoulder into a fireman's carry. With his left hand securing the wounded man atop his shoulders, and his assault rifle in his right, Jim makes his way back to the first wave under their cover fire. The 175-pound burden stays with him as he crouches down and lets his weapon spring to life while his comrades retreat further. Up he squats again, groaning under the weight, then more running, more retreating...

"Cut!" the director bellows through his megaphone.

I dropped to the ground in exhaustion, my breathing deep, exhalations rising like geysers in the night sky. I think, in total, there were ten takes of that shot. It felt like I was back in university doing stadium repeats with the boys in blue, but in actuality, I was right where I was supposed to be: on a movie set doing what my dance partner had designed for me.

Maybe Malcolm was on the other end of that phone as it rang while I sat in his backyard. Sure, his voice had *sounded* like a casting director from New York, but either way, it had gotten me back to Manhattan. A short time later, I'd found myself in Virginia Beach as one of the leads in a made-for-television docudrama called *The Navy Seals: The Untold Stories*.

Jim and Jimmy were in their glory as this gig was every kid's dream. Where else can you get paid for running around like you were seven years old again, playing army? Or in this case, navy. The series would re-enact three special-ops missions of the navy seals: Grenada, Somalia, and Panama. Jim was selected as one of the five leads featured in the three episodes, which also introduced him to weapons training.

This was the real deal, or as close as one could get. "Hollywood rounds" was the term used for live weapons inserted with blanks. This was a far cry from Jimmy's *Star Trek* phaser on the streets of Cydot. Now Jim found himself holding a variety of weapons: handguns, assault rifles, a sniper rifle, and even a shoulder-mounted rocket launcher, with which he himself took out Noriega's private jet in the third episode. Regardless of being loaded with blanks, weapons training was a discipline and was treated as such on the shoot. A team of special effects and weapon professionals would be on site to ensure education and safety.

The men stood around J.T Rockwell, who was instructing Jim and the others in safety protocol. He was a gentle man, average in height, with a non-militaristic approach to his delivery. A friendship soon developed for the length of the shoot, kicked off by an off-the-cuff comment J.T. made:

"These weapons are a bit easier to use than the muskets on Mohicans."

Jim's head snapped to attention. Muskets? Mohicans? That could only mean one thing.

"The Michael Mann film?" the wide-eyed actor quickly responded.

"Yup, the one with Daniel—"

"—Day Lewis!" Jim said, interrupting the man in his shock and amazement.

Well, that was all it took. If anyone on production was looking for Jim between scenes, he could be found over at the weapons trailer, listening to stories from J.T.'s time on *The Last of the Mohicans*. He would tell Jim of the time Daniel came by at the beginning of the shoot and made arrangements to get a musket each morning so that he could run up and down the mountain in character, two hours before call time. Daniel's character Hawkeye was born out of an intense discipline to create. As were many of his other iconic roles with similar yet different "all in" methods.

Well, I didn't run up and down a mountain each day down there in Virginia, but I did feel the shift into character when sitting in a makeup chair while they applied camouflage paint to make me an intense bad-ass mofo. When I secured my digits around that sniper rifle, it was game on. I even got to perform my very first stunt, leaping over a small space between rooftops to evade an incoming hand-held rocket. As pyrotechnics went off around me, there I was, channeling Little Jimmy, who was channeling the mustard captain on a perfectly executed Kirk roll. It was glorious.

Pure joy when I think of that time down in Virginia Beach with a bunch of strangers, shooting guns, and playing navy dress up. It was one of the reasons why I wanted to be an actor so badly, to experience things that I normally wouldn't ever get the chance to in real life. I have my universal dance partner to thank for those memories, or maybe (just maybe) it was Malcolm giving me the answer I needed most.

The Attitude Era

"Are you *REEAADY!?*" The rough and gruff voice blasts through the speaker system of the arena and to the jam-packed Triple Inn faithful. Jim and the regulars are on their feet, much like the sell-out crowd in attendance in person at the show. This was the WWE, World Wrestling Entertainment, and nothing could hold a candle to Monday Night Raw as it would play out each week.

Back from Virginia, Jim had built quite the following of wrestling fanatics at the bar who would show up every Monday for the lights, rock and roll, and scripted pageantry that was the Attitude Era. They all eagerly awaited what would happen next.

Triple H, the cerebral assassin, stares directly into camera one more time. His jacked-up muscles fit his growling delivery perfectly. "Let's – get ready to—"

The crowd inside the Triple (as well as everyone in the full stadium) scream in unison with him:

"SUCK IT!"

Little Jimmy, Jim, and even James (the author) still loves wrestling. From backyard leaf-pile jumps and the leg drop of the immortal Hulk Hogan to the Macho Man and the "suck it" rebels of D'Generation X of the Attitude Era, we were all in. Yes, it's fake. That's not the point. It's about selling the drama, and going all in each and every match, putting one's body through the ringer for the love of entertainment.

Jim was caught up in the spectacle, and really, that's what it was. The lights and music, the entrance onto the stage, and then the walk to the ring. That bloodlust for applause was pumping through Jim's veins alongside the wrestlers on television. The louder the better for the returning navy seal. He was addicted to the rush.

Of the myriad of legendary performers that hit the ring each Monday evening, there was one in particular who seemed to captivate the "millions and millions" of fans around the world (to quote him directly). The People's Champ, The Rock, aka Dwayne Johnson was something new to this large arena of play. His unparalleled ability to own the microphone, coupled with his uncannily raised "People's Eyebrow," seemed like a magnet for attention. Simply put, everyone liked him. Including the charismatic boy wonder of Cydot who was soon to "smell what the Rock was cooking," directly across the street.

Jim was cooking with gas on a set of incline dumbbell bench presses at the gym, his muscular frame handling the load of some heavy weight as he grimaced his way to the end of the set. His headphones were locked and loaded with the usual suspects, driving him onward with sonic intensity. As the dumbbells returned to the black mat, Jim sprang off the bench and strummed a perfectly timed strike to his air guitar, lost in his own world. As he spun around, he froze, a deer in the headlights, or in this case, the blazing glare of an aura, cast by a 6'5" beast of a man, surveying the iron landscape. In what seemed like a few minutes but was actually mere seconds, the figure approached.

"Hey, man, I'm gonna need a few spots in a bit," he said as he threw his towel on a bench beside Jim. The big man stretched out his hand. "What's your name?" asked the People's Champ.

"Jim," the much smaller responded, accepting the offered hand and shaking it.

The Rock took one look at Jim, patted him on the shoulder, and simply said, "Alright, Jimmy, let's get to work."

Just like that, I had a workout partner. I wasn't nervous, nor was I truly in awe of this soon-to-be even larger Hollywood icon. I was simply me, finding an even playing field on the floor of the gym arena. I mean, I may have increased the weight on my next set of dumbbell presses, but do you blame me?

The Rock was in town for his first of many *Saturday Night Live* spots, in addition to the opening of a WWE themed restaurant in Times Square. Whenever he was in town, it was Jim's gym that he would train in. Dwayne didn't forget Jim's name either and would (on occasion) let the name "Jimmy" echo across the iron paradise upon his arrival.

I often wondered if he sensed the inner child in me, using my old namesake as he did. He was and is a big man after all, with the heart of a child beating from within. Regardless, back then, I could sense his tremendous work ethic and knew he was destined for greatness. But it was something else. He also had this air of grace and humility about him as well. I could feel it. I had but one half of that celebrity equation courtesy of rowing. My grace and humility was taking a back seat to my bloodlust for pageantry and applause, spurred on by the thrill of wrestling's heyday. Another door was soon to open. Oh, crossroads, what devilry is this?

A Bow Tie and a Cape

The gladiatorial lights, with their pomp and circumstance, and the roar of the crowd filled a void in Jim, namely the desire for more large-scale attention, a desire that would soon find this gladiator shrugging his shoulders, thinking, *I could do that,* and signing another contract with the shadowy figure at the dusty intersection.

Chippendales, the famous male revue, was starting back up again in the city and was looking for a bunch of new lead dancers to put on the prestigious bow ties and cufflinks. The announcement was made via *Backstage* as usual, and there was Jim with his eagle-eye homing in on the opportunity, salivating at the idea of being on stage enveloped in the lights and music. He busted out his tightest pair of designer jeans and old cowboy boots and sauntered into the big-city audition.

The saloon doors swung open to another kind of circus, full of paparazzi, cameras, lights, and chaos. Jim was familiar with this, but many of the other men milling around were definitely not in their element. Each person was herded inside like cattle, first to the registration table to sign waivers and then on into a holding area. He was surrounded by giants of men and muscle, a world he had no idea even existed. Men were doing pushups, smearing extra lotion on their skin to enhance their on-camera chiseled look, and preening around like stuffed peacocks. Jim, on the other hand, quietly peeled off his shirt as a megaphone sprung to life amidst the chaos.

"Okay, everyone, let's line up!" said the ringmaster, taking command.

The men were prompted into lineups for examination and a once over by the camera. Jim and the men were inspected like slaves in a Roman marketplace. Some of the men would turn into crowd-pleasing gladiators provided they could do one thing: dance. *Chippendales* was not a Jersey Shore bachelorette experience. It wasn't about crotches in ladies' faces. It was a show and an experience much like the WWE. A choreographed story of dance, lights, and music... and flesh too.

A tiny man emerged from behind a small table and moved out to a spot in front of the men. He began to choreograph a small series of dance steps that the lines of man flesh would repeat on cue. This is where it got quite entertaining. Now, I was in shape back then, far removed from my scrawny rowing frame, but those damn beefy guys began to move around like thunder giants before the asteroid hit. Some had two left feet, while others had two left feet encased in cinder blocks. My cowboy boots seemed to glide along effortlessly as the music was introduced. I just focused solely on the little man leading the group. *Just focus and flow*, I thought to myself, trying not to be distracted by the camera, viewers, and most of all, the other gladiators going all sorts of ways, each a slave to their own lack of rhythm. In total, the audition lasted about thirty minutes before the lines of testosterone were released back out into the concrete jungle.

Just a few short days later, I took the call underneath the Christmas lights of the Triple Inn and was welcomed into the *Chippendales* family as one of the lead dancers. To be fair, the glory days of the organization were long since gone, and this new resurgence would only see the group performing one night a week with some travel gigs, but those legendary bow ties were as crisp and clean as ever. Rehearsals commenced right away with the squad learning various dance routines for the group numbers. There would be six lead dancers and three backup "real" dancers that would come together for specifically designed themes and musical numbers. The solos took a bit more time to plan and design based on each dancer's personality.

Kind of ironic when I think about it. Jimmy got his stage legs in front of the candy stripers of the pediatric ward, and here was Jim about to add an extra "P" to the second word of their title, taking the stage in front of two hundred screaming, fanatical women. The solos in *Chippendales* were also unique in the way they would unfold. They were actually called "kiss and tip" numbers. After their solo on stage, the dancer would have a specific song and time frame to go out into the audience and secure all the waving dollar bills. To maintain some order, the dancer was escorted by another (clothed) dancer carrying a small bag, which would be stuffed with the bills once each cheering woman was greeted with a hug and a kiss on the cheek. The faster one moved, the more money would get stuffed into the money sack. And so, through the mob they would go, hell bent on the waving green candy. Yup, ironic indeed, as was the sock.

Jim stood backstage in the dressing room, holding one of his gray dress socks and an elastic band. *Everything serves a purpose*, he thought to himself. Even that stint as the sought-after detective had proven useful as he now knew exactly what to do with the sock. It was for protection after all, not to signal a flagrant foul to the director but rather to keep things hidden under the confines of the dreaded thong. Why this piece of undergarment was invented, especially for a man with dangly bits, Jim had no clue. *Hence the sock,* he thought. No one wants their junk falling out on stage, or even worse, at the hands of some rapid animal clawing at you. All in the name of ego. With that, Jim secured his package and put on his dress whites. He was up next.

The soft tap of piano keys punctuated the dimly lit stage as the crowd contained their cheers, processing what was happening. The piano continued its instrumental opening as the lights grew. It took fifteen seconds before the first lyrics announced the song and cued Jim to appear.

The angelic voice of Mariah Carey echoes through the venue, singing the opening line of her hit song "Hero," as Jim appeared, taking the stage. His perfectly pressed white navy uniform sent the crowd into a frenzy. In an ode to *An Officer and a Gentleman*, he would be joined by the other dancers, all in their navy whites, doing a series of militaristic parade movements.

The hero does lie within, somewhere. How and why that song was chosen for me, I have no clue. All these years later, all I can think is this: *Of course, it was.*

Slowly, the other officers would leave the stage one by one, finally leaving Jim alone in his white uniform among a sea of prying eyes. As the white coverings were removed, the noise grew, the women stood, and the frenzy magnified. And then there was Jim, his blue thong standing center stage as the lyrics ended. *A hero* does *lie in me,* he thought, amused, as Mariah's softly crooning voice fell silent.

Jim punctuated the lyric and the number with a synchronized salute to the crowd. The lights slowly dimmed on the piano outro until he was enveloped in darkness, the screaming applause fueling his soul.

So, it went for quite a number of Saturdays. Each week, we would come together, have a few drinks backstage, and go make some extra cash. Occasionally, we got to travel to parts unknown to do shows in remote cities, and that's when it got really exciting. Celebrity life, I guess. Pictures, autographs, and solicitations. It was its own circus, that's for damn sure. I even got to be in a book and featured on the cover of *In the Kitchen with Chippendales*. Nothing says "chef" like an apron and spatula... and a bow tie, I guess.

It also opened up my eyes to how different or world is, and operates, depending on whether it was seen through a masculine and feminine lens. The shows were fun, make no mistake, but being immersed in a world that mirrored how women are treated and perceived was an eye opener. The timid kid sitting on a folded chair now had the world at his feet. But being clawed and mauled and seen as a piece of meat reminded me of the whip-cream nightmare. There was no hiding the sleaze of it, and like a tiny splinter just beneath one's skin, it festered. Misalignment to one's truth always shows itself; someway, somehow, it just does. For me, it came with a "pop."

Three lucky ladies sat in three chairs on the stage, excited at what would happen when the lights snapped on. Jim was behind the curtain somewhere deep in Pennsylvania, waiting for his cue. He was doing his best to pump up before his grand wrestling-style entrance. This was his moment. This was the participation number that drove everyone batshit crazy. He took a few steps back, prepping for blast off.

What was supposed to happen was that he would make this magnificent jump, far greater than into an old leaf pile, and soar through the air like Superman, landing smack dab in front of one of the women in time with the musical drop. To ensure the dancers' safety, the grounds crew would wipe the stage in between numbers to remove any excess lotion and oil that they used to enhance their physiques under the lights, like the crew at a basketball game, cleaning the court.

The red flag went down, and Jim exploded from the starting blocks, inspired by the hundreds of screaming women. Through the air he flew, timed perfectly as always. As he landed exactly where he was supposed to land, his right foot found a grease spot that had been missed by the crew. The roar of applause turned to a unified gasp of horror. Jim's right knee hyperextended with the loudest "pop," as though Chuck Norris' sniper rifle had taken him out on one of those crazy YouTube videos. He went flying across the stage like a crumpled-up ball of paper.

Jim didn't know what happened, but as he quickly stood up, he buckled to the stage once more. It dawned on him then that he was now basically operating on one leg. What's that saying? The show must go on? Indeed, it must, and he knew he had to finish regardless.

Jim immediately found himself in an episode of *Keystone Cops*. A comedy of errors ensued, with him fumbling around the stage like a baby giraffe. The crowd knew it too and were doing their collective best to keep him going despite a few more slips and falls.

There is a lot of strength that comes from surrendering, whether you're naked in a thong or deep in the wilderness of life. When force becomes flow, everything seems lighter. That beautiful transition is found in acceptance, the objective welcoming of the past or the beautiful loving presence of what is transpiring in the here and now. For Jim, this overarching current of ownership wouldn't happen for many years later. But that night, in that present moment, he found the flow by just giving in and going with his instincts. Like an actor ditching the script, he made shit up on the fly, playing off his limps and falls as if it was all part of a choreographed slapstick act. The crowd loved him for it.

When it came time for his signature move at the end of the song, which involved one of the lucky seated ladies, Jim didn't expect it would go as planned. How could it? All he knew was that it would go... some way. He approached the seated woman and lifted up her legs, wrapping them around his waist so she was straddling him while still in the chair. He then bent down and picked her up, chair and all, moving with her to the music. The mob went insane as Jim struggled to keep his knees from buckling. When he put her down, however, the leg of his chair landed directly on top of his right foot. Quickly trying to adjust the weight that was now crushing his toes, he shifted, which caused the tiny little round end of the chair leg to perfectly find its way under a shoelace and hook him like a fish. As he went to move backwards, down he went again like a stone, riffing on his poor knee once more. All he could do was throw his hands up in the air in surrender.

I think that was the loudest ovation I ever received on stage. Sure, they felt bad for me, but I like to think they also saw the sacrifice in it. "All in" does come with a price of admission, especially when the ego leads the cavalry charge. That night, I remember standing on the stage a bit longer than normal, basking in the sound of appreciation.

The following morning, as the dancers were preparing to load the bus, Jim could barely walk. He leaned against the side of the vehicle, his phone to his head, handling a call with his agent regarding his next gig: a commercial.

"Listen, I can barely walk, but I'm just standing for the shot. It's not like I'm running around or anything. Look, I need this," he pleaded.

"It's going to run all over Europe." Taking a deep breath, he continued more forcefully. "Work your magic. Thanks."

Jim had one day to recover from a knee that was two sizes too big. There was no way he was going to concede a paid commercial gig, especially if he just needed to stand in front of a green screen. He downed half a bottle of Advil and iced his knee as much as he could. The following day, Clark Kent hobbled his way into a dressing room, collapsing in a chair, too exhausted to stay upright. The wardrobe assistant entered with a pile of red and blue spandex, took one look at his face and his outstretched knee, and said, "I'll help you get it on?"

"Please," he said, nodding and smiling playfully. "Between you and me, I'm a train wreck."

The assistant helped the (eventually) dressed actor make his way to the sound stage, where he was greeted by three stagehands, who lifted him high atop a large wooden box, his final destination secured. There he stood. The strong and impervious Superman with his hand on his hips, cape blowing in the wind, and a look that defied any evil that might come, which included a torn ACL apparently.

That was a good bookend to my own "Attitude Era" I suppose, with many things coming to an end. I opted for surgery only to have complications, including two infections and a wack of other issues, which left me with a brutal scar. All because of a six-inch grease spot and a G-string.

The Triple Inn chapter came to a close right around the same time as I felt the urge to spread my wings and search the city for a new adventure, and perhaps, a higher profile venue from which to sling drinks and climb the management ladder. The curtain closed on a big part of my life, and looking back, it felt like I was granted an intermission, a short time in which I could gather my breath and reset. Instead of being on the stage, I opted for the crowd, and it was ten years in the making.

Rhody Roadies

The pre-show music fades. Cue house lights in "three, two, one." The lights dim to black, which ignites the roar of the crowd. The anticipation builds as the sell-out crowd at the Beacon Theater waits for a sign. And then it hits, that melodic tidbit of ambient background noise with the tick of a clock summoning the arrival of a progressive rock juggernaut. The flashing Tri-Ryche logos are perfectly synchronized to the clock, ticking louder and louder. The time is at hand, and the New York City crowd knows it.

It begins with one guitar laying down a slow, moving freight train, its chorus growing in intensity while the cymbals from the man behind the chains begin to punctuate the build. Then, the second lead guitar springs to melodic life, weaving in and out of the mounting score. Just a few more measures of momentum until the drums spring to life, helping to raise the stakes in this soon-to-be musical experience.

The 'Intro' is now in full swing. The rhythm section and the two lead guitars climax their final push, building fury while the entire crowd waits for the musical drop of the searing song that is "Revolution Calling." Another measure, and then it hits the crowd like a sonic atom bomb: the crescendo of the drums and the shredding guitar with its scalp-blazing signature riff. Oh, it's a revolution alright, and the crowd knows what's next.

The lyrics hit as if from an other-worldly being. Somewhere in the darkness, the man and microphone become one. From the shadows, he sings and begins the saunter out from the darkness and moves to his downstage mark, sending the rabid fans into a state of chaos. It is the voice, the aura, and storytelling personified in Mr. Geoff Tate.

He points his finger into the crowd while holding the note to his last lyrical word: "on." That finger points right at the two Rhode Islanders in the crowd, on their feet and screaming. Maybe it wasn't directly to them, but for Jim and his childhood best friend Dave, their ten-year Queensrÿche following had reached its own crescendo, make no mistake.

Their playful adventures of youth had gotten an adult upgrade as the two had embarked on the first of three stops, following the band to various cities along the New England coast. They had seen shows from the front row before, but what made this Y2K outing different was that the heyday of arena rock was now a thing of the past and smaller more intimate venues were the norm. The band had also decided to offer backstage passes to fan-club members. Well, it was a good thing that the Cydot boys were long-time cardholders because Jim was finally going to meet his musical hero.

"Revolution Calling!" The two joined Geoff and the rest of the Beacon faithful in a full-blown vocal attack, arms raised in unity.

The house lights had been brought back to life, and with them, Jim and Dave could clearly see the small group of lucky pass holders assembling by the stage. Upon closer inspection, they also realized that all of the other fan-club members were still stuck smack dab in the eighties: full-on mullets, leather, and concert T's were everywhere, which kind of bothered both of the Rhody boys. The band has always been more than your typical eighties offering. Ever since 1990, the band had presented itself with music and style like a hip and harder version of U2, not leather-laden boozehounds cruising the Sunset Strip. But in retrospect, it worked out brilliantly as there they both stood, the pretty boy with the accountant best friend in a group of metalheads.

The side door to the stage soon opened, and the band filed out. The man himself approached the group, moving in slow motion, or so it seemed to Jim anyway. One thing was for sure, he approached Jim first, causing his heart rate to skyrocket. Geoff was dressed in the latest fashion, looking more like something out of *GQ* than *Metal Edge* magazine. The two met at last, eye to eye.

Geoff stuck out his hand and said, "Hi!" as Jim extended his.

You are the most incredible fucking singer/songwriter on the planet! What was it you said in the middle of "Roads to Madness?" What was it like in Montreal, seeing that nun dancing with a teddy bear!?

These thoughts went through my head like a machine gun while I calmly said, "Hi, I'm Jim. Thanks for your continued inspiration."

We shook hands, then he and David did as well. In all, we spent about five minutes with Geoff and with each of the other band members. The time didn't allow for anything but small talk really, but the die was cast. We also struck up a conversation with Geoff's wife, Susan, who would become the band's manager and be at all the meet and greets. I don't know if being the pretty boy in a sea of metal was the reason or not, but as Jim and Dave headed north to follow the band, they would continue further discussions on a first-name basis. As did his wife.

I like to think that a tiny friendship formed, but I'm not that naive. There was, however, a level of respect that did form as I wasn't just a fan sitting around eating Cheetos with headphones and reminiscing about the glory days. I was trying to make it about the entertainment business and conducted myself as a professional, or at least, I think it appeared that way to them when I spoke. Geoff took an interest in my movie-script writing, and over the coming years, our conversations evolved into an even playing field of creative artists. So much so that Geoff's first solo album would contribute to a future creative endeavor of mine and fuel the opening to the movie version of *Schools of Fish*.

Those brief moments with a musical hero felt like stamp-certified "dreams become reality," of which the boy from Cydot was always trying to remind me. Geoff is still going strong now, and I know that if and when we meet again as the two older men we are now, his heroic aura will still be there. Those three shows back at the turn of the century were just what the doctor ordered for me as my Big Apple time was pivoting. The intermission was coming to an end, and I was quick to find out that Geoff was correct in his song, "Real Word." I was about to see for the first time that "you can't find the real world alone."

Day One, the Earth Stood Still

The promenade up Fifth Avenue was a beautiful display of marquee pre-war buildings on one side, boasting elegant architecture with cano-pies extended outward to the street with an army of doormen to greet the inhabitants. Equally dazzling on the opposite side of the street was Central Park, with its magical green allure an escape from the concrete hustle and bustle. For Jim, the walk up this stairway to heaven con-cluded at 995 Fifth Avenue and the corner of 81st Street.

His neck craned upward at the rows and rows of windows perfectly situated to look out over the vastness of Central Park. This was the Stanhope Hotel, one of the many Golden Age icons now looming over him. Jim was familiar with the Stanhope, thanks in large part to those

Sunday evenings with Malcolm. His grandfather would play old Charlie Parker records with the warming sensation of Scotch running through his body. The Bird, as he was known, was a legendary jazz virtuoso whose mighty saxophone would speak other worldly melodies in the forties and fifties, a true genius who passed away upstairs behind one of those windows at thirty-four years young. Jim took an extra moment reminiscing about those Sunday evenings with Malcolm before he made his way down the red carpet and through the doorway that would lead him to a world of marriage, murder, and mayhem.

The other side of that doorway was indeed a whole new world. My friends and circus-sideshow peeps from the Triple Inn would soon be replaced by east-side socialites, designer "everything," and a sense of entitlement. Hell, even their dogs would command me to fetch them water for their bowls. My smoke-ridden jeans and sleeveless T-shirts were replaced with slacks, shirt, tie, and a vest. The bar was pure class. Dim mood lighting replaced the pub's Christmas bulbs and string lights. Underneath it all was a veil of romance. The classy setting could even make an old countess and her bunions look beautiful. This was the world of the reserved elite and the world I needed to be in. I knew there would be more money behind each pour of a pint, pop of champagne, and conversation. The history of the place did seem to evoke a sense of magic, and it didn't take long for me to feel that soft breeze of possibility blow in.

When Jennifer Aniston walked in under tow of a much older man, it didn't faze Jim in the slightest. This was New York City after all. As the two bellied up to the bar and ordered two pints of Sierra Nevada beer, Jim knew it wasn't actually Jennifer, but it could have been. The hair was spot on. The cheekbones and eyes conveyed that disarming "girl next door" quality. This woman had a way about her, an ease of grace in her tone and demeanor. The dingle-balls she was with, however, his mouth had one speed: full throttle.

It didn't take long for Jim to start going through his mental rolodex of old bartender tricks to shut the egomaniac up, and even better, try to create an opportunity for him to ask her what the hell she was doing with this guy.

"Hey, Slick," the man barked at him, "two more pints since you're not doing anything."

If I had some Visine right now, mothaf— Jim thought to himself as he smiled politely at the chooch and poured the drinks.

Ah yes, Visine, the eye-drop solution. It was an old trick from back in the day. A few choice drips of those refreshing eye drops in a beverage and that jackass ("chooch" in Italian) would have been taking trips to the shitter for about an hour. Moral of the story: Don't piss off a bartender.

Instead, Jim just delivered the two pints as the ever-gracious host, catching a few wayward glances from the woman in the process. As the night progressed and the glances continued, he wondered if their paths would cross again.

A few days later, Jim was dancing his white linen cloth around the edges of a wine glass when two ladies entered. He immediately slowed his polishing and put that energy into a smile. She was back and had brought her roommate along for the visit.

The two grabbed seats at the bar, the same two as last time. "Sierra Nevada?" Jim suggested with a smile.

"Yes, please," she said with her Aniston-like voice. "I'm Poppy, and this is my roommate, Lori," she said as she hung her designer purse on one of the bar hooks beneath the bar top.

Jim knew he was in the land of preppy socialites, but he had not been expecting a name like that. He wanted to respond, "My name is Biff," but reasoning got the better of him. "Poppy?" Jim said, leaning in a bit, making sure he'd heard correctly. "I'm Jim." He smiled.

They were soon chatting the night away, in between Jim's bartending duties, and built a solid connection. He knew right away that she was a different breed of woman than those he had been exposed to. She was simple in her naiveness, a farm girl from the west coast now living the designer-apparel dream in Manhattan and working for Estee Lauder.

The idea of being a starving artist was lost to her. He also knew instinctively that she didn't have the passion for life that artists do but rather was full of life anyway, from a different source, one that had all the answers and would always provide her with lightness in the dark: religion.

As they went on more and more dates and fell deeper into each other over late-night wine, rainy sidewalk kisses, and romantic conversations, Jim knew that the religion thing was something that couldn't be avoided. He was a monkey man after all. Human evolution was his bag and having a science-based mind and sitting across from someone with a completely faith-based response to everything can be a recipe for disaster. But then there were those eyes... and the sweeping romance was hypnotic.

As Poppy became a fixture at the bar, another woman also made her presence known at the Stanhope and would always reserve the corner table. She was one of those upper east-side socialites that carried an air of royalty wherever she went.

Generosa Ammon had just moved into the hotel while renovations were being done to her newly purchased Brownstone mansion. Her quaffed hair and long cigarettes added to her Cruella Deville mystique (minus the Dalmatians). She was married to Ted Ammon, an uber successful Wall Street financier and investment banker worth in excess of eighty million dollars. Unfortunately, all that money couldn't buy happiness apparently. The two were in the middle of a divorce, and like most divorces, it got nasty, especially when someone with gasoline in their veins entered the scene.

Danny Pelosi was her general contractor, electrician, and soon to be "all things Generosa." While Generosa would float across the bar to her appointed seat each day, Danny would enter like a bull in a china shop. That was him. Straight from Long Island with his heavy Italian accent, tattoos, assortment of chains around his neck, and a loud infectious laugh. He brought smiles to even the coldest prude in the establishment. But above all, Jim would come to find out that his heart was his most valuable asset, besides his "golden glove" winning hands, which had won a boxing title during a misguided youth that was as long as his rap sheet.

Each day, the two would enter the bar and hold court from the corner booth, each discussing the day's events at the renovation site or how bitterly Ted had treated Generosa that day. The two maintained a professional air about themselves, but as the drinks began to flow, it became obvious to Jim that there was something going on underneath. *Bunions*, Jim thought to himself. *Time to rub the bunions.* He knew

Danny was going all in on this potential opportunity, swooping in like a vulture with his charm and boyish antics.

Danny's personality was infectious. It hooked me too back then. With each passing day, I grew closer and closer to both of them, perhaps also infected by Generosa's magic. I knew that, with a wave of her finger, she could grant me freedom from my financial prison. Regardless of the shenanigans that were playing out, I connected to these two souls, and they opened their hearts to me and Poppy.

It hadn't taken long for me to introduce my girlfriend to them. On my days off, we would join the two, holding court all together. Generosa and Poppy were cut from the same cloth and became bonded. Much the same could be said for Danny and me. It was like being reunited with a neighbor from the Cydot days, two guys just being guys without all the frivolous frosting. We left that to the ladies.

This additional moonlighting lifestyle only added to the romantic air that Poppy and I were consuming each day. Whether it was fueled by the alluring taste of what could be or just the romantic fire that burned within us, we soon found ourselves booking a trip to Italy for a magical getaway. After only three months together, we planned to spend four days in Rome, three days in Florence, and two days in Venice. And to top it off, Generosa secured the Venice portion of our trip with a stay at a ritzy premier hotel.

Membership has its privileges, I thought. It wasn't like we used her for her fame and money; it was a byproduct of our growing friendship with both her and Danny. They truly became our first friends as a couple, and that friendship would continue to grow.

I didn't know back then how much travelling was within my DNA. The history, the culture, the romance of ghosts, and conversations on cobblestone streets is something that calls to me every waking day now. In my youth, I had travelled a bit courtesy of my parents and the school French club. But as an adult in Rome, I heard the whispers from the archaeology books of my youth. I began to see the depth and romance in every single stone and person as they walked by.

On the last day in Rome, I woke extra early for a run and made the deserted city mine. I approached the Roman Forum and the Coliseum as the sun began to rise, bringing its golden hue of life. My pace slowed to a crawl, and then I stopped, unable to continue. Before me was a once bustling civilization now covered in dirt and fencing, and decrepit in appearance. The image of the yellow Wickford sanctuary, losing its battle against time, floated through my mind. Time rolls on, and the relevance of everything only lives in memory. I remember crying at this unavoidable thought as I stood frozen by the ghosts before me.

Florence was much the same as I recall. Never have I felt so at home in a strange place. The city famous for the birthplace of the Renaissance, and whose energy still holds sway over me to this day, felt so natural. The old roads and buildings of Rome had been replaced by a blend of old-world architecture infused with a New Age cultural essence. Science and the adventure of exploration had replaced the worship of gods in togas.

But it was Venice, with its stunning canals and backwater pathways, that found the two travelers caught up in the magic. The voice was unrecognizable, but the tone was unmistakable: It was the voice of romance, serenading Jim and Poppy on a gondola ride. A large, plush, crimson blanket covered their legs while they sat swept away on the current of the moment. Jim slowly reached under the crimson covering, his hand retrieving something from beneath the warm darkness. It was small, something that could be concealed in the palm of his hand. The gondola came to a stop at a place the strategist within the romantic had planned.

Jim unveiled his hidden secret, his fingers peeling back to reveal a ring. "Will you marry me?" asked the boy from Cydot through the man.

Poppy paused for a moment and then responded, "Yes." Her eyes were full of wonder, and in them, Jim felt the earth standing still.

Back in New York City at the queen's corner booth, Jim and Poppy were greeted by Danny and Generosa with hugs, congratulations, and champagne. As the romantic veil of adventure waned, the undercurrent of their religious differences kept gnawing at Poppy. For the thirty-three-year-old Jim, he could sense it too. Was getting married the right thing to do? Was it time to anchor his ship of dreams, walk ashore to begin a settlement, and burn the boat for good measure? But he kept coming back to one thing: For the first time in his life, he felt he needed to save someone.

Months earlier, Jim had sat glued to every word dancing off her lips as she told him the story of how, in her first marriage, she had been living the simple life and involved with her parent's almond business. Her husband at the time had had one too many the night before work and had been trying to pull the sick card. Well, Poppy wouldn't have any of that nonsense; it was her father's business, and she took great pride in being a part of it. She would be damned if her husband was going to choose to drink and be hung over versus showing up for his shift that morning.

"Get your ass to work," she'd said.

He knew he had to and did.

"That was the last time I saw him," she said to Jim.

Still somewhat drunk from the night before, he'd made his way to work, hopped on a tractor, and driven off into a field for the day's work. Somehow, he must have slipped off, gotten pinned under the tractor, and passed away among the warm winds of the California heartland.

I still remember hearing the conversation for the first time. The strength in her voice. The ownership. This was a strong woman who had left that chapter for a new one in Manhattan, where every line would be written by her unwavering faith. I felt the unmistakable urge to save the damsel in distress, even though she didn't need saving at all.

We ended up walking the red carpet at the Bellagio in Las Vegas and were soon pronounced husband and wife. As the festivities moved to the Venetian Hotel, the movie continued to play out. As newlyweds, we rode an indoor gondola this time, in celebration, passing by beautiful fictitious set pieces while Italian music serenaded us with a velvety falseness. Those billboard ears of mine, however, were hoping to hear the loud cry of "cut!" from the director.

Day Two, the Earth Stood Still

Apparently, Mr. Spielberg didn't get the memo, so back to New York we went. I moved into Poppy's tiny studio apartment on the upper west side, and we began a new chapter in our lives. I also said goodbye to the comfort and poshness of the Stanhope Hotel to work side by side with my new wingman in life, Danny. Cash is king. Especially if driven by ego and needing it to secure a foothold to build a new life: a married life.

I had never really done any manual labor, but I found myself on the job site, Generosa's property to be precise, surrounded by an interesting cast of characters. They were all Danny's inner circle of friends and family members. Each day, I showed up to a scene from *Goodfellas*. There I was, Rhody Jim with the broom, Joey Bag of Donuts on the jackhammer, Vinnie Voom Botz on the table saw, and Johnny Big Nose the electrician. Some days, we worked hard, other days we fucked the dog, but regardless, we got the cash.

The new scenery also kept the Gardiners in the circle of Generosa and her vast influence, which was growing more and more dynamic with every waking day. The divorce battle was heating up. At this point, Danny made no effort to try and hide the fact that he was living high on the hog. The two would be seen everywhere, enjoying "champagne wishes and caviar dreams" as Robin Leach would say. But underneath it was a darkness looming. Court and custody battles ensued for Generosa's two children, whom they had adopted from the Ukraine. There was an investigation into Ted's vast fortune, some of which was unaccounted for. There was talk of offshore accounts, enemies, and betrayals. Danny himself filed for divorce from his estranged wife. It was a gong show with one big flipping g-o-n-g. Even so, amidst all of the tabloid speak and gossip mongering, there was Danny and Generosa and Jim and Poppy.

That summer, we would be invited on several occasions out to the Ammon's huge estate in the playground known as the Hamptons. This was the lifestyle of the rich and famous, where all the glitz and glamor from the big city could be found soaking in the summer sun. It was nice kicking back in the plush surroundings, watching my wife sip a luscious French Bordeaux from a wine glass while engaged in a frivolous conversation with Generosa over the difference between Gucci and

Chanel. Danny's coarse hand held a can of cheap beer while a cigarette dangled precariously from his lips. It was as if two worlds had collided on impact, and I was floating somewhere in the collateral debris, not sure which side I felt more comfortable in.

Jim got up from his leather chaise lounge to leave the scene of the crime for a reprieve out in the crystal blue warmth of the always neutral sunshine. The air was warm, and the sun's touch on his forehead brought him back to the summer days on Cydot. To a time where there was no status, no big questions, and no underhanded intentions or lurking evil. Just play. I wondered what Malcolm would have thought of my current situation and the interesting soap opera I found myself in. I figured he would have some smart-ass comment to make, so I raised my glass of twenty-five-year-old Scotch to the blue sky in his honor.

It was a few months later when Jim found himself thinking of that toast to the crystal blue on a walk home from a morning workout. The September sky was piercing in its blue boldness. Its sharp hue was uninterrupted by any sign of white brush strokes, and there was just the tiniest whispering hint of autumn in the air. A change of seasons was soon to arrive, one that would echo humanity.

The dark black plume of smoke rose up into the air and dispersed into that crystal blue, destroying the serenity of the morning. Jim's mouth slowly gaped open, his eyes mirroring the chaos on the television screen before him. No one knew what was happening at 8:46 a.m. that morning, not even Matt Lauer and Katie Couric on the *Today Show* as the events unfolded for Jim and millions of others across the country. At 9:03 a.m., the chaos turned into sheer panic as the second plane hit the south tower.

I don't think I sat down for hours that morning. I was glued to the television for the events that were taking place just a few short miles down the road. It wasn't until all the news reports came in about the sheer magnitude of the moving pieces of Armageddon, conspiring on this devastating attack, that I began to feel the fear rise within me. When the south tower collapsed at 9:59 a.m., followed by its twin at 10:28 a.m., I knew the state of the world as we knew it was over. The world stood still again. Any semblance of that boy inside me was snuffed out just like the souls trapped in those buildings that had collapsed in front of my eyes.

When I finally had to leave the confines of the studio apartment and venture outside at around noon on September 11th, I walked into a changed world. As I meandered the streets, so did so many others, lost and confused at what had happened and what was yet to come. It was like a zombie Apocalypse unfolding before my eyes. People were milling around, dazed and confused, some even staggering under the weight of their contemplating minds.

But it wasn't until the herds of people walking up the avenues came into view for Jim that he saw the magnitude of impact firsthand. Hundreds and hundreds of people took to the avenues, a mass exodus from wherever they were to get back home. Public transit had been halted, and now people roamed the once bustling roadways. The city's heartbeat was gone. As the day progressed, the gentle winds increased, bringing the awful smell of burning metal, jet fuel, and chaos uptown. The smell was unmistakable, infecting everyone with heartache and loss.

As the crystal blue faded into night black, something remarkable began to happen. Jim and Poppy, like so many others, couldn't stand to be inside "alone" any longer. There was an irresistible pull to embrace the city that had just been devastated. The married couple walked the streets only to be greeted by strangers everywhere who, after the day's events, were not strangers anymore. They were family. Random hugs and hellos began to inject a life rhythm back into the amazing city. There would be drinks shared on the front steps of buildings and relationships fostered. It was the start of unconditional love rising from the smoke. Jim could feel it in the warm gaze of each unknown passing soul, in the silence of a stranger's embrace, and in the laughter that would somehow find a way to shine in the dark. That shining power of love's currency would continue to resonate with him and his travels, always. But that night, he was drawn to a sound and began to listen. He could hear the city's heartbeat beginning to thump again.

Mr. Peacock in the Study with a Taser

It was a transitional time for the world, the city, and even for the new-lyweds. Less than a month later, Jim and Poppy moved into a larger apartment on the east side of Manhattan. It had been almost a year of Jim being removed from any actual creative calling. He was too busy sweeping up construction zones by day and hobnobbing with the rich at night. But like anything anchored in unmistakable truth, there was no avoiding the fact that his creative fire was beginning to burn again. Thankfully, he had the bank of Danny to help ignite his purpose.

Their friendship had grown strong over that first year, and while Danny could give two shits about the arts, he did respect Jim's passion to follow his dreams. Support from him usually always came in the form of a big laugh followed by money. Jim's scheming plan was to repurpose his *Schools of Fish* one-man play into another indie film. What he didn't realize was that he was about to be cast in a real-life ominous play, one destined to be a bestseller.

"Everyone stop what they're doing!" Danny shouted while his hands shook, attempting to light a cigarette.

Jim and the crew waited while that extra-long hit of nicotine filled Danny's lungs and gave his wavering soul some semblance of balance.

"Ted was found murdered at the Hamptons house," Danny continued.

Shock instantly hit everyone's faces. Immediately, they knew that Danny would be prime-suspect number one. It wouldn't be long before the cops would be breathing down his neck. The divorce had gotten financially nasty, and there was the matter of his rap sheet. The man was a criminal with less than stellar friends and associates, a group of which Jim was now a part.

Jim felt a sense of panic shoot through his body. He looked around at his surroundings, and at the crew before him, none of whom he knew very well. The *Sesame Street* song "One of These Things is Not Like the Other" played on repeat in his head.

"Everyone, go home!" Danny commanded. He then pointed to his nephew and another worker.

"You two, stay with me."

Needless to say, the job site was shut down, indefinitely. Jim and Poppy spent hours, bewildered by the chain of events that kept unfolding. "There's no way Danny did it. No way," Jim would utter to his wife. The guy had everything wrapped with a neat little bow from the outside, but regardless, the newly married couple found themselves smack dab in the middle of a big shit sandwich.

The news of the murder took the city by storm. Reporters began to follow Danny everywhere like a swarm of insects, hell bent on sucking the life out of the man. He quickly became public-enemy number one, and gossip about the two scheming lovers became the topic of every water-cooler conversation.

Jim's phone would ring, with Danny summoning his "friends" for support. They would answer and be there for the two among the sea of paparazzi back at their corner roundtable at the Stanhope where the journey had all started. But Jim could sense the change in Danny—in both of them for that matter. It was like they'd aged overnight. Danny's head would begin to tick like a clock, always looking over his shoulder as if Joey "Two Shoes" was coming to whack him.

"Just remember, you haven't seen anything. I don't care who asks you, what they ask you, you say nothing." His thick Italian accent laid down the law to Jim from across the table.

I don't know if it was the accent, the man's somewhat crazed state, or my own naivety, but I remember taking that loving advice from Danny as a threat. Like he was informing me that I had seen too much and was in too deep. I'd never felt paranoia before, but in the coming days, it began to surge in like a stormy wave off the Atlantic.

Especially as more and more details began to emerge about that ominous night. Ted Ammon had been beaten to death in his home, possibly by a bat. But it was the information that came next on the evening news that had sent Jim reeling, grabbing his coat and heading out into the night's chill. He zipped up his jacket to its farthest point while navigating around strangers on the sidewalk. His thoughts drifted to a scene he'd witnessed months earlier at the job site. The work cronies had gathered for their pre-work coffee banter, goofing around as usual.

"Do it!" a few of them shouted to the young man. "Do it!"

Succumbing to peer pressure, one of the workers raised his shirt, exposing the skin on his stomach. As Jim moved closer, he saw that one of the other men was holding a hand-held taser. The stun weapon found its way against the exposed flesh. The shocking noise filled the room, and it took a millisecond for the man to cry out in pain and be knocked backwards.

Pedestrians were quick to dodge Jim as he abruptly stopped in the middle of the sidewalk. The impact of this re-lived memory froze him with its underlying meaning, which tied directly into the news report. Ted had been incapacitated by a Taser prior to being beaten to death. The cold darkness began to intimidate him. Faces of strangers now became possible detectives following him. Or worse, some of Danny's less desirables stalking him. Did he know too much? Was he a liability? Had Danny really done it or was it just a coincidence?

I am not sure how long I walked the streets of midtown that evening. Maybe it was a few hours or maybe it just seemed that long. One thing I remember clearly was that things were adding up against my friend, against the couple who had played such large roles in my life in such a short time. I was trying to distance myself from the emotional connection to them both and be objective. But another salvo of allegation missiles would soon launch, sending both Poppy and I reeling again.

The security cameras of the house had been tampered with, or more precisely, the hard drive had been removed prior to that fateful weekend. Guess who those cameras had been installed by? Yup, Danny. They were allegedly there so that Generosa could "spy" on her shady husband. And the big cherry on top? Ted Ammon had yet to finalize any changes to his will after the couple's split, which meant that Generosa would inherit his ninety-seven-million-dollar estate.

I wanted so desperately to believe that Danny was the patsy in all of this, framed by some other enemy of Ted's. When he called, I did my best to try to distance myself, but our friendship got the better of me one night. The tone in his voice was unlike the bravado I was used to. He sounded like a broken man needing a friend. When he asked me to take a ride with him out to see his cousin, I obliged. But as we drove over the Brooklyn Bridge, it dawned on me that I was now trapped.

When they finally arrived at his cousin's house in Long Island, Danny put the car in park and pulled out a cigarette. "Stay here. I'll be right back," he said as the lighter flame lit his chiseled and worn face. Jim rested his head against the passenger-side window, lost in one thought. How had he ended up way out here, far from his wife and the safety of his apartment? It was a few minutes before a knock on the window jolted him back to consciousness.

"Get outta da car," Danny said. "We're gonna go in the backyard for a bit."

Jim got out as ordered and walked with his friend towards the back of the small house, situated on the bank of an inlet.

"Jimmy!" Danny's cousin called in his booming Italian voice. I had known A-man for quite some time. He seemed a nice enough guy, but then again, as I was learning, what's lurking underneath the surface was what really counts. He stood there, his small frame leaning up against his picnic table, doing his best Joe Pesci impersonation, with some Danny DeVito thrown in for good measure.

"Took you guys long enough. I ain't gettin any younger," he offered in his usual smart-ass way.

The two cousins went off for their own little sidebar, leaving Jim propped up on the picnic table to take in the view. Nearby, A-man's boat was gently moving with the rhythm of the water, causing Jim's mind to drift back to Malcolm's boat and the times spent out on the paradise of Narragansett Bay. He wouldn't let himself get fully lost in the memory though; he was too amped up for that. One of those billboard-prized ears of his was trying to get a sense of the hushed conversation that was unfolding.

"Nice boat, A-man!" Jim chimed in to remind them both that he was still there.

"Go check it out," Danny's cousin responded.

The two approached Jim, who now removed himself from his perch in case he had to channel his inner Carl Lewis and run for the gold to safety. "I'm good," Jim said. "My grandfather—"

"Come on, just check it out with us," A-man interrupted, with his infectious-host voice.

I remember walking towards the dock, flanked on either side by two men, two frigging characters. The Joker was with the Penguin, and I was stuck in the middle without my goddamned utility belt. I hesitated before crossing the threshold onto the boat. I knew that step would remove me from my last bit of safety.

"You first" the Penguin quipped.

Jim hopped over the railing and into the boat. Trying to be cool and nonchalant, he checked out his surroundings and entered the main galley with a nod of approval. When he turned, he saw that the Gotham criminals were blocking his only exit.

Trying not to signal his growing fear, Jim decided to move forward into the galley towards the sleeping cabin. He lowered his head for a peek inside.

"Cozy," he said, only to turn and see the two men were right on him.

"It is. Go on." A-man's host voice had now been replaced with something darker.

"No, I'm good, thanks," he answered defiantly.

"Don't be a baby. Just check it out," A-man said, punctuated the statement by pushing Jim into the cabin.

This is it, thought Jim. The elf from Cydot was going out by way of a customized pair of cement overshoes, or perhaps he'd be buried in the endzone of Giant Stadium after all. So many things went through his mind as he stood in the middle of the tiny sleeper cabin. He even decided to look down at his feet to see if he was standing on any sort of drop cloth like in the movies. His eyes closed, and he took a deep breath. He stood in complete silence, frozen not only in fear but in surrender. After all, there was nothing he could do. He's escape route was blocked by two men and a tiny doorway. When he finally had the courage to open his eyes and face his would-be murderers, he inhaled deeply and spun around to see what the universe would dish out.

There was nothing but an open doorway and the view of the two men now standing at the back of the boat. Taking another deep breath, Jim gathered himself and began to make his way out of the cabin, the galley, and off of the boat. He eventually made it back to that picnic table, without his weary legs giving out, while the two men resumed their personal sidebar.

"Nah, he doesn't know anything," A-man whispered to Danny.

This time those ears were tuned in, and that message was received loud and clear. I'd thought I was going to die. There's no way around the events of that night, no matter how many times I have replayed that scene in my head through the years. I'd thought it was game over. But then all I wanted to do was get home and change my shorts.

Thankfully, I did and soon found myself subpoenaed to appear before an inquiry led by the DA. I was on stage again, this time in front of a room of people both from the legal system and from God knows where else. The inquisitor tore into me, grilling me on dates, whereabouts, what I saw, who I was with, and most importantly, time-frame moments leading up to the weekend of the murder.

I'm not sure why I felt guilty, sitting there as the questions came fast and furious, but I did. Perhaps, it was embarrassment for even being involved. Perhaps, I knew I was sitting there because of my ego, because I was willing to play Russian roulette with the rich and famous and ride the coattails of easy street. Worse of all, I knew that, in the minds of everyone before me and the attorney giving me the gears, I was just another one of Danny's lackeys.

As the spotlight faded from that day, the entire support community around both Danny and Generosa seemed to dissipate further into the shadows. Just one day after Danny's divorce had been finalized with his first wife, he married Generosa, less than one year after the murder. They loved each other to some degree—well, perhaps, Generosa did more than Danny—but sadly, no lovers could weather this storm. The heat continued to come down on Generosa, and the DA began pitting them against each other, causing deals to be struck and a wake of collateral damage. The two separated for a time, which resulted in Generosa cutting Danny out of her inheritance. To top it all off, for added dramatic effect, the gods of fate penned one last ironic and sad chapter to the story.

Through the stress of it all, Generosa succumbed to breast cancer before the prosecution could press murder charges against her. Danny carried out her last wishes by bringing her ashes to the corner table at the Stanhope Hotel one last time. This time, there would be no Jim and Poppy for company. Just a broken man and a cocktail in her honor.

Danny had spent all of the buyout money from Generosa on lawyer fees. He was broke and soon got his former bank teller pregnant too boot. She delivered him a son after he was shipped away in 2004 to a life sentence in Attica Prison, where he was given a nice orange jumpsuit for his troubles.

I visited him only once in that first year of prison. It was my one and only time behind the barbed wire and guarded gates. He maintained his innocence and was seeking an appeal. However, the ride was over for all the players. This Shakespearean yarn had come to a close. The heiress had passed away, and the two young children were whisked off to a new life somewhere under the radar. Danny's friends and coworkers vanished all over the country, and one innocent man had been taken away from the world and his family. It was a story that would spawn television movies, a dedicated episode of *Law and Order,* and a book. As I hung up the phone and nodded goodbye to Danny through the plexiglass partition, I knew I would never see him again. I got up from my chair and walked out, not giving in to the urge to look back one last time. Both Generosa and he will always have a place in my memory. I just choose to remember the smiles.

Celebrity Cocktails

That feeling of shame brought on from the Spanish Inquisition spurred two large heel kicks into the side of Jim's giddy-up as he had to let go of the high-life imposter role and get back to the creative fire that burned within. Distancing himself from the upper west side, he found a completely new path, one leading to the hip and younger Manhattan nightlife. The rowdy average joes of the Triple Inn and the stuffy quiet elite of the Stanhope would now yield to the mecca of who's who, jockeying for notoriety and attention. It was the world of celebrities and wannabes, and each evening brought with it an incredible anticipation of who would be looking you straight in the eye from across the stone bar top.

The first step on that giddy-up train was the Chamber Hotel. This boutique midtown offering had an adjacent restaurant inside called "Town." This was the era of hotels creating their own magical rhythm section to the symphony of the night. Town restaurant was *the* place to eat, to be seen, and to work. I remember being greeted by the Austrian Master of the House with his European suit and thick accent.

Albert Trummer was not a bartender. That was an insult. He was a bar chef and ran the lounge and restaurant like a fine piece of Swiss timing, except he was Austrian. This world-renowned mixologist took Jim under his wing, teaching the secret Jedi ways of mixology and alchemy as it related to getting people hammered and charging them a good price in the process.

As the bell chimed for the witching hour, Jim would adjust his suit and tie and make ready for the onslaught. Behind the bar, his weapons lay ready for the inevitable wave of energy that would hit. Mini Bunsen burners and small frying pans for sautéed toppings were locked and loaded for the night ahead. The top of the bar had the finest antique-looking containers containing many of Albert's magic potions and tinctures. To round out the perfect setting was the latest hip lounge music imported all the way from Paris and the famous Hotel Costas.

One thing I do remember from all the years of slinging drinks and hobnobbing is that everyone looks better at night in Manhattan. I know it sounds silly, but it's true. I don't know what it is per se, other than the lights, mood, and atmosphere, the thrill of where the evening will go, and the anticipation of the unknown. Maybe that's it in a nutshell: You never really knew what you would see, or who you would see, every waking moment. That "celebrity right around the corner" psyche was something that was strong for me back then. Through the years, I've amassed quite the rolodex of celebrity interactions, not that they really meant anything other than a sign that I was on the right path to my dream. At "Town," it seemed to be a nightly occurrence.

"Keyser Soze! Keyser Soze!" Jim was dying to say it, probably just like everyone else at the bar. One of the *Usual Suspects* stars, Gabriel Burn, approached, but the energy in his eyes told Jim that his impulse wasn't a good idea. It was an art that he honed, gauging celebrities and how far to push interactions with them. Like most things, it was a dance. When Gabriel's movie running mate Stephen Baldwin showed up with his brother Billy, the bartender sensed the green lights of banter. Stephen was one of the most approachable dudes he ever met. Jim even found

himself in a penthouse apartment with a bunch of people from the other side of the bar, Stephen included. The two shared a long conversation about the movie *Moulin Rouge* and the visual brilliance of its director, Baz Luhrmann, as it played on a large television for ambiance.

Night after night, the shenanigans seemed to unfold, coming to the full-on crescendo with a full-circle moment. Jim nearly fell over when Robert Plant approached the bar and ordered a round of drinks. Now to be fair, he wasn't 100 percent sure it was the legend, but when the man dropped his credit card, there was the name as clear as day: Robert Plant.

Jim picked up that card, and in his mind, he went back to middle school. Two distinct chops of the card on the counter concluded his mental visit. He leaned into the former lead singer of Led Zeppelin and said, "Mr. Plant, eight and half minutes and a steel chair is what I remember about every school dance."

Robert smiled and patted him on the shoulder. "Last dance, huh?"

Jim nodded before turning away to complete the credit card transaction, smiling from ear to ear.

The hotel restaurant and lounge business was yet another brotherhood in the city, with multiple owners partnering in multiple spots to monopolize the night life. It just so happened that one of the owners of Town was also involved in another hip and trendy hotel located in the SOHO district, at 60 Thompson Street (which was also the hotel's name), and he wanted Jim to go man its helm. It had two lounges and a restaurant owned by a predominant French-Swiss restaurateur named Jean Marc. The two hit it off and soon Jim's sweat-soaked tailored suit was replaced with a specially tailored black-on-black uniform from a local city designer.

The hotel's Thom Restaurant became Jim's sandbox, and he assumed the captain's chair each night. The downtown crowd was a bit edgier and definitely rowdier than midtown. There were chaotic evenings with endless rows of patrons all wanting their fix, and more subtle and gentle late afternoons, which allowed for intimate conversations.

Jim popped open the ice-cold bottle of Heineken beer and plopped it down in front of Sandra Bullock. There was no one in the entire place except himself and Sandra, just talking. Those thirty minutes spent with her would stay with him always. Who didn't have a crush on her at some point? But he kept it together. That was his superpower. He loved just being the guy who was simple and unassuming when he opened his mouth, encouraging the same in others, celebrity or not.

That superpower opened the door to a special friendship. Not with Sandra unfortunately but with one half of the dance duo from *Footloose*: Chris Penn, who was Kevin Bacon's dance makeover in the film. Brother to the more famous Sean Penn, Chris became a regular whenever he was in town. Chris and Jim bonded, and their friendship extended out of the bar to bi-coastal phone calls when he was back home in Los Angeles. The bar top became his pitch table, as Chris was always excited to share some of his screenplay ideas and get Jim's unbiased feedback.

It was kind of surreal having discussions with someone you'd seen prancing around on the big screen with two left feet, never mind just deciding to make a call and having him always pick up to talk. But that was the sort of big-hearted soul that Chris was. When he passed away unexpectedly a few short years later in Los Angeles, my heart sank, and the only thing I could think of doing was cracking open a cold one, dusting off my old cowboy boots, and kicking back to watch him and Kevin light up the screen one more time.

I guess these acquaintances, interactions, and brief sightings were just part of the Manhattan territory. I guess I got what I wanted in a sense: a taste of fame or (at least) the tiniest glimpse into the reality behind the people I saw on the screen and more assurance that I was walking the exact same path.

That glimpse went a little bit further when Michelle Johnson walked in one evening. She looked the same, well slightly older, but still the same gorgeous woman that had made her screen debut in 1984s *Blame it on Rio*. This romantic comedy was the story of a much older man, played by Michael Caine, who meets a very young woman, played by Michelle. The role had put her on the map and infatuated every teenage boy across America in the process.

As she sat there at the bar, Jim was reminded that another child-hood fantasy was now literally three feet away. Conversations and laughs continued throughout the evening. At closing time, the two found themselves out in the darkness of Thompson Street underneath the magic of the Manhattan skyline. The small talk had all been exhausted by this point, leading into the pondering silence of what to do next. That silence finally broke with a smile and a hug as the two ships of the night passed in the night, continuing on their respective courses, never to meet again.

Celebrity sightings and interactions in New York happened often to many wannabe actors and bartenders. I realize that. But to the dreamer and movie star in me, it kept me walking onwards towards my destiny and fueling my need to be like one of them. To be famous.

Fade in on "Nogara"

The rain pours down over the dark European city street, its lampposts doing what they can to illuminate the old and weary cobblestones. Gothic architecture encases the old throughways, bridging the gap between the world of yesterday and the modern age. Poised up high in the belfry sits a watcher, a death dealer, and a protector.

The opening of the movie *Underworld* saw the one and only Kate Beckinsale, in her sleek black assassin outfit, ready to spring into the ageless battle of vampire versus werewolf. It was an iconic opening from a movie that reinvigorated the timeless myth with a new mythos, look, and feel. Helming the movie was Kate's husband, Len Wiseman. He was a fairly new director on the Hollywood scene, but after his *Underworld* entrance, would go on to a solid career.

I think sexy KB and her vampire mythos, along with *The Lord of the Rings* film journey truly launched me into the uncharted realm of fantasy as both a dreamer and a writer. I have always been fascinated by the concept of good versus evil, as well as immortality, so much so that I would devote the next five years of my life to writing a screenplay and creating my own mythos of immortality, religion, sword play, and adventure.

"God then spoke to Satan. 'The wager will be this. The feathers of your wings will be scattered across the world, hidden over time. Forty-eight men and women will be granted with the gift of immortality, twenty-four of your choosing and twenty-four chosen by my hand. They will wage war over the hidden feathers, living through the centuries with their human emotion and weaknesses as you call it. Only if you acquire all two hundred and sixty-two of them will your wings be reformed, the chain unlocked, and your freedom to reign over the earth begin.'"

Jim used everything at his disposal to go deep into this world and create its own lore. Concepts and ideas from some of his favorite films and musical weapons would be used in the creative process. An entire world full of immortal sword-wielding warriors, religion, myth, a nun and priest, and a brooding hero would all lead to an epic showdown. The three thousand-year-old wager between light and dark would end on the streets of Rhode Island. This was to be Jim's crowning achievement. This was *Nogara*.

It was the first time I'd thought creatively in terms of a business concept including multiple marketing angles. I hired a designer to sketch the characters and create visuals for branding. The backstory lore would lend itself to graphic novels, video games, and action figures; it was designed to be a mini fantasy world unto itself. I dare say, at that time in my life, I was convinced that I was creating my own magnum opus. Above all, the younger me knew that one person and one person only would be the one to direct it. It had to be Len Wiseman. I was confident that, when the time was right, some way, somehow, I would get it into his hands.

The mad scientist aspect of Jim that ensued was "all in," as you can imagine. Even his universal dance partner showed up to add to the creative momentum and stamp certify his mission with good luck. He was on the receiving end of a Sears national commercial that earned a year's income in just forty-five minutes of work. His creative and acting goblet filleth over. However, the all-in price to be paid was his marriage.

Even after two years, the married couple felt like they hardly knew each other and were victims caught up in the romance of a faraway land.

Each day Jim's fantasy of marriage was eroding. Not even the creative fire of *Nogara* or the biggest of miracles could help.

Cat's in the Cradle

The slow rise and fall of skin against Jim's cheek brought memories of a boat partnering with the slow waves of the ocean. His eyes closed in harmony with the moment. Soon he pressed his ear more firmly against the rising flesh, searching for the tiniest whisper of movement. The tightness of the skin over her stomach amazed him that day. It was another canvas, and together, their masterpiece lay hidden underneath.

As his wife's stomach began to grow, so did Jim's anxiety. He wasn't ready to be a father, or at least not what it meant to be one in his eyes. They weren't stable; the thought of raising a child in a concrete playground seemed ridiculous, especially given Jim's storybook upbringing. But nonetheless, here they both were, with a baby on the way.

I could feel the walls closing in around me daily. The pressure of fatherhood, the religious albatross that was always looming, and worst of all, the lack of emotional glue between me and my wife was suffocating me. For her part, she was happy. Who wouldn't be with a beautiful baby inside? But she was also naive to my boiling turmoil. I felt trapped, and not even my acting face could keep my smile from diminishing more and more on a daily basis. The only air of freedom that I could sniff was found on a roof deck overlooking the Empire State Building.

Jim stood among the countless stars in the form of lit office windows high above 37th Street. A slight spring breeze ruffled his hair as he gazed directly at the two remaining Manhattan skyline landmarks, the Empire State building and the Chrysler Building. The city always looks different from a bird's eye view, more majestic and spanning than the endless concrete walls that accompanied people on their daily, ground-level travels. This would be his throne atop the world for the next handful of summer months as manager of Rare View.

This new rooftop oasis was an addition to the successful Rare Bar and Grill Restaurant on the ground floor of the Shelbourne Hotel situated at the corner of Lexington Ave and 37th Street. Rooftop destinations, with

188 | ALL IN WITH LOVE

their stunning panoramic views, were a premium in the city. It didn't matter that they would serve premium cocktails from plastic cups and charge an arm and a leg for them. It was sexy, and everyone wanted in.

When the new bartender walked in for her first day of work with a name synonymous with New York City, he knew he was screwed. The history of those countless sideline gazes from middle school caught up to him, and when she appeared, he had no choice but to make her dance with him. She was a blonde, supermodel-esque woman dressed in black, a metallic bottle opener tucked in her pants, and she meant business. Brooklyn was tall, fit, beautiful, and had a personality that was completely magnetic. Everywhere she walked, all eyes seemed to be captivated by the large windows of her soul. She would become Jim's wing-woman behind the bar, and together, they made the cash register ring and the patrons happy.

I was definitely caught up in the magic of the evenings as they would play out into the wee hours of early morning. As I came back to my current reality and climb the flight of stairs to my second-floor apartment, I could feel the safety of the rooftop vacating me. Some nights, I would enter, and some nights I would sit in the hallway for a little while longer. Lost and helpless is a godawful feeling, and it became my reality. I knew that Poppy didn't deserve any of this. Damn the consequences, and curse you, Frank Green.

The nights that I did make it inside the door would be spent on the couch, pretending I had fallen asleep watching television. She would go to work, allowing the air to return so I could breathe and focus on my opus, while Geoff sang some lyrics from my theme song: "Someone Else?"

I was trying to stay afloat, and my rooftop damsel, Brooke, became my life raft in the stormy seas of self-hate. In one defining moment over a life that has had many, I got off the couch, took a deep breath, and made my way down the hall to the bedroom.

The ominous creek of the door announced Jim's arrival.

"You're up?" he asked as he moved to stand by the foot of their bed.

His wife was sitting up in bed, reading a passage from her Bible. She sensed her husband had come in for a reason and slowly closed the book, placing it gently on the nightstand. The devil before her spoke.

"I don't want to be married anymore. I... I will try to be a dad but not a husband. I'm sorry. I can't."

The always stoic Poppy sat quietly in contemplation. A tear formed in her left eye as she slowly reached back for the solace of the book, unable to speak. She opened it and found what she needed within. The miscast actor exited the bedroom with his words still echoing in his mind.

Jim ran through the corridor of the hospital until he reached the elevator. Multiple impatient presses on its "up" button killed the time until the doors parted. Inside he dashed, obviously in a rush.

Out of the elevator, he flew and quickly scurried down the hall, being mindful of the room numbers as he whizzed past them. The destination was finally in his sights, which only increased his speed until he entered. His momentum slowed to that of a walk, and then a rest, once again standing at the foot of his wife's bed. No words this time; he couldn't utter any. Jim stood in silence.

Poppy was holding his son, wrapped in a white blanket with the tiniest beanie for a hat. I had missed my own son's birth into this world. I'd known it was a gamble when I'd taken a modeling gig an hour out of the city for the money. Of course, I couldn't have foreseen the accident and the traffic that had made it a three-hour drive back, but Poppy's look was devastating. She'd handled my denunciation of the marriage like a saint, but to miss their only child's birth truly was the work of the devil.

We didn't exchange words when I finally had the courage to approach. I hesitated to extend my arms but did, into which she conceded my son. I wish I could write of the tiniest hint of an elf nose or the making of billboard ears, but I can't. All that stays with me now is the swirling emotions I was feeling back then. The anger, the disappointment, the regret, the hints of joy, the shame... They were all there, and here now still. They swirl around in a concoction of sadness that has never left me.

Moving day came quickly. Poppy was going back to California to be with her family, and she was taking her son with her. Jim climbed the stairs one last time. He opened the door to the scattered remnants of a once vibrant dwelling. The only things greeting him were a few arrant boxes and a legion of dust bunnies. Poppy appeared from the kitchen, holding their baby.

"Would you like to say goodbye to your son?" Her soft voice echoed in the emptiness around them.

Jim nodded and carefully secured his son in his arms. He turned from her and made the long slow walk down the hallway and into the empty bedroom. The door closed behind him. The emptiness of the room, of the life that was, perfectly matched the void in his heart. But as he stared into the tiny eyes that looked helplessly back at him, he felt the grief of abandonment.

"I'm sorry, Jayden." Jim could barely utter the words. "I'm sorry."

His athletic physique transformed to a mass of jelly as he slowly slid down the wall, holding his son. For the next twenty minutes, Jim would share his soul in a one-way tear-filled conversation, sharing all his mistakes and misguided attempts at life in no particular order.

There was a lot that I shared with my four-week-old son that day, much of which will remain between us. I do remember begging for forgiveness over and over and wiping my snot-filled nose on my sleeve as I showered my cheeks with tears. I was sorry I couldn't save his mother; the knight had failed miserably at that as well. It was a goodbye. I realize now that it was a goodbye to two boys that I loved very much: Jayden and Little Jimmy. Life had arrived, and with it, I had distanced myself from the Jimmy I used to be, as well as the Jim I'd thought I would be. Although my life with Brooke would continue onward towards that famous Hollywood sign, all this older man wants to do now is sit with Jayden a little while longer, alone in an empty room while the savagery of the world outside played its tune.

CHORUS: *THE GALLOP WEST*

Thunderous hooves now announce the escape from the concrete scars that line our warrior's heart. Parts of his sweet youth lie on the floor of that receding arena and give way to the fame and legacy that surely waits beyond the westward fold. While accompanied by his future queen, he is unaware of the council that travels with him. Unseen forces lay in the shadows of our hero and linger in the gray twilight of underachievement.

His spirit burns so, and quick to turn his eyes frontward, away from the pain of the past, we join him in the glory of what lies ahead. The call from the mythical sign of childhood beckons from afar, causing his pace to quicken.

Engage our eyes and hearts, eager for his victory and the land that awaits the thrust of his flag. Enter to the scene a boy, not yet severed from the man. Onward they go, sword in hand and dream in tow.

LOS ANGELES ARENA

A Back Seat to Heaven

We are going to meet Steven. You know. Steven Spielberg!! I'm so excited. "When you wish upon a star, makes no difference who you are!" La - la - la... I can't remember the rest.

Finally, I get to take the wheel! Well, not really, but I get to speak. Cappy is driving. Oh, you know him as Jim; he's my captain. Well, next to Mr. Kirk.

We are going to dreamland! You know the one: H-O-L-Y... Wait, right... double L's... H-O-L- L-Y-W-O-O-D!

Hollywood!

I'm making sure Cappy keeps his promise. To me. To our dream.

Did I mention how excited I am!?

Jim and Brooke loaded up their Jeep Liberty to the brim for a one-way trip to Los Angeles. When they left Rhode Island, in early September, Jim was feeling loss, like a part of him was being torn away. He had said goodbye to his high school wingmen and his Cydot brethren, but it was the drive away from the yellow house and his folks that stung the most. They were getting older, and Jim wasn't sure when he would see them again. No one knows what life has in store, except in each specific moment. For Jim, there was an air of finality about it all, like a volume of a book closing only to be put onto a dusty shelf and forgotten. As he drove away from the comfort of the only home he had ever truly known, Brooke gripped his hand tight and helped ease the sorrow of his wet eyes.

It's okay. When we get there, you'll be on television, and then you will be able to help Mom and Dad with all the money you will make.

The Midwest was as romantic as I remembered in the movies of my youth. Brooke and I could see why settlers wanted to flock to the great frontier and live off the land. Our tiny speck of silver moved through the open landscape on a course due west, the moist air of the Atlantic but a distant memory.

The new chapter began with a trip through the vastness of America on their way to the coast of sunshine and suitcase dreams. Unlike the fantasy Jim had shared with Tanya about taking the southern Route 66 passage, he convinced Brooke that the northern route held more romance. Soon that tiny speck of silver found its way into the great plains of the Dakotas and the Badlands. This legendary geographical region contains rock outcrops and secret passageways with, let's face it, a kickass name. It was a land rife with mystery and myth that greeted the two travelers as they stood atop a promontory, taking in the vastness before them. Jim could feel the ghosts of pioneers urging him down the open road.

The map of adventure played out perfectly as each wondrous stop on that journey (some planned and others not) led to beautiful moments of reflection, freedom, and joy. That mythical northern route led them to "1880 Town," a small roadside museum dedicated to the film *Dances with Wolves,* complete with Buck, the horse that had carried a suicidal Kevin Costner across the bullet-whizzing frontline of the film's opening battlefield. A gentle pat on his majestic head brought visions of Jim's own frontier journey in a faraway land. *Maybe a wayward wolf will join our caravan like it did for Colonel Dunbar,* he thought to myself. There would be visits to Mt. Rushmore, horseback riding in the sweeping pines of the Black Hills, deep excursions into forgotten gold mines, and our own "close encounter" at Devil's Tower. But it was the city of Deadwood that would forever leave a mark on their souls.

The two stumbled upon it, or perhaps were guided to it by some grand design beyond them. The open road began to narrow as the sentries of pine trees steered them into the Black Hills and towards a small town that was just a name on a map, like so many others. Deadwood had become a household name, thanks to HBO, just a year earlier and a favorite song selection of theirs, from their cross-country co-pilots Big-n-Rich. Their song, "Deadwood Mountain" told the story of Wild Bill and Calamity Jane and others that had frequented this makeshift gold-mining town, wrought with chaos, debauchery, and calamity (pun intended). It was a destination based on an inquisitive interest. What transpired in the day and half spent there was a full-blown love affair.

Jim and Brooke made their way down the bustling streets past saloons, restaurants, and small casinos. The air was full of magic, and everyone seemed to have some of that old-west swagger. Jim sure did, his cowboy boots having never felt more at home. Stepping inside the room where Wild Bill had played his last hand of poker, he was greeted with a warm sense of familiarity. He closed his eyes and imagined the fastest pistoleer in the west, pulling his famous "deadman's hand" before being cowardly shot in the head from behind.

It didn't take long for Jim to finally stumble upon the true portal of days gone by. He stopped Brooke on the sidewalk, feeling the pull to enter. Before him, the swinging saloon doors stood idle, waiting for his entry. There was something romantic about pushing open the doors and stepping onto the old wooden floors of yesterday.

They swung open, and in walked cowboy Jim, or rather tourist Jim, but he was acting the part anyway. He did his best sauntering old-west walk while taking in the moment.

Throw some Captain Kirk in that walk too, Cappy! Sway the shoulders a bit with the hips… Any green women?

Jim reached the bar and assumed the position, one foot perched on the brass railing. Then the moment came for him to say his line, straight, to the point, and said as perfectly as had ever been done in a hundred movies.

"Whisky." He nodded at the bartender.

The bartender, who was dressed the part right up to his handlebar mustache, knew exactly what this cowboy needed. A shot glass and a bottle.

Two shot glasses now accompanied Jim and Brooke as they took up seats at an adjacent poker table for a few hands against strangers, and the ghosts of Wild Bill and the gold rush. As the day progressed, and it became time to hitch their wagon and continue westward, they had one more stop to make first.

The two city folk climbed the steep terrain to stand before the stones of Mt. Moriah Cemetery on Deadwood Mountain. Since his days in colonial New England, Jim had loved spending time in cemeteries with their cultural and artistic significance. He stood before the graves of Wild Bill and Jane, among many others who had come west, searching for elusive treasure and adventure. There was the scent of legacy permeating the air, and with it, Jim couldn't help thinking about his westbound trip into the unknown. Perhaps just like Deadwood, amazing opportunities would be right around the corner. Leaving home is always tough, but there can be magic found in every step forward out that front door. The air swirled in through the pines and among the stones of the cemetery.

Softly at first, it came to his attention and then grew more pronounced. It was the gun-toting ghostly whispers of "all in."

Their trip continued down south towards a horse-riding experience in Albuquerque, New Mexico. Chuckling to himself, he thought, *I knew I shoulda made dat left toin at Albakoike.*

When one grows up with Bugs Bunny on Saturday mornings, you don't shy away from finding out why he always said that classic line. Opportunities like this don't come around often. So, Brooke and Jim did the only thing they could think of once there: They looked left, because they weren't going that way, and then took the right turn at "Albakoike" and charted a course to the red rocks of Sedona.

The Native American energy that permeates the place is palpable. Even ten years before I would eventually grow into spirituality, I remember feeling the primitive energy pulsating around me, not only in the red clay rocks but in the trees and sky. It was everywhere. Years later, I became aware that Sedona is synonymous with energetic vortexes, convergent points of powerful magnetic energy that attracts spiritual people from far and wide to stand in its awe as the native dwellers did long before. On this trip though, it was just a peripheral awareness without any moving force on my soul or deeper meaning. What did move my soul in our short time in Sedona was the open sky and the winds of adventure.

The rush of air while clutching his handlebars on Cydot Drive was replaced by the wind in his face at a thousand feet. Snoopy and Woodstock from New York went searching for the elusive Red Baron via a bi-plane ride complete with epic Maverick-style turns and drops in altitude. With their goggles and helmets, they kept peering eyes ready for a dog fight with that pesky German ace. However, the only fight that ensued was with their own stomachs, which they narrowly won.

When it was time for the silver spaceship to get back on the road once again, the journey was nearing the end of its long westward voyage. The American Southwest is so vast in its landscape, none of it more eye-widening than the Grand Canyon. For any would-be traveler it is the non-negotiable place to see. When the two New Yorkers climbed aboard the safari vehicle and headed off through the adjacent underbrush to a secret, isolated lookout, they both felt like kids on their way to the ice-cream shop. The fifteen-minute walk down a narrow pathway grew clearer until the small group arrived at the view of all views. The small number of tourists that were there just grew silent. There were no words to speak at the magnitude of creation before them. For Jim's part, it was the first time in his life he truly ever heard the powerful sound of silence.

Jim squeezed Brooke's hand a little tighter as the two stood at the edge of the canyon. His eyes took in the universe as it laid out before him as far as the eye could see. After a moment, he released his grip and took a few extra steps forward towards the steep edge. The view was too powerful to share even with her.

I was frozen at the steep cliff, not with fear but with awe. I felt called to bear witness to the greatest masterpiece this planet had ever created, and to do so alone. The vastness of this creation called to me as a private experience, and it awoke something in me that grew from a spark, standing at the Roman Forum, to the need to hoist my sail and explore throughout my older days. Life in all its majesty calls to me in a certain frequency, and that sonic symphony plays out on my individual quest to experience all of it.

WOW... I think Hollywood and Mr. Spielberg can wait a bit. This view! Yeah, I'm going to leave Cappy alone for a bit. He's in "wonder mode." I love that feeling.

While Jimmy may have dreamed about the magic of the universe, it was Jim who felt the profound convergence of time, space, and energy that day. The universe had created perfection, and he was there to bear witness. As the sun slowly crept beyond the horizon to light the southern world, the legacy lights that were hidden in New York came back into focus. Jim looked upward at those markers of the sky, remembering the boy, and a father, and the hall of heroes that was calling to him.

Koi Nurse

Okay, the Grand Canyon was great. Yes. But you haven't seen wonder like THIS!

It was there, on top of Mount Lee (Lee, like my dad...)

When we stopped, I jumped out to get the best view.

The nine white letters stood majestic at forty-five-feet high, each one thirty-some feet wide. The two cross-country travelers had arrived at their desired destination: Hollywood.

(Sniffles can be heard) WOW! It's SO beautiful!

A short detour found Jim and Brooke now standing behind the great banner of dreams and looking out onto the valley of possibility. Los Angeles. Endless is a word that comes to mind. The roving streets, avenues, and highways continued onward, spilling from one county to the next. In the far-off distance, the Pacific Ocean sits beneath the haze, a barrier at least on one side of the entertainment capital of the world. The entire valley was blanketed in a dry brownish hue, not the rich earth tones of Jim's homeland but more of a sunbaked, overlaid treatment as far as the eye could see. But to Jim, it was still beautiful. That sweet scent of make believe will always be a perfect pair of rose-colored specs.

This is HOME for me and Cappy. I can feel it! The awe of make believe. Here is where I belong. Where WE belong.

Together we are going to become MOVIE STARS!!

When the silver steed finally came to its home in a designated parking stall, the strangers in a strange land had situated themselves smack dab in the middle of the glam-metal glory days. Ground zero to start the next chapter of their lives would be an apartment between Hollywood Boulevard and Sunset Boulevard, directly across the street from the legendary "Rock and Roll Ralphs" grocery store. It was everything that Jim remembered seeing on television and on MTV. The vibrancy brought with it a renewed energy in him. It was his destiny after all, a calling from when he was a child. The rearview mirror held the brooding cold streets of the concrete jungle while this new landscape presented him with warmth, light, and excitement.

When the sun finally fell down behind the west horizon, the Sunset Strip came to life. This short one-and-a-half-mile throughway connected east with west and was lined on either side with boutiques, shops, clubs, and restaurants. Bands like Motley Crue, Poison, and Quiet Riot were born on these streets and made cruising it the cool thing to do. Jim was going to replay that very scene out for himself. He turned up the dial on his radio, and Poison took the wheel. Jim's offkey vocals did the rest.

The silver spaceship continued down the art gallery of LA life. Sprawled out on the sidewalks was a supporting cavalcade of characters coming together, mingling in the pulse of the Strip. The socialites, rockers, the punks, the artists, the hookers, the trannies, and the homeless, each gave their own color to this visual masterpiece. The old hunting grounds of bands like the one blasting in the Jeep were still marquee destinations, if for no other reason but nostalgia for a simpler time.

It didn't take more than a couple of days out and about to determine one thing: Everything in Los Angeles was based on status. One didn't need a business card. You had your car to showcase how successful you were. The inhabitants themselves came from a cloning facility; God's conveyer belt rolling out gorgeous women and handsome men with an assortment of wardrobe choices at their disposal. The most notable look at the time was the designer jean and retro T-shirt look, along with a pair of crisp Chuck Taylor Converse sneakers. You had to look your best because everywhere you went, you were bound to run into a famous person, or a producer, or a director, and they held the magic wand to celluloid immortality.

YES! We are going to be famous!

Los Angeles has a way of sweeping one into its web. Jim wanted to play like all the other clones walking around. What's one more to add to the collection searching for a poof of the wand? Brooke, bless her, was the opposite. For such a beautiful woman, she would just *be*, absent of ego and all the shit that usually came with a package like that. That's why she always touched gold wherever she went (Jim being the one possible exception). She made friends, made contacts, and was loved wherever she went.

I really like Brooke. She's nice.

She'd had a few friends from New York move here so at least they knew someone among the sea of nameless faces. Brooke's world, or rather the world she and her friends came from, revolved around the music industry. Her two closest friends both happened to work for Larry Rudolph, the famous music manager. Larry was a huge name in the business at the time and was specifically noted for managing Britney Spears.

At this point in her career, Britney had moved west from New York as well and was in a transition period, getting rid of Larry and replacing him with Brooke's two friends, one as her manager and the other as her assistant. Brooke's friends were "in."

Maybe they could help us, Cappy?

Before Jim and Brooke could begin their ascension to fame like her friends, they needed money. For Brooke, her gift was working with kids. Sure, she was one of the best bartenders Jim had ever seen, but she had a motherly quality about her that was put to use working as a nanny on the side. It didn't take long for her to get referred to a high-level exec at Warner Bros looking for someone to watch over their two children. Each day, Jim would drive in and out of neighboring Burbank as her personal chauffeur, leaving him to audition by day and get situated back into the work nightlife when the sun went down.

Koi Restaurant was a who's who of city dining. Jim had been a key manager in opening its elegant baby brother back in New York at the Bryant Park Hotel and was now set to helm the owner's newest endeavor: Bridge Restaurant. It was slated to open soon, but until then, Jim was afforded some shifts at the celebrity hotspot. People flocked to this Asian fusion eatery for just one thing: to be seen. Behind the small bar, Jim had a front-row seat to watch the play unfold.

Get your popcorn ready!

They came in pairs, or occasional trios. It was like Noah's Ark for the famous wannabes and the already established. Let me tell you, "King Kong truly ain't got nothing" on Denzel Washington when he walks into a room, any room, never mind up to the bar to get a drink from Jim.

With the women, let's just say that Jim wondered if Los Angeles was overrun by those of the female persuasion. They always milled about in packs, most of them trying way too hard for the image they were aiming for. They appeared like mythical fairies, aloof with their laughter and playful antics, which was the direct opposite of the east-coast race of females and their straight-shooting real-life energy. In the city of angels, if you were fortunate to cross paths with a straight shooter, rest assured, you would know it.

It was the end of his first week behind the bar at Koi when just such a creature walked in. The actress Michelle Rodriguez from *Girlfight, Swat,* and *Fast & Furious* fame entered the establishment and beelined it straight to Jim. She was on a mission, and Jim thought to himself, *Hell, Denzel ain't got nothing on this chick.* She was tenacious, and he loved it.

"Two shots of Patron Silver, cutey," she said while eyeing the blue-eyed bartender in front of her.

Oh no, here we go again.

Jim cracked a smile and quickly poured the two shots. He instinctively knew that Michelle was not the type of girl that needed training wheels, no salt or limes for this woman. She bent her index finger, signaling Jim to come closer while sliding one of the shots towards him. Up the two small glasses met with a clang and then down the hatch. Michelle then leaned in, and without hesitation, grabbed Jim by the back of the head and laid a kiss on him.

I wish I could remember what the heck was running through my head other than a flashback to the spinning coke bottle of my youth as a scared little boy.

Hey, hey!! Wait just a minute, I wasn't scared!

With the kiss complete, she just winked, and then off she vanished into the sea of customers and the nightlife before me. *I have arrived*, my internal voice egotistically triumphed once again, the spinning shot glass landing in my hand with a timed smirk. *This is my destiny.*

What a great word. The mythical destination of a warrior code. Perhaps destiny is what we all truly seek, an acknowledgement that we have arrived to honor what is divinely ours. For me, all signs were pointing to the golden land of make believe. Everywhere I turned, there seemed to be affirming moments that I was right where I needed to be.

THAT is what I mean! Movie-star destiny!

Jim began settling into his groove in Hollywood, exploring the city during the day and slinging drinks at night. One particular night at Koi, a waiter approached and asked him if he could make something special for his dear friend Majel, who would be coming in to celebrate her birthday. Those ears of the boy wonder perked right up at the name, one which he'd only ever heard referencing one person in his life.

"Majel?" the wide-eyed bartender replied. "As in 'Majel Barrett?'" The waiter's nodded response only made Jim's eyes grow wider.

With his voice wavering, he asked for confirmation once more. "You are friends with Nurse Chapel, aka, Mrs. Gene Roddenberry?"

The waiter laughed. "Yup, and if you make a good drink, and she likes it, I'll introduce you to her."

Star Trek! You see? You see, Cappy? What did I tell you?

Ladies and Gentlemen, shit had just gotten real. Into the apothecary style books Jim dove, working on crafting a cocktail that would beam his ass from the bar to her table for a chance encounter. He would get one shot and one shot only, so into mad-scientist mode he went, preparing and tasting his creations.

When the widowed wife of the *Star Trek* creator entered the establishment, followed closely by her friends, Jim didn't really get a chance to see her. She moved quickly to the back seating area for her party, which would be composed of about fifteen people. When the word came from the server, Jim prepared his special elixir, a blackberry martini complete with a foamed egg-white topping.

Then he waited... and waited. He thought, *Okay, I just fucked that one up.* He reminisced about the conversation he'd had with Robert Plant without a care in the world, and yet now, he had sweaty palms at the thought of meeting a small character on the show. But a big one in awakening the hero within him.

> *It's Nurse Chapel, Cappy! BE excited. She was McCoy's right hand! Had a secret crush on Mr. Spock and made him cry in the episode "Naked Time!"*
>
> *Wait, wait... Here he comes.*

The waiter turned the corner and approached with a smile. "She would like another, with a special request," he said, almost toying with Jim, who spread his hands in a gesture that said, *"Of course."*

"She would like you to deliver it to the table." The waiter's grin matched Jim's.

> *Yes!!*

Internally, I pulled a Kevin from *Home Alone*, with holler and a fist pump. I mixed up another of the special drinks and set out. Navigating the twists and turns of the jam-packed restaurant with my fancy drink was nerve racking, all the while making sure my hands were steady on the black tray. If that dollop of egg white slipped off the top, disaster would ensue.

When Jim finally arrived with his offering of friendship, the waiter calmly introduced him to Majel, who immediately complimented him on his drink creation.

"If you have a few minutes, I would love for you to sit and join me," said the wife of *Star Trek,* while pointing to an empty chair beside her.

Jim could feel his armpits begin to dampen his black dress shirt. It took every ounce of energy to keep his hand from shaking as he placed the cocktail down on the table. He then took his seat beside her and was introduced to the others in her party. For the next fifteen minutes, there was small talk, Trek talk, and unfortunately, slurred talk as Majel had been at the booze even before showing up at the restaurant. There was a turning point when the fun of the conversation that was feeding Little Jimmy turned solemn. Jim began to feel sad, as it became obvious that this woman was a lost soul, here in the present, and slated to always live in the past. She was holding court to all she had left. Her husband and most of her co-stars were gone, and all that remained was a tired woman whose destiny seemed reached long ago. She would join much of her cast among the stars just two years later.

She seems so sad, Cappy. Why do you think that is?

Jim and Majel concluded their time together with a hug. As he walked away back to the reality of life, Jim couldn't help but wonder what destiny truly had in store for him in this land of make believe. He knew the brass ring was here, though. He had to find it, or at least be in a position for it to be bestowed upon him. He began to wonder if it was hidden amidst the serendipitous brush strokes of the universe.

A Picasso of Chance

After just a handful of months, Jim and Brooke decided they better not chance the fashion citations that would surely come if they kept risking showing up in public places with non-hip attire. Off to the mall they went on a shopping spree and a little retail therapy for the ego.

I always get super excited when we go out. Who are we going to meet?! Who? Who? (Laughing) Ha! I sound like an owl!

The two gazed up at the long escalator leading from street level to the first floor and back again. These conveyer belts held the power to raise up all celebrities and normal folk, and bring them down to earth, figuratively and literally at the same time.

As they moved upwards, Jim noticed who was coming at him, gliding effortlessly on the downside: It was Morpheus, the one and only Laurence Fishburne. He remained frozen as he descended, stoic in his appearance. As the two converged side-by-side, the man turned his head just the slightest bit and nodded.

Red pill. Blue pill. It didn't matter because I was definitely entering the matrix. What is life other than a series of micro choices that make up the fabric of our existence? The perceived reality is all that matters at any given time, so-called destiny or not, and I didn't need a pill to remind me that it was all smoke and mirrors. Still, I loved it anyway. Soon, Brooke and I found ourselves wandering the mall matrix, a world of glitz and glam with designer shopping bags and people dressed to the nines, hell bent on a mission. It was a perfect place to people watch and see if any "glitches" in the matrix would appear.

Folklore states that a pot of gold can be found at the end of a rainbow. Well, that glitch showed itself that day at the end of a twelve-year rainbow. By this time, Jim and Brooke had split off on their separate shopping excursions, and he came face to face with his "Somewhere Over the Rainbow" muse: Elizabeth Perkins—twelve long years after he'd last seen her on the cold and rainy New York City street, after a long day of holding the tether of a "Macy's Day Parade" balloon, and chastised himself for his lack of courage. Now she was here, right in front of him.

Lack of courage? No. You were scared, Cappy.

"Elizabeth," he calmly said to the actress who stopped upon hearing her name. She smiled, and Jim stepped closer. "We met a while back in Manhattan. Well, kind of. I was an extra on the *Miracle on 34th Street* remake.

I couldn't believe how it just flowed out of me, like a subconscious imprint of what I should have done all those years ago. I perfectly recreated our moment of connection on that cold and wet day.

Her eyes lit right up, and to this day, I don't know if it was because I had recognized her or because she remembered our fumbling encounter. What I do know is that we spent the next handful of minutes talking and feeling each other's flow and energy. We were in the dance that wide-eyed boys and girls get into when the twinkle in the eyes meet the butterflies in the stomach.

Get her number! Magic wand, remember?...
POOF... remember?!

As their time drew to a close, they graciously parted, and this time (at least for Jim), there would be no moping his way home as he had done on that cold day over a decade earlier.

No!! Wait! (large sigh) You didn't ask her. You're being stupid.

Whether in the mall, the local takeout place, or a coffee shop, it just seemed to me that I always had one foot in the door of fate, just one step away from stardom. My chauffeur routine to Burbank provided a suitable mobile office at the Starbucks situated close to the Warner Bros lot. Even back then, I knew much of life is a visibility game. You have to put yourself out there so that unseen energetic dance partner will come your way. Destiny is also a choice, and I made the choice to set up shop there every morning, working on my screenplay and acting like I was "somebody." I couldn't have picked a better spot, really. This location was ground zero for the who's who of the film industry as they fueled up prior to stepping foot onto the lot of make believe.

When Billy Baldwin stood next to Jim in line, the two former New Yorkers struck up a conversation, even reminiscing about meeting once at Town Restaurant. Not only did Billy wish him good luck but also footed the bill for Jim's Venti black coffee. Back to his makeshift office Jim went to enjoy the free coffee and work on his *Nogara* screenplay while waiting for the next sign from destiny.

The large coffee had only a few sips remaining when a woman approached his small table. Jim looked up at her from behind the laptop.

"Hi there, I'm Anne," said the woman in a British accent. "If I may... who are you?" She didn't beat around the bush.

"Just a kid from Cydot Drive," he quickly answered.

Nice one!

He stuck out his hand for a shake and then confidently continued. "Jim."

Is this the one? The golden ticket? he thought to himself. The two spoke for some time, and the next thing he knew, he was feverishly working on a British accent for an audition. Presto! Nothing up his sleeve! Then "Poof!" a casting director offers him the chance to read for the lead role in a film. When opportunity hits, it can hit fast, and after he nailed the audition, he was heading for a table read with other possible actors, surrounded by producers looking to back the film.

The tornado of chance landed Jim at the head of the table, the potential lead finding himself in the captain's chair once again. The cast went through the reading, each doing their part to bring the typed words to life so that the producers would open their funding purse strings. There were a few moments during that read where Jim took his eyes off the page and took in the scene before him.

This is why we came here.

I loved every damn second of those eyes on me. That beautiful moment ended, and the following days became weeks, and then the project stalled indefinitely as they couldn't secure proper funding. Just as quickly as opportunity presents itself in this magical land, revealing a glimpse of fate, it can also vanish and dry up. In an instant. A microcosm of the fragility of an actor's career, I suppose.

No biggy. We just gotta keep going. Mr. Spielberg is out there.

I kept thinking that if I could just land another Sears or Domino's pizza commercial spot, it would buy me more time financially. I was hitting the pavement a lot, thanks to my agent, and I kept getting close. But as Malcolm would say, close only counts in horseshoes and hand grenades.

(softly and innocently) I miss him. A lot.

That Scottish wisdom became annoyingly redundant. Jim would exit each audition, and a day or so later, his phone would ring, and his agent would speak the familiar phrase: "You're on hold, with the right of first refusal." It played out over and over. He'd get down to one of three actors, but he just couldn't break through to the other side of that lucrative doorway.

Thankfully, a small reprieve came in the form of a print campaign that appeared through a set of swinging doors (saloon doors, in a sense). *Thank God for Deadwood*, he thought to himself as he donned his jeans and cowboy boots one more time for the cover of a PlayStation 2 game. The wardrobe department provided a large belt buckle and an official cowboy hat to complete the look for *CMT presents Karaoke Revolution Country*. His swagger returned, and with perfect timing, as the new restaurant was about to open.

Whatever it takes, Mr. Movie Star!

A Hitched Captain and his Bridge

I can't believe all the people waiting to get in. I mean, it isn't a movie premier. It's just a restaurant.

But these people? In their fancy clothes? Cappy is in charge!!

With the pedigree of Koi LA and Koi New York, it didn't take long for the owner's newest creation to become one of the most talked about restaurants in Los Angeles. As patrons entered Bridge, they would be greeted by a stunning hostess who would steer them one of two ways. To the right lay the restaurant, a large open-spaced room gorgeously decorated with brown wooden trim and stunning off-white light fixtures. There was a large wall dividing the space, which was in fact a huge wine cellar valued at some absurd amount of money. On the other side of this sommelier's over-indulgence was the multilevel bar and lounge area. A long bar, with a beautiful back bar display as tall as the vaulted ceilings, took center stage. Bridge restaurant brought sexy back to Los Angeles before Justin coined the pop phrase, and running the bar show was Jim in all his swaggering glory.

I'd be lying if I said I was living up to the appointed position without any ego. I mean, I literally did hold the keys of entry, and every major so and so who wanted to hold court in the lounge had to come through me. The excitement of this new stage coincided perfectly with the warm fuzzies that began to circulate through my soul.

Those first few magical notes instantly transported me back to wonderful times. Cydot times. The Christmas season commenced with holiday carols following me around wherever I went.

> *Hold on! I have to take a minute here in this story to say that Christmas IS the Hollywood of life!*
>
> *The fine print under the 25th says, "Approved by Jimmy." It's the most beautiful day in the world, and I love him for never forgetting what it means to us. Thanks Cappy!*

To this day, no matter how heavy things are or how much stress may be present in my life, the sound of a Christmas carol will always diffuse the bomb, at least temporarily. There was a growing sense of unease that had been building since the concrete streets of New York and was not letting go on the sunbaked ones of LA.

Anxiety can truly be a faceless man that comes in many forms. I couldn't avoid the fact that I was still reeling from my lack of nobility as a father and the Poppy fallout. That shame, coupled with Brooke's predisposition for financial stability and planning, was a whispered opposition to my "shoot from the hip" philosophy. Lastly, there was the matter of Brooke's work visa, which was expiring. Being from Canada I knew she needed to get her green card pronto. But thankfully, I was armed with something other than festive tunes to help ease that. I loved Brooklyn and she loved me, all of me, including my previous marriage baggage. She was a special woman, the sort that doesn't come around often, and even my dimwitted younger self was bright enough to see that.

The morning of the 25th had reunited a cast of old characters as Jim sat around the Christmas tree with Brooke and her family up in Vancouver, Canada. The young couple took their positions across from the lit tree, their cozy jammies and Santa hats on for good measure. Little Jimmy was there somewhere, and if you looked hard enough, you might be able to catch a glimpse of Rusty the red squirrel sitting alongside the mustard figure of Captain Kirk, helping Scuttle the mouse keep the wharf rats from interrupting the festivities. This was a big day, and no one wanted to miss what happened next.

Brooke looked bewildered as she sat with a large gift-wrapped box on her lap, wondering what this last present under the tree could be. As she dove into the dismantling of a less-than-perfect wrap job, she realized that another wrapped box lay inside. The artist and romantic in Jim wanted to build the suspense because he knew for sure Brooke was not expecting what lay within the last package.

After discarding three progressively smaller boxes, she reached the holy grail, the remaining tiny box that held their future. As she opened it, Jim got down on one knee, with the pom of his Santa hat hanging off to the side. The Christmas elf softly spoke.

"Will you marry me?"

The tears flowed from Brooke's eyes. "Yes," she said quietly.

That moment on the floor among the remnants of wrapping paper still seems like a far-off dream, or at least a moment of true love in the long exhale of life. Destiny had revealed itself yet again with a commitment made on the most magical day of the year.

When the two arrived back in Los Angeles post holidays, they made an appointment to deal with Brooke's looming Canadian status. On Valentine's Day, 2006, the two love birds walked into city hall and came out husband and wife. No fanfare, no friends, just a simple exchange of "I do's," two signatures, and presto, they were newlyweds. In just a couple of short years, marriage number two was now official, and Jim and Brooklyn Gardiner would begin to chart their course as newlyweds should: together (though one of them was ever mindful of the actor's yet unfulfilled dream).

Mustard Destiny

The golden hour in Los Angeles is one of the most stunning sights to behold, as the warmth of the early evening meets the sun's descending light, as all before it basked in an unmistakable hue. That hue illuminated a left hand as it released its grip on the steering wheel for its owner to gaze upon, a silver band his focal point.

Jim sat parked in the silver Jeep like he did most early evenings at this time, outside a house in Burbank, waiting for his now wife to get off work. He couldn't help but get lost in the thoughts of life, roads travelled, and what unknowns still lay ahead. Besides, that is what dreamers do, especially when their current world seems at a standstill. He must have looked at that ring fifty times a day in those first few weeks of being part of an officially married couple. It definitely held sway over him in comparison to his first failed attempt at happily ever after. There was a finality about this one, as if the destined commitment would inevitably pull him further away from his dreams. It was just a whiff of intuition but one that Jim homed in on as his hand resumed its grip on the steering wheel, a little tighter this time. But then the heaviness lifted. There she was, glowing more beautiful than that golden-hour hue, walking towards her chauffeur. *She is beautiful, and she is my wife,* Jim thought to himself as she approached with that disarming smile of hers.

When I was with her, the heaviness always lifted off my shoulders. It was during the loneliness of the day, between the pressure of booking a gig or working on my *Nogara* screenplay, that I needed escape. That time left me alone with my mounting thoughts. Once again, I would turn to movies for medication, specifically the world of Terrence Malick. His visual and poetic style of filmmaking had moved me immensely ever since I'd first seen *The Thin Red Line* back in New York. To me, his films are a poetic insight into the human condition, and now I was about to take another trip down Malick lane.

> *Cut! Or stop reading, depending on whether you're a book person or a movie geek like me: Jimmy. This is 'my' chapter, remember. I finally got one, so I need to talk about two things:*
>
> *Number one: (deep breath) It's okay that he's moved on from Steven's movies. You know, like "E.T.," Jaws, and "Indy." He wants something deeper. Okay.*
>
> *Number two: I can't BELIEVE what is about to happen!*

Brooke was working a bit later while the husband and wife she worked for enjoyed a quick dinner out, which allowed Jim to sit down and watch Malick's newest offering. *The Brave New World* was the re-telling of the Pocahontas story, starring Colin Farrell and Christian Bale, both of whom Jim admired. With the press of a button, he began to feel that pressure lift. In typical Malick fashion, the music swelled in unison with romantic images of Indigenous people playing and enjoying life while the large-masted ships from overseas made their way up stream to impending change. Jim was almost drooling with anticipation when the moment was crashed by the ringing of his cell phone. The caller ID showed that it was Brooke.

Well, if you didn't know any better, you would have thought the Flash was in the apartment that early evening. Jim hung up the phone and was gone in about 2.2 seconds, leaving a vapor trail in his wake, making a beeline for Burbank to grab Brooke. On the other end of that phone call was a celebrity sighting, but not your average celebrity that's for sure. Luckily, the traffic was fairly light that day, and he didn't stop grinning the entire way there. Speed records were set, laws broken, and maybe even glimpses of cats and dogs living in harmony, because this was all about destiny. Especially to Jim (well to Little Jimmy too). This moment was thirty years in the making.

Thirty-ONE years! WHOA!! Dreams, dreams, oh my gosh!

(singing) When you wish upon a star… Yes!!!! They DO come true!!

When the silver Jeep arrived outside of the house, Brooke quickened her pace. The family had made its way home and stood at the doorstep.

"Good luck!" the wife of the couple said as the two left in another vapor trail.

Hurry up! Let's GO!

When the Silver spaceship finally reached its intended destination at the parking lot outside a French bistro, the two travelers exited the vehicle and made their way to the front door. Jim took a deep breath and gazed at Brooke with a smile. Then inside they went.

My heart was beating like Mom had just given me a shot. I walked in, and I knew exactly where he was. Right away.

(excited gasp)

It was HIM!! I couldn't believe my own eyes. My hero was sitting RIGHT THERE!

As the couple took their seats at the bar, Jim had to look over and take in the view. There he was in the far corner: William Fucking Shatner. The man in mustard, the little toy that Jimmy had clung to so tightly, was now staring Jim right in the face. He knew enough not to stare back.

Really? I couldn't stop myself!

We ordered some food and some wine while I schemed, working on my next move. Little Jimmy wanted to run up to the table like an innocent child, waving a cocktail napkin for an autograph. Although to be fair, I am not sure he would have fully recognized the man. He vaguely resembled the dashing young Captain Kirk, never mind the physicality of the action figure.

Ha! I saw him before YOU did! And of course, I knew!

I mean, well... he was fatter—Shoot, Mom told me never to use that word. Sorry. Bigger? No yellow shirt either.

Well, I suppose that is what time can bring to the dinner party: a change in weight, hair, stature, and a weary edge that seems to age many. Beneath it all, however, I could still feel that childhood wonder associated with the man just thirty feet away.

Jim was carefully gauging the wine consumption at the table, deciding whether or not to offer up a token of fandom with another bottle, on the Gardiners' dime. Just as he decided to pull the trigger on the offer, his hand raising to flag down the bartender, a waiter arrived at Shatner's table, delivering a second bottle. Jim's hand quickly dropped to the bar with a defeated thud. *Now what?* he thought.

Ummmm... You were too late, Cappy! We-we have to wait.

Brook frowned. "Are you *really* going to wait for him to finish that—"

Yes!

"Yes!" Jim responded with a look that said *Duh! As though anything else is even an option.*

Time passed, and the restaurant emptied. With each tick of the clock, the hour drew nearer until, out of the corner of his eye, Jim caught a glimpse of movement. Shatner and his dinner companion had stood up, and now the two gentlemen were getting ready to leave. This was Jim's shot, and he knew it. As Jim Kirk left the Bistro, heading out into the blackness of the parking lot, Jim Gardiner knew he would soon follow.

"Elvis has left the building," he said to Brooke.

Who's Elvis again? Oh, never mind. Let's GO!!

"Good luck," she responded with a big smile.

He stood, gathering himself and making sure his legs didn't buckle under the weight of his nervous energy. A deep breath, and then it was time to meet destiny face to face.

The blackness of space beyond the doorway was broken by intermittent beams of light radiating down from above, choice spotlights greeting the legendary actor and the actor wannabe. Up ahead, the two men exchanged goodnights, and when Shatner's wingman banked right toward his vehicle, Jim knew it was time to spring into action.

Captain Kirk was making his way to the captain's chair of his silver Porsche, as Jim approached from behind.

I raised my arms... I was going to hug him!

Captain James T. Kirk?

"Mr. Shatner?" Jim's voice cracked with anticipation.

The short and portly former Starfleet icon slowly turned around, half bent over, trying to get into his car.

I... Oh my gosh, I...

"I just wanted to say what an honor it is to meet you, a real hero from my childhood." Jim was somehow able to get this out without stuttering.

Ditto.

Jim's extended hand followed his words, hoping to establish a mutual connection in the moment. Shatner caught the hand coming towards him with his eyes and then continued his full turnaround to finally meet the gaze of the man towering over him.

(a big, exasperated inhale of excitement)

To be honest, I wasn't sure if he was still bent over or not. I'd already learned that he was somewhat vertically challenged, but it did catch me a bit off guard. After thirty-one years, there I stood with the man who had forged my destiny and championed me to my own captain's chair. There was one more thing that I was quick to deduce as well. My hero was . . . absolutely hammered!

What the—

The parking-lot spotlights beautifully highlighted Kirk's bloodshot and piercing eyes, which quickly deduced that I was yet another lunatic fan. His demeanor shifted, and I could almost see his thought: *"Am I not bloody safe anywhere?"* He begrudgingly extended his hand to meet mine with a calculated captain-esque word choice.

"Yeah, yeah. Thanks," he blurted out, totally dismissing me.

(a gasping inhale)

With that, he was off on another mission. The silver Porsche space-ship tore out of the parking lot at warp speed with Jim's hero, an inebriated Captain Kirk, behind the wheel.

I can see myself standing there, half stunned by the phaser blast to my soul. I was grasping at how to feel, especially after the diss. I was an adult after all. It wasn't like I was seven years old and getting the cold shoulder from one of the characters at Disneyland.

(sniffling) Easy for you to say.

I was a grown man with a boy tucked inside somewhere that had just gotten to meet a legend. From my much older perspective now, it's easy to shrug it off. "It is what it is." But to Jim at that moment, it was much more. It was a destiny moment. One that began to plague him with an unanswerable question: Can my fantasy life be my real life?

An emptiness overtook him as he slowly walked back into the restaurant. He felt a sense of loss, as if a veil of possibility had been ripped from him, leaving him in the coldness of his own "space."

> *(sniffling and sullen) The final frontier. These are the voyages of the Starship Enterprise.*
>
> *(big sniff)*
>
> *I stayed there a little longer. Maybe he would come back for that hug. (sigh) Nope.*
>
> *Cappy had his head down by the door. I still don't know what this word destiny means...*
>
> *Hmmm. Movie star. A movie star needs a movie. Ah, his screenplay? Yes, we should focus on that. That will get Steven to notice him!*

Fade Out on "Nogara"

Can my fantasy life be my real life? It took an empty parking lot and a dejected fan boy to give life to that internal question, which would become synonymous with each step I would take forward from that point in my life. I began to question all the dreaming and fantasy escapism that Jimmy had concocted when he was alone and dealing with asthma, and even those damn witches from the hospital. I began to wonder if the power of dreaming was a curse or something.

> *He doesn't mean that.*

After all, everyone has a curse, even the immortal vampires that entertained Jim from a large movie screen on Hollywood Boulevard. He was knuckles deep in a large, buttered popcorn, enjoying the opening day of *Underworld Awakenings*, the much-anticipated sequel, with his onscreen-crush Kate Beckinsale and its director, Len Wiseman. The debate of whether or not he was guilty of building a fantasy around his actual reality was put on hold when the universe's latest offering hit the theaters. It was exactly what Jim needed to dive deeper into the dark and sweeping romantic world of his screenplay, *Nogara*. Knowing that he was now living in the same city as the director he hoped would helm his opus, he would soon find that elusive swing once more, and the result would be a gloriously artistic creative rhythm—one which immediately allowed his dance partner to surface.

When he received a call from his agent for an audition, it was just like any other casting, this one for the role of a futuristic bounty hunter for a gaming company, something similar to the "Halo" game concept, or so he gathered.

"Jim Gardiner" the actor read off his name for the camera slate. He then turned to both sides for some profile shots before standing like the hobbled superman from his New York days, with hands on his hips in a dramatic pose. After a few more pans of the camera, the audition was over. In and out. Easy peasy.

A few short days later, while Jim was feverishly putting the finishing touches on his *Nogara* rewrite, the phone rang. It was his agent, and he was delighted to get a second request for the bounty hunter game job. At the call back, the director would be there to walk the actors through different action sequences based on the storyboarding, which wasn't unusual for certain types of spots.

"Jim Gardiner" the all-dressed-in-black actor slated once again.

Now, just like we used to do back in the Cydot days . . .

Jim took his place on the mark while the casting director operated the camera. Two men sat at the back of the room behind a folding table. The one gentleman spoke up and began guiding the actor through a series of moves. Jim was soon to find himself playing, miming things like holding a large laser cannon, digging a grave on a cold barren planetary landscape, and walking as if encased in a large cumbersome space suit. After about ten minutes of playing Cydot Drive space soldier, he was escorted out by the casting director.

Jim climbed back into his silver Jeep and began the drive home across Los Angeles, feeling indifferent about the audition.

Well, that went well! Do you think you'll get the job? I'm so excited!

Out of sight, out of mind. That was how Jim was approaching it. He'd come to the realization a while earlier that booking the jobs he auditioned for was something outside of his control, and so there was no use in worrying about whether some arbitrary man in the back of the room thought he was the right fit or not.

Doesn't mean you can't be excited.

The only thing that *was* in his control was the work he could put into forging his own way via the screenplay. He needed to get home and fire up the computer before his evening shift at Bridge Restaurant. While the laptop was taking its sweet time to spring to life, his thumbs were busy messaging Brooke from the keypad of his blackberry. He was just about to hit send when his agent's name came up on the screen. He answered the call.

Leaning back casually in his chair, he said, "This is Jim... That's great... Awesome... Yeah, sounds good. What time's the fitting?" He scribbled down "10:00 a.m.," still listening to his agent and replying as needed. "...Yeah, he seemed nice. Pretty straight forward in the room, like most directors..." Jim wasn't sure where his agent was going with the conversation but nodded along, until his agent explained who the director was and he was left with his mouth hanging open and scrambling to respond without sounding like he'd just shat a brick.

"Uh, y-yeah... super cool... I heard that, yeah. Another *Die Hard* film is up next for him." Shaking his head in disbelief, he was trying to sound calm. "Okay... Yup, call me back with the details. Thanks so much." With that, Jim hung up the phone and stared at it in shock.

I still shake my head at the divine timing and destiny of it all. While I was 100 percent sure that Len Wiseman would one day direct my screenplay, I hadn't even recognized him walking me through the moves at the audition. Yup, the man who'd married Kate Beckinsale and helmed the two *Underworld* movies was directing this spot. He wanted me, and I wanted him.

Ha-ha-ha-ha! Good one, you dolt! (as Dad would say).

It was a sign. That's a destiny thing, right?

Unlike his usual battle cry of excitement and proclamation of it being a sign, he sat thinking to himself, *What if this is another let down? Another fantasy that doesn't meet reality moment?*

No way!! After almost five years?? It's a gift!

Jim slowly smiled a childlike smile.

✧   ✧   ✧

The importance of those steps towards the front door of Tatopoulos Studios in Burbank was heightened to say the least. The studio was owned by Len's right hand man, Patrick, who created special effects for such Hollywood films as *Stargate, Godzilla, Independence Day,* and the *Underworld* films.

The door soon opened, and there was Patrick, granting him permission to enter a world of magic.

I can't believe all the amazing things I'm seeing! It's like Christmas! This is the best present ever!

Jim meandered through all the larger-than-life set pieces and animatronic creations. The notion that these very items had been used on the big screen was somehow romantic to both the man and the boy. Jim and Patrick chatted, and it was quickly evident that Patrick was appreciative of both his enthusiasm and his film savvy.

About fifteen minutes later, the door opened and in walked Len. The two film brothers embraced, and then Len acknowledged Jim with a handshake.

"Let's get to work," the fired-up director said, rallying the troops.

Patrick went off to retrieve my outfit while Len explained to me what he was looking for. As he started to discuss some of the movements, it took all of my energy not to think of how I could bring up *Nogara*, if the situation presented itself. As well as the fact that I was enamored with his wife.

Hey, hey. None of that stuff now. Stay focused.

Sometimes I do wonder about you, Cappy.

However, my attention was quickly brought back into sharp focus when Patrick emerged with a large space suit.

Getting into that damn thing was a feat unto itself, but Jim managed with guidance from the two men. Last but not least, a large helmet was secured over the boy astronaut's head, taking him back to the days of his space-exploration fascination. Jim's view for the next twenty minutes or so was through a wire-mesh screen. The helmet provided a barrier for him, and inside it, Jim could feel his guard lower so he could really relish the moment.

You did it. You are here! Remember this, Cappy! Movie stars are discovered! This is it!

Well, DiCaprio has Scorsese, and Russell Crowe has Ridley, Jim thought as he stood toe to toe with a director holding that beautiful wand of access. When the time came to peel out of the suit and gather his things, Jim was greeted once again with handshakes, and gratitude for his time. Then it was time to leave the playground of wonder and hop back into his silver steed.

That was soooo amazing!!!

I was so happy for him. We drove with the windows down and dreamed about the red carpet and living the Hollywood life.

The dreamer in Jim was in full effect; that's for sure. Once again, he felt hypnotized by all the signs and steps leading to one internal thought more than any other: *Finally, the movie-star dream is here!!!* Now, it was about the wait.

One epic and inspired day bled into another less-inspired one, then quickly into an anxious one. By the fourth day, he was in was full-blown anxiety over the silent phone. At 3:15 p.m. on the fourth day, he finally heard from his agent while sitting in the middle of his desolate parking garage. Jim removed the phone from his ear and sat motionless.

What? What is it? Did you get the job?

Jim's head dropped down to the steering wheel, his forehead connecting with a thud.

Ahhh. Okay, Cappy. We need to keep going. Next! Right?!

Cappy!? Right?

Jim's head raised up from the steering wheel and tossed his blackberry over his right shoulder into the back of the vehicle.

Hmm, maybe I'll just let him be for a bit.

Jim sat staring out the window into the neon-filled underground structure. Lost. For forty-five minutes, he sat there in utter failure. The scenario played over and over in his head, and he wondered how Len could have chosen someone else. Destiny had lined this up with open arms. It just didn't make sense. No matter how many times he played it over in his mind, it just didn't make sense. He felt like a fool and a failure.

Cappy's in panic mode. He needs warp speed, fast!

Jim didn't really know what to do or think anymore. He'd seen everything so perfectly... and now complete chaos. He felt like throwing in the towel right there, but he decided to make one more move on this chessboard before tipping over his king. He printed out the latest edition of *Nogara*, with a nice cover letter, and was going to hand deliver it to Len's production office.

You got this. It's . . . that destiny thing.

King Kong ain't got nothing on you!

Jim came to a stop at the top of the stairs before the door into the office. He took a moment to gather himself. Redemption lay on the other side.

We've been waiting for this our whole lives.

Jim nodded to himself and entered. The open space greeted him with desolation from a dead-end western town.

Oh no.

The production office landscape had three desks, two of which were unoccupied. In the third sat a young production assistant, finishing up a conversation with someone on the other end of the phoneline. Her raised finger told Jim to hold on a second. That time allowed him to take in the starkness of the office. He knew this was it. When the assistant finally concluded her call, Jim didn't bother asking whether or not Len was in. He knew that he wasn't.

"Could you please make sure Len receives this? He is expecting it." Jim did his best to act the part. He passed her the package and about faced onto the other side of the street, the one on which dreams and all the amazing clues to its path are nothing but a crafted crock of shit.

"Signs, my fucking ass," he muttered to himself as he exited the building. "This plus this, multiplied by this . . . is supposed to equal *this!*" Jim processed the last five years of the *Nogara* journey, hell the last thirteen years and all the various signs that had ensured his destined path. It was all a bunch of shit.

The Apparitions of Fate

White was all he could see, accompanying the feeling of his warm breath floating back at him as he exhaled. "Hurry up!" the boy's voice decreed.

"Hold still, Jimmy," his mother responded while she gauged where his two excited blue peepers would fall beneath the white sheet.

> *It wasn't my first costume ever, but it was the easiest. Where I grew up, everyone was fascinated with ghosts. Old creepy mansions, spider webs, and ghosts floating in the hallways.*

With two dots, his mother marked the spot with her black pen and then removed the sheet, unveiling the boy.

The little elf stood with his eyes wide, his bowl-cut disheveled by the removal of his costume.

"How much candy do you think I'll get tonight, Mom?" he asked with boyish anticipation.

> *I got a lot, in case you were wondering.*

Jim was still fascinated with the idea of ghosts all these years later. He'd begun to understand that they were everywhere, and more importantly, that not all of them are the tormented souls who had done wrong but rather visions, memories, and foreshadowings of thought that can befriend or plague the conscious mind. In the city of angels, it seemed that he'd begun to gather a fan club, which would grow over the coming years.

There are moments of great let down in life. It's unavoidable, and as many of the great inspirational pundits tell us over and over, "Out of failure comes our next educational moment. Blah, blah, blah." Something like that. To James, it is 100 percent true. To Jim . . . well, let's just say that those continuous kicks in the groin bag by the industry, the universe, and God's wicked sense of humor were beginning to desensitize him. He began to feel like one of those tortured souls, roaming the halls of some cobweb-infested mansion.

> *Cappy, this isn't like you.*

Jim stood in silence before the congregation arrived. The pulpit was surrounded by liquid escape, the alcohol bottles the keys of his pipe organ, upon which he would serenade the inevitable eyes that would soon be on him. His dream felt like a big old destination nowhere. He kept losing himself in the purgatory of past triumphs, close calls, and perhaps unrealistic expectations, the price of the crown he had chosen to pursue.

His hand reached for a glass, which found its place on the stone bar top. Then a bottle of clear liquid found its way into the glass. Not much, just a mouthful to wash down the white pill that he'd removed from the pocket of his black dress slacks. In his profession, you could get anything: in this case, a pain-relieving Vicodin tablet. You just needed to know the right people. Down the hatch they both went, the liquid and the pill, his eyes closing and welcoming the strange communion. It was one of the few times where he'd "taken something" to help him over the threshold. It didn't happen often, but when it did, it provided just the right tipping point.

I always hated pills. I don't understand this. (sigh)

It was now time to hold court and feed off the congregation. Being the man in charge held status, and for Jim, it was the only thing he had left to cling to, damn the consequences. The nights blended into each other. His phone would be on fire with choice people wanting to bypass the outside line and secure a spot down below in the lounge. Money would be slipped into his hands and eyelashes would be batted for free drinks. For his part, he welcomed all of it as it was an indication that he mattered.

I soon decided I needed a status upgrade in the form of a two-seater sports car. The silver Jeep went bye-bye. I didn't even ask Brooke. My God, the thought of it makes me cringe, and to make matters worse, I knew Brooke couldn't even drive a standard. In reflection, I believe I did it to get back at her in some way. My love for her couldn't overshadow the fact that she was the one who stepped in gold-plated puddles while I seemed to eat shit sandwiches. Things always went her way, and when she landed a new nanny job, I think my younger self somehow took it as another blow to his persona.

"Whoops, I did it again" had rung through Jim's head two-fold when Brooke unveiled her recent Midas touch moment, this time securing a new nannying position for the pop diva Britney Spears.

Why can she do it and not you? What makes her special, Cappy?

Just like that, Brooke was frontline in the A-list world, being swept up in the current of celebrity life thanks to her two closest friends. Both Brooke and Jim were quick to find out how insane the pop star's life was. While Jim was home pondering his next move, feeling stuck in the rut of life, Brooke would be orchestrating a great escape for Britney from her Malibu home, which would include wigs, multiple cars, and bait-and-switch techniques, all in the name of getting Britney a few choice minutes alone. Whether it was a walk on the beach with Brooke or a simple conversation, it usually ended the same way: captured by the lens of some intrusive paparazzi. Even Brooke was at their mercy. On a trip to Florida with Britney, she was photographed on the back of a golf cart and plastered all over the internet as this "mysterious bikini friend of the pop star." No one was safe.

That time Brooklyn spent with Britney was hard for Jim to swallow. It was the world and perhaps the lifestyle that he had wanted growing up. Los Angeles can be cruel that way, allowing one to be smack dab in the middle of it all and yet so far removed at the same time. That was a dangerous equation upon which to balance self-worth, and when he wasn't playing make-believe celebrity with his sports car or shifts in the lounge, he went into full-on retreat mode.

A finger presses the remote, stopping the credits as they roll on the television screen. Jim stares blankly at it while the remote slips from his hand. He has finally finished *The Brave New World* and sits in his post Malick trance as the explorer's ship begins its passage out into the mythical watery blue. The ghosts of Captain Smith and Pocahontas are still dancing with Jim, and a resulting state of melancholy seems to drip from his being.

It was sad.

Like all great stories, it was a love story first, which spoke to the adventure within the colonial ancestry of my soul. But more than that, this confirmed that director Terrance Malick would command my spirituality, with this and future films, each experience culminating in his pinnacle of film faith, *The Tree of Life*. He had the ability to connect me directly to the wonder of childhood, the innocence of love, and the great depths of the soul. It was and is poetry of a visual kind and moves me beyond measure.

The ferry toll into the Malick world, of course, came with a price. Namely the lost feeling when Jim resurfaced in the real world, where that unanswerable question (Can my fantasy life be my real life?) continued to blur. It left Jim with a sense that his real world was an uninvited dinner guest.

> *Dreamers get lost sometimes.*
>
> *When Cappy and I began to part ways after Cydot, I noticed he liked sad movies.*
>
> *The movies with adventures, bullwhips, aliens, and even a giant shark didn't make him feel enough. He felt better with sadness. (sigh) He felt at home.*

Jim stared at the countertop as his bar rag moved back and forth for no apparent reason other than to keep that hypnotized Malick state going. It was early evening in empty bar when the universe decided to have some fun with his psyche. He saw a man out of the corner of his eye approaching from the other side. As he walked down the bar, Jim quickly processed the universe's latest offering. It was Sonny Crockett. It was Captain John Smith. It was Colin Farrell.

Earlier in the week, Jim had gone to the movies to see the sleek *Miami Vice* remake, and he had literally *just* finished a three-hour jaunt with the man now in front of him. All he could think was a sarcastic *Really!?*

> *Hey, that's the—*

"Hey, man," Jim casually said.

Colin leaned in and rested his forearms on the bar. "How's it going?" he said with that Irish voice of his.

He ordered a drink, but Jim could only focus on what to think of yet another serendipitous moment.

Talk to him, Cappy?

Small talk doesn't exist in a situation like this. This had some universal design to it. So, as Jim approached and placed the drink in front of Colin, he just assumed a similar position, leaned in, and led with his heart.

"I literally just watched you on screen all afternoon, and here you are. That's fucked up," Jim said plainly.

"Oh, yeah?" Colin said, smiling and taking a sip of his drink.

Jim began to recount his afternoon spent in the clutches of Malick and the emotional state it elicited. He could tell that Colin wasn't expecting to hear about the Malick film, since it wasn't a typical mainstream movie, especially with the *Miami Vice* remake currently in theaters.

"It was a beautiful piece of poetry, man. I loved it." My voice was as honest as ever.

Colin pushed up off the bar a bit, looking thoughtful. "Yes, yes, indeed it was poetic. It was a great experience and thank you for reminding me."

(clapping) Good angle. I will say that.

I know in my soul that it was a heartfelt recognition between two lovers of cinema. Sure, one was famous and the other infamous, perhaps. But there was no celebrity or bartender in that moment, just two men appreciating the search for poetic verse in life and art.

After a few minutes and a few more sips, he shook hands with Jim and disappeared around the corner back into the restaurant. Five seconds later, the name "Jim!" preceded his entrance back into the bar area. He was holding a twenty-dollar bill.

"I got so caught up in the conversation, I forgot to pay," Colin said with a smirk. "Keep the change, and that's not because you liked my film." With a smile he was gone.

You make sure you go and talk to him, Cappy. After dinner.

Jim turned to head back to the center of the bar, staring at the bill in his hand.

Cappy?

Jim didn't know what to make of universal moments anymore. He was drawn to his own reflection in the glass, his aging face staring deeply back.

He knew he was still young, but he was growing weary of these sparks, these situational "can't make this stuff up" moments. A big part of him wanted to be excited about the Colin Ferrell interaction, but he was tired of hearing himself rally the troops around one divine sign or another. As he looked deep into that mirror, he could see a face that was changing.

To this day, I still don't know what it is, but throughout my travels, I have always had a face that everyone thinks they know. Brothers, cousins, actors, musicians, it always comes up that I remind them of "so and so." My New York days were filled with a "you look like" carousel of interactions. A few of the people I frequently reminded people of were actors Ralph Fiennes, Treat Williams, Bill Pullman, and rock front man Scott Stapp from Creed. There was a time when I almost got mauled by a bunch of rabid David Duchovny fans outside *The Late Show with David Letterman* because I jokingly mentioned that I was David's younger brother. A stage manager and Triple Inn alumni got me backstage to meet one of my fan boy look-alikes who also had a monkey named after him. The look on those women's faces when I was pulled out of the crowd and brought inside, after I told them of my fake Fox Mulder lineage, was priceless.

I sat front row, watching my apparent twin up there next to Letterman, and wondered if I would ever get to sit in that seat. I also wondered if, just once, someone would say that so and so reminds them of me instead. Watching Duchovny on stage felt eerily similar to the old days and my cold steel middle-school chair.

(sigh) I remember that show. And those school dances.

Jim's mind came back from his time portal with The Late Show and focused back on his reflection. The image of his younger Duchovny self was just another ghost to join the dinner party, one whose table seemed to be gaining seats. However, there was a spot reserved for Jim's other famous doppelganger, one that would haunt him as an older version of what was to come. He too paid Jim a visit this very night.

Jim's eyes squinted closed while the fingers of each hand firmly rubbed his temples in a clockwise pattern. Whether he was trying his best to negate a stress-induced headache or trying to rewind time in his own mind was for him to answer. The speckled lights from his tight squint filled the blackness behind his closed eyes. It didn't take long before he heard it, like a wind blowing through the rustling leaves of home, the sound of a chair being pulled out, which morphed into the sound of a scraping chain, its heavy weight abrasively moving along the floor. A Charles Dickens style voice broke through the darkness of his closed eyes.

"I wear the chain I forged in life," the ghost said. Jim's eyes blinked open at the eerie sound and statement. "Hi there," it continued. "Can I get a shot of Tequila please."

Scrooge Gardiner turned, and there was his real-life reflection, albeit an older version of it. Jacob Marley forced a smile, and then appeared the unmistakable grin of Robin Williams, the famous actor/comedian and Jim's other apparent clone.

(excited gasp) It's Mork from Ork!

I used to watch that as a kid! He was so FUNNY!!

Jim immediately sensed that the type of tequila he chose didn't matter. It was evident that the comedian's lighter side had not been invited to this dinner out with his friends, from whom he had separated to come to the bar for a shot. Robin's head hung low, only gazing upward at the sound of the bartender pushing the shot glass towards him. He raised the glass to Jim and threw it down the hatch with barely any emotion.

"Please add that to my dinner tab," Marley spoke as he went back to his table.

Jim watched him walk away, weighed down by the chains of something only he knew about. *"It is a ponderous chain."* Jim's thought preceded the cold chill that came over him as he thought about his own depressive cycles and the emptiness growing within. Like the Dickens Christmas classic, Jim would be visited three more times that evening by the ghostly older reflection of the man in the mirror. With each subsequent return to the bar, the marquee persona of Robin Williams that everyone knew and loved would begin to show itself a bit more, the fuel of alcohol easing his pain.

Each time Robin turned the corner, Jim had two shot glasses at the ready on either side of a bottle of Cazadores.

"It's against the law to shoot Tequila by yourself," Jim said to his older reflection.

Robin smiled and cheekily responded, "Why thank you."

The "clink" of glasses signified the union, and the two men let the liquid disappear into their bodies. On the third and final toll of the bell, the ghost of what was to come made his appearance. Between the drinks at the table and the side shots, Robin was beginning the downward slide into drunkenness. He stood before Jim, eyeing the empty glasses like a dog eager for a treat. Jim took a moment, staring deep into his eyes, and saw his own potential journey. Overcome with emotion, he began to pour two last shots. Jim raised up his glass, and Mr. Williams did the same.

"Captain, my captain," Jim said in honor of one of Robin's most famous movie lines, and in honor of the man before him. Their glasses touched, and Jim did his best to hold back his tears.

(softly) *I love you, Cappy.*

I felt vulnerable and unsure of what the heck was going to happen to my life. Would I follow in the footsteps of the ghost before me? Mr. Williams soon vanished with a goodbye, and I was left pondering my own meaning of the word "happiness" and what to make of this latest universal offering. My fire was dying.

A Spartan Reprieve

He won't listen to me. Stupid Len Wiseman, not hiring Cappy.

(exhaling snarl) He just wants to sit around and... Mope. I think that's the right word.

And now he has other things taking away his focus!

The sound was majestic. It resonated around the small room and into the ears and souls of the husband and wife who were there to hear it. The thumping was both elegant and dainty, announcing a whole lifetime ahead with each musical beat.

"You see that small line?" the clinic technician pointed with her pinky finger.

Jim bent down and squinted to home in on it. "Congrats, you're having a girl," she proclaimed.

That second year in Los Angeles found the soon-to-be parents living in Burbank. The spare bedroom of the apartment unit became a little girl's room. The two went to town, painting it and doing what eager parents do. Jim got rid of his two-seater ego car for a "family" vehicle. Everything seemed to be falling perfectly into that purgatory place of the mundane that most of society are herded into, either by their own choice, or as Jim had been, forcibly.

I knew this would happen. I knew, I knew, knew...

Just wait! Soon, she will want a normal life too! I need help.

On a ride one afternoon through the outskirts of Burbank, Jim was lost in his thoughts and his music as usual. His eyes drifted down to a new tattoo he had recently gotten in honor of Brooke and the hero he needed to be for her, them, and himself. It was the sword of Achilles, the legendary warrior and Greek hero. That day, the fresh ink also whispered to Jim to keep on his quest and "look to the right." Jim obliged and looked that way. The sign on the building immediately caught his eye, especially the first word: "sword."

It caught my eye too! And then I saw it: that spark in Cappy's eyes.

Jim had stumbled on the home of SwordPlay LA, a combat studio that trained men and women in the art of weaponry. *Oh, destiny, what devilry is this?* Jim thought at the mocking, teasing sign. While his white flag was certainly climbing up the pole, it was not waving a full and utter surrender just yet. He hit the blinker, indicating a right-hand turn.

Finally... something. If Cappy is holding a sword that will keep the dream alive! Great! A Star Trek *phaser always did it for me!*

Yes, I will go on record as saying that I am one of those guys that would totally get dressed up in medieval garb and go swing a sword for fun. Although, sadly, I never did play dress up outside of Captain Kirk rolling around the backyard, I had started taking some sword lessons back in New York when my *Nogara* screenplay had been just beginning to take flight. I had enjoyed it, and I have to say that holding a sword in my hand felt as comfortable and natural as a toothbrush. What I didn't know was that I would be entering into another sort of brotherhood, one I desperately needed, and one that would provide me with my swan-song acting gig.

Jim entered into the modern-day ludus for weekday and weekend gladiators with a curious spark gleaming in his eyes. This training ground had walls that were surrounded with an assortment of different weapons ready to be unleashed. As Jim came to find out, there were also opportunities in film work. A handful of the group members had just completed some large scenes in the sequel to the *Pirates of the Caribbean* movie opposite the swashbuckling Johnny Depp. After hearing this, it only took a few minutes for Jim to pull his all-in card and join the group.

YES!!! I knew it! Finally, a way in! Gosh, it's good to be
excited again!

He had been missing that team dynamic in his life and very quickly
found himself as one of the core members. It was a much-needed break
from the grind of work and pending family life. Plus, it offered him a
sense of romance that seemed lost. The way one dances with choreography and a sword seemed to stir a deep inner fire.

I'm doing my happy dance right now!

It didn't take long for destiny's divine hand to feed that fire some
gasoline. The world was talking about the anticipated release of *300*, the
story of King Leonidas and his men of Sparta, holding off the Persian
army at the Hot Gates. Jim was well aware of this legendary story of
bravery and sacrifice from his school days, geeking out on ancient history.

In typical Hollywood fashion, networks and movie companies
were pushing to ride the coattails of this film juggernaut. The History
Channel had secured the rights to broadcast a docudrama based on
Steven Pressfield's classic narrative of the story. *Gates of Fire* was going to
be the source book, and the production team was looking to cast actors
proficient in combat, preferably from the same fight team, to play King
Leonidas and his frontline warriors. Jim auditioned and found himself
going to war, Spartan style.

Television movie, here we come!!

This may sound crazy, but I actually remember thinking it was a
good thing I had been in Chippendales awhile, torn ACL aside. My
natural coordination combined with the fluidity of choreography made
me stand out during the fight scenes. It truly was a dance—an aggressive
dance, but still a tango with your fight partner over the orchestrated
moves. And just like during my time on the Navy Seals mini-series, my
inner child was in hog heaven.

I know you didn't ask, but hog heaven for me was rolling around
on my back lawn like Captain Kirk.

Spartans were notorious for bravery, combat tactics, and of course, their shields. "Come home with your shield or on it" was their motto and for good reason. Their shield was their life, and the life of the man next to them. Jim immediately felt the power from holding these robust badges of honor. Learning how to use it as an extension of the body came naturally. As did using his seven-foot deadly spear with the blade on one end and the spiked metallic club on the other.

Rehearsals lasted for a few months and with good reason. These were dangerous weapons, and if there was a misfire during the intricate maneuvers, the result would be blood. There was plenty of that anyway, along with bruises, during the controlled chaos of the grueling choreography.

> *Finally! Fourteen years of trying, and I can't even count how long since Cydot. This was it!*
>
> *SO EXCITED!! Okay, breathe, Jimmy. Breathe. It was our FIRST time EVER on a Hollywood sound stage!*
>
> *Costumes! People! Oh, LOOK at those rolling lights!*
>
> *(big, excited inhale) OH, MY... Trailers! Like, private dressing rooms for the movie stars!*
>
> *And there!! That's where the director sits! Behind all those televisions! Like Steven with his baseball hat and scruffy beard!*
>
> *There is no way Cappy will walk away now.*

As the armored breastplate slipped down into position, Jim began to feel the portal to the past emerge. But it wasn't till he adorned the epic Trojan style helmet that the portal opened. He could feel a connection spanning centuries. He grabbed his weaponry and took his place on a large stage, standing before a huge green screen. It was time for the Spartans to defend the hot gates and for Jim to exercise his own demons.

> *I sit in the corner, ready to watch! WOW... I am so excited! This is like Elliot riding his bike with E.T., or Quint and Sheriff Brody chasing the shark!*
>
> *Finally, Cappy! Finally.*

In weapons and stunt work, there is a fine line between performing with energy and believability and maintaining safety in every nuance of movement. For a few days on a backlot studio, Jim pushed that boundary to the limit. He became a Spartan possessed, going all in with every ounce of his soul for each take. The crash of his sword against an opponent's would elicit visions that he was trying to vanquish. Ghosts of failure, underachievement, his son, his parents... they all ran through his mind with each choreographed onslaught. Just like Little Jimmy on the tennis court against his asthmatic ghost, he was now battling an internal foe.

I knew this was it for me. The emergence of the ghostly tone of surrender rang in my heart. I was a warrior trying to expel every last ounce of energy so that surrender came easily. The final curtain was drawing in on my time as an actor, and I could feel the pain rise as the spotlight began to fade.

The seven-foot spear twirled like a tiny baton over Jim's head until he brought the full force of it crashing onto his opponent's shield. *"I can't breathe, Mom,"* echoed in the vacancy behind his possessed eyes as the warrior took a deep rhythmic breath, spinning his body to block a kill shot from behind. His shield thudded from a sword strike against it.

Jimmy's body grunted from the powerful force of a missed baseball swing and a wooden rowing handle being slammed into it. That elusive swing had found the warrior as his shield moved like a left-handed sword strike, crashing into a Persian body. The powerful blow knocked the enemy's hands into the air as the sound of applause filled Jim's head from the east-coast stage.

The choreography continued with a backwards sway and pivot, timed with a twirl of his spear once again. Down to one knee he dropped, as his weapon now thrust forward with unwavering tenacity. As it landed its powerful kill shot on his Persian enemy, the spartan warrior's head dropped, as it had done in the underground parking garage after the universal let down at the hands of his wish-list director, Len.

It's easier to see now that destiny was being tied up in beautiful little bows of finality like the ending threads of a story. Perhaps it was the universe's way of providing me some comfort as I began my journey north to a far-off land.

"Cut!" bellowed the director.

YAY!!!! THAT'S HOW IT'S DONE!!!! I can't stop clapping.

A sweat-soaked Jim remained down on one knee. He was exhausted from the day's shooting, but for now, those pesky little apparitions had been silenced. Like the Spartan he courageously embodied, he was now coming home on his shield. The universe had spoken: Destiny was not to be found in Hollywood.

Huh? What? I don't understand... You just... What are you—

"Shut up!" I remember saying to myself and to that younger ghost while rising up from bended knee. There was no way the dream could continue to live. The wonder was over.

(softly) Cappy... (sniffs)

E.T. was leaving me again, and there was nothing I could do to stop it. I began to get so angry.

Jim continued through the motions of life for a while, paying attention to the end of the little chapters in his life as they happened. The daily walk to Starbucks from his apartment soon found himself and the members of Queensrÿche together again. One last rekindled conversation with Geoff Tate and his wife about the New York City days and east-coast shows brought them all back. It was a fitting send off to an eighteen-year love affair, and the last time he would see Geoff, forever a hero at his roundtable.

Big deal. Some hero you are, Cappy.

Another hero would assume his position next to Geoff from a nightly encounter at one of Jim's remaining shifts at Bridge Restaurant.

"Where are you ladies from?" Jim asked the bachelorette and her entourage of ten ladies while pouring champagne.

"We are all from Dallas," she responded with the southern twang synonymous with his paper-hero quarterback on Cydot Drive.

Whenever I would run into someone from Dallas, I always had to let them know I was a huge Cowboys fan and that I grew up with a Roger Staubach poster on my wall. Why? I have no idea, but I did and still do.

"Really?" the bride to be responded. "My dad is good friends with Roger."

See!!! Magic, everywhere! This is your dream!

"Really? That's cool," Jim said, but his reaction didn't seem to have the fire it once would have. The night concluded with a goodbye and his address, as per the bride's request. She wanted to thank Jim for his outstanding service and hospitality.

It did shock me when about a month later a package arrived from Dallas, Texas. The contents contained a personalized thank-you letter and a signed NFL football from my paper hero. I may have lost that wall poster to time, but the signed Roger Staubach football sits proudly on display to the left of my laptop as I type these words. A reminder of kindness.

Love Raises a White Flag

I'm still mad at him. I don't know what to say.

The white tissue pulled from the box just in the nick of time as liquid snot spewed from Jim's nose. The credits began to roll on Darren Aronofsky's brilliant emotional film, *The Fountain*, and the blubbering mess that was Jim was left alone as usual to ponder its heavy meaning on his life. Like the futuristic version of the main character in the film, Jim had to let go of his fear of death, or in his case, of leaving a dream, for the potential to be born again. It was a slow and agonizing walk towards that flagpole.

When the magical family day arrived, there would be no mad dash to the hospital this time. I would be there to welcome my baby girl into this arena of life. Brooke was in labor for a total of twelve hours before we welcomed my daughter onto this pale blue dot. I remember crying over this small and gentle creature nestled in my arms. I recalled one of my favorite film lines: "Sometimes there's so much beauty in the world, I feel like I can't take it, and my heart is just going to cave in." That was me that day. Her innocence brought me back to the days when I still had mine, before the world began to eat away at it. I knew it would happen to her one day, and a feeling of being powerless took me. It didn't take long for me to realize that this stupid life of dream after dream, rejection after rejection, and my need to "be somebody" would not serve this beautiful little angel who was now dependent on me. I also knew that our isolation in the big city without any family would not serve Brooke either.

As the Gardiner three settled back into their apartment lifestyle, Jim marveled at Brooke's ability to handle everything. It was like she had been doing this all her life. Breastfeeding and pumping milk, no problem. Changing diapers and bathing, check. Rocking their baby to sleep, easy peasy. Being a spectator to this also stirred thoughts of something in him that had been locked away in his heart and mind: his son, Jayden.

It had been almost two years since he'd last seen him on a quick visit while his ex-wife was in Los Angeles. Not that Jim didn't want to see him more, but it was as if it were too painful for him to comprehend, especially while the dream that was Los Angeles was crumbling. The winds that blew in from up north signaled change, opportunity, and support. In one last twist of universal gift-giving, Jim was able to orchestrate a reunion in Los Angeles, bringing his parents out to meet their granddaughter and their grandson, Jayden, both for the first time.

The drops of water danced around Jim in arcs of happiness, each exploding on the surface with the sound of joy. It reminded him of the summers at the beach, watching the lights dance across the sky on the Fourth of July. A three year old Jayden was frolicking in the shallow end of the pool without a care in the world, his floaties keeping him safe. All Jim could see was the baby-toothed grin swimming at him, his arms opened for his dad to grab. Jim knew he was still too young to comprehend all of his new life as it was playing out. But he also knew his son would understand it at some point, and that thought hung over him even as the innocent play did its best to silence it. It was then that Jim's dad emerged from the upstairs condo, swim trunks on and towel in hand.

The three generations sat together on the edge of the pool, their feet dangling into the aqua cool. Jim's heaviness gave way to the beauty of the moment. Three males, no words, just love. I am sure there were words, but I can't remember. I wish I did. I wish I could go back to that very moment in time and say to my son, "I am sorry" one more time. To tell my dad, "I am sorry that you will never see him again." And to myself... God, the things I would say. But I can't.

When we three returned upstairs, wrapped in towels, we were greeted by the women of the family. Brooke, the proud new mama, was sitting across from Carolyn who was holding a six-week-old baby girl in her arms. Jayden walked right up to his grandmother and leaned in to gather a closer inspection of the baby. A strange unease filled the apartment that day, a mix of confusion, contemplation, and a generational changing of the guard, if there is such a thing. No one in that room, kids included, would have imagined that life would be playing out the way it is now.

It's simple. Stay. STAY!

As the time came for Jayden to say goodbye, the little boy innocently gave his grandparents one more hug, and kissed his tiny half-sister on the forehead. When it was Jim's time to say goodbye at the door, he dropped to one knee and hugged his son, eyes closed. In his mind, he could feel his hands pulling on the pole tethers, the flag rising further upward into the wind.

"See you," the wide-eyed son said to his dad.

Jim knew that he would not. The words "I hope so" finally emerged with a tussle of his hair.

Jayden walked away, holding hands with Poppy, the two happy at their own reunion. Jim stayed in the doorway, watching their retreat, his eyes and heart wanting to speak but muted by fear.

I love you! I love you!! Say it, you idiot!!

All these years later, my inner voice is still screaming at myself.

For some reason, I couldn't back then. I disappeared back behind the door, another battle lost. I signed the adoption papers for Poppy and her new husband a short time later. My folks and I haven't seen him since, and for my parent's part at least, they never will.

It was soon time for the elder Gardiners to leave and head back to the east coast, back to their home. A big part of Jim wanted to go due east with them, but he and Brooke would be making their own pilgrimage north just three weeks later. Another parental goodbye similar to those before was at hand, but with each passing day turning into years, these reunions and goodbyes became few and far between. Jim could sense that leaving both grandkids behind had caused his parents a lot of sadness, and with that knowledge came his own guilt for living a life that deprived them of the opportunity to watch them grow up.

He stood now in a familiar scene. Another empty apartment, once teeming with life and possibility, now lay dormant and barren. The image of the Grinch burned in his mind. Jim was one of the Whoville kiddies who went to bed with dreams and wonder only to wake and find the house desolate, every ounce of Christmas removed, leaving just emptiness and crushed dreams. His fire was gone. His sword too heavy.

Jim backed away from the emptiness and turned to exit.

STAY!!!! You promised! You promised me!!

He stopped and turned back one last time to the scene of the crime.

Across the empty room, leaning up against the wall with his arms crossed, Little Jimmy exploded into anger.

> *You coward! I will NEVER forgive you for this! I will HAUNT YOU! You GAVE UP! Captain Kirk wouldn't! Roger never did! Indy always fought! Don't!!! Please, don't—*

Jim took one last look, and then closed the door on what was. With it, his warrior spirit ceased to exist in the land of "one step away."

In the beginning of August 2007, Brooke and Jim climbed into a full U-Haul truck, a trailer hitched behind it carrying Brooke's car. The soon-to-be travelers were accompanied by their co-pilot: a beautiful nine-week-old girl, secured firmly in her car seat between them. The end of a dream is never an easy pill to swallow, nor is the idea of a warrior turning away from what flows in their blood. They were now heading to the northlands of Canada to take a crack at living a normal life.

Jim gazed down at his sleeping daughter and tried to steal some of her peace, but it didn't work. There was, however, his wife. Her eyes were alive with excitement at the thought of going back home to begin a new life. Jim forced a smile and shifted the U-Haul into drive. They moved past the parking lot that had witnessed his encounters with Captain Kirk and the boys from Queensrÿche, the Warner Bros studio growing progressively smaller in the rear view. Jim couldn't help but think of Jimmy, somewhere deep within, sitting with his head in his hands, sobbing. New York and Los Angeles, fourteen years on the run, chasing a dead-end dream.

His hands continued their pull on the tethers until the white flag reached the top of the large pole. There it stood, its white signal waving proudly in the prevailing winds of change.

The sounds of crying and sniffling fill the air. Anger has floated away and been replaced with profound sadness.

> *It was more than fourteen years. It was our life. Our dream. (sniff)*
>
> *Please come back. Don't leave me here alone without you. All I ever wanted was to live in the world of make believe.*
>
> *I'm . . . I'm gonna wait here till you come back. I won't give up on you. I can't. (sniff) Find me. (sobbing sounds) Please, FIND ME.*
>
> *I know what E.T. would say: "I'll be right here."*

CHORUS: *THE NORTHLANDS*

Pray you, go gentle into the dark night with our beaten warrior for the dream is dead. The boy is gone. What now remains is a shell of the man who "could." The bleakness of this forthcoming land is the perfect stage to find death and rebirth, to surrender and bear witness.

Have no fear for this warrior is still tepid in his lust for life. Hope awaits at the extended hand of new life while the decaying castle of home crumbles in the far-off distance. This mythical land of good and evil will give rise to moments of greatness, a brotherhood reborn, and a loving arrival of legacy. But be warned, beneath it all lies the dark plague of emptiness that continues to spread its wicked hold on his worth.

Come now, entertain a land trampled by his feet, its soil laden with tear-filled regret. But hope circles in the air, as do the apparitions poised to strike. Thus, to the northlands doth our scene take flight.

VANCOUVER ARENA

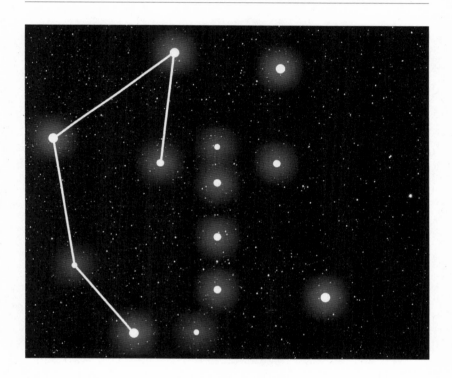

Same Shit, Different Steak Suite

I. Middle Earth

The air of the northwest hangs heavy with moisture as it sweeps in off the Pacific Ocean. It is a mythical place, make no mistake, one of killer whales, bald eagles, and teaming wildlife. Vancouver Island is a huge piece of land almost the length of the New England coast of Jim's youth.

A few sandy beaches are vastly outnumbered by jagged rocks and bluffs calling for adventure. Mountain ranges line the isle, dividing east from west and projecting their superiority over the endless rows of subservient pine trees. The energy of this land was different from what had made up the first thirty-six years of Jim's life.

The surrendered warrior found himself at the only place that felt familiar in this new land, perched upon some rocks overlooking the ocean. His internal banter was screaming as loud as the chorus of sea lions swimming offshore. It was time to begin anew and find some happiness in the responsibilities of life, and maybe over time, those voices of regret would diminish. He had to get to work, literally. The starving artist's lifestyle was a thing of the past; he had a family to provide for.

The Gardiner three set up base camp at Brooke's parents' mini-estate. It would be about eight months until Jim's immigration papers would arrive, but thankfully, he was able to secure work with her dad's island-wide grocery-store chain. For the first time in his life, he went to work each day without a dream.

He walked in and took in the sights, sounds, and smells of the surrounding warehouse. He felt small standing before the endless storage rows of items found inside any large grocery store. A looming smell of damp cardboard permeated the air and welcomed him to this foreign landscape, from the glitz and glam of Hollywood to this present-day Island of Misfit Toys.

Toothless grins accompanied the honk of forklift horns as they whipped around the aisles like go-carts. The warehouse crew was unique to say the least, poster children for the Walmart most-wanted list in the world according to jaded Jim. Of course, they were good people—well, most of them were anyway. They were quick to brand him with a nickname, Hollywood, which only reminded him of the land he'd just left. The cold concrete and endless rows of cardboard became his prison. All he had to do was look around and see the fruits of his life's labor so far. The sentence dished out by the universal warden was solitary confinement, which suited him just fine.

The once ego-labelled jeans and outfits were replaced with grungy blue-light specials from the local five and dime outfitter. His solitary days would begin and end the same, riding a motorized picker through the various aisles to assemble a palette of supplies to be delivered to the large grocery stores. Round and round he would go until the Fred Flintstone whistle blew, and he was allowed a reprieve from the prison. That prison gave way to another: the negative self-talk that filled his mind, accompanied for the very first time in his life by heavy drinking.

I cringe thinking of Brooke eagerly waiting all day for her husband to come home only to be shunned as I gave my daughter a kiss on the cheek, loaded up the vodka, and took my place on the couch of despair. If there was a gold ring forged in the fires of Mount Doom, it was in my pocket that's for sure. I was turning into my father, the weight of depression growing.

Brooke could sense it. Her parents could sense it. Everything was chalked up to an "acclimation phase," I think she called it. It was a 180-degree shift from the last fourteen years of my life, and it was slow paced. Slow as in even the crickets seemed to be too lazy to sing at night. My only hope rested on my official status coming in the mail and the three of us moving to the mainland where the pulse of life seemed more welcoming.

With Christmas fast approaching, the air began to lighten a bit for Jim as usual. This was his daughter's first magical Yuletide experience after all, and being the first grandchild in Brooke's family heightened things a bit for everyone.

Her tiny hands gripped and shredded the assortment of gifts, way too many for a seven-month-old, that's for sure. The love and wonder in her big, beautiful eyes caught her father's and she stopped to smile. Jim let that smile in, for a moment anyway, and felt a hint of the joy that seemed abandoned with Jimmy in the land of dreams.

The holiday proved to be a shot in the back of Jim's arm, helping to get him over the hump. His Canadian papers were soon to arrive, and with that light at the end of the tunnel was some fresh air. His attitude and mood shifted somewhat, and he even decided to forgo the booze, something he would do for the next fifteen months until another reunion called for a celebratory toast.

After eight months, the three found themselves on a ninety-minute ferry ride to mainland Vancouver, and back to city living. The needle on the record player of life found its groove once again with Brooke securing a nanny job and Jim taking up bar duties at a downtown place called Bogart's Steakhouse. Same shit, different steak indeed.

II. A Sort of Homecoming

The ocean navigates its way around much of the downtown portion of Vancouver. A portion of this modern-day Camelot juts out into an evergreen oasis that greets the Pacific. Stanley Park is a magical place, an escape from the city, and a glimpse into an untamed wilderness that stands defiant against the swirling sea. Like an ancient castle, the park is surrounded by a seawall that extends around the perimeter, marking old- and new-world divisions. Jim stands at one end of this wall and can feel nostalgia starting to pump in his veins.

A large wooden building is situated at the end of the inner harbor, the gatekeeper to Stanley Park. With its white trim and white doors, it stands proud as a hub of history, a cultural beacon for a sport near and dear to Jim's soul. Built in 1886, the Vancouver Rowing Club was a throwback to the collegiate boathouses of Jim's youth and the famous structures that lined the Charles River in Boston. Jim now found himself before its entrance and the faint cries of an extinguished brotherhood started to whisper. It had been fifteen years since he'd last crossed the threshold into that defining arena. He always knew he would return at some point; he just wasn't sure that this was that moment. But the warrior in him stepped anyway.

The club itself was steeped in tradition and folklore, the way he always envisioned it after his *Oxford Blues* movie initiation as an eighteen-year-old. The building's old wooden smell permeated through the massive shell bays housing equipment, rowing ergometers, and rows and rows of oars. The adjacent rooms had showers, a gym, and meeting rooms that led to a beautiful bar for members only: an athletic oasis among the hustle and bustle of the city sirens and chaos. Jim found himself before the endless award cases containing trophies and photos of warriors past, each with a forgotten story captured in time. This was the club's history, an ode to mythical combatants, including Canada's first ever Olympic gold medal in the 1950s.

He stood there examining the homage to glory days, and the thought of his own storied past flooded back. Of his first time in the Rhody boathouse and the wall of framed heroes, which now held the iconic picture of his strokeman Kevin, standing up in the boat, from the boys in blue silver-medal run. But these faces before his older self were strangers, unknown tales bound by the common denominator of love for this ancient discipline. A similar sensation came over him like a charge of electricity. It was a whiff of unfinished business mixed with the welcoming smell of the shell bay that took hold of him. As that air circulated within his soul, something else magical happened. The display glass that housed his observing reflection offered a glimpse of a gentle and joyous smile on the face of its owner.

The grip from the throttle seemed like a long-lost handshake reuniting two friends. Jim sat in the stern of the small coaching boat with one hand on the outboard motor while it carved its way up the inner harbor. The serenity of Narrow River back in Rhode Island had now been replaced by the thousand-meter stretch of real estate they had to work with here. Unlike the east-coast haven, this was a never-ending minefield of pleasure crafts, tourist ships, seaplanes, and floating debris for both the coach and the rowers to navigate.

This was now his territory, thanks to his wife. Brooke had found a job posting that was looking for rowing coaches, and just like that, he was re-immersed in the world that had forged him. It started with teaching a "Learn to Row" class, but once his rowing background got out among the club members and governing board, he was offered a coaching position for the competitive masters squad at the club. His mission was to replace the current coach, who had come to the end of a long and storied career, and bring some of the big-boat culture back into the club.

It should be noted that masters rowing traditionally refers to anyone over the age of twenty-seven with different categories of competition based on age. With adulthood comes a myriad of responsibilities that athletes have to navigate, making sweep rowing more challenging. Vancouver Rowing Club (VRC) was no different than most clubs in that the majority of its rowers were small-boat scullers. But now with Jim at the helm, there was a renewed energy with the squad and a chance to put together some bigger sweep boats for competition.

Speaking of energy, it didn't take long for word to spread outside of VRC, and he soon found himself at a little club nestled in the tranquility of Deep Cove. This small hamlet was situated between the roaming hills of North Vancouver, with a vast water landscape upon which to row for endless miles. Unlike the juggernaut of the city club, this small rowing team consisted of eight master athletes who only rowed in small sculling boats. With a rowing schedule that was opposite of VRC's, it fit perfectly into Jim's routine. In the span of a month, he was now the head coach at two programs, hanging his hat on this reacquainted love affair.

The early fall mornings at the Deep Cove Rowing Club also marked a notable mention in my life. It had been fifteen years since I had developed any true bonded friendships, and now I had two that would withstand the storms of time. Matthias was a large and powerful German rower who rowed with the grace of a ballerina. His gentle teddy-bear interior was a perfect balance to the grizzly bear raging within his pint-sized wife, Leslie. She was a glorified coxswain in stature, one who fiercely took up the challenge of competing as a rower and did so at a very high level. Conversations with these two after our early morning rows fueled a friendship that will never diminish under the weight of time.

The fall chill in the air matched the tingle of the water as it surrounded his lower legs. The view before him was a pristine aqua-blue landscape with endless possibilities awaiting his reunion. It had also been fifteen years since Jim had last situated himself inside a rowing single.

He had forgotten the emotional impact of the sport, the sensual nature of the rhythmic dance and the oneness with the morning glass as it slid under his gliding craft. That wind from Cydot Drive began to rise once again, hitting his face with each and every stroke he took. It was a moment once lost in time that gloriously reconnected the young boy and his quest for adventure, the young man and his quest for identity, and a man adrift on what lay ahead. The three souls embraced this beautiful, joyous reunion set against the morning sun.

I still remember that specific moment, about forty-five minutes out on my solitary row, when I stopped to turn around. The shell glided to an eventual stop, and all fell silent. Around me, a truly mystical view of mountains and fir trees created a backdrop of awe. I sat still, reflecting on my life and how this sport had been instrumental in my stepping into adulthood. So many memories flooded my mind, none more powerful than the season with the boys in blue. Suddenly, I had a desire to go fast, to relive those powerful life lessons found in the sixty-foot rowing shell. That addictive air of competition began to swirl around my shell and followed my long and joyful row back to the boathouse.

The swirling air followed Jim over the next few weeks, building to a gale force wind that he encountered one rainy morning at Vancouver Rowing Club. The drowned rat was in the process of changing when the club captain approached. Angus was an English chap and former competitive skier who had taken up his oars later in life despite his smaller stature. He wasn't built like a rower per se, but his heart would tell you otherwise.

The conversation that ensued was mostly one sided, with Angus telling Jim about a prestigious race that would be taking place at the beginning of May. The Opening Day Regatta was held in Seattle and was an invitation-only event that included not only collegiate competitors but masters as well, with one very important distinction: The sprint-racing season in masters rowing is only one thousand meters, unlike the two thousand meters for collegiate and international competition. However, this event would be the full two thousand meters, allowing the older athletes to take a journey back in time to their younger days and chase big-boat glory over the full distance.

"Eighteen seconds?" Jim's eyes bulged in horror and cleared his throat. "That must have been brutal, mate?"

"Downright embarrassing, to be honest," Angus immediately responded.

VRC had fielded a men's eight in last year's regatta and been trounced by the undefeated rowing powerhouse, Pocock Rowing Club. Jim could sense what was coming next.

"Would you help us get an eight together and see if we can't redeem some pride this coming May?" asked the club captain, plainly.

"What about Mike? He's not done coaching just yet."

"Mike is in, if you are," Angus fired back.

Jim stared at the floor for a moment, feeling his body temperature rising. He looked back at the club captain and the two locked eyes. A campaign of destiny was ignited.

The seven-month quest to achieve old-man glory was now in play. While I was quick to give Angus a hell-yeah commitment, there were a few things that had to happen for me to, in fact, be all in. First and foremost, this had to be my show to run. I needed full autonomy to design the training and race plans to maximize our chances. It would be done via a selection process whereby anyone could try out, but the eight chosen would be committed to the boat like the days of old. Practices would be held in the eight itself, meaning the rowers had to shift their priorities to allow for full attendance each session. There were two more pieces of the puzzle to round out the terms: One, Coach Mike (in all his sixty-extra pounds of coxing glory) would squeeze into the shell one more time and get a chance to go out in a blaze of coxing glory; two, I would sit in the stroke seat one more time and lay down the rhythm for the men to follow. The governing board at VRC agreed to the terms, and the dotted line was signed.

The training plan I created was geared towards pushing the boat's physical limitations and adapting it to handle the two thousand-meter race. I would begin to log miles and miles of extra volume in the rowing single to build my aerobic base. A combination of intensity and base training would make up the indoor ergometer components, while the water sessions were about unifying the power application of the eight rowers into a symbiotic unit of speed and efficiency.

The selection process wasn't without its friction given the nature of some egos at the club. When the dust had settled, the seats to potential glory weren't all the fittest or best rowers at VRC, but they were the best combination of athletes who would stay committed to the course, and above all else, believe in the process.

The black marker went to work on the large white board, feverishly writing down numbers and lines. In fact, the only thing missing was some quantum equation or the theory of relativity. The men from the boat sat around the shell bay as the mad scientist unveiled the all-important start sequence he wanted the boat to use for the race. Summoning his university days, they would opt for a high and prolonged start sequence to get them off the line. It was designed to be a two-tiered approach with the first ten strokes at a very high stroke rating and a secondary shift of ten strokes at a slightly lower rate. After the initial twenty, the crew would then bleed down over a number of strokes to the desired race pace. Jim's thought was that the other crews in the race wouldn't be so ballsy as to implement something similar with two thousand meters being uncharted territory for many of them. Of course, it was also unfamiliar for those who sat before Jim, their eyes wide in horror at the scheme he'd laid out. He wanted to leverage the element of surprise, believing that Pocock and the others would be scrambling to pick up the pieces.

The men were willing to trust their coach and give it a shot. However, getting this concept to work in practice didn't come as easily as it had on the scientist's white board. The stroke rate wasn't where it needed to be, and the boat felt heavier than it should have. Jim's next gamble came in the form of taking the tiniest man in the boat, the English bloke Angus, and moving him all the way from bow seat to the prestigious seven seat in the hopes of adding more quickness to the stroke. If the start concept didn't do it, this positional change surely raised a few eyebrows among the squad. But the underlying fiber of every good unit is trust.

Each and every practice, the men showed up and brought 110 percent to whatever workout was at hand. The air around the club shifted as other members began to marvel at their ability to go deep into the suffer bucket and come out the other side with a playful smile. That is what warriors do: They go all in, especially when the impending battle is approaching.

The trumpets sounded, the war drums beat loudly, and the ritualistic pre-battle rigging of the boat had begun. The air of any race day is an epic mix of emotions: pressure, fear, confidence, and belief. Jim took an extra deep breath that overcast morning in Seattle; the Opening Day Regatta had arrived.

It had grown into quite a large spectacle through the years. Sure, there were traditional elements one would expect from a rowing regatta, such as monogrammed sport coats and champagne in the hands of the elite. However, never before had Jim seen the rowing elite standing next to a bunch of earthy free spirits playing the bongos. Heck, there were even cheerleaders and street performers. It was a carnival atmosphere that lined the banks of the racecourse, and it was magical.

The race itself would start out in an open area of water, marked by logs on either side that would guide the boats down into the "cut." This long stretch of racecourse would be bookended by two banks with masses of spectators perched atop its stone walls. The course itself was quite narrow and only wide enough across for four boats. Because of the walls, the sights and sounds of racing paired with the screams of the spectators to form a tunnel of audible chaos for much of the race. It was pure electricity.

Jim had been removed from this scenario for almost sixteen years. The environment, the sight of boat trailers, and all the crew jackets made for an overwhelmingly emotional shot to the chest. He had found his way back home and now stood in the pre-race huddle with a new brotherhood. The boys in blue lived on within the men in red. It was a four-boat race, but only two mattered: Vancouver in lane one on the inside wall and Pocock in lane four on the outside wall. The men broke from the huddle with a thunderous "VRC!" cheer, grabbed their racing shell, and took the long walk down to the loading dock.

Up at the start, the light drizzle had dissipated, and the flat water was a gorgeous shade of gray. As Mike was lining the boat up, I remember thinking how incredible the warm-up section was. That elusive swing was found on the very first stroke and never let up. It was a great feeling to be that linked again, with each man completely in tune with the other. If we could manage to recreate that over the next six minutes, fate would perhaps deal us a different result than it had the previous year. But at the end of the day, we really didn't know how fast we were.

"I have alignment," the portly cox said into his microphone.

Jim gave Mike a smirk and whispered, "Tight fit?" which was a running joke between the two. It didn't matter that those sixty extra pounds would equate to an additional handful of seconds they would have to make up for; the men wanted the coxing legend exactly where he was.

"Sit ready," he said calmly.

Jim sat at the starting position, his hands loose around the twelve-foot weapon. As Jimmy had once done, he looked to the stroke men in the other boats. *Not today*, he thought. A quick tap on his back from the tiny seven seat, and the crew was poised for action.

"Are you ready?!... Row!" The starter's voice echoed across the channel as the red flag unleashed the powerful chaos.

The big red machine went to work. They pried the boat forward with the first three strokes and then began to build the power and rate, which immediately launched the white rowing shell forward. Instantly, Jim could feel the boat on his right falling back. As Mike coolly counted off the end of the first ten strokes, the VRC boat was almost half a length ahead of the two closest boats and roughly a seat or two up on Pocock. But now came the roll of the dice. Mike shifted the crew into their second ten-stroke part of the start sequence. Just as Jim had envisioned, the other crews dropped to their race rating to conserve for the longer race. VRC kept the gas pedal pinned, and as they approached the last three strokes of the sequence, it was clear as day that it was now just a two-boat race. Mike looked to his left and then back to Jim.

"Bleeding down in two!... One!... Two!... Hit it!"

Jim and Angus went to work, slowly shifting down the rating over the next ten strokes to the desired race pace. As the boat began the descent, Mike cracked a wry smile and fired off the words the men wanted to hear: "Three-quarters length on Pocock." The boat was moving exactly according to plan. That glorious swing was in full effect with each subsequent stroke. The men could feel it and now anticipated the words from their coxie.

"We cracked em! Open water on Pocock!" Mike barked.

The VRC men now needed to stay composed and trust the training and their ability to respond should there be a challenge.

As the boats entered the cut, the roar of the crowd began to swirl, creating an ominous undercurrent of screaming that seemed the perfect musical score to the can of ass whooping that was being opened. Nothing had changed in the standings, with VRC maintaining a length lead over the green hometown beasts from Seattle. As they approached their fan base along the wall, the screams and chants of "V-R-C!" took over the arena. It was a surreal moment for many of the club supporters to actually see what was unfolding. The mighty home team that had spanked VRC by an embarrassing margin was now at the receiving end of a reciprocated offering. Mike kept the boys under control the rest of the way and only added in one shift in rating as the finish line approached. Discipline and dedication with unwavering commitment yielded trust in their ability. The outcome was never in doubt. When the horn sounded, Jim punched his fist in the air and let out a victory scream. The men in red finished exactly one length over the dejected hometown heroes.

After the air re-entered their lungs, and the total body burn began to subside, the men in red became young boys in the sandbox once again. Laughter, hoots, and hollers echoed down the boat and gave additional flavor to the circus that is Opening Day. Now it was just about getting back to the dock and the champagne that awaited them by the trailer.

As Mike commanded the men to roll the boat into stretchers, their seven-month mission finally concluded. Cheers filled the air from all the club spectators that had made the trip in support, while the men in red hugged one another. It didn't take long for the champagne to pop and the bottle to make the rounds, each member acknowledging a special moment in time.

The journey for this crew had indeed been special. No one in that boat thought they would experience a "true" crew concept as those years had seemed lost long ago. Unlike in college, when rowing "is" life, these men all had their own lives to juggle, and in effect, put on hold to go after a burning desire in their twilight years. And why not? Why does time or age have to dictate one's playground? The sandbox is always sweeter with others, and I take great pride in knowing that I had played a part in putting those smiles on their faces. The twilight campaign with the men in red will always stand as another top rowing moment for me. Once again, I had gone all in to find some sense of purpose... and now I had to pay the toll.

III. The Rosetta Stone Cracks

The dirt would fly into the air and spread thin, like summer fireworks raining back down all over Jim's daughter. The toddler loved dirt. She was fascinated with it and could spend hours just playing in it. Jim had actually carved out some time away from the water to sit on the edge of a playground sandbox and watch over his little shield maiden. The past year had flown by and brought many changes, with his success down in Seattle adding more duties to his coaching carousel, including a head-coaching job at Simon Fraser University. He would take the lead for that team, and in just a few short years, build it into a viable rowing culture, producing athletes that could compete against the larger and better-funded programs. It was a skill to juggle the three different clubs, personal-training clients, and his own training, but he needed to in order to meet the family's financial goalposts. He was exhausted. But the success in and out of a rowing shell seemed to fill some vacancy of self-worth within him. Why he couldn't find that in being a husband and father was beyond him.

But this particular day on the playground was all about the view before him. Tireless, boundless energy was on display in the form of pure wonder, and he had a front row seat. He marveled at his daughter's innocence, a reminder to him that everyone has it at some point in their lives. He couldn't help but drift back to Cydot and those expectation-free days of child wonderment. He floated along the breeze on a bike ride into town and a trip to his grandfather Malcolm's house. The joy of first love and high school. The awe and wonder of walking into a boathouse for the first time and stepping into a calling.

His eyes came back into focus on the other adults milling around the playground, each seeming to be fixated on their phones while the very joy that they all sought was right before them. The distractions of real life are unavoidable. He himself had fallen victim to the bicoastal institutions that offered dreams, but in reality, had hardened him, leaving him older, unhappy, and devoid of simple joy—something that not even the love of his playdate next to him could alleviate.

The internal language of love seemed to be slowly rewriting itself, word by word, sentence by sentence. Even through his journey of those ego-driven days in the concrete jungle, he'd never stopped evolving, though one constant remained: the need to understand the game of life. That's what helped him grow, seeking answers to life's riddles as they were laid out before him through his past failures and triumphs. But sometimes stages of growth become dependent on a dance partner to bear witness, hold space, and allow one to be fully seen. The angelic woman next to him was an excellent standalone addition, content to be just that and assume her simple place on the bookshelf of life. A part of Jim, as he existed at that time, envied and loved her for it.

I, on the other hand, have seemed to amass a "life series" of volumes, adding more and more to the complexity with which I view this place we call earth. This latest edition was full of deeper soul-searching questions and desires. Most of which fell silent on Brooke's ears. I began to realize that there was so much power in being "heard" and "seen" by another that the lack of it began to crumble the foundation of our relationship. I was crying out, from the couch days of high school innocence, but no one came. We loved each other, and yet I felt like she only knew a fraction of the real man inside. I was on a journey to understand my own Fibonacci sequence, that evolutionary growth spiral to the root of my soul. I'd already lost Little Jimmy, and now I could sense that I would lose her too.

IV. A Few Nights at the Opera

The curtain peeled back on the morning of November 2, 2010, as the Prima Donna took the stage for her aria to begin. It took precisely twelve minutes, unlike her big sister who had taken a more leisurely approach to coming into this world at around twelve hours. In fact, the newest addition to the Gardiner family didn't even want to wait for the doctor, which left the attending nurse and Jim to handle the dirty work. Poor Brooke didn't even have any time for pain medication; it was just push and go. The newest addition made her arrival known with an operatic scream to the heavens.

She was soon exhausted from her belting performance and found herself resting peacefully in her older sister's arms. Jim's eldest's chipmunk cheeks expressed the pure joy of having a future wing-woman to play with. The now Gardiner four were all gathered in a room, taking in the silent serenity of the moment with the older love birds acknowledging the sheer beauty of the two masterpieces before them.

I have thought about that scene often over the years, especially when the cares of the world seem to be knocking dauntingly at the door. It reminds me of a gentle and peaceful time when the four of us were all together and our hearts were one. It was a perfect moment for an imperfect man. Sometimes, I wish I'd never walked out of that hospital and could just sit in that scene longer before the unwelcoming call of "Cut!"

It was a few days later when the script did, in fact, change. Brooke started to bleed. Her woman's intuition didn't disappoint, and soon she found herself undergoing a DNC procedure. It was determined that there was a piece of placenta still inside her uterus, which needed to be removed.

Brooke, whose nervous and anxious disposition was put to the test, made it through, and she was now resting comfortably at home. Jim was doing his part, hopping back on the coaching carousel while keeping an eye on his recovering wife and baby. The new family addition, compounded by the stress of the previous week's scare, mixed perfectly with his youngest's piercing screams and his quest for financial stability. Jim found himself the frog, the one who doesn't jump out of the pot but rather tries to stay and adjust as the water gets hotter and hotter.

Tiny bubbles began to rise to the surface when Brooke shouted for help from the bathroom. Jim pushed open the door only to find a horrific white face gazing up at him. She was bleeding again, this time in coagulated lumps. Immediately, they left for the emergency room, where upon arrival, her white complexion and delirious state got her whisked off into a room for immediate examination. She continued to uncontrollably pass more blood clots, with Jim himself using a small waste bin to catch the cranberry-looking projectiles.

Helpless. That's all I felt at that moment. My wife's blood volume was critically low, like "at death's door" low, while I was playing catch with blood clots and waiting for someone to get their ass back into the room. At this point, Brooke was out of it. The memory of being alone with Malcolm when the phone rang sent a cold shudder up my spine. Here

I was, for the second time in my life, staring at the possibility of death. Her large, helpless eyes could barely focus on me.

The door crashed open, and a team came in to whisk her away again. Jim leaned down and gently brushed aside her hair.

"It will be fine," he whispered and kissed her on the forehead.

In a flash, she was gone. That was the moment when I stood among the cold silence and wondered how I could raise two girls without her. Those feelings of loneliness that had haunted me in the empty apartment in New York, and when leaving Los Angeles, crept back in. *This world is just too much*. I cradled my head in my hands. The frog felt helpless.

It took Brooke a few months to fully bounce back after another procedure and two blood transfusions. The doctors had surmised that, in the first DNC procedure, her uterine wall must have been accidently cut open. The pieces of placenta had been removed; however, the resulting gash was in a high blood-vessel area, which had led to the internal bleeding. Thankfully, the dust began to settle and the newly anointed Gardiner four could now begin to find some normalcy.

That is, if normalcy comes with window insurance. Every day with his tiniest angel was a crap shoot. When she was unhappy, the whole townhouse complex knew it. The legendary opera front runner was diagnosed as being colicky, not that identifying the issue provided any relief for the eardrums of Jim and Brooke. There was no escaping it, and every night, the performance would begin again.

When Brooke was finally better and getting out at night to exercise, that left Jim to deal with the baby. Take a stressed and helpless man, throw a colicky baby in his arms, and the result is implosion. Back and forth, he would walk across the living-room floor, more bubbles forming in the water with each subsequent pass. Finally, in a fit of rage and aggravation, he blew his top and screamed, "Shut up!!!"

The feeling I get in my stomach when I think of that moment never changes or goes away. Every parent yells at their child at some point, but this was more than that. The feeling that scream carried was directed at my sweet daughter, and beyond her, to life itself. It was a soul-purging exorcism. I went upstairs immediately, put her in the crib, shut the door, and ran away to the basement to hide from her—and maybe from the world—like a coward.

When Brooke returned to our daughter's screams and found me sitting in the downstairs office, the look of disappointment on her face was mixed with anger. She just shook her head and proceeded up to the top floor to come to the rescue of our daughter. Again. The feeling of inadequacy and abandonment that had been festering since my empty-room conversation with Jayden was now fueled by the fact that I just couldn't understand my role as a father and provider. My life, with all of its Jimmy dreams and schemes, had been fooled by the boiling water.

V. The Ghosts of Home

At thirty thousand feet, the ominous Rockies seemed only a few feet away through the window. A sprawling expanse of mountainous peaks and pathways with nature at its best, unapologetic and majestic. Just the day before, Jim had completed a very successful four-day stint at the Canadian Masters Nationals, coming away with numerous medals and a national championship in his age category for the men's single scull. The August heat and battles had claimed its victim, who now just surrendered to whatever comfort he could find in his seat. His eyes fixated on the view out the cabin window on his way back to Rhode Island. Wondering.

Those eyes now found the sights out a taxi window as it sat idle in the parking lot of the infamous town dock of his youth, trying to connect the dots of lost familiarity. After a moment, Jim signaled to the driver to continue on to their destination.

Much can be said about Main Street and its once glorious prom-enade of colonial houses and flags triumphantly proclaiming youth and freedom. There was no mistaking that the town that he loved so much had withered over time, with the ghostly voices of play vanishing. It was as if, in the blink of an eye, time had erased the memories and three hundred years of history both.

I have come to understand that perception of anything is everything. Those days back home had lost their vigor because I had. Specifically, I had lost the wonder of life as seen through the eyes of my younger self. My inner child hadn't made this trip, and now that absence of joy kept me company as I made my way through town, knowing that my end destination would have the same lusterless view.

I exited the vehicle and stood silently. The once beautiful yellow hand-built Cape Cod house of 92 Prospect Ave was decaying, just like its owners. Thirty-plus years saw Malcolm's playground now old and stale. The yellow paint had faded, with parts of it losing its battle against time. The mighty green shutters hung slanted and tattered, the shrubs and landscaping overgrown and forgotten. But it was one distinct sight that will forever haunt me: a large red dumpster smack dab in the middle of the driveway.

I was afraid to walk into the house, knowing my parents would mirror the once-flourishing oasis. They were in no position, physically or financially, to keep this nostalgic treasure. I knew that, but the thought of a lifetime lived with only a garbage bin to show for it didn't sit well with me. I've always been guilty of being nostalgic, but to me, this was the end of something. I remember feeling extreme guilt that my mother had to leave the only comforting thing she had left in her life. This was the house her dad had built, and then rebuilt when she'd survived a fiery lightning strike when home alone. Guilt rose in me as I walked past the dumpster. I'd left to globetrot, traveling the country and chasing a dead-end dream, and left them to manage on their own. The struggle of an only child, I suppose. But there was also anger, as I began assigning part of the blame on the other male culprit in the family.

Jim entered through the screen door as he had done so many times in his youth. There he was, Leigh Gardiner, his dad, laying on the couch and smoking a damn cigarette. Yes, he'd been dealt the short straw when he'd lost his job, but for God's sake, get off the damn couch and get motivated to live your life! Here Jim's mom was, at seventy-one, still working full time, while his dad sat on his duff all day. As much as I will always love my dad, it still burns my ass even now.

Jim's dad groaned as he pulled himself up off the couch. "Carol!" he growled with his deep voice. "Jimmy's home."

She emerged from the kitchen, looking ten years older than he remembered her looking only four years ago in Los Angeles. She looked worn and tired as she nestled into a hug from her only son.

"It's good to have you home. We missed you," she said lovingly.

"I missed you too. Besides, you can't move all on your own."

✦ ✦ ✦

Jim's neck craned upward while standing in the small closet. His eyes locked on their target: the wooden hatch that led into the attic. He hadn't been up there in years, probably not since his early teens when he'd looked everywhere for his next adventure. He pulled down the folding ladder that his grandfather had built and began to ascend into the unknown.

The beam from his flashlight illuminated the dark, showcasing the dancing rhythm of dust as it moved through the air with his unannounced entry. The attic contained many items that were once revered as treasures when young Jimmy went exploring. Old suitcases and travel items from the aviation era of the 1940s, with their worn-leather look, sat against the wall still waiting for their owners to whisk them away for exploration. Books and countless mechanical manuals from Malcolm's time fixing the airplanes lay thrown in a box.

As Jim combed through one of those dusty coffins, he picked up a tattered, off-yellow magazine. He blew the dust off it, which travelled through the air like a plume of smoke. *Aviation,* the oldest American aeronautical magazine had a closeup picture of his beloved F-4 Corsair airplane on the cover. Jim squinted to see the smaller writing and read it out loud to himself, and maybe to Little Jimmy (in case he could hear).

"From Vought-Sikorsky comes this new fighter, hailed as America's fastest. The power is provided by a Pratt and Whitney double wasp… the most powerful engine ever installed in a fighter."

Jim smirked. *Of course,* he thought. Malcolm would only work on the best.

Now with heightened interest, the flashlight scanned for more goodies. He reached a heavy item towards the bottom of the box. When the beam of light gave it life, Jim knew instantly what it was but had completely forgotten its existence. It still had its metallic silver glow from the day his grandfather had shown it to him. It was an engine piston from *"the most powerful engine ever installed in a fighter,"* the one Jimmy would pilot in countless dreams.

I remember the day my grandfather had shown me this. He cherished it as a token to the pilot he'd never become and to the aircraft he'd spent hours and hours working on. It was from the last F-4 he had ever serviced, and now it lay dormant in a box, in an attic, with other items that had outlived their usefulness. I sat among the ruins of a period in life and reflected on my own usefulness. *Where does it all go?* I wondered. *This concept of time and relevancy.* This was a graveyard of memory, and I hated it.

Jim got up and moved past other boxes containing decorations for his favorite holiday and towards the far corner of the attic. There was something that caught his eye about the object that sat underneath a series of large blankets. He approached, shining the flashlight so his hands could begin to lift away the dusty coverings. As the last blanket pulled away, a shroud of dust began to float through the beam of light that brought to life the secret beneath. A large wooden house, roughly three feet by three feet and two stories high, was now exposed. The light scanned each room, bringing it to life before moving onto the next. A living room complete with wallpaper and fixed furniture gave way to a kitchen with small wooden appliances. A family room and den met with a staircase leading to the second floor, containing bedrooms and a bathroom. So much beauty in the details. Jim knew what this had to be; truth has a way of landing like that, in an instantaneous thud of emotion. A single tear streamed down from his left eye and over his cheek and then dropped to the dusty floor. This hand-built creation had stood the test of time much better than its big brother. This had been handmade by Malcolm, a doll house he'd made many moons ago for his only daughter, Carolyn.

The following day, Jim followed closely behind his mother as they ascended the stairs to the bedroom. He paid attention to how the years and her knees had slowed this climb she made each evening. At the top, she opened the door to the spare bedroom and entered. This was the spare bedroom now, but back in the day, this room had been hers. A sanctuary of play as it should be for any child.

Once in, it didn't take long for her eyes to reconnect to a forgotten piece of her soul. Jim could see and feel her energy shift as she moved closer to the house. It was like she was transforming back into the little girl he had never known. Into each room she went and relived a moment in time that only she will ever remember. Jim held his breath and dared not utter a word. This was her moment.

When her inspection and childhood journey was over, she stood upright and gently pushed her glasses back up her nose to their correct resting position and took a seat on the edge of the bed next to her son. Her head soon found its resting place on his shoulder.

"Grampy made that for my birthday," the old woman surrendered.

She began to cry, and Jim put his arm around her, doing his best to provide comfort. Those swaying breathing dances of Jim's asthmatic youth were now being repaid in kind. Some moments happen without any understanding of their importance or repercussions even years later. This was one of those moments for Jim, the magnitude of which would compound as his mother began to struggle with her own memories and fall victim to Father Time.

The graphic of the hurricane showed its trajectory up the east coast of the States with tiny little Rhode Island in its path. The meteorologist was estimating landfall in two days' time.

"Might get stuck here for a bit," his prone father muttered from his couch, cigarette dangling as his left arm reached down to the floor and picked up his Manhattan on the rocks.

Jim just nodded, still eyeing the television. "Sounds good to me."

Two days later, the sideways rain pelted the side of the house, and the winds blew in right on cue. Jim's flight had been cancelled, buying him a few more days before he would have to return to Vancouver, saying farewell to Malcolm's slice of heaven. Ms. Irene battered the coast in full-on hurricane fashion. It didn't take long for the power to go out and envelop Jim and his parents in blackness. Flashlights had now replaced the kerosene lanterns of Jim's youth, and each sat with their individual torch by their side. It was a special moment as the three nestled in on the couch with Jim in the middle.

He reached for his cell phone and began playing videos of his girls for Mom and Dad. His first born had grown so big in the four years since they'd last seen her. His youngest, not quite a year old, would make the cutest faces while her big sister unleashed dance moves to random music. The three silhouetted figures watched the videos over and over, and for Jim's part, he hoped the moment created one last good memory for his mother. He was sure to take the memory with him when he left as well. It would be his last memory of a house that felt like a part of his soul.

His job was now done, and it was time to leave, John Denver style, on a jet plane, and truthfully, Jim didn't know if he would be back again. The adventurer was off, once again leaving his folks to cope with life on their own terms: isolated, friendless, and for the most part, penniless. The life of the yellow house at 92 Prospect Avenue was coming to an end. Another edition in life's encyclopedia that takes its place on the shelf of memory, and partly, in a fucking red bin. As he breathed in the last whiff of Atlantic air before boarding the plane, he was overcome with sadness like the weight of an extra carry on. He stopped at the top of the stairs, leading to the inside of the aircraft, and looked back, not expecting to see anything but hoping for everything.

I don't know how it happened or what it looked like, or even felt like, for my mom and dad as their red Jeep pulled out of the driveway for the last time and made their way to a tiny old apartment. I do know one thing however: The vastness of the empty house will forever be filled with the ghostly sounds of play, life discussions, Scottish humor, and the delicious aroma of Malcolm's signature pancakes that could cure any sadness on earth. And through the open space leading upstairs, and into a spare room that used to be a little girl's sanctuary, there are a set of stairs in a small closet. Up those stairs and into the attic of yesterday, the new owners would eventually find nothing except one item, sitting in the corner; a large, homemade, sixty-six-year-old dollhouse, removed of dust and left within its big brother. With it, a whisper of a young girl's laughter fills the air.

VI. A Starry Sky

The ocean breeze blew in, picking up some gentle grains of white sand as the setting sun cast its fading orange glow. Two more years had gone bye in a blink of an eye, and Jim still found himself coming up empty handed. Not in the rowing medals or the ice-cold beer that he held onto while swaying in a hammock, but rather in his quest for financial stability. He felt like the family couldn't get ahead, and when they did, or when they got to experience something, it was due to the bank of Brooke's dad. His beachside happy hour was no exception. Her father had purchased a multiple-week getaway in the Mexican Riviera for the entire family.

The oceanside hammock brought him clarity and reconnection. It was in these moments that it became clear. The surrounding pressures of life receded when he could connect back to that little kid and find the joy in the simple moments. The movement of the hammock called to the memory of his grandparents and to backyard cheeseburgers, cooked Malcolm style. But it was the history of the world that took a stranglehold. The adventure and archaeology of the Mayan ruins was where Jim began to hear the spiritual whispers of those before him. Curiosity and wonder was found in touching the ancient stones of Tulum. A profound sense of connection overcame him, not just in the physical sense but in a timeless, spiritual way, feeling as though he were a part of "everything." The untold stories and crumbling legacies seemed to call to the ghost within him, that warrior seeker who needs to search the world for never-ending connection. It was a glorious, renewed partnership made even more magical with the four eyeballs that greeted him each morning, smelling the same air of excitement.

Cydot Drive was alive and well within his two girls. Here, Jim's kids could be kids. They were in a paradise where each turn gave way to exotic birds perched on their arm, an ocean kayak, or a pool swim with dolphins that brought tears to their dad's eyes and pure awe to theirs. Cave exploring and dinner with a monkey was as routine as the sun rising. This time away was all about play.

"M" is all I remember. The significance of that letter and the words that followed landed in mid-swing of the hammock. It occurred to Me in that Moment that the Monotony of life could be More Manageable with the Monster of Money allowing pockets of play like this. I had become a reincarnation of Houdini, the master escape artist and dreamer, looking for a way out of my reality into the wonderful breeze of possibility. I often reflect on the moments of escape I have had over the years and realize that they have allowed the pressure cooker within me to stabilize, coming at the precise time when needed most. Money, travel, and women seemed to be keys that would unbind the straight jacket I felt enveloping me.

There in Mexico, one other thing became as crystal as the liquid oasis now surrounding Jim's feet. Namely, that these pockets of real-life escape needed deeper pockets to fund it. Much deeper than he had or was able to provide as a rowing coach. Jim felt strongly that money giveth life and taketh it away. His parent's situation reminded him of that very fact every waking moment. Money held the keys to the playground.

Like many things, an escape can begin as a whisper, the tiniest seed, and then that seed can grow into opportunity. During the family time that ensued nightly, Brooke's dad would often talk about business and investments with his son-in-law. Most recently, along with the other two brain children behind the grocery store empire, he'd purchased an old seaside inn and restaurant on Vancouver Island. It was a gorgeous piece of property in dire need of a full makeover to breathe life back into the sleepy little town of Qualicum Beach. With Jim's restaurant background, it didn't take long for Brooke's dad to drop one of those well-placed whispers, suggesting that Jim oversee the property.

"Fuck no," Jim jokingly responded.

The family laughed, in part because of Jim's lightning response but also because working for the three wise men, as they were known, was a death sentence. They'd built an empire on old-school sweat equity, and when you were in a management-type role, they owned your ass for life. Jim knew it, and Brooke knew it too. Hell, everyone on Vancouver Island knew it. To be fair, it wasn't just that which had garnered the snappy response. Jim also knew deep down that his former life in that industry had done nothing but feed his ego, create unhelpful opportunities, and force him into a slave-labor mindset with late and long hours. On the other hand, it could feed his pockets and perhaps provide the key to more doors of wonder. The whispers continued throughout their stay in Mexico and those conversations lasted about as long as the tequila each night.

The very last night of the magical stay was upon the family, and each would enjoy it in their own special way. Jim dug his bare feet into the cool of the evening sand, but he wasn't alone. A smaller pair of bare feet did the same by his side. Darkness enveloped the two figures that stood against the backdrop of unseen waves crashing against the far-off reef. Their necks craned upward to the sheer beauty of heaven's pincushion. Thousands and thousands points of light spread across the blackness, each a beacon of possibility. Jim's thoughts went to the memory of his own father, easing his crying after an unsuccessful school dance by pointing to the stars and connecting those dots of imagination.

His knees now landed on the soft sand as he knelt next to his oldest angel. He gently took her hand and folded in all her fingers except one. A tiny index finger became a pointer of dreams as her dad started to trace out the different constellations that hadn't dimmed since he was a child.

With each slow movement over the belt of Orion, or the handle on the Dipper, or the "W" of Cassiopeia, his daughter's excitement blossomed. "Wow" would repeatedly fall innocently from her tiny lips in complete wonder. The scene was accompanied beautifully with the rolling waves increasing their tempo against the snare drums of corral. The receding water danced like the slightest tickle on the ivory keys of a Steinway, while the wind through the palms ushered in a string component to the magic that was unfolding.

This is another moment in time that I will never allow myself to forget. It was perfect in every sensory way, the magic of two kids lost in imagination before the gateway of 'what if.' Love in every millisecond of each second on that beach is all that is needed to understand the power in being present in life. I remember my daughter running back to the others to brag about the stories of Orion the hunter and Queen Cassiopeia. My daughter's heart was beaming as big as her beautiful eyes. For me, I took some more time on that beach. My knees gave way to a full-on surrender to the sand, my prone body providing me an unobstructed view to the Sistine Chapel of the universe.

An outstretched finger traced more points as Jim's imagination took over the captain's chair. Perhaps those vast points of light held his own heroic journey, just as his younger self had thought all those many moons ago. He could see parts of it taking shape, the warrior in the night sky forged in the different arenas of his life. But the image wasn't complete. The constellation of his hero was far from being brought to light. In that moment, Jim knew his journey wasn't close to concluding, that some unforeseeable mythology had yet to play out for him to take his place among the heroes of the sky.

The smile slowly eroded as he sat up from his trance-like view. The sonic symphony that was scoring his ecstasy was gone, replaced by his internal chaos of worry and doubt. It was on that sandy beach where an innocent whisper began to take hold and find its roots in his soul. Frodo reached slowly into his vest pocket and fondled the shiny ring of opportunity. The whispering held power. It held security, material possessions, small-town fame, and above all, the key to the playground of adventure. The tranquility of the sandy shire was fleeting, and Jim Baggins could feel the pull of its call.

CHORUS: *THE WEARY KING*

Our sacrificial lamb charts a course for the last outpost at the edge of sanity. It is a tribal realm, one devoid of joy. Only whiffs of this fleeing emotion travel up from a forgotten land, holding prisoner the boy and the dream.

The dark lure of wealth has seized our flawed hero. His pitted sword and shield have been strengthened by something far more sinister: unlimited power. A throne and kingdom are soon to be his but will further wrinkle his troubled brow. Forward he trudges, and not even the power of love can prevent him from standing before the edge of the abyss.

Save fret for rays of light doth break the canopy of darkness. A holiday reunion of generations will shine brightly for our hero like the stars he seeks to take his place among. Further tales of conquest shall be written as heroes return to their founding shores to battle once more. But make no mistake, the time of the sword is coming to an end.

And so, our longing eyes shift their gaze to this marveled land at the edge of the jungle, ever mindful that out there in that darkness, beyond the great walls, lies a ravenous beast. Come now. The haven of this small-town outpost will find the soon-to-be king surrounded, his faithful queen and two daughters standing by. Normal life has indeed begun, and the thrust of the flag finds his feet, firmly grounded.

VANCOUVER ISLAND ARENA

The Shire and Green Goodness

Vancouver Island's perfect blend of reality with Middle Earth fantasy seemed fitting for the final showdown of good versus evil. A culmination of a life journey would take place here among the wilderness, among the mountains that extended along the westward fold, and then sloped down like a beautiful sonnet, soft and effortless until they kissed the ocean.

Just eight months after that Mexican whisper, Jim found himself standing with his girls and Brooke in the driveway of a house in the sleepy oceanside hamlet known as Qualicum Woods. The excommunication from Los Angeles had beaten him into submission, his wounds, open for the past six years, were now going to be closed tight by a financial tourniquet. For the first time, an air of hope blew in as Jim moved to insert the key into the door of their new castle. The two little girls charged into their new home with the excitement of Christmas morning. They scattered down the hallway, quickly picking out their respective rooms and claiming "thou shall not pass" entry into their domain.

Brooke's folks had come to the rescue yet again, this time purchasing a small rancher for their extended family to live in. I knew the moment I walked into the house that it was the one. The neighborhood was a throwback to Cydot Drive and a time when kids could just roam and ride their bikes without the hustle and bustle of real-world chaos. It warmed my soul, knowing the girls could experience a real childhood of innocent play and adventure in this modern fear-based world. Truth be told, I was also "all in" on this particular house because it had a small separate studio out back, complete with heat and electricity. Perfect for my indoor rowing machine. Make no mistake, I wasn't hanging up my oars quite yet.

One of the hardest things was saying goodbye to my rowing friends. Our conquests were many and our awards too numerous to count. Gone would be the boathouse culture, and the only true friends I'd had, in Matthias and Leslie, over the last four years. I kept the faith that we would be reunited once more at the water's edge. Until that time, I had only the rowing ergometer for friendship and three loving girls for company.

Qualicum Beach itself is like Sleepy Hollow, an aging town where the majority of the residences have one foot in the grave. It is a retirement community, and at one point, noted for having the most millionaires per capita in all of Canada. It was simply gorgeous, and the town center was just a short bike ride away, much like the Wickford of Jim's youth. Only a few quaint commercial streets absent of name-brand businesses and corporate power made up the town's central hub.

Down the hill from the center of town, and about a forty-five-second drive from Jim's new house, lay the soon to be Old Seaside Inn. It was smack dab across the street from the ocean paradise that would greet its eventual patio users with a stunning view. The property itself was a long way away from opening its doors, still deep in the renovation phase. Its predecessor was a small motel with a restaurant that had stood the test of time until time itself decided that people weren't interested in a seventies- and eighties-style Dutch atmosphere. The big machines were called in, and what remained now was a skeleton of its former self. This new property would be a complete makeover, which would see the Dutch nostalgia turn into a chic modern-deco thirty-two-room boutique hotel with an amazing circular dining room. Even more majestic would be the outdoor patio area that could sit another hundred people under the moonlit starry sky. All the while, the ocean breeze would blow in from across the street. It was slated to be quite the oasis.

But for now, it was just a construction site, and that is where Jim showed up to work on September 1, 2013. Life sure has its training grounds when we look back and connect the dots. Much like the first day when he'd sauntered onto the job site for the Italian crime lord Danny and his band of marauders, he would soon find himself surrounded by another group of construction workers.

I was back, immersed in the world of drywall and timber. That smell was unmistakable, and as I shook hands with the construction company owner, there was a certain calm that overtook me, like I'd done the right thing by being there at that moment. Everyone on the site knew I was there because of my father-in-law, but I simply did what I always do and found common relatable ground and was liked.

The three wise men's master plan was to immerse me in all areas of the project and understand everything and anything having to do with *every* aspect of the property. Over the next year, I would do just that, having my hand deep in the cookie jar of every phase of construction, renovation, bar design, and room furnishings. In a sense, I would become an encyclopedia on all things Old Seaside Inn (or the OSI, as everyone in town would come to call it). But first thing's first.

"Start with that wheelbarrow and move the dirt pile to the back lot," the owner of the construction company barked. Jim went to work.

When he returned through his front door that first evening, he looked like he had been in a coal mine all day. Standing in the shower with the water cascading over him, he knew he was in for the long haul. This life choice was going to be an endurance event, and he'd signed a contract on the dotted line with the Qualicum mafioso. But out in the living room post shower, the concerns of the freshly washed father of two melted away as he took up his mantle on the softness of the couch with his prized angels on either side. It was his haven after a long day of work and the impending 4:30 a.m. alarm cry.

Warriors get shit done, mafia contract aside. Jim had committed to spending a year on the backyard iron maiden day in and day out, getting fitter, stronger, and hopefully faster. The blueprint to getting back on the racecourse consisted of working at the OSI, acquiring enough money so that he could buy a rowing shell in about one year's time. There was a huge lake he had scouted approximately fifteen minutes down the road that he could train on—alone, but training nonetheless. His ultimate goal was to race the summer of 2015 and reunite with his athletes at the racecourse. The plan was set, and another dotted line signed, sealed, and... as far as delivering? Two words: ALL IN.

It was in these moments that I felt the most alive. I had a passion and a purpose, each demanding attention and focus with that warrior spirit. It drove me each day as I began my new life on the island. The early mornings out back fueled my passion, that sanctuary of time and space when the effort, the discipline, the commitment, and the music came together in a symphony of chaos, creating dreams fueled by a burning desire. And then the crescendo of completion, that sweet moment of silence when body, mind, and spirit return to life. With the passion box ticked, I could navigate the purpose part of the formula and provide for the well-being of my girls and Brooke.

I nearly tripped over him a dozen times in those first few months. The "tile guy" wouldn't offer much in the way of conversation. He just plugged away on his hands and knees, doing his work, lost in his head-phones. It was one day after he got a whiff of my athletic background that he just looked up and asked me, "Have you heard of Rich Roll?" With that simple question, this quiet, unassuming guy changed my life.

Rich Roll had written a book called *Finding Ultra* that chronicled his path of life reversal from an overweight, forty-year-old alcoholic who thought he was having a heart attack to becoming one of the fittest men on the planet, competing in the Ultraman Competition in less than a year. This 320-mile mega triathlon brought together the fittest and perhaps craziest athletes in the world. If that wasn't enough, he would then find himself in the Epic Five—five full Ironman Triathlons completed in the span of a week.

But it was Rich's secret weapon, which the tile guy shared with Jim that afternoon, among the sawdust and chaos, that really changed things. Rich had switched to a completely plant-based diet on that journey. Jim had always looked at food like fuel, regardless of the time of day. Eat and eat often, things like a huge bowl of pasta for breakfast. He also knew that every athlete's body responds differently to the physiological stress of training and to the breakdown and utilization of nutrition. He thought about his own signs, his mood swings and spikes in energy, and the fog that sometimes enveloped his brain. By the end of that nondescript conversation, Jim had committed to going to Chapters book store and purchasing *Finding Ultra*. With the opening of the cover, Jim stepped into a whole other world.

There was an instant connection to this man on his quest for sobriety and self-discovery. In addition to the training and nutrition, it opened Jim's eyes to spirituality as a way of living. Meditation, mindfulness, and yoga all seemed like fairy-dust tools to the sweat-equity mindset of the rower who made shit happen in his life. But for some reason, it just seemed to land through Rich's story. It is here that the idea of grace and flow first began to lift off the page and infuse its lure into Jim's subconsciousness. Rich went about establishing a new mindset and self-growth code based on discipline, commitment, and the universal laws of gratitude, grace, and personal forgiveness, fueled by plants. Jim began to find his next adventure within a blender and followed many of the tips and tricks within the book to refuel him post workout and throughout the day on the job site.

It took only one week for Jim to feel like he'd been hit over the head with a brick, woken up, and found that the world had changed. He felt an internal buzzing, with all his senses seemingly more alive and in tune to the world before him. The stiffness in his body, which he'd attributed to the mileage of training, had all but vanished. In addition, his energy and mood levels seemed to stabilize. He became acutely aware that his daily energetic dips had levelled out. Well, if those shakes were the Kool-Aid, he was going Jonestown on this plant-based shit. Next up, he removed gluten and dairy from his diet, to which his tightness and internal inflammation completely disappeared. In addition, his training output and recovery shot through the roof.

Well, that was it, a pure game changer, and there would be no going back. The nutrition train was full steam ahead and now blew the whistle on the self-growth locomotive. Jim began diving into the world of the Rich Roll Podcast. It was here that Rich, with his diverse guests, would spin tales of inspiration, athletic achievement, spirituality, and personal development. Rich, his guests, and a plant-based lifestyle became Jim's immediate circle of influence, which did its best to protect him from the pressures of life and arm him with the knowledge to be more than he currently was as a man.

While I was playing Tony Robbins, Brooke found a suitable school for the girls, which happened to be a three-minute drive away. Like a mother protective of her cubs, she ensured that the next handful of years spent there would be the best choice for both of them. Roots were being firmly dug in, and finally, it seemed time to cement our family flag. I finally did it. I conceded and embraced the life manual that was handed to us when we crossed into adult life. You know the one, where Page 173 states, "Thou shalt settle down and raise a family within the guidelines set forth by societal norms and financial expectations." And so, it is written, and so, it shall be.

The Road to Mordor

The Old Seaside Inn became a stunning and classic call back to the glory days of Hollywood. Gorgeous stone and woodwork met the tiled floor in a mesmerizing composition of beauty. It was class all the way from the moment one entered to the moment one left.

Jim would be overseeing the bar-manager duties and helping the restaurant manager and overall general manager the wise men had hired. Knowing that the captain's chair would be his one day, Jim went to work, creating big-city inspired cocktails, hiring the appropriate staff, and working on creating the bar lounge's aura, which would include wall-mounted televisions playing classic films from the golden age, like *Casablanca* and *From Here to Eternity* for the guests as they sat and enjoyed an evening out.

Now the wise men had established themselves as brilliant business owners; however, it should be noted that the grocery-store business is not the restaurant business. Regardless, the powers that be had decreed from their lofty throne atop Mt. Olympus that the OSI would open on Mother's Day. If you listened carefully, you would have heard Homer Simpson chime in with the biggest "D'OH!" all the way from Springfield. Mother's Day is the busiest day of the year in the restaurant world. But orders are orders, and so the doors opened.

Day one of the OSI exploded over a series of special sold-out seatings throughout the day and into the night. The team did their best with the high-paced environment, which was an old friend to Jim. As Mother's Day rolled to a close, so did any further semblance of normal life for Mr. Gardiner. The restaurant exploded with business and never slowed down. In a blink of an eye, day one became day fifty-six without a single day off. The whispers on that Mexican Beach had now landed him bound for life.

The first dramatic turn of events happened only one week into the opening and directly in line with the owners' track record of hiring unworthy team members. They abruptly shit-canned the hotel's general manager not because he didn't know what he was doing but because he didn't want to do things their unconventional way.

Boom. I found myself running the entire property and holding down the restaurant and the bar of one of the busiest properties on the island. It was insane actually. I planted my flag in the sleepy town of Qualicum only to have it feel like I was transported back to Los Angeles each evening. Then it happened. I don't remember which night or which interaction caused it, but I felt that tingly sensation in the back of my arm. The needle going in and the rush of adrenaline churning through my body. All of a sudden, I was somebody again as the eyes and glances would come my way. The conversations. The invites. In retrospect, this was exactly why I'd given my father-in-law an "F" bomb response back in Mexico. I knew I was powerless to stop it once it returned. That powerful ringing began to take hold once more.

With almost two months without a day off, Jim was becoming more and more disconnected from his family. They seemed like shadows that would come and go in the early stages of one's sleep and then a distant memory upon waking. The ninety-hour work weeks took hold, and the trifecta of chaos that had been so prevalent in the big-city scene began to feed on his soul once more.

Behind the bar, and from deep within his pocket, the ring of evil called to him. The consistent *stress* was now at an all-time high, and the steel cage was closing tightly on any semblance of roaming freedom in the world. Behind Jim, and in his very hands, lay the dark instrument of *alcohol*, its effect just enough to find the will to keep going and create an alternate reality to which he could escape. But it was the *attention*, in combination with these other elements, that truly pulled him into the darkness. The evil eye of Sauron came in the form of women that clamored and swooned, lining up to engage in conversation with the would-be traveler, actor, athlete, and whatever else they thought Jim might be. Each night, Jim would slowly lose hold of himself, till eventually, he couldn't handle the dark pull any longer. He would soon don the dark mask of shame.

The environment that Jim swore he would never return to was eating away at him once again, challenging his will. He could feel himself slipping, losing control of reason, until one fateful night, he pushed the boundary too far, and there was no going back. That blurred line between fantasy and reality, between flirtation and action, was crossed.

I saw the red flags. Heck, so could anyone else who watched this scene playing out. Instinctively, I knew that the flags would be replaced by screaming trumpets should the line get crossed. Boy, was I bang on! Hold your pet bunnies close, ladies and gentlemen. This woman became completely infatuated, like one step away from hiding a boiling pot in her designer bag.

It was a rough go for me, and I sure wish I'd made a left instead of a right. I wish I hadn't done a lot of things I did in my life, but the reality is that every action has a reaction. I knew the fallout would eventually come, which only added to my volcanic stress. The glances and whispers began. All of this under the very roof my father-in-law had built and entrusted to me to run.

A Yuletide of Blue Redemption

Salvation from his transgressions and stress-filled slave labor came in the form of a Christmas present a handful of weeks early. It was too large to be wrapped, but the twenty-seven-foot-long blue racing shell fit perfectly by the side of the house. Each morning, it would take its position on top of Jim's vehicle for the fifteen-minute drive to Cameron Lake while the late-fall air signaled the hopeful change to the most wonderful time of the year.

It wasn't exactly the perfect lake to row on, but at the same time, it was. It fit the self-purgatory blend of reality and fantasy in which Jim was stuck. The morning landscape at the lake was primal in its surroundings and energy. The waterway was dark and mysterious like the eerie, mythical legends that accompany its 5.5 km length. There were countless tales of the cold, unknown fathoms of its icy waters. Planes, trains, and automobiles have apparently disappeared into its murky depths. Yes, that is a movie title and with a highway on one side, an old train track on the other, and small planes flying overhead, you get the point. The lake also had steep mountainous bluffs rising on all sides, as if the gods themselves would gather to watch Jim wage war every day.

The accompanying score to the drama was stone-cold silence in all its mysterious wonder. Depending on the day, the winds would channel in through the mountain pass and bounce around the stadium walls, creating waves and chaos. This lake was unpredictable at best, but the warrior in him would hone his skill of assessment and decide whether or not to challenge the gods and venture out into the blackness all alone. This became his arena, and unlike other rowing waterways, he felt it was his and his alone. Just one man, seeking redemption through physical pain and dedication with only the morning silence. Valhalla had arrived...

Santa's sleigh was also on its way in the form of two fully purchased tickets for Mom and Dad Gardiner to come for a visit. Dad's health had been on the decline since Jim was last home to help with the "farewell to Prospect Ave" move. He knew the grand clock of life was ticking, but it was more about the proper reunion with the warmth and love that colored lights and Christmas carols can bring. His parents had never met his youngest daughter, and only once met his oldest, at just six weeks old. This was about bonding with their grandkids and hopefully reinvigorating that holiday wonder in their old eyes. It had left them both when their boy elf had become a man and moved to New York City.

The two girls bounced on their toes with excitement, their hands and face pressed up against the large window, waiting for the tiny plane to arrive at the single-strip runway. The small group of travelers then descended the tiny ramp, and the world slowed down for Jim. The girls' rhythmic up and down motions began to slow, and their words turned into a faint hum. There his parents were now, standing on the tarmac, and a blanket of safety seemed to warm him while the holiday tunes danced like sugar plums through his head. The pain of his hotel escapades seemed to recede as his mind transported him back in time to his mom's gentle touch while rolling up his sleeve, the needle delivering him a reprieve from suffocation.

The thump of feet hitting the wood floor and then the pitter-patter scurry down a dark hallway announced that the magical morning had arrived. As he pried himself out of bed, he realized that this was what Jim's parents had always heard in those long-ago mornings. He always made a point of getting up before Brooke (or in this case, any adult in the house) and soaking up the excitement that was unfolding in two sets of wondrous eyes. The girls would jockey for position among the unusually large number of gift-wrapped presents that year. Innocent banter consisted of self-proclamations of what this was or that was. Careful consideration was given to the strategic opening order as only a seven- and four-year-old can. Jim just sat on the floor with them, his coffee in one hand and his heart in the other. There were no words to add to this youthful bliss as his two mischievous elves peeked, shook, and weighed each present like young Sherlock Holmes and Watson on the scent.

I'd like to think that there were six children around the tree that morning, each of us in our own bubble of joy. I can't help but remember the feeling of this being a fresh start for me, as the sights and sounds provided a sense that everything would be okay. The girls took turns attacking their plunder of holiday treasure while laughter and smiles poured from the older kids in attendance. As an only child, I couldn't help but wonder if they would serve as compasses for each other in adult life, and what roles they would play as the beauty of youth faded. They were so happy. As were my parents. They sat surrounded by kids on Christmas morning for the first time in their lives, and their eyes were alive with the scene. I wondered if they'd missed this sort of moment as much as I did. My answer is yes, and that's the end of that story.

That magical morning was pure joy in its most lethal form: love. It oozed from the crackling fire of early morning. It permeated the air with the scent of apple cinnamon mixed with freshly brewed coffee, the glow of the early morning lights, and the soft holiday music layered beneath the joyous smiles and wondrous eyes of magic. By my own design, with the support of Brooke and perhaps with the help from the universe, I was able to reconstruct a bridge back to innocence. For me, it became my ultimate Christmas reality. One that has vaulted to the top of the list of those mythical days of the calendar.

The holiday memories were capped off by an entire family dinner at the OSI. Jim's parents' time on the island was drawing to a close, and with it came a growing feeling that this would be their last trip anywhere. His dad's health was declining, and the pulmonary disease COPD would claim all but thirteen percent of his lungs, reducing him to a life tethered to oxygen. Jim's mother's brain would slowly begin to show signs of decay, its once sparkling radiance now becoming a mere lightbulb at the end of too many clicks on the switch of time. But at least the family felt whole in this moment, spread out around a large table, generations together in life's ultimate equation of happiness... Or so it should have been.

I looked around at everyone's smiles and loving laughter, at the innocent kids misbehaving and the older men at the table encouraging them to do so. The once pristine walls around me were now becoming a prison, and thoughts of a jailbreak began to seep into my mind. There was no way to escape the ghostly whispers of failure and betrayal that seeped in through the gateway, attacking my smile and eroding my heart.

When goodbyes were exchanged at the airport, I wanted to climb into my folk's suitcase and feel the safety of long ago. The kids hugged their grandparents a little longer this time, perhaps knowing that they would never see them again. As the door to the small plane closed, I felt the final nail being driven into the lid of my coffin. I stood just as Little Jimmy had done back in the far-off land of dreams, thinking, *Don't leave.*

The Council of Ghosts

There was no magic spell chanted or ancient puzzle piece reconstructed to open the portal. It was as simple as seeing his parents go and realizing that the holiday fantasy was over. The eerie voices flooded in through the crack in his soul, haunting his every move. They would begin in the cold dark of the morning as Jim sat alone in the kitchen with the silence of coffee.

"How did you end up here? What happened?"

Those taunts would continue on the vastness of Cameron Lake in front of the spirits that would gather along the mountains to watch the spectacle unfold.

"All your medals can't hide your betrayal and failure."

Jim would wage war against the shadowy figure that was relentless in its pursuit. Some days, he would be victorious, and some days, the entity would stand atop the podium. These morning battles would dictate the strength and resolve to handle his other visitors, whom he would surely witness during the day. If he was fortunate enough to see his girls before the endless workday, the ghost of Little Jimmy would stand with his son on either side of the girls in the kitchen.

> *"Why did you have more kids? Gonna abandon them too, probably."*

When his wife would give him his send-off kiss, the ghosts would claw at his legs, trying to scrape away his sanity.

> *"That's the only kiss that should matter, you scumbag."*

The real test each day was when he set foot in the haunted house of his workplace, surrounded by prison walls oozing with shame.

> *"You piece of shit. Everyone knows."*

With each passing day, these whispers were unavoidable and followed him around the grounds of the hotel. His stress was mounting, made worse by the recent owners' decision to fire the restaurant manager. Now Jim was the only management figure overseeing the restaurant, the bar, the hotel, and all the staff.

When I had to fight for a few days off to make it to the racecourse in the summer, I drew a line in the sand and managed to get the wise men to concede. Even though I won that battle for sanity, the war was beating me. Sometimes, the sun rises over a dark horizon when we least expect it and brings with it a glimpse of light that illuminates an escape hatch. This latest ghostly presence arrived out of nowhere.

The apparition was the owner of a resort and golf community up island in the Comox Valley. He had invited me to lunch to thank me for being a good ally to the manager of the neighboring property he owned. *Free lunch never hurt anyone,* I thought, so I was happy to take the offer.

This guy, the Kingpin (as I like to think of him), was schmoozing me like no one's business. He was recounting the exceptional service I'd provided him and his lady friend one evening while at the OSI and complimenting me on the tight ship I ran. The owner's rough and

286 | ALL IN WITH LOVE

unpolished personality and ego fit perfectly with his role as carnivorous land developer and business mogul. Who else could create a community with its own postal code, complete with golden fire hydrants?

It didn't take long for Jim's phone to ring a few days later. The Kingpin invited him up island to see the resort firsthand, complete with a guided tour. Now things got interesting. When Jim pulled up to the seven thousand-square-foot resort clubhouse in all its majestic splendor, complete with two restaurants and a golf shop, he knew he wasn't in Kansas anymore. The ninety-eight villa units were scattered in different sections on the surrounding land, adjacent to parts of the eighteen-hole golf course. This was paradise, and a drop of saliva began to hang from the corner of Jim's mouth. Once inside, his eyes beheld a large, double-sided staircase that led up to banquet rooms and the owner's cigar-scented palace.

As Jim cut through the dense vapors upstairs and took a seat, he realized that this was the big time. Living on an island only had so much opportunity for vertical growth. The Kingpin began his pillow talk of inclusion, with Jim realizing almost instantly that he himself was being presented the keys to run this empire. The weight of the moment was profound, and Jim knew that this was perhaps a golden opportunity.

As the piece of paper slid across the desk, and he saw the number written on it, a deal was struck, though not officially. When he gazed upon the six-figure salary staring him dead in the face, his fate was already sealed. The Kingpin would give him everything he would ask for: a normal work week with humane hours, time off for all his rowing events, a large corner office, and free reign to build the empire.

The ride home for me that day was extra-long. I had never seen money like that, nor did I feel worthy of it. I wanted it but still felt confused by it all. If I was alone, I would have paid the toll and taken that walk instantly. But this was a family decision, one that would require some serious discussions with my wife and her father.

I sought an answer in the only place that could deliver it: inside a rowing shell. Among the tribal council of apparitions that gathered at the lake, I found it, during one of the last grueling sessions before the upcoming championships. I decided to stay at the OSI and honor the work I had started and the life I had signed up for, damn the consequences.

Jim was milling through some paperwork in his office when his father-in-law entered through the glass doors. "Take the job up island," he said plainly. "They won't change."

Confusion filled the air while Jim processed what was going on.

"They won't hire anyone to help you out," his caring father-in-law said. "They just don't get it. Go. They won't give you what you need," he softly advised.

The fact that my own father-in-law, one of the mafioso himself, told me to get out, made me so proud to be married to his daughter, and yet so bloody nauseous that I had betrayed him as much as her with my shenanigans. It left me no choice but to pick up the phone and accept the offer.

To date, I believe nine managers have gone through the revolving door of the wise men's OSI. But that day, the universe took the wheel with my new job commencing in one week... as soon as I got back from reuniting with some friendly ghosts.

The way the sun kisses the water in the early morning is a poetic painting; on race day, it is a complete universal masterpiece. I was finally standing at the water's edge once again, before three long days of racing, when a calm fell over me. The weight of the OSI had been lifted, and I felt my shoulders rise. The air of possibility and new lands was now in my sights, and despite all the ups and downs over the past two years, and hidden secrets, I felt a sense of peace. My old running mates were back by my side, and together, we would share some epic racing moments in the days that would follow. I don't think I was ever more prepared at the starting line than I was back then after spending a full year out back in the dark on a cold steel rowing machine. It was my time, and I took full advantage of the moment. The weekend concluded with four gold medals and one silver to add to my collection. With it, another page turned on my insatiable quest to find "me."

The Magic Castle

The director of operations assumed his conductor-like position in a large decked-out corner office, complete with a commanding view over the domain in front of him. He began forging a new cultural identity for the resort, and the symphony of success would come from all the key players contributing their unique and individual gifts. In total, 250 employees lined the orchestra pit, each with a part to play in the overall composition, one whose energetic and uplifting score would change the aging and old perception of the resort across the land.

Jim could feel the surge of excitement as he entered the mahogany boardroom for his first management meeting. It was a fresh start with free reign and team players to help make his time at the resort a success. Like his days in the boathouse, he brought the vigor and bravado to rally the troops. On his right was the food and beverage manager, Slick Nick. He was a young and energetic man who seemed to have one too many hands in multiple cookie jars, always working the angles. Next to him was an old buddy of Slick's, Charles, the head chef. Napoleon himself might have been taller, but even his arrogance would be dwarfed by the big-city chef now living on the island. Across from Jim was Rob, a fellow American and head of the golf department, who had the honor of being married to the owner's daughter. Lastly, the banquet and special events coordinator, Jessica, a single mother doing her part in this world to make a living and raise a young man.

If the top-secret plan had a code name, it would have been "Injection." The resort had become associated with the old stuffies living atop the hill in their own kingdoms, which frankly, they did. Jim and his merry band of men and women needed to inject vitality back into not only the resort but also the Comox Valley's perception of it. This three-part prime directive came from the cigar palace atop the dual staircase: bring a young and youthful energy back to the resort; have the most profitable upcoming fall and holiday season ever; and create a unique family Christmas experience. Oh, you bet your bottom dollar that last one perked up those billboard ears on the Cydot elf. Mr. Christmas was given the green light to build a holiday destination to be experienced by people coming from far and wide.

The mad composer began to pen the symphony, starting first with the title. "The Holiday Resort Walk" would be an interactive extravaganza of lights, music, fires, outdoor movies, games, and a do-it-yourself s'mores station, all in the name of a few chosen charities. This undertaking would require bodies, and what better way to foster community engagement than getting the surrounding residential community to volunteer? An unused downstairs section of the clubhouse was converted into the appropriately named "Santa's Workshop," where helpers would get to work on crafting Jim's scheme.

Upstairs in his vapor palace, the Kingpin shifted through some of Jim's makeshift sketches of the soon-to-be Christmas spectacular. Jim waited, his eyes squinting from the smoke.

"Jimmy," the man growled, his stogie tucked safely in the corner of his mouth, "I knew... I *knew* you were the one."

I don't think he ever called me Jim, as a matter of fact. But as I sat in that chair, I felt like I was in the presence of Don Corleone, and far be it from me to correct him. Next, he casually flipped me a paper document from the mess in front of him.

"See what you make of this. I want us to go big, baby," he said. "We didn't pull the trigger on this last year, but with you, Jimmy, might it be time?"

Jim looked up from the document and smirked, another cog in his creative wheel beginning to turn. It didn't take long for his trigger finger to find its mark.

Jim descended the dual staircase under the warmth of focused lights. The cameraman captured the scene while the director of operations and now television host spoke about the magic of the resort and surrounding real-estate community. With a charming and natural delivery, the once-upon-a-time actor found his spotlight again.

The Kingpin's suggestion saw Jim signing a contract with a local television provider to sponsor a series of commercial segments showcasing not only the resort but the surrounding businesses in the valley as well. The frosting on this creative cake was that Jim himself was slotted into the host spot. Immediately, things were firing on all cylinders at the resort and some joy crept back into his life.

Back at home, Jim would enter through the front door at a reasonable time and be greeted with the most amazing jump hugs from his daughters, their tight squeezes filling his heart. His eyes would catch those of his wife, witnessing the love from the kitchen. The rose-colored optics of money and momentum had certainly delivered the Gardiners a lovely hue of red.

One morning, he sat at his computer, balancing his youngest on a knee and sipping coffee while scrolling through some rowing websites. "Holy sh—." He realized his daughter was staring at him and caught himself before inviting the backlash from Brooke.

"What is it?" Brooke chimed in from the adjacent kitchen.

"They just announced that the US Nationals will be on the east coast next August. In New England actually, at one of my old racecourses." His voice sounded younger and inspired.

He didn't see Brooke's eye-rolling reaction, but he could feel it from behind the wall. He shifted his little one off his knee to the nearby couch and grabbed a scrap piece of paper. A pen began scribbling down some math. "2015 minus 1992." The result was circled: "23." Jim smiled and sat back in his chair, swiveling around just once before picking up his cell phone.

The connection at the other end was fumbling chaos. His dad was notorious for having more than two thumbs, which caused his phone to always dance widely in his gorilla mitts.

"Thumbs!" his son decreed.

"Shocking," his dad responded, half chuckling at his own goofiness.

"How's that new pacemaker treating ya?"

"Ah, good actually. Don't even know it's there, to be honest," his dad said. "The damn oxygen tank is a pain in the ass though, that's for sure, but I think I'll live a few more years."

Jim smirked at his dad's sense of humor, negative as usual. "Good, because I need you to stay alive until next August," he said, offering some cheeky humor of his own.

There was a hearty laugh. "Why's that?"

Jim's finger landed on the scrap paper. "It has been twenty-three years since you and Mom last saw me race."

Jim continued on about how cool it would be for them to see him race again and threw in some serendipitous sprinkles of full-circle moments for good measure. The course itself was barely an hour's drive north for his parents. The real question would be how well his dad could navigate the walking, with his portable oxygen man-purse, and deal with the August heat. That aside, the phone call ended with an agreement between father and son.

The phone no sooner clicked off than it sprang to life again with text messages to Matthias and Leslie, his old rowing mates. If Jim was going to make the trip for high-level competition and a shot at home-turf glory, he wanted his best mates by his side. In the coming days, a small contingent representing the Vancouver Rowing Club would be his wingmen and set a training cycle in motion for a reunion with a river that had helped forge his destiny.

Her young neck craned upward to get a glimpse of the star fifty feet in the air, which to a five-year-old was right up there with the real stars. All the large fir trees surrounding the resort clubhouse were adorned with rows of holiday lights, illuminating the surroundings in hues of festive bliss.

"Look! It's the Grinch!" her older sister blurted out, pointing.

They were gone then, off to see the Grinch and other famous characters, leaving the adults to stand by the warmth of a cozy fire that burned from a large steel barrel.

"I think I nailed it on this one," Jim offered while putting his arm around Brooke.

It was the opening night of the Holiday Resort Walk, and hundreds of people had come to the Magic Castle atop the hill, some for the very first time. It would be the first of nine nights that would welcome thousands of people when all was said and done. Jim took his wife's hand and began walking through the winter wonderland, feeling the love that it gave its visitors. The rented surround-sound system was set at just the right volume for all the best holiday tunes. Flashes from cameras would capture the children's faces as they stood next to their favorite holiday characters. A life-sized gingerbread house would gather thousands of signatures on the inside of its walls. Kids would skip through the Candy Cane Forest, leading them on their way to photo ops with Mr. Claus on his red throne. Everywhere one turned there were sights and sounds associated with the most wonderful time of the year. Outdoor movies would play, and families would sit by an open fire to make delicious s'mores treats together. Jim's scanning eyes returned to his approaching little ones, each coming to grab his hand so the world would know he was their dad.

I like to think that, in that moment, I had made them proud. Sure, they loved my rowing medals, and they loved that I had been on television and so forth. But that night, I truly felt they loved me for creating that experience for them. In retrospect, perhaps I had... and for Little Jimmy as well.

They were soon to find a place upon each knee before the large outdoor movie screen. I did my best to explain why *It's a Wonderful Life* would stand the test of time for holiday movies. Under a red and green haloed night, James Stewart, aka Jimmy Stewart, spoke to the Jimmy lost inside me and to my girls. Little did I know that I was also speaking to the James in me who had yet to emerge. I softly glanced first to my right and then to my left; my angels were lost in the large screen. I pulled their heads closer to my chest and surrendered to the moment, hoping that it wouldn't escape me like those conversations with my Cydot neighbor Dave on the edge of a dock so long ago.

From the screen, the movie angel spoke. "You see, George, you've really had a wonderful life. Don't you see what a mistake it would be to just throw it away?"

The Losers, The _____, and The Crumbling Wardrobe

The holiday came and went, and with it, the highest seasonal revenue in the history of the resort. By the end of December, Jim was labelled a hero, but by the beginning of February, he was quickly becoming the red-headed stepchild. Cocaine can do that. Jim's two main team members got caught doing blow at eleven p.m., while he was home asleep by nine.

The Kingpin found out and began to grow what would become two pancake-sized boils on his arse named Slick Nick and Stubby Chef. He wanted them both gone, and it was Jim's job to send them packing.

To be fair, it wasn't just their descent into the lure of white-powdered rails that was their demise but more so their attitude about work. The arrogant chef only wanted to offer food that he deemed worthy of his culinary paygrade. Meanwhile, when Don Corleone wants a flipping omelet on the dinner menu, put a flipping omelet on the dinner menu. Jim called them out on the drugs but still tried his best to rally the troops. They were a big part of the resort's success after all. But they wouldn't give the owner what he wanted. So, the Kingpin lost trust in his commander in chief, who lost faith in his lieutenants.

Jim straightened his tie and adjusted the same nicely fitted blue suit he'd worn on his very first day at the resort. A knock at the door announced the executive chef, who took the firing with a nod of his head and very minimal conversation. Next up, Jim's closest partner at the resort, Slick Nick, was going to present a more heartfelt discussion. The two had spent hours and hours together over the past eight months, crafting this new improved version of the resort. The conversation was as classy as it could have been, and then the two stood, shook hands, and exchanged well wishes.

Jim emerged a short time later to the eerie quiet of the desolate lobby. It was wintertime, and the lack of golf and guest traffic compounded the quiet. He could sense the ocean receding slowly, silently trying to catch him and the resort off guard. There was an unsettling energy that Jim could feel, though he couldn't identify it. When the two now ex-employees appeared, carrying their belongings, there were no words exchanged, not a glance or even a gesture, at least at first. Then Napoleon turned and saluted his time at the resort with his nub of a middle finger.

I went home that evening and told Brooke of the two buffoons and how the firing had gone. I have to say that I felt bad for them, and for myself, I guess. The key team had just lost two people, and I'd lost some of the respect of the owner. Oh well. Not my monkey, not my circus. My head hit the pillow peacefully that evening, and I slept like a baby. Meanwhile, the ocean was still receding.

The following day, Jim was pulled aside by a co-worker from the kitchen while on the way to his corner office.

"I just want to say how childish that was," said the interim chef, "and that I have no respect for either of those guys."

"Childish?" Jim responded, unsure of the context.

"Yeah. Texting the staff old pictures of you. Bullshit."

Jim began to move backwards toward his office, feeling panic rising. The bottom had just fallen out of his stomach as the wave of anxiety crashed the castle. The tsunami hit in the form of a twenty-year-old stigma.

I had known that someday, somewhere, it would come back to bite me right in the ass, and it finally had, taking a chunk right out of my designer suit. Those two weaselly little bastards had uploaded a bunch of pictures off the internet of me romping around as the T&A boob detective from twenty years before. For good measure, they'd included captions like "This is your GM" and "Nice ass, Mr. Big Shot." The tsunami's fall out was massive, with text messages having been sent to *all* the food and beverage staff and anyone else in the business for whom they had contact information. A fit of anger came over me like none I had ever experienced before (or since).

Jim stormed out of the clubhouse hell bent on finding them. He spent hours driving around town on this mission, heading for hot spots they were known to frequent. He was ready to open a can of whoop-ass on them both and wasn't scared in the slightest. The one prick was kneecap high and the other a scrawny wet bag of dicks. He would opt for Napoleon first, taking out the short, bigmouth while the bone rack cowered in fear. Jim's ego wanted payback. The last time he'd seen red was outside the Triple Inn in New York when he'd boot stomped some abusive drunk into unconsciousness.

Potential hot spot after hot spot yielded no prey, and as time marched on, the anger that was boiling inside of Jim began to shift toward damage-control mode, and then to panicked shame. *What the fuck do I do? How do I recover from this?* By the time a few hours had passed, all the anger had turned to depression, and he stood before the large doors of the resort clubhouse. He took a moment and then opted to turn back to the sanctuary of his own vehicle and the long drive back home.

He pressed play on another Rich Roll podcast, trying his best to surround himself with positive, inspirational energy. He would choose not to tell Brooke about the pictures and text messages right away. The anxiety and embarrassment it would create for her, coupled with his own shame, was too much. He was supposed to be the family's provider, the rock, the hero. Instead, he was nothing but a resort eye roll, a man crumbling under the weight of his own poor choices and an old stigma.

The Losers, The Witch, and The Crumbling Wardrobe

The lightning crashed, and the thunder rolled, announcing her presence. She rode in from the north, surfing the gale force winds like a point-break champion. Her silhouetted figure was illuminated by each lightning bolt of the gods. She tightly clutched her custom-built broom, her cape trailing in the wind of her descent toward the unsuspecting people below. When she arrived on the grounds of the Magic Castle, the earth shook with fear and the employees retreated to the shadows. Flames would follow her up and down the hallowed halls, and those upon whom her gaze fell would turn to stone. Broom Hilda had arrived at the resort.

Jim sat stunned in his office. The Kingpin had circumvented him and hired Hilda to be the new food and beverage manager. As the owner, he could do anything he wanted, but it was a clear sign that he had lost trust in his captain. But Ms. Hilda had a reputation as long as Danny Pelosi's rap sheet. She was a former employee turned manager who (as legend would have it) had been fired not once, not twice, but three times already. Apparently, she was a miserable wretch of a human who would berate staff and guests alike. No one could understand why she was back, but the whispers among the staff who had lived through those dangerous times told of smoke-laden romantic interludes in the upstairs palace that may or may not have happened. Regardless of all the stories, she was back, and she brought hell with her.

"We got a lot shit to clean up around here," Hilda proclaimed within milliseconds of meeting Jim. "Send me all the current staff schedules, asap." And just like that, she vanished to her downstairs lair with no time for pleasantries.

Now to be fair, I always—and, I repeat, *always*—give people the benefit of the doubt regardless of their past track record. I mean, I've spent most of this book telling you about Jim and Jimmy's innate ability to "get" to people, find that common denominator, and be able to bridge the gap to create a co-existing environment. I gave her some space for a day and then decided to approach her downstairs lair to break the ice.

Her snake-riddled head was buried in work on her desk when Jim popped his around the corner of her office. "Hope your day is going well," Jim said with welcoming boyish charm. "We should grab lunch and discuss—"

"I'll let you know if I need anything. I have a menu to build." Her eyes looked right through his soul and began to turn his powerful rowing legs to stone.

"Okay, you know where to find me," he said, trying his best to disarm her before retreating to the safety of his upstairs office.

He would continue to try, over and over as a matter of fact, until he exhausted every strategy in the playbook that had worked so well in his life to that point. It took exactly four days for the first unsuspecting banquet server to burst into tears from Hilda's reign. She had spewed words like "useless" and "pathetic" at the poor girl, barely a young woman, and left the server a blubbering mess. This was just a precursor to Hilda's problematic behavior, like charging snakes-first into Jim's office unannounced and demanding insights into this or that or openly dismissing him in team meetings, which were supposed to be led by him.

There were times when he cowered in his office, and there were times when he stood up and demanded respect, but the bottom line was that he knew he was walking a very thin line. One misguided curse word or derogatory remark, and she would get what she wanted. She could call him a dick, and did, but he couldn't call her anything. If he uttered anything that held the slightest hint of impropriety, that would be all they needed... "they" being her and the Kingpin, of course.

She had been deputized by him. I knew that the Kingpin couldn't shit-can me that too soon after the embarrassing boob-detective incident.

That would be too obvious and allow me leverage to go after him for unfair practices. So, they proceeded to make my life a flipping hell.

We've all met people who seemed to have been miserable their entire lives, and Hilda was one such person. It's a shame because at some point, long ago, I suspect that she wasn't like that. It's sad. It was just so foreign to me to be that miserable and to have that much hate running through one's soul. It was this moment in my life when anxiety really began to surface in me, something I'd always thought really only affected other people. I was wrong. Deep, restless anxiety began to creep around inside and take hold of my essence. Perhaps it had been there unnoticed for a while, like a slow growing moss, but with Broom Hilda came the magic fertilizer needed to make that anxiety grow and start running rampant.

The telltale signs followed me home, and the jumping hugs from my girls and innocent gazes from Brooke ceased to happen, or perhaps I just couldn't allow myself to relish in their sanctuary. Brooke became my therapist, to whom I would deliver my daily confession of anxiety. As the turmoil grew over the months that followed, I had no choice but to tell her of the pictures from the movie and the incredible shame and embarrassment I was dealing with.

Even the liquid safe haven of Cameron Lake wasn't impervious to the state of my life each day. Thankfully, the pact I'd made with my father still held sway, but even that was beginning to lose its power as Hilda's spell cast its shadow even across the hallowed expanse of Cameron Lake. With about three weeks to go to the big race back on home soil, I imploded.

The life of a single sculler and all that comes with it couldn't compete in a mental world already chock-full of anxiety, depression, grief, and guilt. I was alone in life and on the water... and the ghosts were relentless. The pressure of not performing in front of my folks grew; my fatigue, both mental and physical, seemed to get worse and worse as the nationals approached. The boat wasn't moving the way I wanted during a handful of practices, and so the shadow of doubt grew into a full-on solar eclipse when I broke rhythm during an all-out race workout and gave up. The only living being on the lake began to sob uncontrollably. Soon the tears became mixed with anger, and my screams echoed from the mountainous walls, creating an ongoing chorus of pain.

298 | ALL IN WITH LOVE

I remember feeling so defeated as I made my way towards the club-house after that morning of surrender. My intention was crystal clear once I sat at my desk. The only thing between me and turning on my computer were my headphones, through which streamed the voice of Rich Roll, directly into my soul. The episode playing was number 166 and featured the astonishing story of James Lawrence, the Iron Cowboy. James had completed the unbelievable feat of the 50/50/50. This was perhaps the greatest endurance achievement on the planet. The Iron Cowboy completed fifty full triathlons, in fifty states, in fifty days. Let that sink in for a moment.

Jim couldn't stop listening as he settled into his desk. The headphones were still connected as he powered on the computer and sat waiting for it to spring to life. A few strikes on the keyboard and "US Rowing" came into sharp focus on the screen. His surrender would include withdraw-ing from the pressure of the singles race to just focus on the team boats. The cancel button was in his sights, the cursor moving for the kill strike.

"I honestly believe this is one of the greatest achievements in the history of (voluntary) human endurance," the velvet voice of Rich proclaimed, directly into Jim's cerebral cortex. His index finger immediately ceased all motion above the mouse's clicker.

"Just be empowered to do that hard thing in your life," the Iron Cowboy said. *"However low you are, wherever you are, there's someone out there that loves you, and there's someone out there that can support you, and there's a way to climb out of it."*

The defeated soul leaned back in his chair, letting that hand grenade of inspiration make its way to every part of his being. He scanned some of the papers lining his desk, many of them the scribblings of a man in a state of office paralysis. He shifted through a few until he found the one he wanted, upon which was boldly written, "Can ordinary inspire?" This was a stream of thought that he had been playing with recently, the idea of just another bloke being a beacon of inspiration for others, like the banter going on in his headphones.

This is what he needed… what others need during hard times. His mind began to churn; the dusty turbines of creation that had seemed dormant creaked and moaned as they grew to life. He picked up a piece of correspondence from the media company behind the resort's television campaign. Profound clarity struck, and for a moment, strength. He looked back at the computer screen and at that cancel button calling his name.

"Just be empowered to do that hard thing in your life," the Iron Cowboy said again in Jim's mind.

His trigger finger sprang to life on the "x," closing the screen and with it any further thought of surrender. He began to craft a possible weapon against the darkness.

He channeled something that day, and before he knew it, he was going to pitch his own show to the television company, Rich Roll style. He would sit down and host inspirational and motivational people from all walks of life: wellness advocates, authors, athletes, entrepreneurs, discussing their personal empowerment stories, all in the name of self-growth and impacting others. Out of the morning water meltdown, the companionship of Rich Roll, and surrounding pressures, *The Inspirational 30* was born. But first, he would get to enjoy six whole days away from Broom Hilda and her chaos.

Beethoven

The coolness from the tree branches overhead was a welcome reprieve under the August sun. The hustle and bustle of the regatta was in full effect, but even that glorious dance that had called him so many times before seemed to lose a few beats. Time changes people, or is it that people change over time? Regardless, no one, not even the mightiest warrior, is impervious to the end result: The curtain falls and the spotlight fades.

The highly contested event was spread out over four days on Lake Quinsigamond in Worcester, Massachusetts. The US Nationals brought out the rowing legends among competitors from all over North America. This was definitely a much larger and more contested arena than those of the Pacific Northwest and even Canada. Jim was surrounded by the usual suspects of Matthias and Leslie, of course, and there was big John, a powerhouse rower who had been a part of the magical eight down in

Seattle. Rounding out the group was Larry, the elder statesman of the squad who was as tenacious as they come.

When I first saw my folks approaching from a distance, I remember that my heart sank. It had only been two years since that amazing Christmas memory, and yet they both looked years older. I didn't get up right away as I was fixated on my dad's slow walk, his body weight and lack of lung capacity seeming like an insurmountable ball and chain. His new lifelong friend hung down from his broad shoulder like a designer handbag. A clear plastic tube made its way up from the machine, wrapping around his head and ears, and finally plugging into his nostrils. It was the only thing keeping him able to walk at all. By his side was Mom, his trusty companion, with her makeshift waddle gait and her arm securely fashioned to his own.

Jim stood up with a wave. Their smiles grew, seeing their only son, who was quick to greet his mom with a hug and offer a tap on the shoulder to his old man. Next, the official introductions rolled out with the Vancouver posse, including a reunion of sorts with Matthias. So many rowing yarns at the other end of the phone finally turned into a face-to-face meeting. The smiles and banter continued for a while, with Jim being the first to break it off. He had a job to do.

"I didn't come here for a T-shirt." Jim's catch phrase triggered the call to battle in his mind. It was the sparking phase that kicked off his pre-race prep. He wasn't there for the default token of attendance; he was there to compete.

For the men's singles, the field to get into the final was unknown. He knew nothing about the competition other than that many of the clubs in attendance were known for being powerhouses and were sure to produce fast scullers. He looked over to his mom and dad, lost in a simple conversation while he stood with a storm of pressure rising, wanting nothing more than to do "good" in front of them one more time. With a large exhalation, Jim grabbed hold of his boat and began the walk of conquest toward the dock.

I morphed into that glorious singular focus as I rowed towards the starting area. My blades seemed sturdier than ever as they locked into the water during my warmup progression. The power strokes felt smooth and the start sequences fast. Satisfied with my work and feeling ready to go, I entered the chute and hooked up with my starting platform. This was it, game time. There were no ghosts, no voices, no bullying Hilda, just me alone. Most athletes feel the nervous energy that accompanies high performance, and then some have the ability to morph into complete and utter white-hot focus, in which everything else is non-existent. That laser intensity came over me, and with it came a sense of calm as I sat waiting for my cue. It was another moment in time I wish I could bottle: the moment of creation, that point in time like the Big Bang, ready to forge life. I found myself sitting in it, in the beautiful nothingness before everything.

Jim's eyes peered upward to the red flag at its apex, fixating on any whiff of movement. When he spotted it, his blades propelled the boat forward like a beast let loose from a cage. The boat exploded off the line, and Jim began to build power and speed with each aggressive stroke. He was fast off the line and had always known it, but now the field of strangers felt its crushing magnitude. Within twenty strokes, he had a full-length lead over everyone in the six-boat field. As he began to settle into his race pace and continued the assault, it became clear that he had a commanding lead. The furled brow of intensity began to relax a bit. He had what every rower would want in a race: a perfect view of the field sprawled out behind him. This meant only one thing to Jim: His folks would see him rowing in the finals.

Back on shore, Jim reconvened with his squad and parents to enjoy the fact that he was going into the finals. Turns out that he had the fastest time from the qualifying heats, which was a good indicator that he was in the running. He knew he stood a good chance to medal if he could put it together one more time. Yes, one more time. That's the secret. There is always "one more time" in the life of an adventurer, and after the pummeling of years, the "one more time" grew heavier and heavier. *Time changes people.*

Jim tried to stay relaxed, sitting with his mom and dad, but could somehow feel it even in their smiles. That dreaded pendulum swing of expectation was taking place. It's a strange phenomenon where the nervous anxiety about not qualifying for the finals and not being able to showcase all the efforts of hard training swings like an ungraceful hammer to the anxiety of *not* medaling. To get so close and not have any validation was Jim's boogeyman in the closet.

That I was addicted to this need to be stamped-certified awesome, or handsome, or successful, or funny is so clear to me now that it brings me pain. I was an indentured servant to external validation and tangible praise, as getting those things was the only way I knew I was worth something, worth anything. Worse was the fact that the fierce warrior in me grew softer over the years, valuing any podium finish, no matter what color the plated medal might be.

"Do you remember that time I was so scared to swing a bat in little league?" Jim asked.

He was standing by his racing shell next to his father.

"Vaguely," his dad said. "Down at the old field."

"Yeah, the old Indian days, *Coach*," Jim said, nodding and playfully punctuated his title. "Well, I don't suppose you remember what you said to me?"

His dad searched the recesses of his memory but came up empty. "I can't even remember what movie we watched last night," he offered with a self-deprecating laugh.

Jim smiled. "You said, 'Swing and you won't be scared anymore'." The underlying impact sat in the air for a moment until Jim tapped the side of hull. "Time to walk to the plate."

His father nodded, still lost in long ago. "Good luck."

The warrior sat idle up at the starting platform in that beautiful moment of nothingness. There would be no oracle of wisdom that Friday afternoon as he waited on a non-descript lake that was inconsequential in the global scheme of things. There would be no summoning of ravens to broadcast one's fateful destiny. Jim knew in his heart that something was coming to an end. This was most likely his last solo race ever, and only if the rowing gods deemed it so would he summon up the magic one more time. He breathed deeply and honored the sacredness of it.

As the flag dropped, the blue missile hurled forward once again, brought to life by hours and hours of power forged in the discipline of commitment. Here he was blasting out of the start like a fearless soldier charging into the unknown strength of oncoming forces, not reckless but impassioned to leave a legacy of some kind. His course was straight as an arrow, and with each stroke, he could see his opposition falling off behind him. As he settled into his race pace, he could see that he had the lead.

The winner of the other heat was next to him in lane four and sitting almost a length back. A quick, intense scan of the course would gather the information he needed to process. Jim still had the lead, with lane four being the closest in second place. After that, there was a large gap playing out with each stroke. As they approached the halfway point, Jim was rowing smoothly even though the pain was beginning to mount. The speed of the boat next to him was increasing, creeping up and inching its way back into contention.

Soon the opposition was almost level with him, which was okay because that was part of Jim's race plan. Lead or no lead, if he smelled blood, no one would beat him in the last 250 meters.

His mind began to formulate the move as the pain receptors screamed louder and louder in his mind and body. Strategy is always a gamble. That was the beauty of the sport. Jim decided he would let his competition take a bit more water before unleashing the sprint from hell. There was about three hundred meters remaining, and things were playing out perfectly for the soon-to-be hero. He was now in second place, about a half a boat's length behind the leader, and there was still open water between them and the other two boats battling for that elusive bronze.

The crowd was on its feet. The cheers were growing louder, beginning to stretch across the water and make their way to the athletes. Jim was ready and hoped the rowing gods were in attendance to watch him drop the hammer on his unsuspecting victim. He flipped the switch to ignite the comeback.

"Boom!" The shockwave moved out from the blue racing shell with tremendous speed. The pressure increased and destiny was his. Except nothing happened. His brain commanded, but his heart didn't hear the call, or perhaps, it didn't want to listen. Truthfully, something *did* happen. For the first time in his rowing career, Jim wasn't willing to open the hurt locker and step inside to the abyss. He was alone and couldn't muster that fight any longer, the voices of pain and the comfort of knowing he didn't *have* to push seemed way louder than the burning desire to win. *People change over time.*

To most, this would seem a cowardly move, but for Jim, it was his surrender to a pressure that had been mounting for years. As the line approached and the horn sounded, a victory scream filled his ears about one and a half seconds ahead of his own. He crossed the line and glided into the silver-medal position. As the pain leaked out of his body, and the warrior briefly returned to the lost boy, a sense of joy surged through his veins as he thought about his folks.

All I wanted to do was hug my parents. I enjoyed a leisurely paddle back to the landing dock, purposefully enjoying the moment as it would soon only ever repeat in memory. I saw them right away, standing exactly where they'd stood twenty-three years earlier. They waved, to which I responded with a fist pump. Matthias met me on the dock and knelt down beside me.

"You did it," he said softly, "and they saw you do it."

He helped me to stand, steading my weary legs with his big frame. We embraced, and I became overwhelmed with emotion. I couldn't have held back the tears if I'd wanted to. I think they were a release from so many things.

Back at base camp, Jim's dad landed his of paw of a hand on his son's head with a tussle of his hair just like he used to do a lifetime ago.

"Way to go, kiddo!" he said enthusiastically.

His mom followed up with a congratulatory kiss on the cheek for his achievement. It was a wonderful moment that Jim felt he'd had a hand in orchestrating. *We do have some control over making dreams a reality,* he thought while basking in the warmth of the August sun that was outshone by the pure warmth he felt in his heart. At least fantasy and reality were on the same page for this chapter of his story.

With more racing to be done, it wasn't like the veil of pressure had completely lifted from his silver-medal shoulders. The following day, his old Cydot running mate Dave made the drive from Boston to spend the day at the racecourse and hang with him and his folks. It was another blessed reunion, which found his dad and Dave under the cooling tent of the regatta beer garden, enjoying some suds and conversation while Jim went to work with only one word on his mind: redemption. And this time, he'd brought along some friends.

There was only three hundred meters left in the men's quad race, a highly contested battle with their Vancouver boat sitting in second place. This was the exact spot where Jim had let go the previous day, and he knew it. But he also knew that the first-place boat was only half a length ahead, dead in his sights. His nostrils caught one last whiff of blood. It was time. Loud enough so that Big John sitting in the stroke seat could hear him, Jim cried, "UP!" The shift in rating began, kill-switch engaged. "Yes!" Jim barked, feeling the power and the surge.

Now in the red buoys, Jim cried out for another lift in rating. The men went deeper; the boat went faster. "YES!" he cried, as much for his own redemption as for his boat moving back up the leader. He saw the bow man from the other boat, almost dead even now. This was it, the last few red buoys marking the end of a legacy.

"UP!" he bellowed one last time. "Everything!!" he screamed. Matthias let out an agonizing cry, John grunted with each epic stroke, Larry wanted more, and Jim kicked open the door to the hurt locker one last glorious time. The boat jumped forward as the VRC brothers crossed the line with about a four-foot victory. The boys didn't know for certain but Jim did. He knew they had gotten them and secured the gold medal. As they glided into memory, Jim cherished every ounce of the pain surging through his veins and then the subsequent bliss of it dissipating into a profound and beautiful moment.

It was a fitting swan song to cap off a love affair between a boy and an oar, a warrior and a discipline, a man and his identity. This was Jim's masterpiece, his "Ode to Joy," culminating in a perfect crescendo. It was time to let go of the push. The top of the mountain is a precarious place, especially when the base is unstable.

I stood by the red jeep, giving a hug to my mom and dad before their drive back to the solitary confinement of apartment living. They were proud. I was proud. I'm still proud to this day. It would be almost four years before I would see them again, at a time when this weekend wouldn't even be remembered. Little did I know that this would be our last great memory together as a family. When they drove away, a hollow-ness crept in and I thought of my two girls and the potential memories with them that I'd opted out of, and of the ones still to come. Love in all its beauty surrounded me that day. I finally turned my gaze away from the diminishing red Jeep and back toward my girls, who would greet me as I exited the airplane back on the west coast, medals in hand and love in my heart.

A Funeral Pyre

Jim's hands did the trick and popped open the lid to a prescription bottle. A gentle tap with his finger, and one pill slid out onto his palm. It was quickly popped into his mouth and washed down with a fresh swig from his water bottle. For the first time ever, he was trying to calm the fire with prescription medication. His eyes closed, and his mind drifted to a Wickford bike ride and Malcolm's backyard, waiting for the desired effect to transport him far away from his surrounding office.

"Any idea who altered the schedule for the banquet servers!?" Broom Hilda bellowed like a foghorn in the mist as she charged into his office unannounced.

After nearly springing to the ceiling like a scared cat, he took a moment to process the situation, taking time to gather himself.

"Well!?" she demanded.

He lowered his head to examine some papers on his desk, raising his right hand slowly, with his index finger in the air, and shushing her abruptly.

"Shh!" He took a moment to calculate his next move. "Now, go outside and shut the door." He pointed to the exit. "When you're ready to reenter *my* office, knock first, and then wait for *my* acknowledgement. Then *you* may enter *my* office and speak to *me* like a human fucking being."

His index finger retracted, and then he dismissed her with a wave of his whole hand. She turned away and left in a huff. As Jim heard the door shut behind her, his right hand, still in the air, slowly flipped her the bird before falling to rest on the desktop.

She didn't knock or storm back in. I knew she wouldn't. She probably went through the whole clubhouse with her granny panties tied in a knot, bad mouthing me to whomever would listen. Oh, and for the record, to answer her accusatory question from when she'd barged into my office, she had altered the schedule herself. Right after, Jessica, the banquet manager, quit because she couldn't take working with Hilda any longer. The story seemed to pick up right where it had left off. There were days when I lost my shit, days when I calmly called her out, and days when she held the upper hand. After one more month of this abusive and demeaning relationship, I was left with only one option for salvation. I knew it was a crap shoot, with the odds not in my favor, but it was the only move I had left to play for my own personal dignity.

Jim sat up nice and tall at his desk, his gray tailored suit and salmon-colored shirt were carefully chosen, in case this was to be his last supper. His briefcase was positioned on the desk to his left, concealing his cell phone, which would sit out of view of his guests. He looked over a detailed paper in front of him, on which he had chronicled, to the best of his ability, all Hilda's unacceptable behavior and the situations in which she had overstepped her authority and ignored his basic human rights, with a list of appropriate witnesses to boot. He took a deep breath and exhaled peacefully. A knock at the door broke the silence.

"Come in," he said calmly.

Two women entered the office, sisters from the Human Resource Department, or rather, from the administrative office that "acted" as HR when issues arose. It was time to roll the dice. Jim was filing an official harassment claim.

His left hand casually moved behind the briefcase and pressed the large red button indicating that an audio recording had commenced. Mama Gardiner hadn't raised no fool. He would ensure that there were no mis-representations of what had been said in this meeting moving forward. Over the next forty-five minutes, Jim carefully reconstructed the various crime scenes, providing documented accounts, key witnesses, and the *piece de resistance*, his pill bottle, which he removed from the briefcase, shook for good measure (to make sure the sound was recorded), and read off the prescription date. When all was said and done, on that Friday afternoon in October, he knew that he'd just laid down an ultimatum worthy of Frank Green from his New York one-man show.

Damn the Consequences.

The severity of this ongoing fight didn't really land with me until four years later in the height of the global "Me too" movement. While I did not suffer any sexual abuse, I sure as shit suffered at the hands of someone of a different gender. It took nearly half a century for the term "bullying" to actually have any relevance to me. Because of my time with Hilda, I have a more profound belief in human rights regardless of sex, age, or position. My time at the resort in those last seven months disgusts me to this day, even while I know full well that my situation pales in comparison to the unwilling footprint left on so many others. Awareness was raised and a stand taken with #metoo. And I had made my stand that day and was better for having done so, no matter the outcome.

That outcome came a hell of a lot faster than Jim had expected. By Saturday, the next day, he noticed that his work email seemed to have vanished. On Sunday, he was sent a long-winded personal email telling him that his services were no longer required, using the usual vocabulary offered to someone being fired. A box with all of his personal items would be awaiting his pickup, tied up with the pretty bow of a nice severance check.

Even a T-Rex with a peanut-sized brain could see that the "generosity" of Jim's severance had been offered so that he wouldn't make any waves. The same gigantic lizard could also see that he clearly had a wrongful dismissal case, if he chose to pursue it. Let's just say that Jim Gardiner went all in, sliding those chips into the center of the table in a formal complaint to the labor board. *Why not?* he thought. *Why not make sure this doesn't happen again at the resort?* Plus, Jim's ego wanted to raise a few more boils smack dab on the Kingpin's kiester. Before the labor-board claims officer, he presented another well-thought-out and transcribed case and demanded justice. He eventually got it, in the form of a nice settlement (and mounds and mounds of red tape and headaches for the resort).

I am sure the Kingpin's caboose felt the sting. Oh, and in case anyone is wondering what happened to Broom Hilda, I heard through the grapevine that she and her broom were eventually sent packing, shit-canned for the fourth (or was it the fifth?) time. I hope a house lands on her like it did in the movies. As for me? Well, the captain soon found his chair again, this time as a television host.

Phoenix on a Five-Lane Highway

It was now rush hour for Mr. Gardiner's life, post-fallout at the Magic Castle. He became engaged in a mad dash to fill that self-worth bucket of his from a variety of angles, all the while navigating a lingering stigma and an undercurrent of potential doom. Traffic was pedal to the metal, and the margin of error was small.

Lane 1: Television Host

The show, *Inspirational 30,* kicked off in the beginning of December, airing weekly up and down Vancouver Island. Being back in front of the camera and beneath the stage lights was a long-awaited reunion, to say the least. Jim felt like his old self there. It was home, and he knew it. There would be a proud twinkle in his children's eyes when they paid a visit to the set, and Brooke herself loved seeing the youthful Jim she'd met back on the streets of New York City.

The show also afforded him the luxury of being noticed. Coffee-shop visits or grocery-store runs turned into the occasional host sighting with locals greeting him, sharing their admiration of the show. The show itself was well received and would immediately find multiple airings in the station's rotation of programming. A second season was also agreed upon, with an extension of its viewership to include Vancouver and other parts of Canada, including Calgary and beyond. In total, there were twenty-three episodes that personally enriched the lives of his guests, the audience at large, and Jim himself.

Lane 2: Performance Coach

The show itself did many things for me. None more powerful than reminding me that I had an innate ability to facilitate change in people, to inspire them, to nurture them, and to elevate them to whatever their next step was on their path to authenticity. Of course, I had barely even recognized my own true potential yet, but I couldn't shake the growing urge to be "of service." Whether in terms of personal growth or business-development guidance, I felt that my life experiences would be a useful blend for the support of others. In theory, it made sense. In my heart, it did too. Thankfully, like Rich Roll, my inspirational flame, I had the ability (on camera and with a microphone) to do just that.

Lane 3: Triathlon

Speaking of Rich Roll, Jim also channeled his essence in the form of athletic conquest. Morning coffee and an envelope would lead to another lane on the crazy commute of life. The envelope in question had been sealed shut before his excommunication from the Magic Castle. Jim tore it open gently, as though there were a ritualistic undercurrent to it all. He unfolded the piece of paper and softly pressed it out on the counter. It was a registration letter from the Ironman Association for an upcoming event. It was a certified entry into a full-distance Ironman triathlon being held in Cambridge, Maryland.

To say Brooke was not amused is an understatement, and sitting here now, I don't blame her one bit. To be honest, I am surprised that she didn't kick me to the curb right then and there as soon as I unveiled this new grand plan of mine, which would (of course) cost money. But that ingrained selfish warrior took hold and a plan was crafted.

Jim only gave himself six months to train, guerilla style. YouTube videos would guide his swimming experience, of which he had none. He didn't own a bike, so he would train for the next five months on a spin bike while trying to borrow a road bike for the final month of training and for the race. Running was the only thing he was familiar with. Some people thought he was crazy. Some people thought he had gonads of steel. But they "thought" ... and that external attention paired perfectly with his need for acknowledgement.

Lane 4: The Town Secret

With the exile from the land of magic atop the hill came the unavoidable fact that Jim now found himself back in a sleepy town full of whispers and finger pointing. There was no escaping it and no escaping the portal that seemed to open now that he was stuck there. In they came, the ghosts of regret with their voices of retribution and abandonment following him around as he juggled his life and tried to make sense of it all. But all it did was add further speed to the fifth and final lane of his destiny. This one was different from the others, a carpool thruway for Jim and all his ghosts.

Lane 5: Unhappiness

The consistent underlying thought to every facet of his life was how unhappy he was. Call it depression, call it unfulfilled dreams, call it a stale marriage, call it whatever you want, but there was just no escaping that life and every fantasy he'd ever had were underdelivering in terms of his reality.

The stage was set. Life was playing out for Jim at breakneck speed. Now in his mid-forties, he was scrambling to come to terms with his lot in life, with five chaotic lanes all converging in one inevitable outcome. It's a wonder that he survived Maryland at all.

A Clipped Wing

Jim and Brooke arrived in Cambridge, Maryland, in the beginning of October. The early fall weather was accompanied by a lukewarm breeze that blew in off the ocean and drifted through the quaint town, which stood with character very similar to the many colonial towns of New England. Even though Jim was about to step foot in an unknown arena, there was a welcome sense of familiarity that greeted him the morning of the event. Up to this point, everything had played out perfectly. All the training in the three disciplines proved to be both exciting and monotonous in its volume. Six months had passed, and now he was ready to embark on the 2.4-mile swim, the 112-mile bike ride, and the 26.2-mile run. His strategy was set and his nutritional game plan dialed in. Now, all that remained for him was to execute. Brooke was by his side, and his little monkeys were perched at home with their maternal grandparents, awaiting live online feeds for a chance to spot their hero.

312 | ALL IN WITH LOVE

As the early morning darkness gave way to the light of the coming adventure, the competitors were gathering in their respective lineups for the swimming portion of the race. They were segregated like separate herds of cattle, with each group standing in their estimated finish times. Slow and steady was the plan—well actually, "don't drown" was the first order of business—and then slow and steady *with momentum* on the bike.

Internally, I was ready to go. I was chomping at the bit, standing in that swim line for what seemed like an eternity. Two things were at the front of my mind at that moment. First was an eerie sense of peace about what was in front of me, like I could handle whatever the Ironman gods threw at me over the coming twelve to seventeen hours. Second was the knowledge that I should have opted for a bigger wetsuit, as its restriction was growing tighter on my shoulders the longer we waited. Finally, the groups started moving. *Here we go,* I thought. *Just settle in and relax and don't worry about the jellyfish.*

Little stinging minefields awaited all the swimmers. Besides trying to navigate and avoid being kicked in the face, Jim counted three burning stings in just the first few minutes of it all. Slowly, he fell into his rhythm just like he had done so many times while gliding on top of the water. Now submersed in it, he did his best to keep his breathing and strokes consistent. He was about fifteen minutes into the assault when he heard a dull hollow "pop" resonate from the water surrounding him. Instantly, he connected that sound with the searing pain emanating from his left shoulder.

Houston, we have a problem. Jim knew that something had happened that would change everything from there on out. The searing pain soon receded to a dull throbbing ache each and every time he brought his left hand upward and through the next stroke. He could have signaled for help and called it day, but he remembered one unwavering truth: He hadn't come all this way for a fucking T-shirt. So, he put his head down and fought the current, fought through the stinging sea creatures, and tried not to focus on the pain. Survival mode kicked in, and finally, as he closed in on the two-hour mark, his feet touched the bottom. He staggered up the ramp to the waiting arms of race attendees who helped him remove his wetsuit.

Jim wobbled on his sea legs and did his best to scurry into the staging area. When he picked up his bike helmet, he realized that he couldn't raise his left arm to secure the clip in place. A signal for help to an attendant got the job done, but as he emerged from the tent, he knew he was in for it, damn the consequences. Most of the competitors were already off on their 112-mile trek, leaving the warrior to make up some serious ground on the bike, provided he could support himself.

"Wahoo! Let's go, Jim!!" screamed his only fan. Brooke was waiting by the fence close to his bike. He quickly detoured closer to her.

"My shoulder's fucked," he nonchalantly said, pointing to his left wing.

He then grabbed his bike and began running on the grass to the saddle-up point so he could begin his assault. *Time to get back into the game,* he thought as he clipped in and mounted up.

Those first few pedal strokes instantly brought him back to the Cydot days of old. The freedom of the wind and the speed of the road beneath the wheels seemed like yesterday. In his training plan, he'd opted to go without aero bars, meaning those two small bars that extend off the normal handlebars and allow a rider to lay over the bike, reducing drag and fatigue. In and of itself, that was no biggie, as many riders go the more traditional route; however, what Jim had not expected to be riding even more of the traditional style, sitting completely vertical as if out for a leisurely Sunday stroll around the block. He couldn't support his body weight evenly when he bent over into a standard position. His left shoulder screamed at him after mere seconds in that position.

Jim quickly had to learn how to shift his body weight so that his right arm and side were taking the brunt of the load, allowing his left to at least help keep the bike balanced. Regardless of the shit sandwich he'd found himself in, the early stages of the bike ride felt amazing. The back roads of the small colonial town led out into sun-drenched farmlands on their route to the estuary. The 112 miles consisted of two large loops out into a nature reserve adjacent to the ocean. Jim's bike was loaded with all the necessary fuel and nutrition and his plan committed to memory. He would be militaristic with its intake. He set himself to the task at hand; each rider ahead of him was a mini challenge to conquer and a battle won once he passed them.

However, when the force of nature smacked him in the chest like an eighteen-wheeler, no one was around to hear the loud "F" bomb he let loose once the back roads gave way to the serenity of the estuary. The wind blowing inland from the ocean that day was excruciatingly fierce, and his upright position acted like a sail going the other way.

That first trip out into the estuary to battle this unforeseen force was when the dreaded thoughts of quitting began to take hold of his mind. The shoulder pain was one thing, but the inability to move forward seemed too daunting. He could barely stay upright as the blowing wind pelted his upright body, slowing him to a turtle-like crawl. To make matters worse, the competitor inside had to deal with the number of people he had passed now passing him again. He found himself out in no man's land with no lifeline and the only thing aiding his continued survival was the endless spirit within him, the same spirit that had fought valiantly on the tennis court, waged countless battles with an oar, and believed that Jim could do anything if given the opportunity.

The stage and the spotlight is a lonely place. Being out there, exposed, changes people. Jim's wife had seen firsthand how it can dismantle the Britney Spears' of the world, and athletes are no different. Sure, that spark can set fire to the internal drive, as it did for Jim. But it was more. It was the fear of being a failure to himself and in the eyes of the world that truly kept his pedals turning. In his mind, his desire for acclaim and attention turned eyes on him, all peering relentlessly at his performance. The little boy from Cydot had gotten what he wanted, and now, failing on a borrowed bike with a wounded wing while being pelted by gusts of wind seemed just what the composer of life required for the symphony to build.

When that last corner appeared, signifying the road out of the wind tunnel, he nearly creamed his spandex. Finally, the wind was gone, and to make things even more glorious, there was now a long gradual downhill stretch where he could regain some precious speed and recover his energy. He even started to reel in some of those riders who'd passed him a short time earlier, each one another shot in the back of his arm, keeping Jim going.

Knowing what to expect now, he had some time to prepare for the assault out in the estuary for round two. This time, there would be no surprises. His only focus was persevering through it, shoulder pain and all, so that he could go and run a marathon. Now *that* is a sadistic reward for perseverance, to say the least.

When he finally made the last turn off the small Cambridge streets into the transition area, he was able to dismount his bike, coming in over an hour slower than he had hoped. He pulled his wing close to his body and ran over to see his wife, who was waiting by the fence. A quick kiss gave him the energy to run into the tent and get set up for the 26.2-mile campaign.

The warrior soon emerged and went to work. He started his watch and GPS to accurately give him his running pace. Off he went, falling into his running groove like a well-crafted Swiss watch. It took about four minutes before another check of his watch made him literally laugh out loud. His training pace began to plummet fast and furious like Vin Diesel.

No time for caution. Just change the plan. The next logical podium moment of this adventure was for Jim to run as long as he could before he felt the utter need to stop. To stay in the game, sometimes we just need the next benchmark so that the very next step could be taken. Success is based on momentum, and that was all Jim was thinking about. He generated inertia and now was letting that force pull him through the community streets of Cambridge. Unlike the wasteland of the estuary, this run was teeming with life. It was here that he witnessed the full-on spectacle that is an Ironman. Strangers young and old held makeshift signs to encourage all the participants on their respective journeys. Names would be called out like random acts of kindness, adding fuel to the athletes' resolve; each warrior's name on their racing bibs added to the script of the scene. With his left arm hanging down by his side or pinned close to his body, he made his way onward for as long as he could.

The wall finally cracked at two hours and twelve minutes, when he consciously said, "Screw it," and dropped his cadence to a walk. Always forward. Always. Each watering and food station would keep him fueled should he need it, but most of all, it was the lifeforce of water, poured over his head and down into his gullet, that kept his core temperature optimal and pushing onward. He managed to string together another sixty continuous minutes of running before the intermittent walking became a closely loved ally. Slowly, he chipped away at the mileage, and as the sun set and darkness began to bookend this long and somewhat glorious day, Jim made his way through the cobblestone streets and into the final chute that summons all the glory and redemption seekers who'd come out to play this day. His pace quickened, all the pain in the shoulder dissipated, and his fatigue quickly evaporated like the sweat from his body.

The cheers rose as Jim first touched the red-carpet entranceway. The announcer greeted Jim's move through the finish: "You are an Ironman!" He was surrounded by the applause of the large gathering of supporters, and the love and admiration of his two little angels who were home watching the live stream of their daddy's race. He drunkenly made his way to Brooke and greeted her with a big, wet, and sweaty hug. She was there for him, and he knew it. Not by marriage or obligation, but because she loved him. She followed and/or agreed to his dreams and his steering of the ship out of love for him. This was one of the first times he felt it from her, the true sense of pride in "her" man for his willingness to dream and achieve.

Back at the hotel, Jim managed to find the strength to pound down a beer and take a shower. By this time, he could barely move his left arm at all; the pain was too intense. So, another beer washed down a few extra-strength Advil, and he assumed a position next to Brooke on the bed. Yes, he was an Ironman, but every ounce of his energy and resolve was now gone, his body broken. In the coming days and weeks, the mental fallout from this battle, along with the other four lanes on the highway, would destroy any chance to fight the gathering storm. The convergence point was coming, and it would be an extinction-level event. As the alcohol and the meds kicked in, his eyes began to droop. His mind went back to the playground of innocence in which he'd grown up. If only he could stay there.

If only . . .

The Sassenach and the Stones

The landscape was so rich with its earth tones and textures; the greens mixed beautifully with a multitude of browns, providing the perfect color palette to showcase the stunning vistas. The wetness and mud that churned upward beneath the couple riding horseback fueled the savagery of the times. While its epic scope resembled Middle Earth, the ground belonged to the highlands of Scotland. As the Celtic music swelled, so did Jim's heart and his memory, returning to a time when tales of this land would dance from Malcolm's tongue, filling young Jimmy with awe. Now, that young boy turned man was once again captivated by the romance and stories that played out on the television screen. He felt like he was watching himself. James "Jamie" Fraser was a Scottish highlander, much like the lineage of the Matheson clan of Jim's grandfather. But it was Claire, the beautiful English lass with her passionate spirit of love, that captivated both their hearts. Jim felt it deeply and wanted it for himself.

It had only been a few weeks since his return from the soul-depleting excursion to Maryland, and he was now basking in the fallout of emotion from the collision of those five lanes. Depression was grabbing hold, sinking its meaty claws into him, paralyzing him both physically and mentally. All energy seemed to have vacated his being, and more importantly, the will to do anything about it. One undeniable fact loomed over him every waking moment of the day: His current life, his married life and all that came with it, was not what he wanted to wake up to every day. An overwhelming sense of dread covered him like a heavy blanket. Those pesky ghosts gathered around him and held daily council. His soul was in shutdown mode, its life-light fading with each unreciprocated smile from his two angels or his loving wife. His only remedy was the boyish notion of escape, of stepping through a doorway into the queen's comfort on a couch somewhere in the rustic Scottish landscape. That place was the television show *Outlander*.

The gray of a late October day was the perfect backdrop for the crashing waves that pelted the rocky breakers before him. Sure, he was on the other side of the country from his homeland's cathartic surf, but an ocean is an ocean. He leaned up against the outside of his vehicle with his favorite beer in hand, Innis and Gunn (Scottish, of course), and stood staring out into that wet chaos of dreams and possibilities. Like many times in his life, he was accompanied by the deep lyrics and majestic score of Dream Theater as it blasted from the speakers. "Along for the Ride" tells the story of the internal search for control and understanding in one's life only to realize that we are all passengers being driven by something greater than ourselves.

Jim took the last swig of his beer and stood among the sideways rain as surrender overtook him before the sirens of the ocean.

"Please, show me the way. Send me a sign," the warrior calmly said.

His plea was soon carried off by the prevalent winds and vanished over the salty turmoil. Like a hitchhiker, he watched for the universe to pull over and take him "along for the ride."

As the author, I would ask that you, the reader, to pick a female name. Any name that comes to you...

Have it? Good, now take that name and insert it into the following blank space:

_____ arrived through the stones exactly one and a half weeks later. Her name didn't and doesn't matter. She could have been a one-eyed slimy creature from the planet "X," and Jim wouldn't have seen it. He was desperate, and desperate eyes take desperate measures when paired with a desperate heart. Her beautiful curly hair was nestled under a black hat. Her lightly freckled skin shimmered in the glow of a post-workout sweat while her diminutive stature supported eyes that told the story of a heart waiting to be found. She didn't utter a word in that initial encounter, nor did she have to. Love needs no language. It is an unspoken force more powerful than any magical poet could summon up on a page. The scene wasn't the Highlands of Jim's ancestral lineage, but it might as well have been. *His* Claire had walked into his life.

The intensity that only weeks earlier had been calling to Jim from a land glorified on a television screen was now right in front of him. His senses were on fire, burning as rich and colorful as her flowing auburn hair. His Claire was indeed English, a true Sassenach in spirit, and of course, she was a professional nurse too.

Claire came to their dance in a very similar fashion as Jim, lost as he was in the endless sea of a mundane marriage, with the connection of love seeming the only life raft. She also had two children and a husband that worked his ass off both for their family and for the material things that society deemed "important." She had it all, and like Jim, was unhappy. It was only a short time before they would meet outside of the gym and continue their contagious smiles and smitten glances during walks in the woods. Everything was just easy, including their first kiss.

Unlike the bullshit fumbling at the Ocean Side Inn, before I knew it, that spark of connection blew up into a full-fledged inferno of affair. My home life was unravelling. Early evening drinks would numb the impending stress of trying to "pretend" everything was fine with my wife, and with life for that matter. I couldn't understand why I had fallen out of love with Brooke. She was perfect. But in the stress of my heart longing for my Sassenach and thoughts of her consuming my every breath, I felt helpless.

To make matters worse, the holiday season was approaching. The ringing of Christmas bells was in the air and with it the excitement of two little girls. Brooke, however, was a front-row observer to the downward spiral of her husband. She begged him to go seek more counselling, or at the very least, get back on the medication he'd used to deal with Broom Hilda. She thought he was suffering from a bi-polar disorder. In a way, he was, in that he was torn between two lives: playing out a romantic love adventure by day and a depressed unfulfilled husband and not-father by night. Not even the warming of Christmas carols or the crackle of a holiday fire could help. It was an addiction, and as generally happens with addicts, the rational brain eventually takes a back seat to the irrational. It was only a matter of time before something had to give. In those heartwarming days approaching Christmas, the magic veil that should have hung peacefully was pulled off, exposed by a third-party Bigfoot-style sighting of the secret affair. The chanting mob slowly began to form, making itself known via phone call.

"Hello?" Jim answered, knowing already who was on the other end of the line. It was Brooke's sister, and what ensued was a twenty-minute verbal assault—fully warranted mind you—the likes of which he had never encountered. Those small-town villagers came out of the shadows, as did the buried secrets from the OSI. Sinister tales of debauchery were erroneously spun by the angry mob. Their pitchforks were raised, and Jim sat in their crosshairs. It was payback time. As he sat and listened to Brooke's sister, he began his slow walk to the gallows. He offered up one last statement before the noose would find its home.

"Please just wait till after Christmas. I will tell her everything. I swear. For the girls' sake... please, don't take Christmas from them."

The Slow Death of Christmas

The boney finger extended outward from the dark cloak and pointed to the wrought-iron cemetery gates. The man beside the ominous figure took his steps down the dark path into the land marked by stones of those no longer. Again, the finger pointed to a nearby plot surrounded by freshly dug earth. The man stood at the precipice above the blackness below, the final resting place marked by a tombstone etched in honor of the soon-to-be-corpse.

"Jim Gardiner, beloved ego narcissist and wannabe in life"

It stood as a testament to the man's life so far. Unlike the Scrooge of legend, this miser jumped into the shallow grave, accepting his own fate. Just his face was visible from the blackness.

"Spirit, hear me! Why show me this? These *things?*" Jim asked. The hand continued to point to the bottom blackness of the grave.

Jim grew thoughtful. "I must accept it all to find happiness? Must I die to be reborn?"

Finally, the bony hand receded with validation, causing Jim to lie down on the cold, damp earth.

"I am not the man I was!" he cried as dirt began to cover his body. "I am not the man I was!" He screamed until dirt filled the cavern of his mouth, suffocating him—

Jim abruptly awoke to the pitter patter of little feet, scurrying down the hallway while he wiped the feeling of dirt from his face. His glance toward a sleeping Brooke was short lived, broken by the little whispers of excited girls from the living room. He laid there for a moment, just listening to his two daughter's Christmas morning love. A tear fell from the corner of his eye, and he felt it travelling the length of his cheek before disappearing somewhere on the pillow beneath him.

When his now ten-and-a-half-year-old and seven-year-old heard their dad in the hallway, they ran to him and escorted him to the tree and the landslide of presents. They were quick to proudly broadcast their opening order while Jim took up his position on the floor. The blinking of the colored lights and the purity of the moment reminded him that the twenty-fifth of December would never be the same again.

The gift giving had ended, and early morning was now replaced by midday. Brooke and the girls stood by the doorway, bags of presents for Nana and Napa at the ready.

"I'll be down soon," their dad said, as he would follow them to Brooke's parents' house a bit later. They both smiled and moved in for a kiss and a hug, their tiny arms around his broad shoulders. Jim's strong arms held the hug a bit longer this time, trying his best to remember every millisecond of it.

"Happy Birthday!" his youngest offered when she broke from the embrace. Her goofy demeanor and the ode to the famous line from the *Frosty the Snowman* Christmas special brought a warm smile to those final moments.

The girls moved to pick up the assortment of gifts for their grandparents, allowing Brooke a moment alone with me. Her eyes... I will never forget those windows of her soul as they reflected her concern and love back to me. Another moment I would choose to have back, the moment before the impending destruction of her sweet heart... and the hearts of my two daughters.

Don't leave.

The door closed and with it all life left the house. Even the ghosts that tormented me seemed to want no part of this thing that sat in the kitchen like a shell of something no longer distinguishable. The walk to the gallows is a lonely one.

Jim sat motionless at the kitchen counter. The house around him continued its deathly silence, even the musical score that accompanied his life non-existent. Eventually, one sound gave life to the graveyard: the sound of the metal cap of a full Jameson whiskey bottle being forcefully unscrewed. A large amount of brownish liquid warmed the inside of his body and his soul. This special day would also mark the second time in Jim's life that he went searching for an escape hatch at the bottom of a bottle.

✧ ✧ ✧

That bottle stood by, a portion of its contents missing, while the fully dressed Jim toyed with his car keys. It was time to accept the noose and make his way down to his in-law's house for the holiday dinner and judging eyes.

When his phone rang, the caller ID showing it was his wife calling, he thought nothing of it, assuming it was just a courtesy check in from his concerned partner.

"Hey, I'm just on my way down," I said into the phone as I headed to the door. That was the last part of the conversation I can remember or perhaps chose to remember. I pressed the speaker button on the phone and did an about face to resume my position at the kitchen counter. The Jameson bottle sprang to life again while I listened to my wife destroying every ounce of my self-worth.

As the one-liners came fast and furious without reprieve, hitting with the precision of an expert marksman, Jim welcomed it all. If (and only if) he was asked a question would he respond (and truthfully). But underneath all of it, there was one looming question that he couldn't shake, one thing that he cared about more than anything, his girls.

"Fucking Bitch!" Jim screamed at the top of his lungs. Its echo left the kitchen and trailed off... out into the neighborhood.

He crumpled to the floor. Her sister had in fact told her the news directly upon her distraught arrival. The thoughts of his two girls dealing with the crying, the screaming, and all the chaos underneath the lights of the Christmas tree sent a rage through his soul. Screams and more screams followed before Jim had no energy left to give them voice. Christmas was forever destroyed.

Holiday Fallout

Cue the Jerry Springer theme music. Not only had the most wonderful time of the year been blown to kingdom come for the Gardiners but a quick investigation by Brooke had prompted a Facebook message and then a call to Claire's husband. Within the span of an hour, two families were left reeling and four kids' innocence shattered.

Jim managed to survive the night and found himself beach side on a windswept late morning the day after the fallout. Boxing Day in Canada is like Black Friday in the States. The malls open early on the day after Christmas, and families march in through the doors with their freshly gifted money waving in the air. His phone beeped, not any beep but one indicating a message from Claire. He opened his phone to read the following:

"So, apparently Brooke's meeting George at the mall!"

He began typing. "What?! Are you ok? I miss you, hang in there." The blue check marks on the phone app, and the word "typing," indicated an immediate response was forthcoming.

"Miss you, too. Yes, we are all here at the mall. Gotta go. George will have my phone."

Sitting on that cold, damp beach, Jim's intuition told him that Claire didn't have the balls to fight for their relationship. While the thought of all of them standing around talking with four kids in close proximity was nauseating to say the least, he also felt like the odd man out. Warriors, even disillusioned ones, feel the need to fight for what they want.

Jim pressed the call button on his phone.

"Yeah?" answered the voice of Claire's husband. He did not sound happy.

"Hey, George, it's Jim. Let's talk. I'll come over to the house, and we can have a face to face." There was a brief moment of contemplative silence on the other end.

"Okay," George said. "We'll be home in about thirty minutes."

It was time for Jim to fight for the woman he believed was his destiny. Into the frey he went.

Walking up the driveway, I found myself on another man's property, about to come face to face with him and profess my love for his wife.

Although the visit itself would come to nothing dramatic, if I could, I would still jump through a time portal like Captain Kirk did in *City on the Edge of Forever* and appear right behind myself as I exited my vehicle, snapping a rear-naked choke on my idiot self and throwing my dumb ass in the trunk of the car. It would have saved me two more years of chaos and self-abuse. But no, love doesn't work that way. It knows no rules. When it strikes, it shows no mercy. So, Cobra Kai style, I was going in to sweep the leg and take what I felt was mine.

A collected breath accompanied the knock on the door. There he stood, the man whose life had been thrown into utter chaos. George's sad sullen eyes greeted Jim with a look of confusion, anger, and shame. Not much was said at the doorway, but the invitation was granted with a gesture to pass the threshold. They took up sitting positions in the living room: George, Claire, and Jim, in a triangular pattern, facing one another.

What transpired shall remain inside that house, within the container of those awful events. The door opened a short time later, and Jim left the house with a departing handshake from George. He did what he had come to do, but as he walked to his car, his spidey sense was tingling. Love doesn't come with a safety net; his New York days had told him that, but Claire had one in George. Would she champion what she felt in her heart and be willing to start over? That was the question.

The answer came the next day when Jim received a Facebook message from Claire, stating that their relationship was over and asking him to respect the privacy of a family re-building. Right away, he knew it hadn't come from her. George was puppeteering the keyboard strikes, or at the very least, standing behind Claire and telling her exactly what to write. Two days had passed since Christmas, and Jim was truly alone. His only life-raft, in the form of true love, had vanished. But Jim wasn't done. The warrior wouldn't have it. He knew she would come back. He knew they would survive these times. So, he channeled some of that Ironman training and treaded water... waiting.

The Slow Death of Jim

The last of his duffel bags and personal items found their way into his vehicle. Jim took a moment, standing in his driveway that was no longer his. He hesitated for a moment and then remembered the words of Ragnar Lothbrok, the famous Viking, chiming in his ears: *"Don't waste your time looking back; you're not going that way."*

He hopped in his vehicle and moved forward with a blank page, upon which to create his next chapter.

Of course, it's never that simple. Those blank pages and forward movement soon found Jim in a modern-day tangled web of star-crossed lovers caught in a story of intense passion, deceit, family betrayal, abuse, and rampant drug use, scored perfectly by a broken string on the universal cello of destiny.

His first stop was at a friend's house to set up a base camp before figuring out what to do. In reality, he hadn't even fully thought through the events of the past week. At this point, he only knew two things: He wasn't going back to his marriage; and Claire could not break away from him. So, the saga continued.

The goodbye and "thanks but no thanks" from his Sassenach didn't last long. It was about two weeks before the love she felt for him made her cave, and she showed up on his doorstep. This reunion was framed as a "proper farewell," one they both wanted to savor and both felt their love needed and deserved. This time, life ceased to exist, and the world stopped spinning, for a moment anyway.

I was there for her and for us. I secretly supported her through health concerns and doctor visits, as well as her own mental chaos. I would be at her beck and call and waited with bated breath for any sign of life from my phone. It was the only hand I had left to play for any chance at salvation. If true love is worth fighting for and can be won, then maybe, just maybe, we would be vindicated for our affair. That was my alcohol-laden reasoning, mind you, but it was all I had to go on.

But that liquid-fueled dogma only added to the growing inferno of anxiety and started to alter my behavior. I began to obsess, trying to force everything to happen and worrying about the shit that was out of my control, sometimes with good reason.

Claire would soon start to show signs of erratic behavior, not showing up to secret meetings, going silent for a day, sending self-destructive messages, and even occasionally falling off the grid, running away, which became more and more frequent over the next few years. When she didn't surface after an important doctor's appointment, Jim went on the first of many covert operations.

Sometimes, the intoxicated Jim would buzz the tower Maverick-style, desperate to know if she was home, caught in another lie. This time, her house faded in the rearview mirror, his attempt at a sighting unsuccessful. The last stop on this reconnaissance flight path across town brought Jim to the last place he wanted her to be.

We all have had a friend or two with "Trouble" as their middle name. Hell, Jim had become close friends with a convicted murderer for crying out loud. There was a nurse friend of Claire's who was about as straight and narrow as Al Pacino in *Scarface*. This nurse spent more time stealing medications from the dispensary than actually giving them to patients. Her house looked like a rundown shanty shack compared to all the other houses in the neighborhood, and outside of it, he found Claire's vehicle.

When she appeared from the house and walked to Jim's vehicle, her energy had changed. She wasn't excited to see him and instead was a weary and ragged-looking version of the Sassenach he'd fallen for. Still, his infatuation clouded his peering blue eyes and what should have been their rational gaze.

"It's over," she said, sounding defeated. "I can't... I can't do this anymore."

"What do you mean it's over?" Jim responded. "Why?"

"It's too much, I can't deal with—"

"Deal? I left everything for you! For us!"

Her eyes gave way, and her head dropped. If ever there was a scene in real life depicting the standoff between Allie and Noah in *The Notebook,* this was it.

"You gotta fight for your heart, Claire!" He begged her. "It's not over." He backed away from her to his car. He opened the vehicle's door, climbed in, and then spoke again, this time with the conviction of a warrior. "It's not over, Claire! You know it's not over!" The slam of his car door punctuated his decree.

He slowly drove away, hearing that Viking's voice once again, pulling him away from the rearview mirror in which he'd watched Claire moping back to the house. *"... You're not going that way."* It may have been prophetic when it finally took hold, but for now, Jim only saw one life ending, the life of a persona and past that no longer served him. That day, he was summoned by a voice somewhere in the heart of darkness. The course would be deep into the jungle on a quest for himself and that elusive truth of his soul. Ponce de Leon floored the gas pedal. Through the trees and overgrown brush of tomorrow lay the Fountain of Youth at the heart of the jungle. He began his pilgrimage. Jim was no longer.

CHORUS: *INTO THE JUNGLE*

Our story now shifts to blur the lines between Fantasy, Memory, and Reality. Lend no discord to the fantastical journey about to be afoot. Channel the spirit of Ponce de Leon, and journey with our warrior as he searches for the fountain of youth. Entertain a parchment, born from a time of playland adventure, that now guides the man to the unavoidable showdown that must be.

View in tandem with our dethroned king the remnants of yesteryear, relics and voices decaying under the rust of time's inevitable march. And the beast. Let us not forget that each warrior, by his own actions, has created a hideous figure that will track his course through the jungle, stalking him.

Come. Conjecture a torn and tattered journey of a soul bleeding redemption from his open wounds, the falsities of non-serving armor soon to be expelled, and a mythical tree that awaits at the epicenter of a potential reunion. But first to the far reaches of his mind he must go, willing to die at the root of creation and vanquish the dark internal foe.

THE JUNGLE ARENA

The Three-Headed Dragon

The twigs cracked under the weight of his meandering footsteps. The ocean breeze that had given him life for so long was non-existent, replaced instead by stagnant heavy air that mixed with the heat like a thick layer of paste. The jungle was silent, though alive with sight. With each step, he plodded further into the dark unknown until the crack under his feet was rewarded with a distant roar, a guttural growl that echoed through the dense underbrush as a warning to all who dared the path. Another step and another snap from below his peering eyes.

A chair finished clicking into place, and on it, the body thumped. The death of "Jim" was something that gave him tangible comfort in an intangible world. He had never used his full name in his life. Everyone and anyone he met him knew him as Jim. But while sitting on a folding chair nearly forty years removed from a similar chair of exile at the school dance, he knew it was time for it. Simply put, Jim had been dying ever since he'd crossed the threshold into New York adulthood and lost the connection to joy as he'd vacated Los Angeles.

Now James sat surrounded by nothing but the emptiness of a new apartment. Here he was far removed from those big cities and yet found himself once again in the emptiness of transition. His only companions were two folding chairs that now acted as a makeshift couch. His feet took their reclined position on one, and he waited.

Onward James went into the dense terrain of wet green, forging his way through the overgrown path. The bullwhip of his archaeological youth was replaced by a sword, which hung along his spine, its handle sticking up over one broad shoulder just below his brown Indiana Jones style fedora. From his pocket, he produced a worn parchment, his dirty finger tracing the faint markings on the nearly fifty-year-old map. The path of his trek was lined with pictographs and icons faintly resembling things that the warrior recognized.

The finger continues over a body of water to another land mass and to the image of a tree. Taps on the map by the finger indicate that this is the final destination point. James rolls up his guidance system and carries onward. He is soon met by a dense cluster of vines that a swooshing pass from his hand clears away.

Before him is a large rock, or rather a monolith, complete with an etched pictograph that showed a three-headed beast standing tall over a primitive man with nothing but a spear for defense. The monster is ominous, three dragon-like heads sit atop long serpentine necks, each attached to one unified body with two menacing front arms ending in razor-like claws. Its armored tail extends backward, narrowing down to a spiked battering club. Another primitive man was impaled on it. Behind the battle scene are the etched skeletal remains of all those who had waged war against the mighty foe on their quest.

Rhody James pinches his fedora with his right hand, removing it while his forearm wipes away the amassing sweat on his brow. The hat is replaced on his head, and he pulls down the front brim for additional tightness, just like his childhood hero. He then disappears onward into the brush.

Society sure has a way of alienating people without a care in the world. This first head of the great beast was the meanest of the three. The small number of friends James had had up and vanished like a fart in the wind. Brooke's friends were everywhere, and they would each sling their poisonous barbs towards him. He was shunned in the once hallowed halls of dance, where he'd been heralded as a cool dance dad, with downward gazes and intentional snubs. If he dared venture outside the walls of his prison, a scarlet letter was burned into his forehead for all to see—the curse of small-town life. It wasn't just the affair with Claire but also the ghost from the Ocean Side Inn rising back from the grave, and even rumors from his distant past. Speculation fed whispers, which evolved into conversation, from which rumors were born.

The second head of the great beast was **Guilt,** in all its tangled glory. In its dark eyes, James would see the image of his two girls and Brooke; the guilt he harbored for his betrayal of them was felt in every single cell of his body. His children wanted nothing to do with him as they grew to understand what had transpired. Even his own parents judged his behavior and disowned him.

"You're dead to us." Those were the exact words his dad uttered when they'd last spoken. James had hung up the phone and added them to the long line of abandoned souls at the Gardiner train station in life. Guilt and shame were everywhere.

The third and most cunning head of the great beast was **Love**. It was lethal in its ability to betray and manipulate its victims. Claire was still very much in his life. As sure as the sun would rise, she would return. A few more weeks had passed since their encounter outside White Powder Ma's shanty house, and she was back in his arms at his new apartment. But on the other side of the coin was her erratic behavior and her life with George. This foe, love, would be the final test James would need to pass if he were to stand beneath the tree and be reborn. He also knew it would be the hardest enemy to vanquish.

Step by step. he traversed deeper on his quest. His glazed and grimy hands pull back the overgrown green curtain, revealing the stones of a dwelling barely resembling the house it used to be. Like most things, it had once been teaming with life, with dreams, and had now succumbed to the passage of time.

The moment is broken by the sound of a falling object colliding with a rock. James unsheathes his sword and turns the corner. An old, rusted bicycle, its red coloring barely noticeable, lays on its side in the death throes of time. He stands before it, staring.

His tired body now finds support against a corner wall in the middle of the ancient ruin, while the teeming jungle turns nightly quiet. A large stone rests on the somewhat open ground before him. Unlike the other stones, this one calls to him as though it is pulsating with life. A glow begins to emanate from the rock, slowly building to a fixed point of light in the darkness. He has found his company for the evening and basks in the Zenith-like radiance of comfort from a mythical land called Cydot Drive. His eyes fill with its light, while cool liquid from a canteen quenches his thirst.

The vodka bottle retreats from his lips and resumes its place on the carpet between his legs. Each day and night, the three battles would rage, and the beast would come for him. Rumors and false accusations would circulate back to Brooke, whose piercing, poisonous darts would blow up his phone. The shame continued to rise in his feverish blood, the images of his girls, and of Brooke sobbing, were his nightly company. Lastly, the thought of Claire at home with George, playing house, or even worse, attending to his forceful sexual demands, was nauseating. This daily composition of torment was far removed from his childhood "Ode to Joy." Days progressed into weeks, which gave way to months, before a tiny ray of hope shone through the dense canopy.

The Princess of Darkness

James never thought the sight of someone hanging their clothes in an empty closet would give him the warm fuzzies. But the way Claire seemed to dance from suitcase to hanger to closet was heavenly. It had taken seven months, but he finally had what he wanted: a shot at vindication.

Claire had moved in. Seven months of secrecy had given way one Saturday morning when the two were busted by George at a secret rendezvous. There was no dramatic standoff of two warriors each championing their love for the queen. Nope. Just a quick "Good luck" and that was that. The Sassenach and the Scotsman were now together.

Shortly thereafter, Claire's mother, whose smile would jockey with Bigfoot for the title of "North America's Most Elusive," asked the both of them to go on a rescue mission. Her other daughter, from her now third husband, was in need of help, and so it was Claire and James to the rescue. Young Lucy had been in and out of rehab, battling drug addiction, multiple times, but realizing that one of her feet was standing in the hereafter, she had now decided to come home, get clean, and start over.

With one fell swoop, the hero in James had the chance to save the day and earn some brownie points with both Claire and her mother. The *Outlander* couple hopped on a sunbaked romantic ferry ride to the mainland to rescue Lucy and her four garbage bags of clothes. It marked the first time the two had felt free to be together, out in public and away from any small-town glances.

Arriving back in that small town, where she would stay at Claire's house, Lucy was read the riot act with a zero-tolerance drug policy. Of course, George would have to enforce it, while Claire was shacking up with James, but they'd both promised Claire's mom to provide Lucy with a safe environment. Safe. Interesting choice of words given the sisters soon disappeared. James waited for Claire to return from a drop off, and waited, and waited. His anxiety spiked, and he found himself in an all-too-familiar scene. Unreturned phone calls and messages sent him into a state of chaos.

The darkness broke with a message at two a.m. *Finally*, James thought. However, the message contained only a picture message from Claire's husband. Its content was Exhibit A of James' love and charity work for the day. There was George with his arm around Claire and the demon Lucy in the background with her middle finger blazing into the camera and James' soul. Just like that, Claire was gone, returning to her own internal family chaos and all-night benders with the magic dust of cocaine. That evening and over the coming days, there would be paranoia-induced texts fired to James from Claire's stoned husband and from

Claire herself. Behind it all was sister Satan, pulling both their strings and encouraging them deeper into the rabbit hole of white carnage.

Leaving Las Vegas—I Mean Parksville

He stepped into a clearing, welcoming the hint of a breeze that blew in off the ocean. Rhody James had come upon a tiny cove surrounded by high mountainous walls on either side. The only sign of life around him was an unkindness of ravens perched on timbered remnants by the water's edge, guardians of this ancient remain.

Slowly, he approached until the ravens took flight toward the mountain pass. He stood before the remains of the off-yellow timbered hull that spanned the length of the inlet beach. A small figurehead in the shape of a beast peeked out from the intermittently sand-covered hull. The boat's structured ribcage was now partially disintegrated and dissolved into the sandy pillow beneath. James surveyed the length of this colossal sixty-foot skeleton. Only a few instruments of its once mighty power remained, extending outward from the craft like the legs of a large water bug that had succumbed to the drying sun. He slowly fell to his knees as the faint cries of courage permeated the bones of its former life and the eight other hearts, now silent. James began to sob at the grave before him.

"SCREECH!!"

The group of ravens had returned, standing in formation off to his left and breaking the silence. Their necks were craned toward the dense jungle behind him. James quickly turned to see the rustling canopy of trees that were shaking violently. It was coming fast. The ravens launched in formation, heading due west off the beach and back above the jungle with another loud shriek. Rhody James followed the sirens of escape.

The accelerator aggressively kissed the floor of the vehicle. The open windows and sunroof invited in a tornado of air that pummeled James as his car reached speeds of 140km/hr. Journey's "Separate Ways" was turned to eleven on the Spinal Tap volume indicator. The mickey of vodka became his microphone. At the top of his Steve Perry lungs, he sang about breaking the chains of a dying relationship and taking a chance on true love.

The journey had begun an hour earlier at 9:30 a.m. when two things happened: The liquor store opened; and after a loud scream and an irrational conversation with Brooke, he'd decided to get the hell out of Dodge. Fairly fresh off the early morning middle-finger photobomb, those small-town societal rumors had done their job. The final blow had come from Brooke herself, regarding Claire and the widely known drug use of the husband-and-wife duo in the community.

"I'm fucking done!" James had screamed into his phone. "I'm done!"

Make no mistake. I was. I was on a one-way trip north to the most remote part of the island. The sideshow circus of the small town had finally gotten what it wanted and now my naive, embarrassed, and stupid ass was driving at breakneck speed in my own clown car.

Brooke took my current state of mind as a sign that I was going to do something foolish. Indeed, I was. I was going to confront that first head of the mythical beast: society. With alcohol as my co-pilot, I began my pursuit. Its warming liquid and the windstorm of freedom sent me back to a simpler time. My hair felt the wind, and my soul began to electrify at the thrill of childish adventure born into this adult chaos of despair.

Telegraph Cove was the first official pit stop on my way north. It was an old-style marina and community nestled between rocky bluffs in the middle of nowhere. It is noted for its whale-watching excursions and fishing charters, but today it served a different purpose.

The last contents of the plastic vodka bottle dripped into a large McDonald's coffee. Then James climbed from the confines of his rocket ship, allowing his legs to steady for a moment, and then proceeded to walk along the docks and village of the cove. The mirrored reflection of his New England was mind blowing. His thoughts drifted to his parents, whom he hadn't spoken to. Further back in memory was a gentler time, with family vacations to Boothbay Harbor, Maine, each summer to bask in the glory of the lighthouses, shipwrecks, and his old friend the Atlantic. The maritime quaintness of this cove and the salty smell also reminded him of the town dock in Wickford. The buzz from his co-pilot and his cranial nostalgia was a perfect sedative for the meandering walk, which concluded with a squat dockside, his feet dangling over the edge. He looked for his Cydot brother Dave, just in case, but that forty-year-old council between friends was not meant to be. This was a solo journey.

✧ ✧ ✧

The drive continued to take him north with just the right amount of continual liquid bliss. Now well into the afternoon, it was combined with Advil and Tylenol to keep the journey going. The result was a lucid theta state of self-exploration among the whizzing fir trees that passed in a blur.

Barbs of jagged branches ripped his clothes and drew blood on his sweat-drenched skin. He came to a stop to catch his breath, his hands supporting his body while he collected himself. His rapid breathing dissipated, and a quiet overcame the jungle. He looked up to the dense covering behind him for a sign. Nothing.

The rest found him standing in the middle of a flat rocky outcrop caught in a stranglehold of ground-dwelling vines. The precipice was a mere three or four feet off the jungle floor in front of it. Before him, he saw rows and rows of smaller, flat, pedestal stones. It started first as a crack of light that shone down from the dense overhead canopy and connected the ground in a small circle in front of him. Sensing the light, James felt compelled to step toward it. It then grew wider and wider, the spotlight raining down and covering him completely.

Rhody James stood on his acting mark, the empty stone pedestals, occupied by the spirits of those before him, bore witness to his own soliloquy:

> *"Friends, family, judging countrymen, lend me your ears;*
> *I come to bury the past, not live in it.*
> *The mistakes that men make live on after them,*
> *The good they have done interred with their bones and dust.*
> *So let it be with Jim.*
> *The noble James*
> *Hath told you that Jim was a dreamer.*
> *If it was so, that blurred line between fantasy and reality was a grievous fault.*
> *And now James stands before you in forgiveness and acceptance,*

For it is not your fault, the casting of stones and barbs
of discontent.

"Thou art governed by the laws of nature and of society,
Routed by the devious force called expectation,
Your coffers filled with manipulation at the hands of every glance
and wayward vision.
The cunning guise of this deity offers bliss and serenity,
Of things to have, to be, to achieve for the elusive ring of happi-
ness and status,
Only to have its shortcomings create a jealous whisper in
your hearts.

"Oh, for the muse of a tear that stains my cheek for us all;
Innocence has been plucked from the very mortal coil we have
dreamed of,
And now we have turned into judging specters of unfulfilled joy."

James concludes his soliloquy with his eyes moist and heart warm.
"Honk!"
A sound echoes across the jungle floor, causing the spotlight to retract
backwards towards the canopy, faster and faster.

HONK!!!!

James' eyes fly open, and he realizes that his vehicle has crossed the double yellow line. He swerves back just in time to avoid the oncoming truck, which blows by him, the sound of its horn carried off by the speed of the wind. After briefly checking his shorts, his head finds the cushy rest behind it. Something begins to click in his mind: a possible way to defeat his beastly pursuer.

The daylight was making its final stand when James pulled into the desolate town at the north part of the island. It wasn't what he was expecting, but then again, it was exactly what was needed for the scene to play out. The town itself reminded him of a modern-era ghost town, ripped and shredded buildings devoid of life and purpose.

Only one establishment appeared to have any signs of life, and so James entered. He did his best to minimize his stagger once inside the forgotten land of bar inhabitants. Scattered patrons sat about, each in their own self-induced dreamland escape. The dimly lit psyche ward housed its patients, staring blankly, some off into nowhere and others at the framed fishing glory hanging crookedly on the wall. *This will do just fine,* he thought. He approached the bar.

"Large cheese pizza, a shot of Jameson, and... whatever that thingy is," he said, pointing to some cocktail creation depicted on a nearby sheet of paper.

Toothless Sally behind the bar was kind enough to oblige, and James took his liquid medicine and joined the rest of the coma patients in the ward. He carefully placed the brown hue of his Irish bloodlust closest to him on the table, with the unknown creation behind it. The ritualistic moment gave way as he fired the Jameson shot down, followed by half of the mystery cocktail. Within mere seconds, the hue of the ward began to change, the light and its accents morphing slightly. His senses became heightened, giving him the ability to see into the soul of each blank stare before him.

The man directly ahead, whose second child was about to burst through his overalls, disengaged the mug of beer from his white-haired face. The catatonic gaze into nothingness was unbroken by the foam that dripped unattended from his bearded chin. Each drop that fell to its freedom on the table beneath it landed with a whisper: "Expectation... expectation..."

James' eyes scanned the asylum for the next inmate while his head remained dead still. His blue eyes landed on a couple sitting in silence, their gaze downward to avoid the conversation of a failed marriage. James' eyes travelled down the length of the woman's body to her foot, which seemed to be tapping along to some slow death march of time. Again and again, the foot touched the floor, and again the whispers continued: "Expectation... expectation..."

James' finger tapped in time with the whisper, the foot, and the drips. His vacant stare searched the wreckage of life's misfortunes until he locked eyes on a man holding a picture of someone in his left hand. Around him on the table, empty shot glasses had been discarded like wayward soldiers that had served their purpose. The numb soul slid his right hand along the table, reaching for the last soldier still sitting upright and full to the brim. James did the same, a mirror reflection of the man he was watching. Both right hands secured their desired liquid injection while firmly focused on the targets: James on the man, and the man on his photograph. Neither budged nor blinked as the rest of the alcohol filled their mouths and stomachs. Slowly, both glasses returned to the table with a thud, marking even more definitive whispers: "Expectation... expectation..."

James was now almost as catatonic as the rest of the scattered people in the wing. His hand began to punctuate the thud of the common denominator, growing louder and louder on the table. His eyes begin to drift.

"Expectation... expectation... expectation..."

The pronounced thud of the great beast was behind him, in hot pursuit, its mighty footsteps getting closer. Rhody James continued through the muck and darkness of the dank terrain, jumping over a small ravine, and upon landing, slid down a muddy embankment, coming to a stop in a shallow swampy pool. He cleared the soupy grime from his face and found himself in a dank depression on the jungle floor. The meteor "Expectation 1993-94" had collided here all those years ago, when a boy had walked through a doorway into the concrete jungle. A blast radius of collateral damage was now his only company.

Rhody James shifted his body to one side of the embankment, its slope acting like a La-Z-Boy recliner to support his frame.

"This is its fucking den," he whispered.

His head fell back to the muddy pillow behind it as he surveyed the scene. Two jagged tree trunks stood side by side, upright through the floor of the pit. The once mighty towers of ego had been reduced to stumps, their legacy gone. A broken and discarded director's chair, which once supported possibility, was now part of this graveyard, littered with lighting equipment and other old film-set relics. Half-buried picture frames of women won, women lost, and women betrayed greeted his eyes like a cemetery of failed love. Across from him on the other side of the ridge was a skeleton, clad in an orange jumpsuit of incarceration, watching over the pit. But it was the sight of the baby stroller that finally caused Rhody James to move. He shifted his body and crawled on all fours through the sewage toward it. His hand reached for the muddy covering but then hesitated and stopped.

He can't. He surrenders and falls on his back surrounded by the filthy swamp. He lies for what seems an eternity, the water slowly closing in around him while his head sinks lower and lower. The dirty grime begins to engulf his face. His eyes do not blink as they fill with liquid, staring upward into the coming blackness. Blackness. . .

"Mr. Gardiner?" A stern and powerful voice shook James from a catatonic state.

Around him stood four imposing police officers, Canada's finest.

"Uh . . . yes?" (At least that's what I think I answered.) I remember spinning around to see the waitress, holding my fresh pizza in a box.

"Would you mind?" I said to the police officer as we both eyed the fresh pie.

I pulled the actor card and tried my best to bring some down-to-earth cool to the situation. My thumb pointed backwards towards the waitress and the white box.

"My large pie," I said nonchalantly. "I'm taking it with me."

"Would you mind grabbing your 'large pie' and stepping outside?" the officer continued, clearly unamused by the situation.

I have to say I did an Academy Award worthy job of not turning into a newborn baby giraffe when I stood up from the table and began my walk of shame. When I arrived outside, the strobing flash of Christmas red and Smurf blue permeated the night sky. To be honest, I was surprised that this spot at the ends of the earth had a police force like this. Six cop cars (yes, six) and six imposing figures now stood around me as I put the pizza box on the hood of my vehicle.

"So?" I asked with my hands up, wondering what in the bloody hell was going on.

"We've received a call from your wife," the unamused officer said, "stating that you might be going somewhere to do harm to yourself."

James chose his next words and actions very carefully. If he talked about his jungle hunt and ensuing pilgrimage to the Tree of Life, even a little, he could easily find himself sitting for breakfast with people in the actual psyche ward. After a micro-second moment of processing, a bushy eyebrow raised up with the lightbulb that sprang to life in his head.

"Well, that's just ridiculous," he calmly responded.

He opened the passenger door to the vehicle to prove his point. The front seat contained his *legal* co-pilots in the adventure, a handful of self-help books and a journal to chronicle his adventure.

"I needed to drive. I... I wanted to get out of Parksville and just drive and think."

A second officer poked her head in to get a glimpse of the seat. "Brené Brown, *Into the Wilderness.* Love her!" she excitedly proclaimed to the other officers after recognizing the book cover.

"Oh, she's great," James responded, right on the heels of her punctuation.

If her head banks a quick right and decides to check the glove box, I am fucked. The thought resounded in his mind like the blast of a cannon. He'd just remembered that his real co-pilots were dead and buried in the small compartment.

"Let's just say I'm on a vision quest," the adventurer in him boldly said, "which will conclude with dinner for one over by the seawall in my car and more writing."

That destination was about two hundred feet away, practically right across the street. In truth, a blind man could have navigated the drive to the seawall and secured a spot for the night. One by one, the swirling red and blue lights were extinguished. The police scattered back into the darkness of the desolate town, and all grew quiet. Jim's head dropped in exhaustion, but there was still more work to do, a pizza to devour, and a beast to face.

The view through the windshield was black. The night sky and the ocean converged in a seamless palette of eternity. The stars that had guided many a wayward traveler were hidden behind a veil of dancing cotton as a breeze blew in from the north. He reached into the cemetery gates of the glove box, pulling the dead plastic soldiers from their slumber. One by one, he revisited their contents, making sure to rescue any remaining liquid. He got what he was after: one last mouthful to accompany him into the abyss.

His heart was finally beginning to return to its normal rhythm after his showdown with police at the Podunk watering hole. His last shot of liquid transformation began to take its lucid hold on his being. He surveyed the blackness before him, the wind coming in through his open window and back out the passenger side. He felt a doorway open as the present world drifted away. His hand moved for the journal and the pen, bringing them to a rest on his lap. The lid of the pizza box opened, and the extra gooey sponge of sobriety was seized. With a double-barreled assault, he fed his body as he channeled his thoughts onto the pages of the journal.

The grease rolled down his chin onto his leather seats, but the savagery didn't bother him. He stood in that doorway between his conscious reality and the subconscious jungle of fantasy. He sat peering into that world, writing down the energy flowing out from within the great canopy of self-discovery. The pen moved in a staccato rhythm; words like "expectation" and "lost innocence" found life on the page. Short sentences on the passage into adulthood and a life begun under the weighty eyes of society and its rules of engagement streamed to life on the page.

Only one pizza slice now remained from the large banquet feast, his gullet full like the ancient kings of old. The grease and cheese further induced a coma-like state, causing the pen to slow its assault. His eyelids drooped, but he fought the pull through the doorway of sleep, not wanting to give in. The pen struggled to complete the last line of his chaotic composition, fighting the good fight.

"The scars of unserving expectation have maimed us, altering our perception of our truth..."

The black ink had no sooner settled into its final markings on the page when his determination relented, and his eyes fell closed.

James' eyes opened, his blue windows now an array of red hues and moisture. Scars of societal expectation floated through his mind as he laid in the beast's lair. He sat up and looked at his arms, each of them covered with scarred slash marks. His finger traced over his left arm, beginning at the wrist and moving upward, each bump of healed flesh a reminder of a misperceived reality, societal manipulation, and the evil of ego. So many years, so many scars.

Where did it go wrong? *he thought. James had built a life that he'd expected to deliver him worth and happiness. The rowing, the acting, the women, the career, all born out of the insatiable need for a nobody to be somebody. Layer upon layer of false personas were forged externally rather than in the fires of his own heart. That was the missing piece. His internal truth was buried beneath the scar tissue of traversing the jungle of life without a personal compass.*

His ponderous stare was broken by the stagnant watery surroundings, which stirred to life with a ripple, and then another, and another as the ground began to shake. The graveyard of relics began to topple and shift. James tried to scramble up the bank but to no avail. The beast was coming.

James' head hung to the side of the car in complete disregard of comfort. The interior of the car looked like a battlefield. Empty plastic vodka bottles littered the floormat. The pizza box remained open with its now sickening aroma infusing the night air. Napkins, books, more napkins, and of course, the journal and its pen sitting idle on his lap added to the scene. The fifteen-hour day and consistent poisoning had done their duty. James was now locked inside the doorway to the jungle. There was no escaping the showdown.

A loud "CAW!" came from the circling squadron of black overhead. They were back and wanted a front-row seat for the carnage. The ground shook with tremendous force, making it hard for James to find his footing and stand ready. Finally on his feet, the entire jungle grew silent. Dead silent. James looked upward to the black spectators perched in the branches and raised his right hand up to the hilt of his sword above and behind his shoulder. The unsheathing brought the ravens in attendance to a cawing frenzy.

The musical score swelled as the stench of the beast announced its arrival. The slithering first head of the mythical creature appeared slowly at the edge of the pit. Its horned skull and long snout gave way to two prominent fangs protruding downward from the jaw. James twirled the sword in his hands as a sign of courage, which enraged the "society" head of the beast. It sprang upward, his mouth gaping open as the fire formed within. The warrior had to act fast, but there was no way out, no item with which he could deflect the fiery death from above. It was then that he was reminded of the scars of expectation on both his arms.

Ownership, *he thought*. *Those scars covering his arms were his and accepting them not as a mark of shame but rather as reminders of the ultimate power of living one's truth could serve as a shield against any future judgement.* Acceptance. *With this, he stuck his sword into the mud at his feet. He then brought his forearms together, so that the scars on each made one continuous line across his arms, and calmly spoke:*

"I accept my scars as a reminder of the man I was, the man I am, and the man I will be as I walk forward in truth."

The head of societal expectation rained down its fiery breath upon James, but the shield of scars deflected the flames. He stood defiant until the fiery breath subsided, and the beast coiled its head back for a kill strike with its powerful jaws. But the warrior knew it was coming. He knew the next move, and when the beast lunged his mighty horned head downward into the pit, Rhody James grabbed his weapon and spun to his left, avoiding the grasping jaw. A full-circle turn saw him bring his sword down behind the bony skull plates of the head, where it connected to the flesh of its neck. The soft tissue gave way, and the severed head fell to its swampy demise at his feet. The beast shrieked in painful horror, recoiling the neck and retreating back into the dense jungle in a wounded retreat.

As the cries receded further into the background, the squadron of ravens left their perch in a unified takeoff. Rhody James watched them disperse into the canopy overhead as a glimmer of light began to break through the dankness. Below him, the severed head lay among the ruins of his past. A fitting end to the lives, the relationships, and the events that this monster of societal expectation had created. James sheathed his sword and bent down in front of the large head. As he had for the people of his community, he began to feel sympathy for the beast. Perhaps it too had been born out of some primordial egoic soup and genetically fashioned in the guise and will of others. The warrior caught a glimpse of himself in its large pupils, a foretelling sign of the journey yet to come. The black mirror held an image of a warrior standing side by side with a little boy.

A far-off sound echoed through the jungle, its guttural groan making the warrior straighten and take notice. It was more like a gurgle than a roar, a volatile mix of dark undercurrents from a distant, rumbling volcano.

The volcano within was groaning in its need to erupt, to pour forth the magma of its soul and purge the vessel that could no longer resist the need to explode. The rumblings grew while James' head leaned against the window. A single track of wetness dripped from his mouth and navigated the contours of his chin. The volcano groaned more, as the closed windows of the jungle slowly blinked to life and then immediately went wide with impending horror. There was no time for this warrior to calculate. He was already in a ready position. His hand struggled to find the unlock button but managed just in time. The car door flew open, and James cranked his head over the sill of the doorway as the lava came. Its first salvo exploded from his stomach and out his mouth like the fiery breath from the beast's severed head. The awful sound of a body wrenching filled the early morning air.

As the second wave began to build, he somehow managed to exit the vehicle and navigate around the contents of his first purge. He staggered to the front of his car by the driver's side headlight and then braced for impact. It came, and he held nothing back. Vile torrents spewed forth from his mouth, relieving his body of seventeen hours' worth of self-induced carnage and a lifetime of pain. His body convulsed and contorted as the eruption littered the ground around him.

The echoes of his guttural booms dissipated, leaving an eerie silence in their wake. All around James, undigested mine fields littered the ground as he made his way back inside the car. Every part of his body relaxed then until it felt like he was floating between two realms of existence. He reached for his journal and began to write the keywords from his first face-off with the beast, and the power of ownership over his scars and acceptance while trapped in its lair of societal expectation. The word "truth" seemed to be woven into almost every pen strike. James scribbled like a mad scientist, trying to make the most of the portal before it began to close, and his eyes lost the power to see. He concluded the profound experiences of a fiery day (which would come to shape him into the man behind these keyboard strikes) with a final entry: "All in with... love?"

The sound of tiny sharp fingernails dancing on metal announced the morning's arrival. This staccato rhythm eventually stirred James back to life. It grew louder and louder as he became more conscious and left the dream world of Valhalla behind. As his eyes finally regained their focus, and his brain started processing their view, he saw it. Blackness everywhere. Figures surrounded him with black eyes staring at him. James and his vehicle were surrounded by an army of crows. They were perched everywhere: the roof, the hood, and the surrounding ground. It was an infestation of these soldiers of myth. It was quite ominous at first, but James soon knew better. It was really a sign that he was on the right path and that the jungle journey would hold the ultimate key. The crows had gathered to feast on his early morning purge, but they also stood as fellow warriors, saluting the courage he had shown and would take with him back into spotlight of the piercing eyes of small-town existence. They also stood as allies for the battles ahead, and for the man who still had two more demons to vanquish.

A Gorn at the Campfire

With his temporary victory over the three-headed beast in the jungle of north Vancouver Island, James began to harness an invisible shield with which he would deflect any harming blows from the naysayers or status-quo champions around him. It had nothing to do with his ego, just strength of his ability to accept and own what he had done. So, whether it was a casual Sunday stroll on the boardwalk by the beach or a trip to the coffee shop to sit outside, he did it with a bit more peace in his heart.

At least that damn ghost from the OSI was free, and I didn't feel like I was constantly waiting for the bomb to go off. Instead, I was walking around in a post-war apocalypse, living off the rubble and shattered remains while liberated from any further airstrikes of past destruction.

That devastation from thirty thousand feet had turned the lives of my two girls completely upside down, and the sadness of shattering their innocence was inescapable for me. They became war refugees in a sense, struggling for their own understanding of it all. They had been forced through that doorway of lost innocence way too soon, and I knew the inner child of each of them would suffer because of it. My only resolve was to try and help them understand and provide them a safe place to experience a glimpse of the love that would always remain regardless of a marriage ending. I even convinced them to take an adventure with me into a slightly different jungle.

The path through the underbrush was marred by half-buried roots and other small tripping hazards that made our journey cumbersome but still adventurous. The pathway finally led to a spit of land with an endless blue expanse of lake water at its doorstep. The view was stunning.

The two girls had never been on a real overnight camping trip, and it had been nearly forty years since I'd first found the night sky above a tent. We'd decided to blaze a trail and set up camp off the map, which in the modern world means not paying twenty-five bucks for a legally designated site. My rebels and I hiked in from the street to a little-known stretch of land with its own private beach. It also marked the very first time I'd returned to Cameron Lake since hanging up my oars and the pending fallout of my life. I knew this bonding getaway would be emotional on many levels, and I welcomed it.

My youngest was the first to burst forward and run onto the beach.

"This land is ours!" she shouted with her arms to the heavens.

"Let's get our camp set up first and then have some fun," her dad said. He stepped back and took the stance of an army officer.

"Minions, a-tten-*tion!*" he barked. The girls immediately stood side by side at full attention, just like in the movie *Despicable Me.*

Next came an assignment of duties for the three to get the tent set up and the camp situated so that the fun could begin. The two young soldiers gave their affirmations with cheeky salutes and the team was off.

"Don't forget the soda pop," the youngest barked back at her drill sergeant, causing all three to burst out in laughter.

A short time later, the Gardiner camp was set up, and the three stood, marveling at their creation from the comfort of three fabric camping chairs while enjoying some deliciously unhealthy candy and cold soda pop. It was a brief rest before the urge to hit the water and do all things kid-like under the summer sun took over. When that recess bell rang, the three sprang into action and took to the water with reckless abandon, James' heart loving the sanctity of the moment.

As the first hint of summer chill descended with the diminishing sun, the three chairs now sat around a makeshift campfire in the shimmer of its flames.

"Tell us a story about when you went camping with your dad," the eldest said.

"Yeah! But wait! Let me get another pop first" her younger sister interjected.

She popped off her chair and went to the cooler, removing another can of orange soda just like her dad used to drink. She finally navigated the tab release and took a big swig before resuming her throne. "Continue," the young queen decreed.

Smiling, her dad followed orders, and the storytelling began. "I was just about your age when I jumped in a canoe with my dad and headed out across a large lake, much like this one."

Little Jimmy sat up in the front of the canoe, eyes wide with wonder as each stroke led him into the unknown.

"Let's go, Dad. Warp speed," the young Captain Kirk said, commanding his father to pick up the paddling pace.

"I'm given her all she's gawt, Captain," his father responded in his best Scottish accent while pretending to paddle harder and harder.

The canoe continued across the great expanse into a forgotten world of Jimmy's fantasy, blended with reality. His young vibrant imagination began to fuel each pull of the paddle. The canoe slowly passed a tall-masted ship whose glory days had long since passed. Only parts of the ship now remained above its watery grave, and Jimmy couldn't help but think it must have been the pirate vessel that Scuttle the stowaway mouse had escaped from with his hoard of pirate plunder.

Once beyond the ship, the wayward travelers entered the Neutral Zone and said farewell to the last known outpost of the Federation.

"Now begins the real adventure," his dad said from the back of the canoe.

Little Jimmy peered into the coming unknown. It started first as faint vapors, wisps of mist like streams of cotton candy that began moving towards them from all sides. The boy captain gripped his paddle tighter.

"Dad?" he said as the boat glided further into the thick, enveloping fog.

"Just keep paddling, son," his dad responded as the eerie mist began to blanket him in a shadowy essence. Jimmy had to find his resolve; even for a young boy, adventure has its limits. As his father disappeared behind the gray blanket in the stern, Jimmy took a deep breath and slowly turned back around to face forward into the unknown that lay at the far end of each paddle stroke.

His pace quickened through the dense jungle, his feet trampling the overgrown paths and underbrush with total disregard for their wellbeing. He was a man hunting the thing that was hunting him. Onward the warrior charged until he burst through the last of the thick green. A few short steps to halt his pace brought him to a vast rocky wasteland. The humidity of the jungle was replaced with an intense dry heat and an unrelenting sun.

Before him was a partially buried and badly eroded sign across his path. The letters H-O-L-L were followed by what looked like the letter "I" with two broken pieces lying on the ground beside it, preceding a chipped W-O. There was a space indicated a missing letter, and then finally a "D" which now rested belly up on the ground.

James stood taking in the view of these giant letters, which had once held great significance. Confused, he turned to see the edge of the vast green at his back. But instinctively, he knew that his path lay forward. His attention turned to his jungle wardrobe, now replaced by a mustard tunic complete with a Federation-style insignia. The hilt of his sword still peeked over his shoulder.

He took a few more steps forward until he saw them: Large reptilian footprints led past the great sign and across the wasteland. Captain James knew what he had to do and began the hunt. Through what remained of the large "I" and "W" letters, he ventured into the wasteland, into the barren nothingness.

"Dad? Dad!" His littlest one tried to wake him from his trance-like stare. "You stopped your story," she said innocently while shoving another handful of popcorn into her mouth.

James came back to the current moment to see his riveted audience waiting with large eyes. "I haven't thought about that canoe trip in a long time."

"What happened in the fog?" the oldest shot back.

"Were you scared?" her younger sister asked while sipping from her third can of orange soda that day.

Her dad smiled. "I was. An adventure into the unknown can be a scary place." He shifted in his camping chair and stoked the fire with another small piece of wood. "Facing our fears, at any age, leads to magic," he said softly.

His two daughters slowly looked at each other and then back to their dad. In unison, they asked:

"Did you make it through the fog?!"

Their dad smirked and leaned forward on his throne as the warmth of the campfire and the love from his girls became all the audience he needed.

"The fog was thick as pea soup, but each paddle stroke took us deeper into the unknown towards a distant shore."

Little Jimmy's eyes were on high alert. The young captain and his wingman were flying blind. The enveloping fog muffled all sound except those from a raven that cawed in the distance.

"That's our lighthouse," the dad assured his son. "Keep paddling toward that bird sound."

"Bird or pterodacty?" the young boy muttered as he strained to see anything in front of him. Finally, some of the creepy mist began to dissipate, just enough for Little Jimmy's eyes to seize the wondrous sight of land.

"Dad! Dad! Land!" The adventurer began to pump his paddle with vigor. "I see land!"

The canoe drifted up onto the sandy spit of the uncharted planet. Jimmy looked back at his dad, his eyes full of raging excitement.

"Two to transport, Mr. Scott," the boy captain said to his father.

"Aye, Captain," Dad responded with a Scottish brogue.

The two made their way out of the canoe and stood on the shore surrounded by wisps of mist and sounds that were unfamiliar to the young boy. The "caw" from the black lighthouse actually came from above, from a black creature perched like a guardian, welcoming them to his land. The new planet had an eerie sound to Little Jimmy, a humming backdrop that consistently echoed the vastness of what lay ahead. A chill came over him.

"Are you okay, son?" his dad asked.

The boy before the man filled his asthmatic lungs with a deep breath to calm himself. He nodded. "Affirmative. I just wish we had a couple of 'red shirts' with us."

The two would always be linked through the timeless references to Star Trek. This one in particular referred to the poor guy in red that always beamed down to a planet with Captain Kirk to be promptly disintegrated, sacrificed, eaten, and so on.

Their laughter reached the heavens. "Good one!" his dad said. "Now, let's grab our stuff."

"Are we setting up camp here on the beach?" Jimmy asked while grabbing his backpack.

His dad turned to his son and got down on one knee. Guiding his son's vision, he pointed up to the raven high above them.

"See that crow?" he said.

"Raven."

"See that 'raven'?" his dad asked, smiling at the correction. "Now, look slowly to the right, and you will see it."

Jimmy turned his head, waiting for the mist to reveal the target. A breeze ruffled his elf-like quaff and cleared the fog from his sight-line. There it was, high above him: a large rocky plateau that looked like it was kissing the sky.

"*That's* where we will camp tonight," said his dad from behind him. The boy didn't flinch, instead he just cinched up his gear. "You will lead us," his dad continued. It was time for Captain Jimmy to channel Captain James.

Captain James approached it, cautiously at first. Its appearance was cast in rock and sand, but the sight was unmistakable to him. His hand slid along one arm of it, wiping the dirt and years off its control panel. His hypnotic stare could not be broken as he circled the stony mausoleum, perfect in its scale and authenticity. With a deep breath, the mustard-tunic warrior sat in the captain's chair of the starship Enterprise. *He sat alone among the emptiness of the wasteland while connecting to something long since removed from his soul.*

Captain Jimmy was doing his best to navigate the rocky terrain. "What do you think we'll see at the top?" He kept climbing.

"Not sure," his dad responded. "But I bet the view will be amazing."

"I want to see the stars. Just nothing but the stars of adventure," said the dreamer within.

Captain James was now approaching a steep ridge that led to a plateau. But there was something guarding the entrance to the rocky incline. It was small in its stony stature, not menacing at all. He was first greeted by the smallest part of it extending towards him. The creature's short and portly stature was immediately felt in the captain's heart. A thin neck led to a large head with oversized eyes.

James moved toward the bulbous extended finger of E.T. the extraterrestrial, who was waiting for Elliot's gentle touch, a reunion of abandoned child and dream.

"Why? Why do dreams and wonder cease?" he asked the alien softly.

Silence. James extended his own finger, the tip of it meeting the bulbous digit with a gentle kiss. As the fingers touched, a faint glimmer of red began to pulsate from E.T.'s rocky chest. It grew in strength as not even the stony prison could confine its power.

"I'll be right here." The voice of Little Jimmy, locked away long ago in an empty Los Angeles apartment, echoed across the wasteland.

James' eyes closed. Love, he thought. Love in all things is what keeps the child's dream alive. *The heart light of the alien grew more powerful in unison with the captain's thoughts. "The child within needs to dream," said Captain James softly before repeating it as a powerful statement of confirmation: "The child within needs to dream!" He withdrew his finger from E.T.'s with childlike joy and turned to the rocky steps leading to the plateau. Upward he went in a hurry.*

Captain Jimmy was struggling. Nearing the top, the fog was still covering much of the view, and the impending dark of night was knocking.

"I don't know why we couldn't have beamed up there, Dad. Kirk wouldn't have—" The trekkie child's banter was interrupted by the sound of sliding dirt and rocks when the ground beneath his foot gave way.

"Dad!" He cried out as his body shifted down the embankment while he clawed at anything he could reach to stop his descent. After a few seconds, he came to a rest at his father's feet.

He turned to his dad with terror and defeat in his eyes. "Can we camp at the beach?"

"Try again," his father said in a calming tone that Jimmy had come to cherish.

The young captain sighed in exasperation and began the climb upward once again, retracing the steps he had just climbed. The fear of sliding again was building, and he hesitated with each planting of his foot or reach of his arm. Nearing the point of his first incident, his footing gave way again, causing him to fall.

Arriving by his dad once more, tears started to form in his eyes. "I can't do it!"

"Yes, you can. You can do anything, son. Try again."

After a few sniffles, the boy tried again, only to be right back by his dad's feet a few moments later. Now sobbing, with fresh blood on his knees to mark his failed attempts, he quit.

"I don't want to do it I can't!" he screamed between the downfall of full-fledged tears. His dad moved closer among the wisps of fog.

"Jimmy, remember that time you were scared to swing the bat a few years ago?" his dad softly asked. His son acknowledged with a sniffle.

"What happened the very next game?"

A sniffle and then, "I got my first hit," Jimmy answered softly.

"Not just a hit, but a triple. All because you faced your fear with a swing. A try. Life is full of 'tries,' one after another. You will always slip. You will always fall from time to time. Real heroes keep going."

Jimmy wiped his eyes and looked at his father.

"They keep going," his dad said again with one last look into his eyes before standing back up. His son followed suit, standing and turning to face his fear head on.

As Captain Jimmy stood before the last rise of the steep terrain, sizing up the competition, his dad leaned in from behind and whispered, "Sometimes in life, a captain looks for a different path."

His son steered his courage with a deep breath and then the assault began, slowly at first and then with more and more speed. His dad watched silently as his boy approached the falling point. Jimmy paused in a crouched position, his cat-like senses kicking in. His eyes scanned the path, looking for clues, and then he saw it: a series of small rocks over to the right side that could serve as footholds. He shifted, deviating right, his scrawny limbs outstretched with whatever strength his frame could muster. He began to climb. A near slip paused his ascent but only for a moment as he continued on, more determined with each successful inch. Those inches began to add up, as did the smile that the boy unleashed when he realized he was doing it. His momentum up the last part of the rocky climb increased, spurred on by his courageous triumph. Faster and faster, he went. This was his *Rocky* movie moment, and he could hear the famous score trumpeting in his mind. The last few steps were successfully navigated, and the young boy took his place atop the rocky plateau, his boney Balboa arms triumphantly raised in the air as the music swelled.

The words "I did it!" were as loud as the musical score in his head. His dad soon joined him and the two shared the view before them. They stood high above the lake and above the remaining fog to see the night sky begin its twinkle in the glorious magic hour of light between two worlds. It was a beautiful reward.

The surface of the outcrop was barren, marred only by the failed remains of others on quests of their own. Items were scattered about. Renaissance dueling pistols, conquistador helmets, rusted and pitted medieval armor, and roman gladiatorial weapons were all that remained of warriors like James, seeking forgiveness.

The acrid stench of death permeated the air. So many lives and dreams had come to this place to make a stand, and now it was his time. An ominous hissing sound and a word not quite audible to the warrior began to dance across the stagnant plateau, its point of origin a small cave opening at the foot of a rocky mound.

The sound grew in intensity, and the hissing noise morphed into an evil-sounding, serpentine word, drawled from within the cave: "Guilt." *There was an elongated exhale on the "t" sound, and then the word was repeated, over and over, striking Captain James with every slow breath the creature released. But the captain stood strong, unmoved by the sinister moan.*

Finally, the solid dark of the cave opening was broken by the emerging body of a two-legged figure. Moving slowly, it took a few steps before completely breaking free of the darkness. High noon at twilight saw two figures in a standoff. Captain James against the Gorn, a large half-humanoid, half-lizard creature born of the fires of guilt. Its scaled and leathered skin wrapped tightly around its mutated muscles. Unlike its predecessor from Star Trek lore, this beast stood with two heads atop its large shoulders. The head on its left shoulder continued its hissing exhalations: "Guilt… guilt… guilt…"

It slowly approached with one of its huge clawed hands holding hundreds of golden rings hung on a twine loop, trophies of the creatures' countless victories.

Wedding rings, *the captain thought to himself.*

"Guilt…" *moaned the creature.*

Many mighty warriors had lost their battle with this Gorn of Guilt. The sight of the rings, and the emotions that came with them, seemed to hypnotize James momentarily. But then the still air was broken by faint cries, echoing across the wasteland. They drifted in slowly at first, like an angelic voice against the serpentine exhalations. As they grew in volume, the Gorn lowered its trophies and looked around. The sound was foreign to it and this land of death. But to the warrior captain, they were the familiar cries of the Valkyries, summoning him to victory. They grew louder, gaining equal power to the Gorn's exhaled decree: "Guilt!"

"DADDY!" This volley of hope reached the ears of Captain James. His trance broken and eyes now fixed on his opponent, he slowly moved his right hand to the hilt of destruction behind his shoulder.

✧   ✧   ✧

"Daddy!" His eldest's latest attempt to get his attention worked. Her father's gaze returned from the night sky to the orange glow of the campfire and his daughters. "Daddy, did you see any constellations? Like we did in Mexico?"

"So many. I felt like I could almost touch them," her father answered. "My dad and I stayed up for hours, just lying on the ground and dreaming of those lights."

"That was a pretty scary story," said a higher-pitched voice, beautiful in its matter-of-fact tone.

Both Dad and oldest daughter turned to the other avid listener, sitting in her folding chair. By this time, her popcorn bag was empty, and now a bottle of Coke was in her grasp.

"Scary?" her dad repeated, realizing it was the second time she'd described her father's story in that way. "I guess it could be. I mean, it was at times."

James approached from the other side of the fire and stood over his youngest daughter, reaching out his hand. "Come with me."

She placed her small hand in his and let him pull her from her throne. "Where are we going?"

"Just down by the water," James continued, feeling her firm grip. Next up, it was her sister's turn. "Come on," her dad offered with his free hand. She quickly accepted, and the three made their way from the campfire to the water's edge.

The cool of the lake felt medicinal as the warmth of the fire vanished, taking the ambient orange light with it. Now there was just blackness and the night sky.

"Whoa!" the youngest softly said as the stars came to life over the silhouetted mountains. The three stood together, holding hands with only the stars in the sky eavesdropping on their conversation.

"Being scared is always a part of life, girls. It never goes away. Sometimes, it just happens when you're doing something new."

The younger sibling pointed at her sister. "She gets scared in dance."

"I do not!"

He smiled faintly. "I always struggled with being scared at the starting line, sweetie," he said, comforting her. "I..." He let his voice trail off, deciding not to continue.

"Why *did* you stop rowing, Daddy?" his eldest asked. "You were the best."

Deadly silence fell over the lake, engulfing them. The entire ecosystem seemed to be waiting for his answer.

He cleared his throat. "Because... because it was the only thing I truly cared about, trying to be the best, I mean, and being acknowledged for it. More... more than anything."

He let the words hang in the air, knowing that his two children were too young to grasp what he was admitting. *Even more than you and your mother,* whispered the voice of guilt in his heart and mind.

A bloody Captain James' and his torn tunic were in the Gorn's deadly vice grip. It began to squeeze the life out of its weaker adversary. "Guilt..." the beast hissed in honor of its impending victory.

"Y... you... you both..." James' breath was all but gone as he tried to speak.

The pain was building inside, and he could feel it stimy his willingness to speak. But he fought on.

"You... you both suffered because of it," James finally managed to say to his girls, releasing just the tiniest bit of pressure from within. "Your mom suffered because of it," he added, reducing even more pressure. "I wasn't around for you, wasn't there for the family when I should have been," he managed to say as the air found its way back into his lungs, powering him to continue.

Captain James unleashed a patented double-ear slap to the hissing head, causing the Gorn to drop his adversary. Quickly, James followed the strike with a double dropkick to its chest, which sent it staggering backwards. The captain looked for his sword, and finally seeing it on the ground nearby, he dove for it.

But the Gorn was coming. James reached and scurried, finally securing a forceful hold on the hilt of his weapon. Its touch offered salvation, and he spun around, eyeing the beast.

The girls could hear their father shifting his weight on the small pebbles of the beach, and in the darkness, they could just barely make it out his movement as he turned to face them. He was silent for a long moment, and they watched in wonder and anticipation as he dropped down to one knee.

"Remember what my dad said to me on the climb?"

"Take a different path," his eldest responded.

Her dad nodded. "I have to take a different path now. I can't make the climb anymore," his words were simple and direct.

The girls stood still, as any young kid would, just trying to understand a lost adult, absorbing, processing, and ready to listen for more.

"Mom and I have gone on separate paths now," he said. "I will always love her. Always. And I will always love you." Tears began to form in his eyes. "I am sorry that I hurt both of you so very badly. I never meant to do that. I... I love you both very much. And I want you to understand something..."

Captain James slowly straightens, his sword at the ready. His eyes burn into the Gorn, standing still in its own defiance. The sirens of a beach conversation fill the air of the plateau as the father, the captain, the seeker slowly moves towards his opponent.

"Life is about happiness... about joy... about always seeing things the way you do now, with love and wonder." Captain James raised his weapon.

"Don't ever settle for anything but that... in your heart and in your life. I have to trust you will understand one day. But for now, I *need* to start forgiving myself for hurting you."

The water from his eyes seemed greater than the lake itself. James reached out and gently grabbed their tiny hands, pulling them in a bit closer. His eyes pleaded for release from the guilt and shame of the beast within.

"I can work to forgive myself, but I need you to forgive me too." Crying, he completes the exorcism with a soft, final release: "I am sorry."

His youngest bursts into a sobbing cry and lunges into her dad's arms, into his soul. He holds her tightly and then looks to her sister, who wipes both of her eyes with her hands. She joins the hug under the endless spotlights of childlike memories in the night sky above. In this watery arena, a faint whooshing, slicing noise fills the air, one that only he can hear, and with it, reptilian cries of pain and retreat. The three silhouettes will not release their embrace, nor should they. Ever.

Passage to Hope

The mighty sails billowed with life as the rolling seas and their salty mist greeted the wayward crew with a welcoming moisture. A soaring albatross accompanied them on their journey, flying alongside the ancient three-masted schooner as it moved up and down on the waves. A pair of eyes tracked the bird, noticing the way it danced effortlessly with the wind as its large wings spread out over the water below. It was free.

James, however, was not. He sat on the deck of the ship, leaning up against a large oak barrel of rum, drinking cup in hand, after his victory over the Gorn. His mustard Starfleet tunic has been replaced by a suit of armor, its robust agility a cross between the armor of medieval and Anglo-Saxon time periods. The ship's crew of small mice and rodents were feverishly busy with their sailing duties, but the captain of the vessel was sharing a celebratory toast. Scuttle the stowaway mouse sat above James, his tiny legs and pirate boots dangling over the edge of the rum barrel. His blue, buttoned-up jacket and tricorn hat gave him the look of a classy seafaring captain, rather than some pirate renegade scoundrel.

James was booking passage across the Seas of Tomorrow to the Port of Hope before embarking on the deep passage inward to the Tree of Life and its holy grail of truth. Sir James raised his cup to his brethren, and as the voyage unfolded, so did their reminiscing tales of a faraway land called Cydot Drive.

✧ ✧ ✧

The round glass lens did its best to magnify the view between the rolling waves. The tiny eye that was pressed to the viewing piece squinted to catch a glimpse. A few mousey blinks and there it was, coming full-steam ahead between the rise and fall of the churning seas. The spiny dorsal fins of the creature broke the surface. Captain Scuttle removed the spyglass and looked to his mate James. The two knew what was coming.

"You have to get me to Hope," James said to his old friend, standing on the nearby railing.

The diminutive captain nodded while his tiny finger pushed the brim of his tricorn hat up on his forehead.

"It won't come for you here. It can't touch a soul in the company of others," Scuttle offered while jumping off the railing onto James' shoulders. "It only feeds when the soul is alone and exposed," the mouse whispered into the ear of his lifelong friend.

The ROAR of the beast, combined with the sound of water crashing against its scaled exterior, consumed the air. A great shadow soon engulfed the three-masted ship as water rained down from the heavens. The sails blustered in the pulsating flapping noise that made the knight, his captain, and the trusted crew shudder. The great dragon-like creature flew overhead and off towards the horizon.

Scuttle turned to his old friend. "It's got wings, mate. Good luck."

✧   ✧   ✧

A short time later, the ship had made its way into the Port of Hope and secured a mooring. The last few passes of the sharpening stone kissed the blade of the warrior, who sat in the company of Scuttle. The two shared a moment of recognition before Scuttle broke the silence.

From behind a barrel, the mouse dragged out a leather-bound satchel with some modest effort.

"This is for you on your journey," he said to his friend.

James easily picked it up off the deck of the ship. "What is it? Doesn't feel like anything's in there."

"Ha! Easy for you to say, Mr. Muscles." Scuttle then adopted a more serious tone. "If you make it to the tree, you'll know what to do with it. It's not for you."

James sheathed his weapon and nodded to his companion. The knight errant knew that this would be a solo journey and extended his finger to the mouse captain for a farewell exchange. The captain touched the end of it with his own.

The Drum

The brass bell hanging from the print-shop door rang as it was opened. When the *Outlander's* destined magnetic pull drew the television characters back together over the centuries, the present-day Scottish lover couldn't help but feel every inch of the fictional reunion in his present moment with Claire.

James held the car door open for his Sassenach. He took in the nuance of her movement and the way she acknowledged his chivalry with a small movement of one side of her lip. Her self-imposed exile was over yet again, and the love she felt for her warrior had pulled her back from the brink. Back from a loveless marriage and scrupulous friends. Back to joy in her heart. A sense of freedom permeated the air, and the two capped it off with a drive and a tune played with the volume on full. The Bose stereo did its best to not be drowned out by the belting couple and the wind from the open windows. The random and foreshadowing selection of "Free Bird" was the rekindling of a glorious moment for James on that hot August night. The boyish wonder of Coach Cain's convertible, an asthma showdown, a tennis court, and the comfort of a queen filled his mind from a youthful memory.

I think those moments were why I allowed myself to be manipulated by this powerful force of love, or Claire, or whatever you want to call it. She was a gateway to youth for me. The feelings I had when we were together and when things were "on" were simply life in high definition, the way an excited child greets each moment of the day. This was our time, and soon, my closet would dance again with her personal belongings.

The epic guitar solo of the sonic trip down memory lane was paused as the two love birds made a quick pit stop at her house to pick up more clothes to further certify this new chapter for them. When the joyous couple exited the house, bags in tow, the innocence of the moment was shattered. As were all four of James' car windows in her driveway, taken out by a pipe (or something like it).

"What did they do?" you may be asking. Well, in truth, they did what two kids in love would do. They shrugged it off, cleaned off the glass on the seats, and continued on their journey, not looking in the rearview

mirror. "Free Bird" picked up where it had left off, and now they had a makeshift convertible to help Jim bridge the distance back to the tennis of yesterday. Oh, and in case you're wondering, the window culprit turned out to be a best friend of George who'd been doing a drive by, no doubt on his way to score drugs.

Well, Claire moved in again, and again, the carnage of her old life, colliding with the new one James was trying desperately to build, took center stage. Erratic behavior and white-trash drama with her stoned husband and sister crept back in. Her own guilt and pressure from her parents started to mount and she, like James, began to question her own sanity in all of this. He was beginning to hear it: the drum of futility.

Thump... Thump... Thump...

Mirrored Reflections

The Claire and James Show continued on, marching to its underlying beat over the next handful of months. It was now that magical time of the year between Halloween and Christmas, where the November chill is greeted with warm turkey, stuffing, and NFL football. It was American Thanksgiving, the last Thursday of November, and while James had been in Canada for eleven years now, not once had he celebrated the holiday. But that was about to change. Finally.

His job was simple; turn on the football game for ambient visual background, select some classic holiday Christmas tunes for an audio score, and set the table. Claire's job was equally simple: After a quick run home to check on her kids, she was going to the store to pick up the necessary ingredients for the holiday feast. Together they would prepare a quiet evening meal, as couples do.

The bottled wine now lay half-finished on the beautifully decorated table, never mind the one empty folding chair that sat next to James. A perfectly cooked cheese quesadilla adorned the white dinner plate while the evening football game came to a close. There is something quite satisfying about eating a gooey cheese offering with a knife and fork, especially when washed down with chilled vodka that combines with a hint of red-wine residue in a stemmed glass. Ah yes, King James' party for one was in full effect.

As was the war inside me. It was raging, part anger and part embarrassment at my own willingness to subject myself to this bullshit. Pure unadulterated bullshit. Of course, there was some plausible reasoning that was offered via my cell phone from the rolodex of cockamamy excuses. It didn't take a German rocket scientist to see how little value I placed on my own self-worth. Looking back, that was the real quest that would take me deeper into the jungle. Love is the strongest force on the planet, and I was now determined to stand before the greatest of its mighty powers: the love of one's self.

Sir James continued on horseback. He was surrounded by a landscape of grays, browns, and endless earth tones in this land where moisture was as common as the damp chill in the air. Intermittent rocks and dense green patches of moss littered the open countryside.

Slowly, he journeyed, taking his time to marvel at the land, which seemed oddly familiar to his soul. He pondered what lay ahead at the mythical tree and thought of his trusty friend and the gift that had been entrusted to him. He looked down at the small sack, secured firmly by his side, hoping that he could deliver on his promise.

The knight and his horse continued on their quest, travelling farther and farther, until they came to a part of their path that ran along jagged rocky bluffs by a vacant stone fortress that overlooked the ocean below. Endless stone walls riddled the countryside as they did in a distant land of make believe called Rhode Island.

It was over the next rise that the landscape began to change, and finally, a great forest stood like a doorway to yet another world. When a strange darkness started to fall, Sir James at first thought it was a late afternoon cloud but soon realized that the shadow over their position was growing. His neck twisted for a view and got what he wanted. The great beast was coming from some perch high in the sky.

"Hey-ah! Let's go!" The knight commanded his steed. Their only course of action was an all-out gallop for safety. The shadow grew as the beast descended. The race was on.

The dragon was descending, but the expanse of trees was getting closer and closer. As the fleeing knight darted inside, the beast had no choice but to pull up its trajectory and continue over the canopy. A great torrent of wind overtook the forest, throwing up plumes of dirt and fallen leaves that assaulted the knight before retreating back to a deafening stillness. There would be no confrontation today; the knight knew that the dragon was flying north, where their epic showdown was ordained to happen.

The tree itself seemed a bit smaller than he had hoped. Standing at seven feet tall, the height was okay, but it didn't have the width that he'd envisioned. "Are you sure we don't want white lights?" Claire asked.

"Colored lights. Non-negotiable," said the Christmas traditionalist.

What can I tell you? As a Christmas purest at heart, those new-fangled iridescent bulbs don't cut it. I need the old Christmas kaleidoscope of colors on my tree. With Thanksgiving over, the official holiday season had begun. Of course, Claire had resurfaced (the next day, as a matter of fact), meandering her way back into my dumb welcoming arms. Whether her boy had indeed been sick will forever remain just one more mystery in a long line of mysteries, like the cheese quesadilla substitute for a turkey meal with stuffing.

The two scorned love birds wheeled a shopping cart through the aisles of the department store with their new holiday tree in a box. When they could just *be*, away from the anxiety and pressure of life's expectations and their own demons, you would be hard pressed to find a happier couple more in love.

The days progressed, with a blend of good and bad, leading up to the magic of Christmas. James and Claire had spent some time planning how the holiday would work between her family and her living with him. The plan was laid out, on paper anyway. The drumbeats in his soul warned of another plan, one with stained glass shattered all around him. But again, when you have nothing else, least of all your own dignity and self-worth, you will always find a way to cling to hope. Well, ladies and gentlemen, hope is not a strategy. Nor is it a shield against the twisted power of love.

That love was on full display on the second to last day of school before Christmas break—Thursday afternoon, the twentieth of December, to be exact. Cue the dramatic thunder as Thursdays seem to be the witching hour for Claire. She invited James to help her very own daughter make and decorate gingerbread houses at the end of school, among other parents no less. It was one thing to be seen in public but another to be at school as a couple. His heart was full that afternoon.

It was also primed for a vampire-style exorcism like the famous Mercy Brown from the annals of colonial Rhode Island history. On her way home after school to drop off the kids, his Sassenach vanished, disappearing through the stones and off the radar. The anxiety began immediately in the pit of James' stomach within thirty minutes of his cell phone becoming obsolete. He knew something was different this time, and as usual, he opened the freezer to grab his only refuge. This time, the rage began to swell with each swig of vodka, a twisted confirmation that his drumming intuition had been right.

The meandering road through the forest continued onward for Sir James and his trusty steed. Their trek had led them deeper and deeper into the dense woods. However, the once vibrant and teeming forest was now full of ash and death, a sign that they were drawing near. A procession of bodies who'd failed on their own quests now accompanied their trek forward.

"Poor souls," said the knight softly.

Sir James surmised that these men and women had fallen to the purgatory that claims most: the torment of being unwilling to go all in on the quest. It was an eerie reminder that this was a one-way journey for the knight. It had to be, or he too would assume his place in this cemetery of lost truth.

What was left of the ashen forest began to close in on the two travelers, pushing them further towards a small tunnel of grotesque and twisted tree limbs. The rest of this journey would have to be made on foot.

Sir James made sure the satchel from Scuttle was secured as he stood before his horse. A soft touch on its long nose punctuated his appreciation of its valor. The knight took a deep breath and turned to face the blackness of the tunnel. His right hand reached up for the hilt of his weapon and drew it. The knight, the warrior, the man slowly began to disappear into the darkness.

✧   ✧   ✧

The death spiral had begun. The morning after her latest holiday disappearance, James found himself sitting in his car across the street from Claire's mother's house, George's black truck exactly where he'd figured it would be, knowing that her mom was out of town. There was no sign of life except the liquid that drained from the small plastic bottle of alcohol in his lap. One last swig, and he summoned the courage to do what he thought the knight should always do: save the damsel in distress. This time he wasn't going to play nice like he had when showing up the day after Christmas a year earlier.

James approached the house, looking for any sign of movement through the curtainless windows. There was none. He knocked on the front door and peered through the windows. Nothing. No sign of anything. Around back he went to the back patio.

Still nothing. He stepped towards the sliding glass doors. The curtains were open. He looked inside and scanned the main room of the house. His eyes were quickly drawn to the coffee table right in front of him, and exhibit A, with which the prosecution would rest its case. A wallet was in plain sight, not a big deal. Beside it, however, was a small rolled-up tube, a credit card, and a small tray. Bingo! Right out of a fucking movie and in plain sight. Well, James lost his shit and snapped. All the lies, all the bullshit he'd suffered at the hands of a love bound by destiny. To think he'd been so blind to the truth… He started to bang on the windows.

"Claire!!!"

I can't even sanely remember the manic state I was in. I recall darting back around front to bang on that door, trying anything I could think of to get to speak to someone. When that front-door assault was done, I headed back around back, but by the time I arrived, Sister Satan had closed all the blinds and curtains. Man, that woman was fast. One more rap on the window, and lo and behold, Satan's head appeared between two tightly pulled curtains. Her eyes were as wide as the fissure in my heart.

"Leave, or I'll call the police!" she barked.

"Fuck off!" James shouted. "You better put away your nose stash first! Listen..." He paused and managed to find his calm voice. "I know Claire is downstairs. Just tell her to come up and talk to me, please."

"She's not here."

This set him off again. He could have pleaded the fact that her shoes were by the door, her purse, even the damn truck, but he figured she probably wouldn't comprehend anyway, at least not without pictures.

"I'm gonna call the cops!" she barked again.

James looked her dead in the eye. "Do it."

She did. Next thing I knew, I was waiting for the police to come. In retrospect, that was a dumbass move. Not only was I buzzed, with booze in my car, but I had completely forgotten that Claire's stepdad was an ex-cop.

It didn't take long for a female police officer to pull up. James greeted her with his usual charm and as much "sober" grace as he could muster. He pleaded his concern for Claire's wellbeing.

"There's nothing I can do unless Claire herself calls for help," the officer responded.

"Can't you go and at least check to make sure they are alright?"

At this point, I just wanted to know that Claire was okay, and if nothing else, make her feel more like a piece of shit than I hoped she was already feeling. Never mind the pure hatred I felt towards her sister, who had quickly topped Broom Hilda on my despicable-human scale.

Realizing fairly quickly that there was nothing he could do, James gave up. He bid the officer adieu and raised a middle finger towards the house in the hopes that someone was peeking out from behind the paranoid white curtains of chaos.

First stop on the railway into the abyss was the liquor store and a nice bottle of dark rum. Next, a grand tour of all the romantic places where Claire and he would rendezvous through the stones, those magical places where the world fucked off and time stood still. But upon his arrival at each romantic sanctuary, he found nothing but a crater left in the wake of self-betrayal.

I was beginning to feel something that I'd never really felt before: the feeling that there was no need to go on with life. The road I had taken to the northlands of the island had been a crusade, and while accompanied by liquid energy, there had been no ulterior motive other than to escape the expectation of society and confront that head of the beast. This was different. There was a reckless abandon in every waking thought I had.

✧   ✧   ✧

"Death," he whispered. Sir James had emerged from the tunnel of twisted branches to stand in a vast open area. It was the only word that came to his mind. Nothing lived. Nothing remained but scorched black earth. The only glimmer of light came from a distant object.

The thick golden borders came into focus as Sir James drew near. The object stood some ten feet high and roughly six feet across, its pane of glass undaunted by the surrounding environment. Standing alone in this ashen wasteland was a large golden mirror.

James stood before this alien structure, struck by the wonder of it. His perfectly crafted reflection looked back at him, and he took in the weary sight. Slowly, his reflection began to dissolve into roving blue skies and billowing white puffs that danced about in the air. Beneath it was an ocean, its vibrant blue and green pummeling the majestic strength of a lighthouse perched on a rocky shoreline.

Images began to dance in this portal to long ago: A street with a young boy, playing basketball with his father; the same boy being held closely by his mother, a hypodermic needle puncturing skin and a hand clutching an old red stuffy.

Bike-riding excursions through the magic-filled sidewalks of Wickford led to innocent conversations sitting on the edge of a dock. Cool, refreshing sips of lemonade and the laughter at one of Malcolm's Scottish jokes. That loving smile of a happy boy morphed into a sad expression as that same boy sat alone on the cold steel of a folding chair at a school dance.

"Love," the warrior softly said.

"Yes... Love," a deep voice echoed back from the center of the mirror, and then continued as more images appeared before him. "It is the one cell from which all life springs forth." The younger knight is now laying in the comforting arms of his high-school sweetheart post epic sport battle.

"It is a gift to truly love," the mirror echoes. "But peace comes from truly loving yourself. Forgive the boy in the chair."

The last sentence hung in the air—air that began to circulate and churn, sending ash and soot upwards. A thunderous thud shook the ground beneath the brave knight.

"Forgive yourself," the mirror offered as the warrior slowly turned to face the origin of that sound of impact.

The great winged beast stood there in all its epic glory. Mighty wings were outstretched to either side of its massive, scaled body. Protruding from the center of its shoulders was a long, strong neck that held a fierce jaw with rows and rows of teeth. On either side of the neck were two scarred-over stubs that had once held its other heads. The remaining head shot forward and bellowed a ghastly roar that seemed to come from every fiber of its being. The sound of a violin began to rise, introducing the musical score that would signal that the final battle had begun.

A Knife by Any Other Name

Those hypnotic violin strings continued perfectly, setting up the soulful voice that became a staple to James through the years. CUE: the smooth voice of Mr. Andy Williams singing "Have Yourself a Merry Little Christmas"

A glass toast hung in the air, a fitting marker to James' troubles not being even remotely "miles away." Down the pipe the vodka went into the abyss, just like the owner of the glass. His mouth is wiped against his sleeve as the red, blue, and green from the glowing tree twinkled in his eyes. It was Christmas eve, and a haggard James stood alone with a bottle of spirits in his left hand and an empty glass in his right. It had been three days since the chaotic scene outside that house, likely matching the chaos that ensued inside. Since then, he'd had only one contact with Claire, who'd wanted to come and get her stuff from his apartment.

I should have burned it all, torched it in a blaze of glory, but instead, I'd just vacated the building when she and George had come by to grab it. Now it was just me again on day three of a relentless bender of self-loathing that was reaching its boiling point. A new holiday tune swelled and so did my psychosis, as I pondered Bing Crosby's crooning exaltation of dear and faithful friends gathered "near to us."

James cracked himself in the face with his own fist. As it didn't have the desired effect, he did it again. "Crack!" His clenched fist slammed into his right cheekbone, sending him reeling against the wall. A few seconds passed while his brain recalibrated from the blow, and then, like a caged animal, he sprang back to roaring life. The bottle was hoisted to his lips, and he guzzled as much as he could before sending it flying against the opposing wall to shatter all over his carpet.

James and his bloody cheek continued his staggered walk towards one end of the kitchen. His vision and perception of reality was mutating. The holiday music had drifted away to some inaudible background hum. From a closet door at the other end of the kitchen came an odd sound, growing louder. It was the unmistakable scraping of something heavy against the floor, paired with the sound of plodding footsteps. The clink and rattle of chains grew in volume. The door was flung open then, and out of the blackness it came, its shackled feet drawing its chains forward with every step into the multicolored lights of Christmas Eve. The imprisoned figure emerged wholly from the darkness, a ghostly version of the man who bore witness. James was indeed facing a beast, an aged man whose light for love, life, and laughter had been snuffed out. His coiffed elf hair was a thinning gray mess that sat on top of a head that seemed to have withered over the years. His ears kept their prominence and only added to his otherworldly look. Darkened sun spots of time littered his face, and his lips had given way to gums that had receded like a moon tide. Jacob Marley was old, he was miserable, and this version of him... was me.

The ground shook with the last of its footsteps and now the two combatants were idle in their defiance. The warrior made the first move, raising his sword and saluting his foe with a vertical gesture. It was then that he caught his own reflection in the shimmering steel. A glimmer of light reflected back into the eyes of the knight.

The reflection created a mask of light on James' face. His blue windows were fixated on one thing, the blade of a large kitchen knife that was now in his hand. His eyes shifted to the closet door as if waiting for something to return. He waited...

Slowly, the origin of the sound emerged from the darkness, and Little Jimmy stood there... wearing a hospital gown and clutching two items in his hands. This figure did not speak but offered the items to James: the strength of Captain Kirk in his left hand, and the love from Rusty the squirrel in his right. James staggered a bit, his grip closing tighter around the knife.

"WHAT DO YOU WANT FROM ME?!" he screamed.

The gentle boy of Christmas Past was unmoved, and just stood there, holding out his offerings.

"What do you want from me?!" the knight screamed into the gazing eyes of the winged creature. The beast's wings pulsated, and then it shot upward into the air, up into the sky, climbing higher and higher before beginning its strafing fiery death run.

The knight's neck craned upward, his gaze following his more powerful foe into the sky. It didn't take long for James to shift his eyes back down to the ground at his feet. Around him, there was nothing but ash, the remains of people, places, and memories gone up in the flames of his own ego, of the beast and its insatiable lust for more. How? *he thought to himself.* Why? *A sense of loneliness and unwelcomed solitude fell over him.*

The heaviness of being alone blew in like a northeast gale. James staggered a few steps, peering into the living room, at the holiday tree and all that should accompany its colorful beauty. The sound of death was all he could think of in the silence of his apartment, at first at least. Then the sound of children's laughter began to percolate, and he was quick to double check the Christmas tree for his two angels, but they weren't there. There were no presents for them tucked beneath the branches. There was only emptiness.

The laughter rose again. He knew this time where they came from. Once again, he slowly turned toward the closet. The second visitor he'd been warned of by Marley appeared outside the door, the ghost of Christmas Present. He watched his joyous girls, nestled under a tree with Brooke's family close by while holiday music filled the air. That loving and happy vision of his girls then morphed into nothing more than a reflection of the man, or rather what was left of him, standing alone in his kitchen. The only thing he had to show for himself was his own unkempt appearance, bloody face, and a knife. It was a wretched sight, one that even James couldn't stand to look at. He shielded his eyes and raised the knife.

"Go away!" he screamed with every ounce of his soul. The beast descended, its throat ready to expel death and add another victim to the long line of heroic wannabes that had taken up this foolish quest. Sir James waited for it.

"Captain, my captain," said a voice that echoed across the ashen land, catching Sir James' attention.

The face is completely recognizable even to the incoherent James. It is the ghostly man in the mirror, his "doppelganger" Robin Williams. The ghost of Christmas Yet to Come was a sad reminder of his own inevitable path. James could feel the anguish building, the pain and sadness of so much loss and chaos. "No more," he whispered, while his eyes unleashed a wash of tears.

"No more," he said again, more loudly this time. Over and over, he said it, louder and louder as the raised kitchen knife began to shake violently in his hand, a slingshot pulled tight, waiting to be released.

"No more!!!" The pinnacle scream was accompanied by a forceful forward thrust of the knife.

The screaming cry of "No more!" echoed all around as the beast's blue flames engulfed him. Sir James did not cry out. Nor did he cry out when he forcefully drove his sword into his own stomach in an act of self-sacrifice. But the beast did. Its fiery death stopped. Deeper and deeper the blade went until it emerged from the other side of the knight's body as he welcomed his own death.

The creature's agonizing scream shook the land, and then it dropped like a giant rock from the sky, impacting the earth with the force of an asteroid. The resulting shockwave sent the impaled knight flying through the air and into the surface of the great mirror, where he disappeared from the ashen landscape.

The knife was still wiggling from its powerful journey into the wood of the closet door, where the ghost of James' future had been floating only a moment earlier.

On the floor knelt a broken man, surrendering to the pain of a life that was no more and the need to assemble a new one.

✧　✧　✧

James had come back to consciousness in the shade of a great tree. A quick inventory revealed that he was still alive. Nothing was there, no wound, no blood… Perplexed, the warrior got to his feet and removed his armor, tossing it to the green earth at his feet. He firmly held the entrusted satchel and took in the stunning view around him.

The blast radius had catapulted him to the top of a large atoll. Before him lay a vast jungle canopy, and beyond it, crystal blue ocean for as far as his eyes could see. The great tree itself was massive, like the sensual weeping willows and grand oaks from a backyard Scottish playground. Its powerful roots were firmly embedded in a decaying stone structure, but its trunk held the most prominence. It was there that James found his sword, impaled in its thick bark. A light grayish sap leaked from the wound.

James approached and knelt down before the liquid offering. His cupped hands caught the tree's sap, allowing it to fill them, and then closing his eyes, he drank deeply of the fountain's gift. There was nothing but silence as he felt the magic elixir of truth working through him like a fever, spreading fast and furious over his body. A sense of wonder, adventure, and play began pulsating through his veins like a runaway train. Feelings and currents from a land full of dreams called Wickford shot through his being. Profound joy came over him, but it wasn't just any joy…

A shadow began to encroach on him where he knelt. He looked up. The first things he saw were two dirty old converse sneakers, tied with a double bow with room on either end to spare, then off-white socks pulled up high against a pair of boney shins. Slender legs give way to a pair of loose-fitting shorts with an elastic waistband, into which was neatly tucked a baggy T-shirt bearing the number "12." He looked farther up, and watched as the unmistakable smile of Little Jimmy grew from ear to prominent ear on a face surrounded by golden elven hair.

I knew you would come.

James couldn't speak. But he quickly searched for the entrusted satchel. He grabbed it and then calmly presented it to Little Jimmy.

The child's small hands undid the leathered fastener, and his tiny eyes peered to the magic within. One hand reached in and slowly removed its contents, which emerged in all its reddish fluffy glory, with big eyes and an unmistakable tail. The gift entrusted to James by Mr. Scuttle was none other than Rusty the squirrel.

Little Jimmy hugged Rusty so tightly that James was worried he might pop the stuffing. Jimmy then shifted his attention back to James, who opened his arms wide. The inner child leapt back into his embrace and into his soul.

Little Jimmy

"The two would never be apart again," the author wrote, in cursive, in a leatherbound journal. After adding an exclamation point, the author sat back in his folding chair. It was Christmas morning, and James was sitting at a table with a bottle of Advil, a large coffee cup, and a nearly empty pot of coffee next to him.

I was definitely in my holiday-morning Scrooge phase. Even though I was hung over, I had waves and waves of supercharged clarity running through my brain. Flashes of creative lightning kept washing over me like surges of innocent youth. It was a loving, liberating madness.

"I am living in my own movie," I said out loud to myself then. For truly I was. I am. Always. Now was the time for the hero within to rise with me, and together, we would step onto the soundstage of life one more time. Together, we needed to emerge from the jungle and save the day as only heroes do. My day. Every day.

For James, that started on the phone, breaking down a fourteen-month wall between himself and his folks. As he listened to their phone ring, his smile grew, boyishly waiting for what would come next: the fumbling of a phone and an exasperated curse word.

"Merry Christmas," he said to his dad.

"Hey, hey!" his dad eagerly responded in excitement. "Carol! Grab the other phone. Jimmy's on the line!... How's it going?"

James took a moment before answering. "It's great. Things are good. The elf from Cydot misses ya," he said with a laugh.

"H-Hello," came his mom's voice from the other phone.

"Hello, Mother," he said. "Merry Christmas."

Another laugh, another smile as the Christmas morning conversation continued with all its usual components: Dad cutting off Mom when she started rambling too much; Mom making fun of Dad for dropping the phone, twice apparently; Dad forgetting the name of some movie that they'd just watched; and the sharing of old holiday memories from a time that, today, was still alive.

With a press of a button, he finally ended the conversation and leaned back in his folding chair. "Living in a movie, indeed," he said as his hands tousled his own hair in excitement. A messy and disheveled version of Beethoven smirked and turned back his journal. His new "Ode to Joy" was about to begin. He raised his pen like the mighty conductor of old.

"And... action!" he triumphantly barked.

```
FADE IN:
INT. APARTMENT - MORNING

A messy and disheveled man is busy reviewing his
own experiences from the remnants of empty liquor
bottles and internal chaos that has been plaguing
him for days. JAMES (late 40s), has the appearance
of a man with an interesting and eventful past,
and a hint that his best days are yet to come. In
the corner, a beautifully lit Christmas tree does
its best to shine a multitude of colors in the
daylight hours.

He stares for a moment at the fading tunic on
his forty-something-year-old Captain Kirk doll
recently removed from its stored slumber. They
have been together a lifetime, and with a smirk,
James gets to work.

He feverishly writes down a few choice words onto
the pages of a leatherbound journal. CAMERA PUSHES
IN on the page:

"(Truth + Trust) = Acceptance"
```

                    JAMES (Voice Over)
That was the magic formula that came to
me. We all need to arrive at our own
individual truth. Whatever that may be
for each of us. For me, it was my inner
child, that adventurer's spirit, the
dreamer. I will always roam this earth as
a seeker, an artist, and always with the
wonder of a young boy from Cydot Drive.
That truth landed. And when truth lands,
trust begins.

EXT. THE JUNGLE - DUSK

The reunited man and boy, with Rusty in tow, began to
make their long arduous trek out of the dense jungle
and back into civilization. The two walk side by side
down the path as the sun begins to fall lower with each
emerging step.

                    JAMES (V.O.)
Each step forward in my truth was anchored
by the trust in it, a steadfast unwavering belief that my heart will never steer
me wrong. This creates acceptance, the
peaceful feeling about all that comes our
way, past and present. It is an invisible
forcefield fueled by grace and humility. This beautiful blend of masculine
and feminine power helped me emerge as a
Conscious Warrior, armed with the playful
innocence of the hero within.

EXT. PLATEAU - NIGHT

The two halves of one sit among the silence of a small
rocky plateau. The clearing has beautifully allowed
for the night sky to shine its pinhole masterpiece.
Thousands of stars light the moment.

James shifts his gaze to Jimmy, still staring upward at
the wonder. The man examines every nuance of the boy as
he sits lost in the wonderful sight. It soon happens,

that initial moment when the eyes begin to lose their struggle with the tears, and they cascade over the skin below. Jimmy softly looks over to see the surrender of the man. He shifts his body closer as James speaks.

> JAMES
>
> *I don't know where it all went wrong. Not a day went by when I didn't think about you, about our dream. I'm sorry. So many bad decisions hurt so many people. You, my kids, and... and Brooke—*

James starts to sob, and Jimmy reaches for his hand.

> JAMES (cont'd)
>
> *She didn't deserve any of this, the life I gave her. I just... I just wanted to be somebody, not the kid...*

> JIMMY
>
> *On the chair?*

James nods, almost embarrassed.

> JIMMY (cont'd)
>
> *You tried; that's enough. Those dreams are still here. Just walk with me (realizes he had forgotten about Rusty and corrects himself)... us... and never let go.*

James' crying recedes and allows a playful smile to emerge with a nod. Jimmy smiles back, his eyes full of wisdom. He then turns his grin back towards the beautiful lights in the sky above them. James, feeling at peace, does the same.

INT. APARTMENT BUILDING - NIGHT

The sun has set on James, who still is feverishly writing in his journal by candlelight. He has some cinematic SFX: MUSIC playing in the background.

He stops writing and glances at his forearm, specifically to the tattoo from Los Angeles and its
sword. Something comes to him, like a vision that
coincides with his life's journey. He quickly
flips to an empty page and begins to sketch.

EXT. PLATEAU - NIGHT

*The two still sit beneath the evening sky, mesmerized
by the moment. Jimmy slowly reaches for James' hand
once more. His tiny fingers work on the older, weary
hand, beginning with the pinky finger and working
upward, rolling them into a fist until only the
pointer finger remains extended. He then slowly raises
it toward some distant lights, much like the tender
moments from the distant mythical lands of Rhode Island
and Mexico. Together, they began to trace the outline.*

> JIMMY
> *There it is. Do you see it?*

James takes a moment and then clarity strikes.

> JAMES
> *I do. I see it.*

> JIMMY
> *"Our" constellation is complete.*

INT. TATTOO SHOP - DAY

CLOSE UP on the end of a needle as it injects
black ink into reddened flesh. A pair of black
gloves manipulate the instrument while rhythmi-
cally wiping away the residue in an artistic
dance. PAIGE, a beautiful tattooist who is covered
in ink herself, pulls back from her artwork for a
better examination.

The outline is that of a warrior angel whose wings
tuck behind a suit of armor. The Conscious Warrior
is on one knee in a moment of acceptance. His

sword is propped up in front of him and his worn
shield by his side. The surrounding landscape is
full of personal items and powerful markers that
have accompanied him on his long journey.

EXT. OCEANSIDE BLUFFS - DAY

The blustery wind blows its late December chill
across the ocean and smacks into James' face
while his half-fingered gloves turn the pages of
his journal.

"Although that three-headed beast fell silent,
James knew that he hadn't heard the last of
Claire. Even when she resurfaced a few days after
Christmas, he decided not to respond. The self-
love pumping in his heart was too strong even for
their connection. It was done."

                    JAMES (V.O.)
(looking off the page and out to the rolling seas)
     A life full of romance is out there,
     and this warrior poet will seek it. But
     not at the sacrifice of my own truth...
     and Jimmy's.

James looks back to the journal and battles the
wind as he turns the page. He continues to read.

                    JAMES (V.O.) (cont'd)
     Perception of anything is everything. In
     just a handful of sober days, and freedom
     from the beast, my view of everything
     around me changed. Suddenly, the sky was
     a different shade of blue. Even the apart-
     ment didn't seem like the prison of soli-
     tude it was. The rebuild would commence
     each day with me, and my hero, playing.

The winter air is cut by the SOUND of a cell phone
ringing. James closes the journal and removes the
phone from his coat pocket. CLOSE UP on the phone
display, which reads "Parents."

Seeing the call display, James smiles and swipes
his exposed finger to accept the call.

                    JAMES
        Hello.

                 DAD (Off Screen)
        Hey there. You got a moment?

                    JAMES
        Sure do. Shoot.

                   DAD (O.S.)
        Well... they took Mom away to the hospi-
        tal. I don't think she will be coming home.

"CUT!!!" the universal director barked, like a scratch across a record,
bringing everything into sharp focus.

James stood up and listened intently to his dad, all the way from the
other coast, describing a deeply upsetting scene, with his mom setting
out plates for imaginary people at an imaginary dinner party.

"What do you mean imaginary people? Just the other day she—Wait,
how does someone set the dinner table for people who aren't there?" The
concerned son was at a loss.

I stood there trying to be a lighthouse while wave after wave crashed
over me from my father's news. Just like that, Mom's mind had gone,
and now they suspected she had Alzheimer's. I quickly found myself
having flashbacks to being in a similar situation with Malcolm many
years before. Even more quick to arrive was my gratitude that I hadn't
gotten this phone call a week earlier in the throes of my jungle battle.
Now, I had the magic weapon of acceptance on my back, and with that,
I was able to calmly guide my ailing and heartbroken father through his
next steps of what was to be his final role in life: caregiver. My very first
task was to keep him alive.

Friendly Ghosts

The view from right underneath the cloud covering was majestic to say the least. The mountains below were right there at the end of an outstretched hand if one chose to reach for it. The rim of the large woven basket was greeted with two sets of excited hands, one larger than the other. Little Jimmy's head was barely high enough to take in the view as the hot-air balloon sailed east towards its destination. The wind of freedom blew their hair back and filled the sails of their soul. Below them, rivers cut through mighty mountains, rock gave way to great plains, and vast lakes adorned the brilliant landscape.

When not taking in the view, the two would revisit past escapades in the confines of the sheltered basket, storytelling at its finest. Of course, no story is complete without its key characters partaking in the magic. Rusty, Captain Kirk, and Scuttle all nestled in for the ensuing trip down memory lane.

James peacefully stared out the small airplane window from his seat. His hands cradled a thinly wrapped Christmas present in his lap. Sure, the holiday was now behind him, but James had one more trick up his old sleeve when returning home.

Besides his mom's impending mental landslide, his dad had repeatedly shown that he was incapable of taking care of himself. Mom had spent a chunk of her life working full time, paying bills, cooking, cleaning, and reminding her husband when to take his medicine. With her gone, he was useless at just about anything, including keeping himself upright.

Before what would be his third hospital stay in a matter of two months, his father found himself spending the day on the floor of the apartment, malnourished and dehydrated. A ten-day hospital visit was the result, and soon, the healthcare system determined that he was incapable of self-care and approved a nursing-home relocation.

I'd like to think that Malcolm was up there in the heavens, pulling some strings for his only daughter, because the universal powers that be ordained that both Mom and Dad Gardiner would find themselves in the very same nursing home.

The thought of going home was exciting, and this time, I was gonna look for the magic in every single moment of the journey. That's what adventurers do: They embellish the moment within each footstep; that's the riddle to life. The magic of the movies that I so desperately sought had been there all along in the microcosm of movement. The next step on this full-circle life tour would be cleaning out my folks' apartment, in which they'd been living for the past nine years.

I arrived in the evening after successfully navigating the train down from Boston airport. According to my dad, the landlord was to have left the door unlocked so that I could get situated and then begin to deal with things like furniture and whatnot.

As the taxi pulled away from the old apartment building, James was left standing next to his folk's red Jeep. With his suitcase, he proceeded up the stone steps to the front door, which thankfully, was unlocked as promised. That is where the script ended. As he walked inside, it became crystal clear that the apartment had already been largely cleaned out, all the furniture already gone except for (Are you ready for it?) a single folding chair. The screenwriter in him couldn't seriously make this shit up. There was also a small card table and a single mattress on the floor. Everything was covered in dust, which James assumed was from the landlord, who was prepping for the new tenants. Boxes of stuff that had successfully circumvented the red dumpster nine years earlier were left for James' inspection before the great "heave ho." But first things first: He wanted to spend the evening with some old friends, so he pulled up that folding chair and lost himself in boxes of the past. Pages and pages of old ghosts greeted James from dusty photo albums. Even better, they did so with a smile.

Love on the Green Mile

The February sparseness that whizzed by seemed beautiful in its own right. Sneaker-clad feet churned over the small pedals of the bike, which was three sizes too small for James. Scuttle was clinging to his shoulder, commanding the knight to pedal faster. It was a race. Up ahead of them was another red bike with Little Jimmy dodging in and out of the odd winter Wickfordite on the sidewalk. Jimmy's other two lifelong wingmen peeked out the top of the small knapsack on his back. The race was on with the impending finish line, lurking down the end of Main Street on once-hallowed ground.

The sip from the coffee added to his already warmed soul. He sat in the driver's seat of the beat-up red Jeep with its windows down and took in the welcoming view. The town dock had returned to its old glory through the nostalgic eyes of James reborn. He could hear the old arguing voices from the warring parties of fisherman, lobstermen, and quahoggers drift across the empty parking lot. Even Scuttle was probably around somewhere, smiling as he realized that the wharf rats were all bark and no bite.

Ah yes, the memories, like the corners of my mind... I can't sing, but I can hear that classic tune as clear as day while I type this. I had to get out of the vehicle and walk to the exact spot where Dave and I used to spend countless hours waiting for those gentle nibbles on our lines, the tiny white and red bobbers starting to dance on the surface of the water. Adventure, excitement, and wonder, all at the end of what lay beneath the surface. That is life in the moment between two steps. And I welcomed it with every ounce of my soul.

I also wondered what would lay at the end of my next stop, which would take me to the nursing home. It had been four years since I'd last seen my parents for my rowing farewell, before life had taken a decidedly sharp left turn with me gripping the "oh shit" handles. Truthfully, I didn't know if Mom would even remember me. If she did, would she be able to communicate? All these thoughts began to enter my mind as I left my morning reunion with the town dock.

The shift into park came with a heavy sigh. James sat for a moment before adjusting the rearview mirror to gaze at his own reflection. This indeed was uncharted territory for him. While he felt rejuvenated and young in spirit, he knew that the battle had aged him. He wasn't blind to the markers of time staring back at him. Now, here he was, close to forty years removed from his own hospital stays, to see his parents now assuming the starring role once billed for him.

The smell was unmistakable, that nursing-home scent consisting of cheap lotions and industrial soaps sprinkled in with a hint of floral essence, the once or twice weekly rotation of showers, and last but not least, the lingering creep of death. It had first filled his nose all those years earlier when Malcolm had been in the death throes of his stroke and left to ride out the breaking wave of life in a nursing home that doesn't even exist anymore.

Now it hung with him as he continued down the hallway to Room 402. The surrounding landscape would be their final resting place, the last home in which they'd hang their hats, full of mediocre musical guests, weekly bingo, and cafeteria cuisine. The dark gray placque with the silver markings of '402' finally greeted James from its spot on the wall. Below it was a four-legged rolling walker with a portable oxygen device ready for hookup when travel was needed. He knew it was his dad's. He could just tell. Another deep breath inward, and into the room James went.

There he was, sprawled out on top of his bed, his signature puffy belly standing like Everest over the rest of his torso. Balanced precariously on top of the summit was his television remote. It took a moment before his dad distinguished his son from the staff. When he did, he fumbled for the remote in excitement to mute the television.

"Hey! You made it!" he said while his legs swung slightly up and then down, creating momentum to help catapult his body to an upright position.

"Yup, sure did. Without a hitch," his son responded.

He didn't have the heart to tell him about the empty apartment right away and would leave that for a bit later. In the meantime, James assessed the room. His dad shared it with another gentleman, who was sleeping at the moment, and there appeared to be two of everything, except (of course) the bathroom, which they both shared with the adjoining room.

"Gotta jockey for the shitter, I see." James was trying to wipe the dust off their old sense of bantering humor.

"Tell me about it," his dad said. "Lifestyles of the rich and famous." His self-deprecating laugh was familiar, even mixed with the inescapable wheeze from his lungs.

James nods to the sleeping roommate. "How's he?"

"Not good. I think he's on his way out," his dad responded with a gentle whisper.

James knew that it was inevitable for everyone in here. The whole place was one long green mile, down which each resident would ultimately walk.

"Where's Mom?" James asked next, concerned and eager to get to the most important issue.

His dad groaned as he made his way to a standing position. "She's in the ward," he said as he unhooked his big oxygen unit and began his choreographed shuffle towards his outside travel device. "But the mayor has the code to get in," he said, smiling cheekily.

As we slowly strolled down the hallway, it became crystal clear to me that Dad *was* in fact the mayor of the nursing home. Each and every staff member would stop and talk to him, introduce themselves to me, and proclaim that they'd heard about my rowing exploits, my television days, you name it. My heart filled, knowing that my dad actually talked about me and was, I dare say, proud of me. It also felt amazing to know that my dad's personality was greatly welcomed among the staff. I knew from that moment that they would be in good hands during their time on the mile.

The nurses quickly moved out of the way to avoid the charging dreamer. A hospital gown hung to Little Jimmy like an extra-large bed sheet, his bony arms signaling his heroic charge down the hallway. His closest allies enjoy the ride from the comfort of his lap. Behind him his jet propulsion came in the form of a six-foot-tall smiling James, with Scuttle on his shoulder.

The wheelchair swerved and braked with the precision of a Formula One car as it made its way down the hallway, finally coming to an abrupt stop in front of the sacred room.

"Ice cream," he whispered.

"Huh? Now?" his dad asked as he continued his shuffle down the corridor.

James didn't bother to explain. Instead, he observed the few residents who stood like lifeless, frozen artifacts in the various corners of the hallway. This "ward," as his dad had called it, was for the residents whose minds had begun the slow descent into chaos. His mom was confined here while they ran more cognitive tests to determine her status. She was a captive of her mind, and now of the nursing home as well.

Dad stopped his two-step shuffle, turned to his son, and spoke quietly, as though they were on some secret mission. "Now, we have to get her away from the leeches and back into her room." James responded with only a befuddled look but followed his dad's lead.

"The loonies," Dad continued, "they like to hover around her and keep her in their sights like a pet."

When I turned the corner, I spotted her right away. She was sitting just as my dad said she would be: surrounded. People were having one-way conversations with her, some holding stuffed animals while others moved back and forth in their chairs to some internal rhythm. It was a surreal, alternate universe. At the epicenter of it all was my mother, sitting silently and staring into nowhere. Her long, ratty hair was a shade of gray combined with a sharp white that brought to mind images of a senile grandmother from an old horror movie.

There was a blankness in her eyes as I approached, unaware that both her husband and son were just feet away.

"Carol," my dad said in a soft, caring voice unknown to me.

She turned, and that's when I knew she still remembered. Her eyes lit up like the Christmas trees of my youth. Her cheeks filled with color, and that Malcolm smile exploded with love.

Love indeed. It works magic on so many levels. It would be a struggle for her to rise from her chair and escape the pawing hands of her captives, but she would not be deterred from doing what her heart wanted her to do: hug her only son.

Her frail tiny frame was soon engulfed by the warrior, ever mindful not to squeeze too tightly. He pulled back and gently moved the white hair from her eyes so he could stare right into them and fall into the dark pupils of her soul.

The darkness never seemed that dark when she was holding him. Little Jimmy and his young mother swayed softly on the edge of the bed after an asthma attack. Standing off in the corner of the room, by the shelves of Star Trek and other toys, stood James. He watched as his mother's rhythmic movement and soft voice helped him through those dark breathless nights as a child. It dawned on him that his younger self had yet another hero, even back then. It wasn't found in the captain's chair of some deep-space mission or epic hand-to-hand combat to save a damsel in distress. He was right there in her arms. James slowly moved from the corner and sat down next to his mother. His arms reaching for another hero.

The two sat in an embrace on the edge of her bed before breaking the union with even more smiles. James' did his best not to let his reddish eyes start to water, trying to stay strong and stoic for his parents. When she spoke, it would be with small words and smiles. The hardest thing for James was seeing her struggle with trying to formulate words in general. She wanted desperately to speak, but the frustration would continually build until either his dad or he would offer up words to help finish the sentence.

The reunited family of three concluded their first visit by the two main doors that led back into the common area. This is where the mighty James really struggled to hold back the force of love wanting to express itself through his eyes. His mother couldn't understand why she wasn't able to go with them. She would try to wedge her way past both men to freedom only to finally relinquish hope after their calming voices somehow registered.

As she stood by the closing door, only to appear in its rectangular vertical window, her son relinquished control of his tears and let them fall as well. Her hand gently touched his through the glass before she turned away, meandering back down the chasm of the empty hallway with her head down, moving back toward to her captives.

James wiped his eyes as one of the lead nurses approached him and his dad.

"You must be Leigh's son?" she asked with enthusiasm.

"Yeah, that's me," he said while taking one last peek through the window to see his mom turn the far end corner and disappear.

"I've heard so much about you! Your dad has told me a lot!" She was obviously smitten with the man in front of her.

James turned back, sensing it. His eyes caught her name tag, which identified her as Laura.

"What do we have to do to get her out of there?" he asked. "No offense, but most of the people in there are on another planet."

The nurse smiled and held up his mother's chart. "Well, the good news is that she has progressed really well in her assessment. There may—"

"Laura," he interrupted softly, "we both know she isn't a flight risk. And from what my dad tells me, that's the biggest concern."

He turned and gave his dad a look before heading down the hallway with the nurse to continue their discussion. One of his dad's bushy eyebrows raised up like Mr. Spock's as he uttered the character's famous catch phrase: "Fascinating."

The Notebook

The paper bag landed on the kitchen counter with purpose, its sound echoing in the vacant apartment. He had just returned from the nursing home with these new memories that carried more weight than the old ones.

His mother had been doing better in the few short months since her initial diagnosis, and they did determine that she was a "non-roamer." This was not because of his attempts to try and charm the heck out of the shift nurse to push his agenda. Universal timing had simply decreed it to be so. The problem was that the nursing home was full, and there were no beds available, let alone a full room for both his folks. Unfortunately, there was only one way for a bed to free up and that was someone reaching the end of their mile.

I couldn't help but think that the subtle hint I had dropped to the nurse about *The Notebook* being one of my favorite romantic films helped our cause a little bit. It's the bar for those types of films, with its storyline of aging lovers in a nursing home, with the wife struggling with Alzheimer's while being comforted by a stranger's visits, reading excerpts from a book. The stranger, of course, is her husband, and the book is their life story.

James Garner. Do you know how many times I have been referenced to the famous actor from the *Rockford Files,* or in this case, *The Notebook?*

Mr. Garner (*sans* the "d" and the "I,") played the rock-solid husband in that romantic tearjerker of a film.

In any case, at the present moment, I was under strict orders from Leigh Gardiner to prepare some contraband. Back in Rhode Island a full day, and I was already creating a meth lab (at least that's what it felt like I was doing in their almost empty apartment).

James began to pull various items from the large brown-paper bag on the counter. First was a large bottle of Seagram's whisky, followed by a smaller bottle of sweet vermouth. Then three small bottles of iced tea were removed by the former mixologist, who went to work. First up, the iced tea was dumped down the nearby sink until just the empty bottles remained. Placed neatly side by side, James then grabbed the whisky to fill up each empty iced-tea bottle about three quarters full, leaving just enough room for the sweet vermouth to fill each to the brim. The contents of the bottles were sealed back shut and shaken vigorously. Sure, these were rude offerings of his dad's favorite go-to, the Manhattan, but they would do nicely.

With that taken care of, the next item on his agenda was to sort through some of the boxes of personal stuff from his family and figure out which items he would keep, and which would make their way to the middle of the living room (the holding pen for the items doomed to accompany him on his impending ride to the dump). Only a few small boxes could find their way into his dad's room at the home, so he moved the folding chair into position and began his sorting journey.

They looked frozen in love. The camera had perfectly captured their wedding day fifty-some years earlier, a lifetime ahead of them, a child to yet have, and each other to care for. It was all represented in this one snapshot from a special day. Now, he just had to decide which pictures and items to keep and which to discard. James opted for the best solution he could think of and kept one or two of each type of thing and opted to chuck the rest. But like any child in this moment, the "stuff" in these piles was more than just a cheap five-letter word. It was all he had left: pictures and memories. But he still had choices to make.

During the hours I spent over the coming days in the lone room, fighting off sneezes from dust and other pollutants, I made my way through the items as best as I could. It wasn't easy. Some of it was my grandparent's stuff that my folks had kept. Some of it was my own: rowing memories, Boy Scouts, modelling, prom pictures with Allison, and other high school items. I began to make my own pile of things that had to come back to Canada with me, including my high school year-books. But even with those, I had to make a choice. I opted to only keep my junior- and senior-year editions. Everything comes with a price, age and life being no exception. Here I was paying the toll keeper for the roads I'd travelled and the inability to keep most of it. But unlike my mother, I was banking on my memory to keep it alive.

Speaking of "alive," when I showed up at the nursing home the next day with my bag of contraband, my dad greeted me with another famous *Star Trek* line: "He's dead, Jim."

I was a little taken aback until I saw the empty bed in my dad's room, and it clicked. I looked back to my father, who explained.

"He died in his sleep last night. They took him away this morning," he offered, matter of fact. "Is that for me?" He pointed to the brown-paper bag.

"Yes." I was still processing what had happened overnight. It didn't seem to faze my dad at all. He seemed more concerned with my gift. He opened up the bag and took out a bottle for closer examination. He twisted the top right off and took a large swig, which made my eyes go wide.

"Whoa!" he blurted out just as Laura, the head nurse, walked into the room. I quickly sprang into "actor" mode to cover for his outburst.

"Yeah, sorry, Dad. I wasn't sure if you wanted the extra-sweet brand of iced tea or not."

My dad, never one to miss a cue, played right along. "Nah, it's fine. Just went down the wrong pipe, I guess."

I spun back to Laura with a smile. "Hi, Laura." A momentary connection broke when she looked back to her clipboard.

"So, I'm glad I was able to catch both of you," she began. "With Mr. Robertson's passing—"

Leigh's next sip from the bottle of moonshine made him growl a bit, which momentarily interrupted her. I couldn't look at my dad anymore without laughing.

"With your roommate's passing, Leigh," she said again, "we can move Carolyn into the room with you. She can stay here as long as her mind maintains function at a certain level. Of course, this means that you will have to be a bit more tentative with her, as she will be relying on you to help her with the most basic concepts." She stopped, and I turned to look at my dad.

I'll never forget the image of him with tears running down both his cheeks. I don't recall ever seeing him cry. I couldn't help but feel so much love for the man, for whom I admit that I'd held some resentment because of my folk's financial lot in life.

"Will that be okay, Leigh?" asked Laura softly.

My dad nodded with a smile.

"Wow," I said, "that's great news, Laura. Thank you so much."

"Well," she said, smirking at me a bit as she moved towards the door, *The Notebook* is one of my favorite movies. Just saying. And now your dad can keep your mom company too."

"What is it with you, son?" my dad sarcastically offered while wiping his cheeks and adjusting the breathing tube in his nose.

I knew he was commenting on my propensity to make flirtatious connections with the ladies but chose not to address it. "Okay, Dad," I said, moving his iced tea safely out of his reach. "I'm heading to meet Dave and his wife for lunch in Wickford. I'll tell him you said hi."

"Mom's going to be so happy when she hears the news!" said the boy inside my dad.

I stood there watching him proudly combing his hair with his small plastic comb.

"Yes, she will be, Dad."

Full Circle

My memories of the time spent with Dave in Wickford after that nursing-home visit have now blended into a beautiful montage of vignettes accompanied by the gentle keystrokes of a Steinway. Sunshine blanketed the last Sunday in February in a picture postcard of crystal blue with just the perfect blend of early spring warmth and late-winter chill. Dave and I were reunited on hallowed ground and made the most of our day, reconnecting with the historic town that will forever be a part of our souls. He introduced me to his amazing wife, Christine, who was kind enough to hear a day full of ancient stories and childlike expositions of a time gone by.

We strolled the streets and antique shops while hearing the familiar sounds of our adventurous youth floating on the air. Our movement was slower than the steel steeds upon which we used to seek untold riches, but somehow, we were just as happy. The wooden planks at the town dock didn't feel as comfortable as they had forty years earlier, but our echoing laughter would have warded off even the largest wharf rat from the days of Scuttle. I'm sure that, if someone caught the angles of the sun just right, they would have seen that we were both flanked on either side by our younger selves.

Through the small back streets of this colonial haven, we made our way up the grassy hill to a structure now devoid of life. My cupping hands provided me a closer look through the glass window into a world that was. A fallen sign and endless dust seemed to be the only clues to a once-bustling elementary school. The large bay windows that used to be the only exit for the daydreaming kids as they sat in their classrooms now showcased emptiness in all its glory. Nothing remained but faded and empty chalkboards still vainly standing. Waiting.

"Let's check out the old library," my energized best friend offered.

"Hell yeah!" I was quick to respond.

The good old library. Dave and I used to love this place of higher learning. Countless hours were spent shifting through books from different phases of my youth and study time with Allison, my high school sweetheart. As much as movies had influenced me, so did the atmosphere of a library and its books, in which the dreams of tomorrow can be found.

Dave and I traversed the two main floors, feeding off the memories of the past and those potential dreams of tomorrow. But it wasn't till we were about to leave that the real treasure from the day's adventures was found. It appeared on a used bookshelf among other books, with a red dot signifying its sale price: a whopping twenty-five cents. It was the first book I saw when I turned the corner. A small paperback edition of *The Notebook* stood out from the shelf like a lighthouse. It was the best quarter I have ever spent, and it has earned a place on the shelf of life's glorious full-circle moments.

The day ended as it began, with a heartfelt hug from a lifelong friend. I only wish we'd had time to throw the football on Cydot Drive one more time or sit in the backyard of Malcolm's yellow house and share a glass of lemonade. So many things actually... all of which will have to live with the little guy in my soul. He was in charge of those awesome moments, and I knew that he would keep them safe. It was a bittersweet farewell as there was no way to know when, or even if, we would cross paths again, as is always the case when one grows older. Until that day comes though, all I can offer to all my dear friends and that village from a lifetime ago is the promise that you will never be forgotten.

The last few photographs shuffled through his hands as he sat on the folding steel throne. James was taking a final inventory of the images before the fateful decisions were finalized. He wasn't alone for the viewing party. On the floor in front of him, with his legs crossed, sat Little Jimmy, dressed in a mustard Captain Kirk tunic.

A photo of the local Cydot gang dressed for the first day of school stared back at James.

"Ha! Dave and I have matching lunch boxes." James chuckled while turning the photo so Jimmy could see.

"Keep it," Jimmy excitedly chimed in. "Those Space 1999 lunch boxes were the best."

James slid the picture into a plastic baggy with other chosen artifacts that would accompany him back to the west coast. He then picked up a small shoebox and placed it on his lap.

"What do we have in here?" he wondered out loud, removing the lid. He navigated through some soft tissue to get to the treasure within. The first item came out, its red and white signature wardrobe giving it away.

"Mom made that," Jimmy chimed in.

"She made all of them," James said softly while pulling out a couple of the matching pieces.

Neither the adult nor the boy could say anything for a moment, the memories from the set of Christmas figurines speaking to them. But they had to make another of those decisions: let go of the sentimental and keep only the practical, or not. With that, Jimmy slowly shook his head, giving his blessing to let go of a piece of their past. James put them back into the box and covered them with the lid. It assumed a place next to the other discarded remnants of yesterday.

The floor creaked and the old steel radiators hissed, fighting off the outside chill beneath the glass windows. James walked through the old turn of the century apartment one last time, his wrapped Christmas present that he'd brought with him tucked under one arm. The funeral mound in the middle of the living room was now complete. Soon it would disappear and assume its resting place upon a landfill exposed to time. At the threshold of the empty bedroom, he now stood, staring at the only object that remained and weighing its meaning.

My mother's walking cane stood on an angle across the room, propped up against the windowsill. Somehow, it felt like it belonged exactly where it was, a marker of passage or some Tiny Tim movie bookend. I remember gripping my present tight and feeling an over-whelming sense of peace. As I backed away, my mind was drawn to the inevitable full-circle closures both big and small that all these "signs" in life allow us to have. I had once seen them as destiny; now I choose to see them as storytelling gifts… story-*living* gifts. I had one more of these to deliver. The universal director was calling me to the set one last time, with one last cue to hit, and one last moment to create.

Closing Credits

The surrounding light bulbs cast their even light across the face at the center of the mirror. James sits in a chair, his eyes closed while a makeup artist applied the last few finishing touches to her work.

"Mr. Gardiner, they're ready for you on set," came the announcement from a young production assistant wearing a headset and carrying a clipboard.

"Great," chimed Little Jimmy as he hopped off an adjacent makeup chair and approached James. "Let's go! We can't be late for the last shot," he eagerly said while trying his best to yank his older self off his chair and out the green-room door.

The two made their way through the vastness of the soundstage, James holding his gift-wrapped present in one hand. Movie production personnel moved by them with a speedy sense of purpose. The two actors were mindful to step over the electric cables taped to the floor while sidestepping the set lights being pushed on rollers. Lastly, the two had to stop completely as a large rolling wardrobe rack whizzed past with medical uniforms slung on hangers. After it went by, the way was clear to enter the actual set. They didn't need an escort any further; they knew exactly where they were going. All they had to do was follow the signs beneath their feet.

The yellow painted bricks began in a circle and led outward down the hallway. James and Jimmy shared an enthusiastic look, grabbed hands, and took the first step onto the yellow road. Their continued steps took them down a hallway while nurses and residents were ushered into place by members of the crew. This time there were no witches on brooms to duck or a man behind the curtain to see, but rather acceptance… of everything.

As the old actor and the young turned the corner, they reached the end of the yellow brick road: Room 402.

"Please take your marks, talent," chimed the assistant director, who was standing by a table full of monitors and people.

Among them was the director, in a seventies-style trucker hat and beard, who said, "Okay, here we go. Places everyone."

"You heard, Steven," the assistant director called. "Quiet on set!"

Jimmy's eyes grew wide at the man in charge and then turned to his older self with a big grin of completion.

"Roll sound. Roll camera," the director continued.

James and Jimmy continued to hold hands. Jimmy leaned in towards James and triumphantly whispered, "That's Steven Spielberg!"

"And… Action!" The director's voice echoed through the hallowed grounds of the set.

✧   ✧   ✧

I first saw the far empty bed and wondered what could have stalled the reunion. But I was quick to realize that closest to me, lying together in the same bed, were my mother and father.

"Hey, Carol, look who it is," my dad said softly.

A slow smile came over my mom's face as her hand moved to hold her husband's. I didn't say much but moved to the vacant chair and took a seat, still holding my present. The room was in the process of being transformed into their personnel sanctuary, with some pictures and keepsakes about. It would be their final place together, for however long her mind could stay above the threshold. But none of that mattered now. Only them together, and me, enjoying the peacefulness of the moment.

However, as I looked around, I realized that the room was transforming into something even more perfect. It started with the red and green glow of a Christmas tree in the corner of the room. Below it, a whack-load of wrapped holiday presents were being guarded by Rusty the stuffed squirrel. My eyes caught a darting figure running across the windowsill to take a front-row spot for the reunion. Scuttle pulled up a seat on the sill, joining the mustard captain, in all his heroic plastic glory. The Zenith television appeared, and on its screen was Roger Staubach, pausing his come-from-behind win for the Dallas Cowboys to watch me.

My grandparents, Malcolm and Myrtis, joined the performance, each standing on either side of the tree, a glass containing a brown liquid extended from my grandfather's arm in a toast to his only grandson. Myrtis, of course, looked like she was dressed for the royal ball.

Dave, flipping a football in his hands, took up a floor seat against the wall and was soon flanked by my other best friends, Steve and Ed. The long monkey tail of Jimmy Fox sent a Christmas ornament rolling across the floor, but thankfully, it was scooped up by my doppelganger, Robin Williams, who hung it back on the tree with a salute to his captain.

Little Jimmy made his way to the bed and hopped up on it, nestling between my mom and dad as the lights began to dim. Lastly, the three front-row floor spots were filled by my two daughters and my son, all eagerly awaiting their dad to begin.

The hero does lie within, I thought, as I sat in that chair, taking in the magic between the moments. I wanted this moment to last forever. Cue music:

James rests the wrapped present on his lap, looking once more at all the faces and memories before him. He slowly begins to unwrap it, taking his time to savor the sound and feel of the paper. The object now rests exposed in his lap. The book itself was a lot thinner than he remembered and devoid of its original cover. But the engraved artwork at its center was unmistakable, even to a fifty-year-old man. It was that of a mouse—a pirate mouse to be exact. James flipped the cover open, and there was his name, written by his mother forty-plus years earlier. His finger passed over it, the written "Jimmy Gardiner" calling to the now James for one more step onto the stage. James took in the crowd, his aging folks holding hands, and his true hero within: Little Jimmy. The actor began as he had forty-three years earlier:

"Shiver me timbers!" the now aging elf mouse excitedly spoke.

Laughter fills the room as he begins to recount the story of *Scuttle the Stowaway Mouse.* The tale continues in a rhyming rhythm of storytelling, love, and play.

The CAMERA begins its slow PULL BACK, switching from the CLOSE UP of James to a PANNING SHOT of his audience enjoying the moment. The CAMERA then GENTLY exits the room and continues down the hallway over the yellow brick road leaving James' voice to joyously drift away.

                    JAMES (O.S.)
           (softly heard from a distance)
This is my favourite part. (trying to control his own laughter)
This is where he finally gets his new hat and ischased by a dreaded harbour rat!

The FAINT sound of LAUGHTER and LOVE is barely audible...

CHORUS: *BEYOND THE FREY*

And with peaceful resolve comes the gentle ending of our play. The final mark for the actor finds him where the story began, by the swirling seas and the only home he has ever known. With a boy by his side and a full heart, our hero stands steadfast as a beacon for "love in all things." The waves crash in unison, pounding with his childlike heart. It is the call he has longed to hear. The warrior's anthem now rises as the orchestra swells to the crescendo of its symphony. To be "somebody," to be "nobody"... to just "BE." That is the question for thee.

One last cue to the candles of the night as they illuminate the warrior constellation taking its place among the heroes in the sky. It is a Conscious Warrior, who kneels in acceptance of what was and whatever fate will decree. Onward, down the road of life, their journey be.

EXT. ROADWAY - DUSK
ROLL CREDITS.

James walks away from CAMERA, his back to us.
DISSOLVE into frame Little Jimmy walking next to
him. The SOUND of waves crashing from the nearby
ocean fills the air. The fading sun casts a sil-
houette over the two figures as night ascends.
The outline of Jimmy's small hand reaching up
for James' larger one fills the screen. The two
connect, and their eyes gaze upwards. The stars
of their constellation shine a bit brighter than
everything else.

                    JIMMY
     I think you should write a book.

FOUNDING HEROES

A special thank you to all those listed below for supporting the initial fundraising campaign and purchasing an advanced copy of the book. You have all had a hand in bringing little Jimmy's and James' story to the world.

Amber Love

Amy Hadikin

Andrea Groth

Angela Yunick

Annette LaBonte

Ariel Mieling

Barbara Shepard

Barney Ellis-Perry

Bethany Amatucci

Beverly Hannah

Brenda Morrison

Brenda St Louis

Brenda Wowk

Brendan Kane

Brian Clement

Carmel D'Arienzo

Carrie Gettings

Catherine Smith

Cher Nutt

Cherie Darsch

Cheryl Allen

Cheryl Pineo

Cheryl Rowley

Chris Johns

Chris Magdalenski

Christina Benty

Christine Roy

Christopher
Allen Jordan

Christopher Coutu

Cindy Van Arnam

Colin Bender

Colleen Cattell

Corinne Rogers

Crystal-Maria Krolenko

Darlene Cameron

David Storti

Deborah LeFrank

Dinna Finnegan

Dori Howard

Edward Mello

Emily McManus

Erin Watts

Fab Lethbridge

Larry and
Frances Crowley

Ge-an Rijniersce

Graham Giske

Gregg Cerveny

Gregory Witz

Helen Gould

Hemraj Shetty

James Michailides

Jasmin Badrin

Jennifer Davis

Jennifer Hutton

Jennifer Jedras

Jennifer Love

Jennifer Spencer

Jennifer Wright

Joely Ferris

John Metras

Jon T. Chirnside

Jonathan Michailides

Judith Mello

Karen Russell

Kari Millett

Kenneth H Clark

Kevin Hogberg

Kimberly McGillivray

Kimmis Chow

Klara Reid

Kristina Stauffer

Laila Presotto

Lauri Theroux

Lee-Ann Liden

Leslee Montgomery

Libby Lee

Linda Breedlove,
author of the "Rebel on
Purpose" Series

Linette Perry

Marcus Richardson

Mark Bombard

Matt Reis

Maureen Harriman

Micah Au

Michael J Eatough

Michelle Bazett

Michelle Richardson

Milena Pargova

Mira Rocca

Mishell Leong

Nicole Majik

Nikki Robbins

Paige Fahie

Patricia Bevilacqua

Paulina Reves

Peggy Adams

Phillip J Hazard

Steve and Rachel Lawson

Rachel Stewart

Rebekah Aramini Lupo

Reene Seitz

Rodney Prieto

Ross Allan

Roxanne Low

Samantha Lynn

Schicker Kelly

Scott Glynn

Sharon Marshall

Stephanie Mielty

Stephen Michailides

Stephen Peck

Stephen Pilcher

Sue Potgieter

Tanya Cloete

Tanya Memme

Tanya Oliva

Tara Jeffries

Tiffany Szigety

S&T Properties
(Svet and Tina Pargov)

Veronica Orendain

Virginia Fullmer

ABOUT THE AUTHOR

Author James Gardiner has worn many hats over the course of both his personal and professional life, as detailed in *All In with Love: my journey to the hero within*. By telling his life story, and sharing everything (the good, the bad, and the ugly), he hopes his readers will be able to absorb the many lessons he had to learn the hard way and be inspired to embrace their younger selves, walking forward into their futures  with truth, acceptance, and grace, always leading with love.

Though he grew up in Rhode Island, James currently lives in Vancouver, BC, where he globally works with people to find and understand their own fundamental truths and gain momentum on their journeys of personal growth.

To contact regarding speaking engagements and book tours, or to learn more about James Gardiner, please go to: www.theherowithin.ca